AULA ABIERTA
NIVEL INTRODUCTORIO

Jaime Corpas
Eva García
Agustín Garmendia
Carmen Soriano

Claudia Fernández
University of Illinois–Chicago

with contributions by
Muriel Gallego
Ohio University
Jennifer Vojtko Rubí
University of Cincinnati

Portfolio Manager: Amber Chow
Product Manager: Rachel Ross
Content Producer: Cecilia Turner
Portfolio Manager Assistant: Christa T. Cottone
Senior Field Marketing Manager: Melissa Yokell
Content Producer Manager: Amber Mackey
Art/Designer: Pedro Ponciano
Content Developers and Production: Pablo Garrido, Agnès Berja, Agustín Garmendia, Sara Zucconi
Managing Development Editor: Harold Swearingen, Pablo Garrido
Digital Studio Course Producer: Charlene Smith
Digital Media Manager: Julie Allen
Project Manager: Integra Software Services
Compositor: Pedro Ponciano, Difusión
Printer/Binder: LSC Communications, Inc.
Front Cover Design: Difusión
Cover Image Credit: ivanastar/istockphoto.com

Library of Congress Cataloging-in-Publication Data
Cataloging-in-Publication data is on file with the Library of Congress.
Names: Corpas, Jaime, author.
Title: Aula abierta : nivel introductorio / Jaime Corpas, [and four others];
    with contributions by Muriel Gallego, Jennifer Vojtko Rubí.
    Description: Upper Saddle River : Pearson, 2019. | Includes index. | Summary: "Aula abierta
    is comprised of brief, modular lessons that are organized around a communicative goal,
    in which students have the opportunity to show what they can do using Spanish effectively.
    Each lesson carefully scaffolds student progress through a series of pedagogical tasks that
    prepare students to accomplish the final goal. Grammar, vocabulary, and pragmatic knowledge
    are treated more as linguistic resources than as topics of instruction. Throughout each lesson,
    we have taken a comparative, global approach to Hispanic culture, highlighting authentic materials
    from around the world, as well as Latino communities within the United States. The learning
    experience is highly visual, providing students with a compelling introduction to the Spanish
    language and culture"— Provided by publisher.
Identifiers: LCCN 2019026258 (print) | LCCN 2019026259 (ebook) | ISBN
    9780135306932 (paperback) | ISBN 9780135654507 | ISBN 9780135654484
    (paperback) | ISBN 9780135654682 (ebook)
Subjects: LCSH: Spanish language—Conversation and phrase books—English. |
    Spanish language—Textbooks for foreign speakers—English | Spanish
    language—Self-instruction.
Classification: LCC PC4121 .C715 2019 (print) | LCC PC4121 (ebook) | DDC
    468.6/4—dc23
LC record available at https://lccn.loc.gov/2019026258
LC ebook record available at https://lccn.loc.gov/2019026259
    1 2019

Rental Edition
ISBN-10: 0-13-530693-0
ISBN-13: 978-0-13-530693-2

Scope & Sequence

Lección

Preliminar
En el aula

LEARNING OUTCOMES
You will be able to...
- introduce yourself
- communicate in the classroom
- greet and say good-bye

COMPRENDEMOS EL VOCABULARIO
- Words related to the classroom
- Numbers from 0 to 100

Lección

1
Nosotros

Hola, soy Paola.
Soy **mexicana**, de Monterrey.
Soy **fotógrafa**.

LEARNING OUTCOMES
You will be able to...
- give and ask for personal information

PRIMER CONTACTO
- Personal information

COMPRENDEMOS EL VOCABULARIO
- Nationalities
- Professions
- Age
- Pastimes

EXPLORAMOS LA LENGUA
- Alphabet
- The forms of **-ar**, **-er**, and **-ir** verbs
- The verbs **llamarse**, **trabajar**, **ser**, **tener**, and **vivir**

AHORA PODEMOS...
- Create a poster with information about who we are

VIDEO
- "Baila conmigo"

CONECTAMOS NUESTRAS CULTURAS
- Different ways people can be addressed

TEXTOS AUDIOVISUALES
- Watch a video of Spanish speakers making introductions
- Present information about ourselves

PRONUNCIAMOS
- Pronunciation of the letters **c/z** and **g/j**

Scope & Sequence

Scope & Sequence

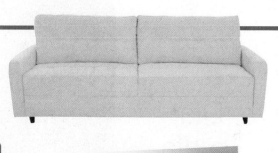

Scope & Sequence

Why *Aula abierta*?

At the University of Illinois at Chicago, I had become aware of a series of important challenges in our basic Spanish program. Many students were finishing their language requirement feeling they had a good knowledge of Spanish grammar rules but could not do much with what they had learned. Many students couldn't hold spontaneous basic conversations that sounded natural; they had difficulty interpreting authentic language (in particular, spoken language); and the language they did use didn't sound pragmatically appropriate. What I wanted—and what students wanted—was for students to be able to use the language in a functional, authentic way, for the real world, at a level that could be realistically achieved after completing the basic Spanish program.

- For guidance, I looked to the ACTFL' s 21st Century Skills Map, whose statement about the goals of a language program helped me further shape our own goals: to develop students' language proficiency around modes of communicative competence that reflect real-life communication. In that sense, I learned what the classroom of today is about: to teach students so they use the language to communicate with other speakers of the language. By contrasting the characteristics of the classroom of yesteryear to the classroom of today, as listed in the 21st century Skills Map, I identified that the goal of learning a language is to be able to do something in that language, as it is also reflected in the ACTFL Standards for Foreign Language Learning and the Can-do Statements. In order to implement these ACTFL Standards and achieve the results I was looking for, I searched for learning materials that would help us be closer to what the classroom of today is about.

- What I discovered was that nearly all the course materials available in the United States still reflected much of the characteristics of the classroom of yesteryear. For example, there is still a grammatical agenda behind the instructional materials, whereby the purpose of instruction and classroom activities is really to practice knowledge of the grammar rules rather than to truly be able to communicate by expressing a meaningful message as speakers naturally do. Then I discovered *Aula internacional* by Difusión, a Spanish publisher. I felt it was nearly a perfect fit for our goals and the type of classroom we wanted to create. We worked with Difusión to modify *Aula internacional* into this U.S. adaptation, *Aula abierta*.

Aula abierta is comprised of brief, modular lessons that are organized around a communicative goal, in which students have the opportunity to show what they can do using Spanish effectively. Each lesson carefully scaffolds student progress through a series of pedagogical tasks that prepare students to accomplish the final goal. Grammar, vocabulary, and pragmatic knowledge are treated more as linguistic resources than as topics of instruction. Throughout each lesson, we have taken a comparative, global approach to Hispanic culture, highlighting authentic materials from around the world, as well as Latino communities within the United States. The learning experience is highly visual, providing students with a compelling introduction to the Spanish language and culture.

We are thrilled to bring *Aula abierta* to other colleges and universities in the United States, opening up an opportunity for your students to effectively communicate in Spanish just as ours have done.

Claudia Fernández

Claudia R. Fernández, Ph.D.
University of Illinois–Chicago

Preface

Introduction to the Program

Empowering Students to Find Their Voice in Spanish. Each lesson of the highly anticipated *Aula abierta* begins with a Can-Do statement and organizes the instructional content around the language students need to successfully complete a task. This backward design approach is a response to the language community's reexamination of students' and instructors' desired outcomes for the 21st century language class: replace learning about the language with learning to use the language.

Aula abierta embraces ACTFL's 21st century guidelines and prepares students to reach Novice Mid by the end of the first semester and Novice High by the end of the second semester. Each lesson is organized according to attainable learning outcomes grounded in these proficiency benchmarks.

The hallmark features of *Aula abierta* include:
- A **reimagined approach** to learning Spanish as a second language, providing a solid foundation for learning in real life.
- **Shorter lessons** (not chapters) that make planning easier and give students a feeling of accomplishment as they progress through the material.
- A scope and sequence organized around **communicative functions**, with grammar points integrated throughout.

Real-world applications for using Spanish in a globalized society.

Realistic tasks, grounded in the ACTFL Can-Do Statements, ask students to communicate authentically.

Cultural information and careful representation of the diverse Latino/a – Hispano/a communities in the US and abroad that promotes **critical thinking and cross-cultural understanding**.

Lección

2

Quiero aprender español

IN THIS LESSON WE ARE GOING TO
identify how we want to learn Spanish

LEARNING OUTCOMES
You will be able to...
- express intentions
- explain the reasons why we do things
- talk about activities in the language classroom
- talk about leisure activities

VOCABULARY
- Words related to language learning and culture
- Classroom activities
- Leisure activities

LANGUAGE STRUCTURES
- Present: regular verbs
- The verb **querer**
- Personal pronouns
- **Para, por,** and **porque**
- Combining verbs and prepositions **a, con** and **de**
- The definite article (**el/la/los/las**)

PRONUNCIATION
- Spanish vowels

CULTURAL CONNECTIONS
- Languages in México

Pérez Art Museum Miami (PAMM).

A Lesson at a Glance:
Primer contacto

This section provides students with the opportunity to explore in an **authentic context** the lexical, cultural, and grammatical elements that will comprise the learning objectives throughout the lesson.

Students engage with the theme of the lesson and **activate their prior knowledge,** giving them their first contact with the language and culture of the lesson.

Strategy boxes guide students to discover patterns and usage in English that help them understand Spanish.

A Lesson at a Glance:
Comprendemos el vocabulario

Vocabulary is introduced in a **visually contextualized** way, whether it is through graphic resources (such as illustrations, photographs, infographics, etc.) that foment strong form-meaning connections or by including these lexical items in realistic texts and/or activities that lead to communication.

> **Active vocabulary** appears in blue, signaling to students the words and expressions they will be asked to reproduce throughout the lesson.

> Activities are carefully sequenced, giving students the opportunity to process new **vocabulary in small chunks.**

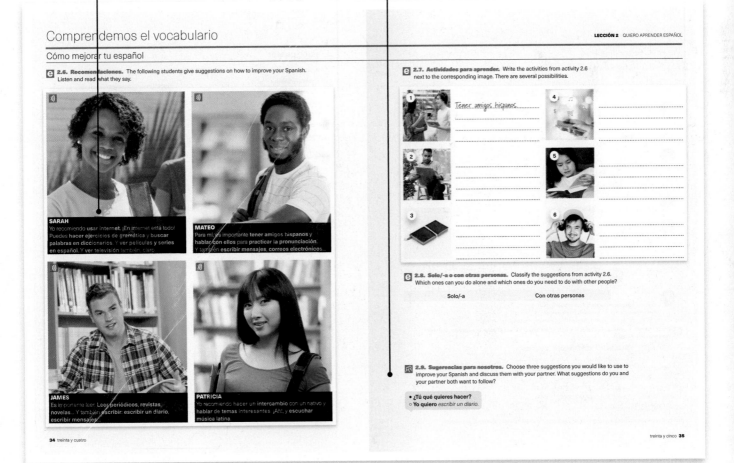

Comprendemos el vocabulario

LECCIÓN 2 QUIERO APRENDER ESPAÑOL

Cómo mejorar tu español

2.6. Recomendaciones. The following students give suggestions on how to improve your Spanish. Listen and read what they say.

SARAH
Yo recomiendo usar internet. ¡En internet está todo! Puedes hacer ejercicios de gramática y buscar palabras en diccionarios. Y ver películas y series en español. Y ver televisión también, claro.

MATEO
Para mí es importante tener amigos hispanos y hablar con ellos para practicar la pronunciación. Y también escribir mensajes, correos electrónicos...

JAMES
Es importante leer. Leer periódicos, revistas, novelas... Y también escribir: escribir un diario, escribir mensajes...

PATRICIA
Yo recomiendo hacer un intercambio con un nativo y hablar de temas interesantes. ¡Ah!, y escuchar música latina.

2.7. Actividades para aprender. Write the activities from activity 2.6 next to the corresponding image. There are several possibilities.

1. Tener amigos hispanos
2.
3.
4.
5.
6.

2.8. Solo/-a o con otras personas. Classify the suggestions from activity 2.6. Which ones can you do alone and which ones do you need to do with other people?

Solo/-a   Con otras personas

2.9. Sugerencias para nosotros. Choose three suggestions you would like to use to improve your Spanish and discuss them with your partner. What suggestions do you and your partner both want to follow?

● ¿Tú qué quieres hacer?
○ Yo quiero escribir un diario.

A Lesson at a Glance:
Exploramos la lengua

As indicated by the title, students explore language within a context that presents structures in a graduated, **inductive manner**. They learn by doing.

In this way, students are trained to:
- be **independent learners**, to approach new texts in the most effective way
- ask themselves questions about the function of the language
- look for answers
- build their own grammatical understanding

The inductive approach has tremendous benefits in the language classroom and even more so outside of class, when students encounter Spanish texts and documents in the real world.

> Learners begin by observing the structure in a realistic context relating to the theme of the lesson. The focus is on **meaning before form**.

> The activities gradually guide students to **draw conclusions** regarding the form or uses of the grammatical structure.

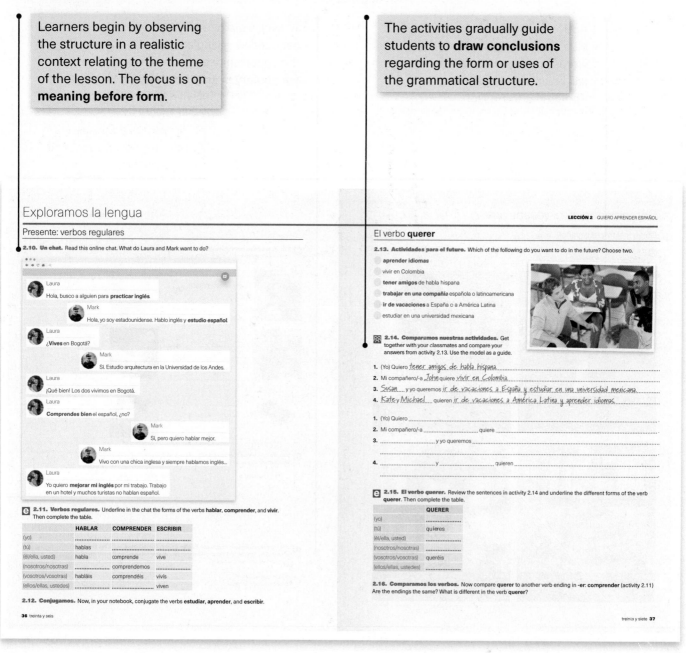

Exploramos la lengua

Presente: verbos regulares

2.10. Un chat. Read this online chat. What do Laura and Mark want to do?

Laura
Hola, busco a alguien para **practicar inglés**.

Mark
Hola, yo soy estadounidense. Hablo inglés y **estudio español**.

Laura
¿**Vives** en Bogotá?

Mark
Sí. Estudio arquitectura en la Universidad de los Andes.

Laura
¡Qué bien! Los dos vivimos en Bogotá.

Laura
Comprendes bien el español, ¿no?

Mark
Sí, pero quiero hablar mejor.

Mark
Vivo con una chica inglesa y siempre hablamos inglés.

Laura
Yo quiero **mejorar mi inglés** por mi trabajo. Trabajo en un hotel y muchos turistas no hablan español.

e 2.11. Verbos regulares. Underline in the chat the forms of the verbs **hablar**, **comprender**, and **vivir**. Then complete the table.

	HABLAR	COMPRENDER	ESCRIBIR
(yo)			
(tú)	hablas		
(él/ella, usted)	habla	comprende	vive
(nosotros/nosotras)		comprendemos	
(vosotros/vosotras)	habláis	comprendéis	vivís
(ellos/ellas, ustedes)			viven

2.12. Conjugamos. Now, in your notebook, conjugate the verbs **estudiar**, **aprender**, and **escribir**.

LECCIÓN 2 QUIERO APRENDER ESPAÑOL

El verbo **querer**

2.13. Actividades para el futuro. Which of the following do you want to do in the future? Choose two.

- aprender idiomas
- vivir en Colombia
- **tener amigos** de habla hispana
- **trabajar en una compañía** española o latinoamericana
- **ir de vacaciones** a España o a América Latina
- estudiar en una universidad mexicana

2.14. Comparamos nuestras actividades. Get together with your classmates and compare your answers from activity 2.13. Use the model as a guide.

1. (Yo) Quiero tener amigos de habla hispana.
2. Mi compañero/-a John quiere vivir en Colombia.
3. Susan y yo queremos ir de vacaciones a España y estudiar en una universidad mexicana.
4. Kate y Michael quieren ir de vacaciones a América Latina y aprender idiomas.

1. (Yo) Quiero ....
2. Mi compañero/-a .... quiere ....
3. .... y yo queremos ....
4. .... y .... quieren ....

e 2.15. El verbo querer. Review the sentences in activity 2.14 and underline the different forms of the verb **querer**. Then complete the table.

	QUERER
(yo)	
(tú)	quieres
(él/ella, usted)	
(nosotros/nosotras)	
(vosotros/vosotras)	queréis
(ellos/ellas, ustedes)	

2.16. Comparamos los verbos. Now compare **querer** to another verb ending in **-er: comprender** (activity 2.11) Are the endings the same? What is different in the verb **querer**?

A Lesson at a Glance:
Comunicamos

In **Comunicamos**, students put into practice what they have learned in the lesson and begin to develop **communicative competency**. The activities, grouped in themes, ask students to reflect on and draw from their own experiences as they express themselves.

The activities align to the learning objectives of the lesson and encourage students to:
- **compare** their own perspectives to that of others
- use language in a **personal and meaningful way**
- show that they can actively communicate about **their own world and ideas**

Activities are carefully designed to build confidence and competency by engaging students in **active conversation** with each other and by reinforcing language structures.

The "¿Sabes que...?" boxes provide additional information to supplement the content presented in the lesson. In this way, students get familiar with the **cultural diversity of regions where Spanish is spoken** as they interact with the target language.

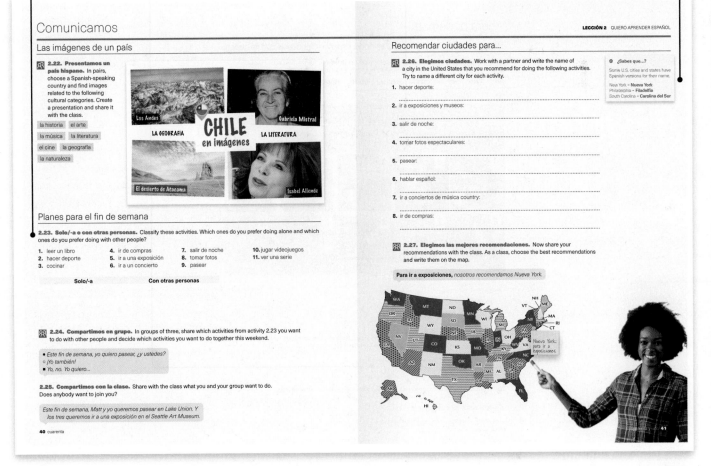

A Lesson at a Glance:
Ahora podemos...

In this section, students collaborate to complete the final lesson task that aligns with the **Can-Do statements**. Here, they work with the language in a way that requires negotiation skills and content knowledge to create a written or oral product that could realistically occur in their communities. The activities in this section stimulate **higher-level thinking skills** as students are creating with language and conveying its meaning.

The culminating task includes having students:
• research, reflect, and create
• identify the information they wish to transmit
• negotiate meaning
• present and share information
• comment and give feedback

Models are provided so that students can focus on the content they wish to present.

Students are guided through the process with prompts, which help them get started and work their way to the presentation stage.

A Lesson at a Glance:
Video

This section and the corresponding video activities found online in **MyLab** are intended to foster the **audiovisual competence** of the students. The objective of the activities—which include Before Watching, Active Watching, and After Watching—is to prepare learners for a world in which audiovisual documents are ever more present, diverse, and relevant. How does this section accomplish this?

- By featuring members of the Latino-Hispano community from a variety of backgrounds in **brief, authentic documentaries**, so that students come into contact with the cultural and linguistic richness and diversity of **Spanish-speaking communities in the United States**.
- By offering comprehension activities that **focus on meaning**.

The introduction gives students a brief summary of the content and a screen capture from the video to **pique student interest**.

As a follow-up to the cultural note, students are asked to **make connections** with diverse communities in the United States and learn more about them.

Video   **LECCIÓN 2** QUIERO APRENDER ESPAÑOL

La niña mariachi

In *La niña mariachi*, we will get to know Yailyn Garcia, a student living with her mother in New York City. Although she was born in New York, Yailyn feels a deep connection to her family's Mexican roots. By studying and performing traditional mariachi music, she is able to combine her passion for music with her love of Mexico.

Pearson MyLab

To find out more about Yailyn and mariachi music, go to MyLab to watch **La niña mariachi** and complete the video activities.

⊕ ¿Sabes que...?

Mariachi music is a style of folkloric music that embodies the spirit of Mexico. Typically a mariachi band is comprised of male and female musicians playing violin, guitar, guitarrón (a large acoustic bass guitar), vihuela (a five stringed guitar-like instrument), and trumpet. All or some of the musicians sing traditional mariachi songs like *Cielito lindo*, *El rey*, *México lindo y querido*, and others.

🔍 Hacemos conexiones

To get familiar with mariachi culture, search the internet to listen to these songs and find pictures of mariachi bands. Share one interesting fact that you found during your search.

cuarenta y tres **43**

A Lesson at a Glance:
Conectamos nuestras culturas

This spread is specifically designed for students to explore fresh, real-world cultural topics, to promote **global cultural awareness**, and to make cross-cultural connections.

The topics are tied to the theme of the lesson and readings are carefully selected to **dispel stereotypes** and overgeneralizations.

The activities that accompany these texts are designed to help students become critical thinkers about **cultural products**, **practices**, and **perspectives**.

Conectamos nuestras culturas

LECCIÓN 2 QUIERO APRENDER ESPAÑOL

El español y las lenguas originarias en México

DÍA INTERNACIONAL DE LA LENGUA MATERNA 21 DE FEBRERO

MÉXICO MULTILINGÜE 69 LENGUAS NACIONALES

En México se habla español y cerca de 70 lenguas originarias. De estas, las más importantes son el náhuatl, el ch'ol, el tseltal, el totonaco, el otomí, el tsotsil, el mixteco, el mazateco, el maya y el zapoteco.

El español tiene una posición dominante y cuenta con instituciones como la **Academia Mexicana de la Lengua**. Fundada en el siglo XIX, su objetivo es proteger la lengua española y responder a las preguntas de los hablantes.

El **INALI (Instituto Nacional de Lenguas Indígenas)** promueve la diversidad cultural y lingüística. Su misión es preservar y fortalecer las lenguas originarias. Además, asesora al gobierno mexicano en políticas relacionadas con esta materia.

ANTES DE LEER

2.31. Conocimiento previo. What language or languages do you think are spoken in Mexico?

LECTURA ACTIVA

2.32. Verdadero o falso. Read the text and pay attention to the image. Then, indicate if these statements are true or false.

	Verdadero	Falso
1. En México existen muchas lenguas nativas.		
2. El náhuatl es la lengua más importante de México.		
3. En México existen instituciones que protegen las lenguas.		
4. El Día de la Lengua Materna solo se celebra en México.		

2.33. Corregimos. Correct the statements from activity 2.32 that are false.

DESPUÉS DE LEER

2.34. Investigamos. Are there any institutions in your country devoted to protecting languages? Research this topic online and share your findings in the class.

44 cuarenta y cuatro

cuarenta y cinco 45

A Lesson at a Glance:
Textos escritos: Leemos y escribimos and Textos audiovisuales: vemos, escuchamos y presentamos

This section provides opportunities for students to learn **how to approach both written and audiovisual texts** for comprehension and to **create their own texts** based on the information they gather.

Students develop comprehension and expression through activities similar to those used in **ACTFL's Integrated Performance Assessment (IPA)**.

Textos escritos: leemos y escribimos

Leemos sobre México

ANTES DE LA LECTURA

2.35. Preparación. What do you know about Mexico? Brainstorm information related to each of the following categories and write it down.

1. Lenguas: ....
2. Turismo: ....
3. Educación: ....
4. Productos: ....

2.36. Comparación. Compare your answers to a classmate's. Are they similar? Have you learned something new about Mexico?

LECTURA ACTIVA

2.37. Lectura. Now read the text and find out more about Mexico. What topic from activity 2.35 relates to each of the facts in the text?

4 DATOS CURIOSOS SOBRE MÉXICO

1. México tiene una diversidad lingüística enorme. El español es una de las lenguas nacionales junto con 68 lenguas originarias.

2. México es un destino turístico muy importante: el principal de América Latina y uno de los más visitados del mundo. Hay 32 sitios culturales o naturales considerados por la Unesco como Patrimonio de la Humanidad.

3. En 1551 se funda la Real y Pontificia Universidad de México (la actual Universidad Nacional Autónoma de México), la primera institución de América en ofrecer clases de Medicina, Teología, Leyes y Arte.

4. México produce gran cantidad de metales preciosos. Es el primer productor de plata del mundo.

DESPUÉS DE LEER

2.38. Interpretación. Follow these steps to extract information from the text.

a. First, circle the number of each detail below that is mentioned in the article (not all are included!).
b. Find in the text the information requested and write it down.
c. In pairs, check you answers. Do you have similar ones?

1. Número de lenguas nacionales: ....

2. Número de lugares reconocidos por la Unesco: ....

3. Primera institución universitaria en América: ....

4. Lugar en el *ranking* mundial de producción de plata: ....

Escribimos sobre México y sobre nuestro país

2.39. Reacción personal. Write a personal reaction to specific information provided by the text "4 datos curiosos sobre México". Justify your reaction.

2.40. Comparación. Create a similar fact sheet about your country: "4 datos sobre mi país". Include the answers to the following questions: When was your university founded? How many official languages are spoken in the U.S.? What kind of products are produced in the state you live or are originally from? Include any images to support your information. Then, share it with the rest of the class.

Arkansas es el primer productor de arroz en Estados Unidos.

A Lesson at a Glance:
Recursos lingüísticos

All the grammatical content in this reference section is presented in the same order in which it appeared in the lesson. The section includes **easy-to-read grammar outlines**, entirely in English, with detailed explanations necessary for their understanding, and examples that clarify the use of the rules in context.

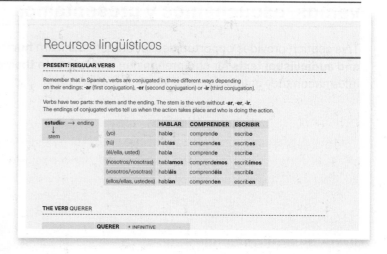

Pronunciamos

This section offers explanations regarding the sounds of Spanish and pronunciation activities specially **created to help English-speaking students** with issues that are usually difficult or that can result in problems with communication. Students become aware of and sensitive to these "challenges", learn through comparison with their own system, and practice with audio recordings.

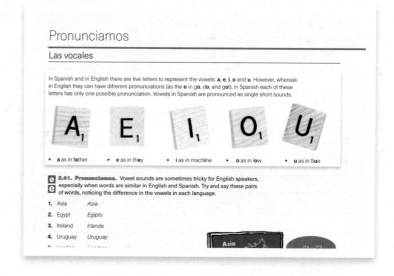

Vocabulario activo

This section summarizes the active vocabulary presented in the lesson. The words and expressions are organized in thematic lists along with their English translations. **Learning strategies** and advice for facilitating the acquisition of vocabulary are also offered here.

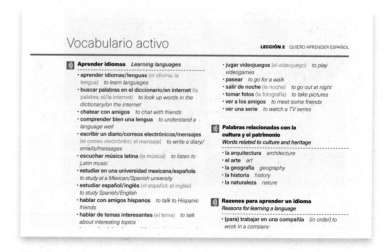

Aula abierta
Digital Resources

Aula abierta features a **MyLab**, which houses
its suite of digital resources.

Student Resources

- **Easy-to-assign modules** that feature all of the *Aula abierta* content curated in a
  learning path. This includes links to eText pages, all interactive activities, PowerPoints,
  grammar tutorials, flashcards, and all downloadable media assets.
- The *Aula abierta* **eText with clickable audio and video** links at point of use.
- A **documentary video series** created especially for *Aula abierta*. In these 15 authentic,
  relatable videos, students get to know Hispanics across the United States and explore
  the linguistic and cultural heritage unique to these communities. Each video is
  supported by pre-, while-, and post-viewing activities to aid students' comprehension.
- A library of **cultural videos** from Spanish-speaking countries across the globe.
- **Practice Activities**, authored by Wendy Mendez-Hasselman at Palm Beach State
  College, were designed specifically for the digital environment and are available
  online only in the **MyLab**. Additionally, these activities feature **just-in-time support** for
  students. If students are working on an activity and need to review something, they can
  simply use the resources provided in the **Need Help** link at the top of the activity.

Instructor Resources

- Abundant teaching resources: **lesson plans**, **syllabi**, **downloadable media assets**,
  audio and **video scripts** are just a click away.
- **Integrated Performance Assessments** use authentic sources and focus on real-life
  contexts that students will find both engaging and meaningful. The IPAs target each of
  the three modes of communication: Interpretive, Interpersonal, and Presentational.
- A rigorous **Testing Program** follows the pedagogy of *Aula abierta* in its focus on
  meaningful production and interpretation of language in real-world contexts.
- **PowerPoints** are designed to support all students and teachers in the classroom. These
  presentational tools provide quick access for instructors to display essential visuals in the
  classroom, while also expanding on the book content to provide a powerful lecture tool.

Acknowledgments

The *Aula abierta* author team is deeply grateful to the Executive Board of Advisors for their assistance in the development of this program:

Yuly Asención Delaney, Northern Arizona University
Ignacio López Alemany, University of North Carolina – Greensboro
Ruth Brown, University of Kentucky
Sara Casler, Sierra College
Devon Hanahan, College of Charleston
Rosalinda Nericcio, San Diego State University
Giovanni Zimotti, University of Iowa
Theresa Zmurkewycz, Saint Joseph's University

We would also like to thank our reviewers:

Tim Altanero, Austin Community College – Rio Grande
Javier Alvarez, Eastern Kentucky University
Jose Ignacio Alvarez-García, Elgin Community College
Daniel Anderson, University of Oklahoma
Guadalupe Arana-Rochel, University of Illinois – Chicago
Corinne Arrieta, American River College
Yuly Asención-Delaney, Northern Arizona University
Anne Becher, University of Colorado – Boulder
Carlos Benavides, University of Massachusetts – Dartmouth
Stephanie Blankenship, Liberty University
Amy Bomke, Indiana University – Purdue University Indianapolis
Cathy Briggs, North Lake College
Ruth Brown, University of Kentucky
Antonella Calarota, Montclair State University
Sara Casler, Sierra College
Aurora Castillo-Scott, Georgia College & State University
Esther Castro, San Diego State University
Isabel Castro, Towson University
Diane Ceo-DiFrancesco, Xavier University
Irene Chico-Wyatt, University of Kentucky
Heather Colburn, Northwestern University
Kelly Conroy, Metropolitan State University of Denver
Scott Cooper, Anne Arundel Community College
Javier Coronado-Aliegro, Elgin Community College
Becky Cottrell, Metropolitan State University of Denver
Amy D'Agrosa, University of Missouri – St. Louis
Daniel D'Arpa, Mercer County Community College
Stephanie Daffer, Santa Clara University
Pilar Damron, Alamo Northwest Vista College
Dulce de Castro, Collin College
Jabier Elorrieta, New York University
Ines Garcia, American River College
Susana Garcia Prudencio, Penn State University
Tania Gomez, College of Saint Benedict
Inmaculada Gomez-Soler, University of Memphis

Marie Guiribitey, Florida International University
Devon Hanahan, College of Charleston
Shenika Harris, Linwood University
Mary Hartson, Oakland University
Eda Henao, Borough of Manhattan Community College
Steve Hunsaker, Brigham Young University – Idaho
Carmen Jany, California State University – San Bernardino
Valerie Jepsen, Winthrop University
Karen Jones, Santa Fe College
Ronald Leow, Georgetown University
Dolores Lima, University of Pittsburgh
Raul Llorente, Georgia State University
Nuria López-Ortega, University of Cincinnati
María Manni, University of Maryland – Baltimore City
Mary McKinney, Texas Christian University
Marco Mena, Massachusetts Bay Community College
Wendy Mendez-Hassleman, Palm Beach State College South
Jeanne Mullaney, Community College of Rhode Island
Alejandro Muñoz-Garces, Coastal Carolina University
Rosalinda Nericcio, San Diego State University
Danae Orlins, University of Cincinnati
Paqui Paredes, Western Washington University
Michelle Petersen, Arizona State University – Downtown
Josh Pongan, Temple University
Dolores Pons, University of Michigan – Flint
Goretti Prieto Botana, University of Southern California
Jennifer Quinlan, Brigham Young University – Provo
William Reyes-Cubides, Michigan State University
Danielle Richardson, Davidson City Community College
Silvia Rodriguez-Sabater, College of Charleston
Nohelia Rojas-Miesse, Miami University of Ohio
Claudia Sánchez-Gutiérrez, University of California Davis
Steve Sheppard, University of North Texas
Mariana Stone, University of North Georgia
Gregory Thompson, Brigham Young University – Provo
Victoria Uricoechea, Winthrop University
Karen Valerio, University of Nevada – Las Vegas
Celinés Villalba, Rutgers University
Sarah Vitale, Loyola University Maryland
Michael Vrooman, Grand Valley State University
Anne Walton-Ramírez, Arizona State University
Justin White, Florida Atlantic University
Karen Williams, Georgia State University Perimeter College – Decatur
Marjorie Zambrano-Paff, Indiana University of Pennsylvania
Gabriela Zapata, Texas A&M University – College Station
Allie Zaubi, College of Charleston
Giovanni Zimotti, University of Iowa
Theresa Zmurkewycz, St. Joseph's University

Lección

Preliminar

En el aula

IN THIS LESSON WE ARE GOING TO

learn useful things for our first day

LEARNING OUTCOMES
You will be able to...

- introduce yourself

- communicate in the classroom

- greet and say good-bye

VOCABULARY

- Words related to the classroom

- Numbers from 0 to 100

Primer contacto

P.1. Presentarse en español. Listen to these students speaking Spanish. Then introduce yourselves like they do.

> Hola, yo me llamo *Phil*. ¿Y tú? ¿Cómo te llamas?

> Me llamo *Hunter*. ¿Y tú?

> Yo, *Jason*.

P.2. Nuestro nombre en un papel. Now write your name on a sheet of paper and put it on your desk so the others can see it.

⚙ **Estrategia**

Throughout the lessons, important words and expressions related to a given topic will be highlighted in blue.

Comprendemos el vocabulario

Recursos básicos para la clase

P.3. En la clase. Read and listen to the conversations taking place in a language class.

1. ¿Cómo se escribe "Jorge"?

¿Cómo dices? ¿Puedes repetir, por favor?

Sí. ¿Cómo se escribe "Jorge"?

2. ¿Qué significa "chévere"?

"Cool".

3. Me llamo Sam.

¿Puedes hablar más alto, por favor?

4. Hola, ¿cómo estás? Me llamo Susan.

¿Puedes hablar más despacio, por favor?

5. ¿Cómo se dice "thank you" en español?

"Gracias".

6. Piececitos... azulosos... de frío...

Lo siento, no entendí...

7. ¿Cómo se dice esto en español?

"Libro".

8. Página 8, actividad 7.

Más palabras

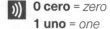

0 cero = *zero*	**2 dos** = *two*	**4 cuatro** = *four*	**6 seis** = *six*	**8 ocho** = *eight*	**10 diez** = *ten*
1 uno = *one*	**3 tres** = *three*	**5 cinco** = *five*	**7 siete** = *seven*	**9 nueve** = *nine*	

e **P.4. Situaciones de clase.** Indicate in which of the situations of activity P.3 the students do the following and how they say it in Spanish.

1. Ask how a word is spelled.

..1..... ¿Cómo se escribe...? ....

2. Ask somebody to speak louder.

....

3. Ask someone for the translation of an English word.

....

4. Ask about the meaning of a word.

....

5. Ask someone the Spanish word for something.

....

6. Ask somebody to speak more slowly.

....

7. Ask someone to repeat what was said.

....

8. Tell someone you didn't understand what they said.

....

> ✿ **Estrategia**
>
> In this preliminary lesson you'll find basic chunks or questions that might come in handy throughout the course. Feel free to come back to this lesson whenever you need it.

Saludos y despedidas

))) e **P.5. Saludos y despedidas.** Listen to these Spanish expressions for greeting or saying good-bye to someone. Listen a second time and indicate the order in which you hear them.

saludos despedidas

○ ¿Cómo estás?   ○ ¡Nos vemos!

○ Buenas tardes.   ○ Hasta pronto.

○ Buenos días.   ○ Chao.

○ Buenas noches.   ○ ¡Hasta luego!

○ Hola.   ○ ¡Adiós!

> ❶ **¿Necesitas ayuda?** *(Need help?)*
>
> **¿Cómo estás?** = *How are you?*
> **Buenos días.** = *Good morning.*
> **Buenas tardes.** = *Good afternoon/evening.*
> **Buenas noches.** = *Good evening/night.*
> **Hola.** = *Hello.*
>
> **¡Nos vemos!** = *See you!*
> **Hasta pronto.** = *See you soon.*
> **Chao.** = *Bye.*
> **¡Hasta luego!** = *See you later!*
> **¡Adiós!** = *Good-bye!*

> ✿ **Estrategia**
>
> All the expressions presented here are quite general across the Spanish-speaking world, but remember that there are many others and that uses may vary even between regions of the same country.
>
> **Buenos días, buenas tardes** and **buenas noches** are related to the time of the day (morning, afternoon and evening/night) and the formality of the situation. Both factors vary a lot from country to country.

Comprendemos el vocabulario

Las cosas de la clase

🔊 **P.6. Las cosas de la clase.** Read and listen to the words in Spanish for common classroom objects.

1 el libro

2 el bolígrafo

3 el cuaderno

4 la pizarra (digital)

5 la hoja de papel

6 la mochila

7 la computadora

8 el celular

9 el proyector

10 el televisor

11 la mesa

12 la papelera

13 la silla

Los números del 11 al 100

🔊 **P.7. Los números del 11 al 100.** Read and listen to the numbers in Spanish.

11	once	26	veintiséis	50	cincuenta
12	doce	27	veintisiete	60	sesenta
13	trece	28	veintiocho	70	setenta
14	catorce	29	veintinueve	80	ochenta
15	quince	30	treinta	90	noventa
16	dieciséis	31	treinta y uno	99	noventa y nueve
17	diecisiete	32	treinta y dos	100	cien
18	dieciocho	33	treinta y tres		
19	diecinueve	34	treinta y cuatro		
20	veinte	35	treinta y cinco		
21	veintiuno	36	treinta y seis		
22	veintidós	37	treinta y siete		
23	veintitrés	38	treinta y ocho		
24	veinticuatro	39	treinta y nueve		
25	veinticinco	40	cuarenta		

P.8. Hacemos inventario. Take inventory of items you can see in your classroom. Then share your figures with the others. Did you and your partner come up with the same number?

- *Libros, catorce.*
- **Yo tengo** *doce.*
- *Yo, quince.*

> ❶ **¿Necesitas ayuda?**
>
> **Yo tengo** = *I have*

e P.9. Escribimos números en letras. Write the words for the following numbers.

1. 44 = ...

2. 55 = ...

3. 66 = ...

4. 77 = ...

5. 88 = ...

> ❶ **¿Necesitas ayuda?**
>
> Although there are exceptions, these are the basic rules to pluralize nouns in Spanish:
>
> • if the noun ends in a vowel, we add -**s**: libro**s**, cuaderno**s**, hoja**s** de papel...
>
> • if the noun ends in a consonant (most commonly **l**, **r**, **n**, **d** or **z**), we add -**es**: papel**es**, proyector**es**, televisor**es**, pizarron**es**...

e P.10. Operaciones matemáticas. Solve the following math problems. You can use your cellphone!

1. 2 x 7 = ...

2. 6 + 2 = ...

3. 50 : 10 = ...

4. 80 - 8 = ...

5. 81 + 9 = ...

6. 24 : 2 = ...

> ❶ **¿Necesitas ayuda?**
>
> | + | más |
> |---|---|
> | - | menos |
> | x | por |
> | : | (dividido) entre |

Comprendemos el vocabulario

Palabras en español

))) **P.11. Palabras en español.** How many words do you understand in these pictures?

P.12. ¿Cuántas palabras comprendemos? Share your number with the class. Then, each of you will say in English the words you understand.

- **Yo comprendo** *10 palabras.*
- *Yo, 12.*

Teatro significa "theater", ¿no?

⚙ **Estrategia**

You'll notice that many words are quite similar in Spanish and English. These are called **cognates** and they may or may not have the same meaning in both languages. Be aware of the context when you find cognates so you can tell if they are **false cognates** (cognates with different meanings). For example, **embarazada** might look like the English word **embarrassed**, but it really means "pregnant".

Vocabulario activo

Información personal
Personal information

- ¿Cómo te llamas?   *What's your name?*
- Hola.   *Hello.*
- ¿Y tú?   *And you?*
- Yo me llamo...   *My name is...*

Recursos básicos para la clase
Classroom expressions

- la actividad   *activity*
- ¿Cómo dices?   *What did you say?*
- ¿Cómo se dice esto en español?   *How do you say this in Spanish?*
- ¿Cómo se dice "thank you" en español?   *How do you say 'thank you' in Spanish?*
- ¿Cómo se escribe...?   *How do you write...?*
- gracias   *thank you*
- Lo siento, no entendí.   *Sorry, I didn't understand*
- la página   *page*
- ¿Puedes hablar más alto, por favor?   *Could you speak louder, please?*
- ¿Puedes hablar más despacio, por favor?   *Could you speak more slowly, please?*
- ¿Puedes repetir, por favor?   *Can you repeat (it/that), please?*
- ¿Qué significa...?   *What's the meaning of...?*

Las cosas de la clase
Words related to the classroom

- el bolígrafo   *pen*
- el celular   *cellphone, smartphone*
- la computadora   *computer*
- el cuaderno   *notebook*
- la hoja de papel   *sheet of paper*
- el libro   *book*
- la mesa   *table*
- la mochila   *backpack*
- la papelera   *wastepaper basket*
- la pizarra (digital)   *chalkboard (whiteboard)*
- el proyector   *projector*
- la silla   *chair*
- el televisor   *television set*

Números
Numbers

- cero   *zero*
- uno   *one*
- dos   *two*
- tres   *three*
- cuatro   *four*
- cinco   *five*
- seis   *six*
- siete   *seven*
- ocho   *eight*
- nueve   *nine*
- diez   *ten*
- once   *eleven*
- doce   *twelve*
- trece   *thirteen*
- catorce   *fourteen*
- quince   *fifteen*
- dieciséis   *sixteen*
- diecisiete   *seventeen*
- dieciocho   *eighteen*
- diecinueve   *nineteen*
- veinte   *twenty*
- veintiuno   *twenty-one*
- veintidós   *twenty-two*
- veintitrés   *twenty-three*
- veinticuatro   *twenty-four*
- veinticinco   *twenty-five*
- veintiséis   *twenty-six*
- veintisiete   *twenty-seven*
- veintiocho   *twenty-eight*
- veintinueve   *twenty-nine*
- treinta   *thirty*
- treinta y uno   *thirty-one*
- treinta y dos   *thirty-two*
- treinta y tres   *thirty-three*
- treinta y cuatro   *thirty-four*
- treinta y cinco   *thirty-five*
- treinta y seis   *thirty-six*
- treinta y siete   *thirty-seven*
- treinta y ocho   *thirty-eight*
- treinta y nueve   *thirty-nine*
- cuarenta   *forty*
- cincuenta   *fifty*
- sesenta   *sixty*
- setenta   *seventy*
- ochenta   *eighty*
- noventa   *ninety*
- noventa y nueve   *ninety-nine*
- cien   *one hundred*

Lección

1

Nosotros

IN THIS LESSON WE ARE GOING TO

create a poster with information about who we are

LEARNING OUTCOMES
You will be able to...

• give and ask for personal information

VOCABULARY

• Nationalities

• Professions

• Age

• Pastimes

LANGUAGE STRUCTURES

• Alphabet

• The forms of **-ar**, **-er**, and **-ir** verbs

• The verbs **llamarse**, **trabajar**, **ser**, **tener**, and **vivir**

PRONUNCIATION

• Pronunciation of the letters **c/z** and **g/j**

CULTURAL CONNECTIONS

• Different ways people can be addressed

Estudiantes universitarios.

Primer contacto

1.1. Algunos datos sobre Muriel. Read the information Muriel has shared on a social network. Discuss with others (in English) the information you can guess about her.

Nombre: Muriel

Apellidos: Gallego Smith

Edad: 22 años

Nacionalidad: argentina y estadounidense

Lugar de residencia: Boulder, Colorado (Estados Unidos)

Profesión: estudiante y mesera

130 Friends   14 Favorites   10 Albums

Marc   Anthony   Jay

Ruby   Selena   Martha

Muriel Gallego Smith
July, 12

1.2. Muriel se presenta. Listen to Muriel as she talks about herself using the information in activity 1.1.

> **Hola, me llamo** Muriel.
> **Mi nombre completo es** Muriel Gallego Smith.
> **Tengo** 22 años.
> **Soy** argentina y estadounidense. **Tengo** las dos nacionalidades.
> **Vivo en** Boulder, en Estados Unidos.
> **Soy** estudiante y **trabajo en** un restaurante.

> ⚙ **Estrategia**
>
> Remember, words highlighted in blue are considered active vocabulary for the lesson.

1.3. Nuestros datos. Now use Muriel's example and write basic information about yourself in Spanish. Be prepared to present it to the class.

Comprendemos el vocabulario

Nacionalidades y profesiones

e **1.4. Nacionalidades y profesiones.** Read and listen to these people from different countries who talk about their nationality and their profession.

1)))
Me llamo Mayra y soy **colombiana**. Soy **empresaria**. **Tengo una empresa de informática**.

2)))
Hola, soy Mario. Soy **peruano**. **Trabajo en un restaurante**. Soy **cocinero**.

3)))
Hola, mi nombre es Ana. Soy **argentina** y soy **profesora de español**.

4)))
Me llamo Ben. Soy **estadounidense** y soy **estudiante de arquitectura**.

5)))
Me llamo Javiera. Soy **chilena** y **trabajo en una agencia de viajes**.

6)))
Hola, soy Paola. Soy **mexicana**, de Monterrey. Soy **fotógrafa**.

Más palabras

))) **PROFESIONES** = *PROFESSIONS*
actor/actriz = *actor/actress*
arquitecto/-a = *architect*
cantante (el/la) = *singer*
conductor/a = *driver*
diseñador/a = *designer*
diseñador/a gráfico/-a = *graphic designer*
médico/-a = *doctor*
mesero/-a = *bartender, waiter/waitress*
taxista (el/la) = *taxi driver*

(trabajo en) **una fábrica** = *(I work in) a factory*
(trabajo en) **una tienda** = *(I work in) a store*

NACIONALIDADES = *NATIONALITIES*
boliviano/-a = *Bolivian*
costarricense = *Costa Rican*
cubano/-a = *Cuban*
dominicano/-a = *Dominican*
ecuatoguineano/-a = *Equatorial Guinean*

ecuatoriano/-a = *Ecuadorian*
español/a = *Spanish*
guatemalteco/-a = *Guatemalan*
hondureño/-a = *Honduran*
nicaragüense = *Nicaraguan*
panameño/-a = *Panamanian*
paraguayo/-a = *Paraguayan*
puertorriqueño/-a = *Puerto Rican*
salvadoreño/-a = *Salvadoran*
uruguayo/-a = *Uruguayan*
venezolano/-a = *Venezuelan*

e **1.5. Nombre, nacionalidad y profesión.** Complete with the information for each of the people in activity 1.4.

1

Nombre: ....

Nacionalidad: *colombiana* ....

Profesión: ....

4

Nombre: ....

Nacionalidad: ....

Profesión: ....

2

Nombre: ....

Nacionalidad: ....

Profesión: ....

5

Nombre: ....

Nacionalidad: ....

Profesión: ....

3

Nombre: ....

Nacionalidad: ....

Profesión: ....

6

Nombre: ....

Nacionalidad: ....

Profesión: ....

1.6. Dos personas que admiramos. Think of two people you admire (one from the United States and one from a Spanish-speaking country) and create their profile as in activity 1.5.

1.7. Compartimos la información. Now share the profiles and tell your classmates why you admire these people.

Yo admiro a *Gina Rodriguez*, **porque es una persona** *talentosa.*

⚙ **Estrategia**

Remember that throughout the course you'll find yourself in situations where you won't have all the words you need to complete a task. Be proactive and train yourself in using an online dictionary effectively. And don't be afraid to ask your instructor!

💬 **Para comunicar**

porque = *because*

**interesante
inteligente
talentoso/-a
creativo/-a
ambicioso/-a
generoso/-a**

Exploramos la lengua

El alfabeto

 1.8. Personas, países y ciudades. Which words in this chart are people's first names *(un nombre)*? Which are countries *(un país)*? Which are cities *(una ciudad)*?

A	a	Alberto	Ñ	eñe	España
B	be	Buenos Aires	O	o	Óscar
C	ce	Colombia	P	pe	Pablo
D	de	Diego	Q	cu	Quito
E	e	Elena	R	erre	Ramón
F	efe	Federico	S	ese	Sara
G	ge	Guadalupe	T	te	Teresa
H	hache	Honduras	U	u	Uruguay
I	i	Ignacio	V	uve	Venezuela
J	jota	Javier	W	doble ve	Walter
K	ca	Karina	X	equis	Álex
L	ele	Luis	Y	ye, i griega	Yolanda
M	eme	María	Z	ceta	Zaragoza
N	ene	Natalia			

● *Alberto es un nombre, ¿no?*
○ *Sí. Y Buenos Aires es una ciudad argentina. Es la capital.*

1.9. El alfabeto. Listen and repeat the letters and the words from activity 1.8.

1.10. Deletreamos nuestro nombre. Your instructor will read the name of a letter out loud. If your name or your last name begins with that letter, say it and spell it.

● *Ese.*
○ *¡Yo! Susan: ese, u, ese, a, ene.*

❶ **¿Necesitas ayuda?**

¿no? at the end of a sentence is generally used to ask for confirmation about something we just said.

Las tres conjugaciones

e **1.11. Pasatiempos.** Read this list of pastimes and indicate which words are verbs.

ir al gimnasio

cantar

ver videos

el fútbol

leer

esquiar

viajar

escribir

dibujar

tocar la guitarra

bailar

el tenis

! **¿Necesitas ayuda?**

Verbs are words that are used to express actions, occurrences, or modes of being (**to do, to eat, to go**, etc.).

e **1.12. Terminaciones.** What three different endings do you observe in the verbs from activity 1.11?

....

1.13. Nuestros pasatiempos. Talk with your partner about your hobbies using the terms from activity 1.11.

Estrategia

Observing the endings of verbs in Spanish will help you conjugate them.

• **Mis pasatiempos son** *dibujar y el fútbol.*
○ **Mi principal pasatiempo es** *leer.*

Exploramos la lengua

Pedir y dar datos personales: los verbos **llamarse**, **trabajar**, **ser**, **tener** y **vivir**

1.14. Pedir y dar datos personales. Listen to the questions and write the answers.

1. ¿Cómo te llamas? ....
2. ¿Cuántos años tienes? ....
3. ¿Dónde vives? ....
4. ¿En qué trabajas? ....
5. ¿Cuál es tu correo electrónico? ....
6. ¿Cuál es tu número de teléfono? ....
7. ¿De dónde eres? ....

1.15. Entendemos las preguntas. Match each question to the information it relates to.

TO ASK ABOUT	QUESTIONS
la nacionalidad / el origen ◯	◯ ¿Cómo **se llama** la profesora?
el correo electrónico ◯	◯ ¿Cuántos años **tiene** Marta?
el nombre ◯	◯ ¿Dónde **vive** el presidente de tu país?
la profesión ◯	◯ ¿En qué **trabajas**?
la edad ◯	◯ ¿Cuál **es** tu correo electrónico?
el número de teléfono ◯	◯ ¿Cuál **es** tu número de teléfono?
el lugar de residencia ◯	◯ ¿De dónde **son** ustedes?

✿ **Estrategia**

Spanish verbs have different forms for each person (**I**, **you**, **he/she**, etc.). Don't panic! You need to study them, but the more you practice, the easier it will become to use verb forms in a natural way.

1.16. Entendemos los verbos. Find the words that are verbs in the questions from activity 1.15 and list the corresponding subject. You can use the verb chart below.

VERBO	SUJETO
se llama	ella (la profesora)
....	....
....	....
....	....
....	....
....	....
....	....

❶ **¿Necesitas ayuda?**

ser = *to be*
I am, you are, he/she/it is, we are, you (all) are.

In Spanish, **it** also uses the third person singular form of the verb even though there is no Spanish equivalent for the subject pronoun **it**.

• *¿Cuál es el nombre de tu universidad?* = What's the name of your school?
○ *Es Loyola.* = It's Loyola.

SUBJECT PRONOUNS	LLAMARSE	TRABAJAR	SER	TENER	VIVIR
(yo)	**me** llam**o**	trabaj**o**	**soy**	teng**o**	viv**o**
(tú)	**te** llam**as**	trabaj**as**	**eres**	tien**es**	viv**es**
(él/ella, usted)	**se** llam**a**	trabaj**a**	**es**	tien**e**	viv**e**
(nosotros/nosotras)	**nos** llam**amos**	trabaj**amos**	**somos**	ten**emos**	viv**imos**
(vosotros/vosotras)	**os** llam**áis**	trabaj**áis**	**sois**	ten**éis**	viv**ís**
(ellos/ellas, ustedes)	**se** llam**an**	trabaj**an**	**son**	tien**en**	viv**en**

❶ **¿Necesitas ayuda?**

We use the verb **llamarse** when we want to say somebody's name. These type of verbs are always used with a pronoun: **me, te, se, nos, os, se**.

***Me llamo** Bob.* ~~Llamo Bob.~~

1.17. Una fiesta. Javier lives in New York and is throwing a party for international students from his school. Fill in the conversations with the correct forms of **llamarse**, **trabajar**, **ser**, **tener**, and **vivir**.

1.

• *Hola, (llamarse, yo)* ....*Javier, ¿y tú?*
○ *Yo, Teresa.*
• *¿De dónde (ser, tú)* ....?
○ *(ser, yo)* .... *colombiana, de Bogotá.*

2.

• *¿(ser, tú)* .... *de Nueva York, Laura?*
○ *No, (ser, yo)* .... *de Puerto Rico, pero (trabajar, yo)* ....
   en Nueva York.
• *Ah... ¿Y en qué (trabajar, tú)* ....?
○ *(ser, yo)* .... *arquitecta. ¿Y tú?*

3.

• *Hola, ¿qué tal? (llamarse, yo)* .... *Óscar.*
○ *Hola, (llamarse, yo)* .... *Molly y él (llamarse, él)* .... *Mike.*
• *¿De dónde (ser, ustedes)* .... ?
○ *Somos estadounidenses. ¿Y tú?*
• *Yo, chileno.*

4.

• *¿Cuál (ser)* .... *tu correo electrónico?*
○ *Sí, (ser)* .... *marcos-marquez_siglo21@gmail.com.*

5.

• *Hola, (ser, nosotros)* .... *Álvaro y Marcos.*
○ *Ah, hola. Yo (llamarse, yo)* .... *Marta.*
   (trabajar, yo) .... *con Javier en el hospital.*
• *Ah, ¿también (ser, tú)* .... *médica?*
○ *Sí, (ser, yo)* .... *médica. ¿Y ustedes en qué*
   (trabajar) ....?

Comunicamos

Todos sabemos un poco de español

1.18. Palabras que sabemos. Write down words or expressions you know in Spanish.

1.19. Nuestras palabras en español. In groups, share your words and explain how you learned them.

1.20. Compartimos palabras. Decide how many of the words are interesting enough to share with the class (because they might be useful, because they are funny, etc.). Then, share them and explain your reasons (you can do this in English).

> *Nuestras palabras interesantes son "gato", "guacamole" y "amigo".*

⚙ **Estrategia**

Talking about the language you are learning can be a great activity. Discussing words (your relationship with them, how you discovered them, what you associate them with, etc.) might help you memorize them or remember them when you need to.

Palabras importantes para nosotros

1.21. Palabras importantes. Think of four important words in your life and write them in Spanish. Use the internet or ask your instructor.

Cine
...

Viajar
...

Amigos
...

Amor
...

> • *¿Cómo se dice "friends" en español?*
> ○ *"Amigos".*
> • *¿Cómo se escribe?*
> ○ *a, eme, i, ge, o, ese.*

1.22. Presentamos nuestras palabras. Share your words with the class and be prepared to answer questions about them.

> • *Cine, familia, deporte y vacaciones.*
> ○ *¿Qué significa "vacaciones"?*
> • *"Holidays".*

Las letras y los números de nuestro país

1.23. Las letras y los números de nuestro país. In groups, you are going to propose six letters and six numbers (between 0 and 100) that relate to your country. Together, decide the letters and numbers (discuss the reasons in English if necessary).

> • **Yo propongo** *la doble ve,* **de** *Washington.*
> ○ **OK. ¿Y un número?**
> • **El** *4.*

1.24. Presentamos y adivinamos. Present your letters and numbers one at a time. Your classmates will guess why you chose them.

> • *La doble ve. You chose it because it is the first letter of Washington D.C., the city.*
> ○ *¡Sí!*

> • *El número cuatro. You chose it because the fourth of July is a very important day.*
> ○ *¡Sí!*

Somos famosos

1.25. Completamos la ficha de una persona famosa. Imagine you are a famous person. Complete the fact sheet with the following information. Use the internet if necessary.

Nombre: ....

Apellido/s: ....

Nacionalidad: ....

Edad: ....

Profesión: ....

1.26. Pedimos información personal. In pairs, ask each other questions to obtain all the information about the famous person.

1.27. Presentamos a una persona famosa. Introduce your partner's famous person to the class.

> *Se llama Idris Elba. Es un actor británico. Tiene 47 años.*

Ahora podemos...

Crear un cartel con información sobre nosotros

1.28. Comunicación interpersonal. Interview a person from your class to obtain basic information about him or her: full name, age, nationality, profession, email address, pastimes, phone number and five words in Spanish that are important to them.

1.29. Presentación. Create a poster with the information you gathered and present it to the class.

3

Nombre:

Apellido/s:

Edad:

Nacionalidad:

Profesión:

4

Nombre:

Apellido/s:

Edad:

Nacionalidad:

Profesión:

1.36. Nuestra elección. Choose one female and one male voice you like the most. Do you agree with the rest of the class?

DESPUÉS DE VER EL VIDEO

1.37. Reacción personal. Would you like to meet one of these people? Who did you like the most? Imagine that you get to know them and you would like to introduce one of them to another person. Write what you would say.

1. Él/ella es / se llama...
2. Tiene...
3. Es de...
4. Es...

Presentamos información sobre nosotros

1.38. Elaboración y presentación. Create a similar video for your instructor so he or she can get to know you better. Select a location where you or someone else can record the video. Greet your instructor, say your name, your age, where you are from and your profession.

Recursos lingüísticos

THE FORMS OF -AR, -ER, AND -IR VERBS

-ar	-er	-ir
estudi**ar**	le**er**	escrib**ir**
cant**ar**	ten**er**	**ir**
dibuj**ar**	s**er**	viv**ir**

THE VERBS LLAMARSE, TRABAJAR, SER, TENER, AND VIVIR

SUBJECT PRONOUNS	LLAMARSE	TRABAJAR	SER	TENER	VIVIR
(yo) = *I*	**me** llam**o**	trabaj**o**	**soy**	teng**o**	viv**o**
(tú) = *you*	**te** llam**as**	trabaj**as**	**eres**	tien**es**	viv**es**
(él/ella, usted) = *he/she, you (formal)*	**se** llam**a**	trabaj**a**	**es**	tien**e**	viv**e**
(nosotros/nosotras) = *we*	**nos** llam**amos**	trabaj**amos**	**somos**	ten**emos**	viv**imos**
(vosotros/vosotras) = *you (plural used in Spain)*	**os** llam**áis**	trabaj**áis**	**sois**	ten**éis**	viv**ís**
(ellos/ellas, ustedes) = *they, you (plural)*	**se** llam**an**	trabaj**an**	**son**	tien**en**	viv**en**

▶ We use the verb **llamarse** when we want to give our name or say someone else's name. It's a reflexive verb and, therefore, always uses a pronoun (**me**, **te**, **se**, **nos**, **os**, **se**) before the conjugated verb:

Me llamo *Connor.* ~~Llamo Connor.~~
Mi profesora ***se llama*** *Pilar.* ~~Mi profesora llama Pilar.~~

❗ Do not translate **My name is Connor** as **Me llamo es Connor!**

GIVING AND ASKING FOR PERSONAL INFORMATION

- ***¿Cómo te llamas / se llama?*** = What's your name?
- *(**Me llamo**) Caleb.* = (My name is / It's) Caleb.

- ***¿Cuál es tu/su nombre?*** = What's your first name?
- *Caleb.*
- ***¿Cuál es tu/su apellido?*** = What's your last name?
- *Davis.*

- ***¿De dónde eres/es?*** = Where are you from?
- ***Soy*** *estadounidense.* = I'm American.
  *(**Soy**) de Michigan.* = (I'm) from Michigan.

❗ There are two ways of expressing where you are from:

ser + **de** + (name of the country/state/city):   **ser** + (nationality/demonym):
Carmen ***es de España.*** = Carmen is from Spain.   *Carmen* ***es española.*** = Carmen is Spanish.
John ***es de Nueva York.*** = John is from New York.   *John* ***es estadounidense.*** = John is American.

❗ In Spanish, nationalities are not capitalized as they are in English.

- ***¿Cuántos años tienes/tiene?*** = How old are you?
- *(**Tengo**) 23 (**años**).* = (I'm) 23 (years old).

❗ To talk about age in Spanish, we use the verb **tener** (*to have*) and not **ser** (*to be*) as we do in English.

- **¿Cuál es tu/su número de teléfono?** = What's your phone number?
- *(Es el) 301-555-8139.* = (It's) 301-555-8139.

- **¿Cuál es tu/su correo electrónico?** = What's your email?
- pedro86@aula.com.

- **¿En qué trabajas/trabaja?** = What's your job? / What do you do for a living?
- **Soy** *profesor.* = I'm a teacher.
  Trabajo en *un banco /* **de** *mesero.* = I work in a bank / as a waiter.

❗ In Spanish we do not need an article (**un/a**) when you describe what your job is: **Soy** *médico.*

GENDER AND NATIONALITIES

Masculine	Feminine	Masculine and feminine
-o	**-a**	
cuban**o**	cuban**a**	belg**a**
CONSONANT	**CONSONANT + a**	estadounid**ense**
españo**l**	español**a**	iran**í**
alem**án**	aleman**a**	
inglé**s**	inglesa	

▶ In Spanish there are two grammatical genders: masculine and feminine. When we say where somebody or something is from, the ending of the word that refers to their nationality will vary according to whether they are male or female.

▶ Nationalities ending in **-o** in the masculine change to **-a** for the feminine:

*un actor mexican**o***
*una actriz mexican**a***

▶ Nationalities ending in **-a**, **-e** or **-í** in the masculine do not change for the feminine:

*Jacques es belg**a**.*	*Jim Carrey es canadiens**e**.*	*Hassan es marroqu**í**.*
*Audrey es belg**a**.*	*Céline Dion es canadiens**e**.*	*Mi familia es marroqu**í**.*

▶ Nationalities ending in a consonant add **-a** for the feminine. If there is an accent on the final vowel in the masculine, the accent is eliminated in the feminine:

*Antonio Banderas es españo**l**.*	*Daniel Brühl es alem**án**.*	*Bono es un músico irland**és**.*
*Penélope Cruz es español**a**.*	*Diane Kruger es aleman**a**.*	*Saoirse Ronan es irlande**sa**.*

GENDER AND PROFESSIONS

Masculine	Feminine	Masculine and feminine
cociner**o**	cociner**a**	art**ista**
secretari**o**	secretari**a**	ten**ista**
profeso**r**	profeso**ra**	estudi**ante**

Garbiñe Muguruza es una tenista muy famosa. Tiene doble nacionalidad: venezolana y española.

Pronunciamos

Pronunciar las letras c/z y g/j

 1.39. Clasificamos los sonidos de c/z. Listen to these words and classify them in the appropriate column according to how the boldfaced letters are pronounced.

cero	**c**incuenta	**c**uenta
comida	**c**ámara	**c**antar
colección	**c**ine	**c**erveza
Zaragoza	**c**inco	**z**oológico

/k/ (como **c**asa)	/s/ (como **c**irco)

> ❶ **¿Necesitas ayuda?**
>
> In some parts of Spain, when the letter **c** is followed by **e** or **i** it is pronounced like **th** (/θe/ and /θi/) in English as in **th**ink.

 1.40. Practicamos los sonidos de c/z. Now listen again and repeat.

 1.41. Clasificamos los sonidos de g/j. Listen to these words and classify them in the appropriate column according to how the boldfaced letters are pronounced.

gimnasio	**g**as	**g**uitarra
jugar	**j**alapeño	**g**eneral
guerra	**j**efe	**j**oven
Jiménez	bilin**g**üe	pin**g**üino
gusto	**g**ol	

/h/ (como **j**amón)	/g/ (como **g**ato)

 1.42. Practicamos los sonidos de g/j. Now listen again and repeat.

Vocabulario activo

 Datos personales
Personal information

- **el apellido** *last name*
- **la edad** *age*
- **el lugar de residencia** (la residencia) *place of residence*
- **la nacionalidad** *nationality*
- **el nombre** *first name*
- **el nombre completo** *full name*
- **la profesión** *profession*
- **Soy argentino/-a.** *I'm Argentinian/ from Argentina.*
- **Soy estudiante.** *I'm a student.*
- **Tengo 22 años.** *I'm 22 years old.*
- **Trabajo en un restaurante.** *I work in a restaurant.*
- **Vivo en Boulder.** *I live in Boulder.*

Nacionalidades
Nationalities

- **argentino/-a** *Argentinian*
- **boliviano/-a** *Bolivian*
- **chileno/-a** *Chilean*
- **colombiano/-a** *Colombian*
- **costarricense** *Costa Rican*
- **cubano/-a** *Cuban*
- **dominicano/-a** *Dominican*
- **ecuatoguineano/-a** *Equatorial Guinean*
- **ecuatoriano/-a** *Ecuadorian*
- **español/a** *Spaniard, Spanish*
- **estadounidense** *American*
- **guatemalteco/-a** *Guatemalan*
- **hondureño/-a** *Honduran*
- **mexicano/-a** *Mexican*
- **nicaragüense** *Nicaraguan*
- **panameño/-a** *Panamanian*
- **paraguayo/-a** *Paraguayan*
- **peruano/-a** *Peruvian*
- **puertorriqueño/-a** *Puerto Rican*
- **salvadoreño/-a** *Salvadoran*
- **uruguayo/-a** *Uruguayan*
- **venezolano/-a** *Venezuelan*

Profesiones
Professions

- **actor/actriz** *actor/actress*
- **arquitecto/-a** *architect*
- **cantante** (el/la) *singer*
- **conductor/a** *driver*
- **diseñador/a** *designer*
- **empresario/-a** *businessman/businesswoman*
- **estudiante** (el/la) *student*
- **fotógrafo/-a** *photographer*
- **médico/-a** *doctor*
- **mesero/-a** *bartender, waiter/waitress*
- **profesor/a de español** *Spanish instructor*
- **taxista** (el/la) *taxi driver*
- **Tengo una empresa de informática.** (la informática) *I own a software company.*
- **Trabajo en una fábrica.** *I work in a factory.*
- **Trabajo en una tienda.** *I work in a store.*

 Pasatiempos
Pastimes

- **bailar** *to dance*
- **cantar** *to sing*
- **dibujar** *to draw*
- **escribir** *to write*
- **esquiar** *to ski*
- **el fútbol** *soccer*
- **ir al gimnasio** *to go to the gym*
- **leer** *to read*
- **el tenis** *tennis*
- **tocar la guitarra** *to play guitar*
- **ver videos** *to watch videos*
- **viajar** *to travel*

⚙ **Estrategia**

Be sure that you learn new words not only in isolated pieces. Try to memorize chunks as much as you can. This will make your Spanish more authentic.

Lección 2

Quiero aprender español

IN THIS LESSON WE ARE GOING TO

identify how we want to learn Spanish

LEARNING OUTCOMES
You will be able to...

- express intentions

- explain the reasons why we do things

- talk about activities in the language classroom

- talk about leisure activities

VOCABULARY

- Words related to language learning and culture

- Classroom activities

- Leisure activities

LANGUAGE STRUCTURES

- Present: regular verbs

- The verb **querer**

- Personal pronouns

- **Para**, **por**, and **porque**

- Combining verbs and prepositions **a**, **con** and **de**

- The definite article (**el/la/los/las**)

PRONUNCIATION

- Spanish vowels

CULTURAL CONNECTIONS

- Languages in México

Pérez Art Museum Miami (PAMM).

Primer contacto

2.1. Imágenes culturales. The following words are related to culture. Match each one with its corresponding image. There are several possibilities.

1. la historia
2. el arte
3. la música
4. la literatura
5. el cine
6. la geografía y la naturaleza

A

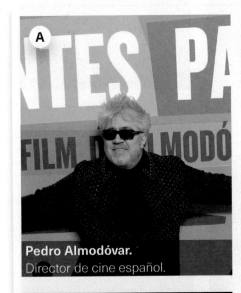

Pedro Almodóvar.
Director de cine español.

B

Mural del pintor mexicano Diego Rivera.

C

Glaciar Perito Moreno.
Argentina.

D

Julieta Venegas.
Cantante mexicana.

E

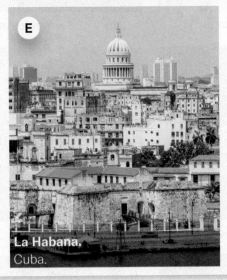

La Habana.
Cuba.

F

Crónica de una muerte anunciada, del escritor colombiano **Gabriel García Márquez.**

2.2. Nuestros intereses. Work with a partner and tell each other which cultural categories you find most interesting.

- **Para mí,** *la historia.*
- **Para mí,** *el cine.*

Comprendemos el vocabulario

Actividades de tiempo libre

 2.3. Actividades de tiempo libre. Listen and discover other activities people do in their free time.

leer un libro

hacer deporte

cocinar

ir de compras

ir a una exposición

ir a un concierto

salir de noche

tomar fotos

pasear

ver a los amigos

jugar videojuegos

ver una serie

e 2.4. Los planes de Eva. Eva has plans for the weekend. Write down what she wants to do according to the images.

Quiere *leer un libro.*

2.5. Nuestras actividades. Share with your classmates your three favorite activities for the weekend. Which are the most popular in the class?

Para mí, hacer deporte, salir de noche y leer.

Comprendemos el vocabulario

Cómo mejorar tu español

e **2.6. Recomendaciones.** The following students give suggestions on how to improve your Spanish. Listen and read what they say.

SARAH
Yo recomiendo **usar internet**. ¡En internet está todo! Puedes **hacer ejercicios de gramática** y **buscar palabras en diccionarios**. Y **ver películas y series en español**. Y **ver televisión** también, claro.

MATEO
Para mí, es importante **tener amigos hispanos** y **hablar con ellos** para **practicar la pronunciación**. Y también **escribir mensajes, correos electrónicos...**

JAMES
Es importante leer. **Leer periódicos, revistas, novelas...** Y también **escribir**: **escribir un diario, escribir mensajes...**

PATRICIA
Yo recomiendo **hacer un intercambio** con un nativo y **hablar de temas interesantes**. ¡Ah!, y **escuchar música latina**.

e **2.7. Actividades para aprender.** Write the activities from activity 2.6 next to the corresponding image. There are several possibilities.

Tener amigos hispanos.

e **2.8. Solo/-a o con otras personas.** Classify the suggestions from activity 2.6. Which ones can you do alone and which ones do you need to do with other people?

Solo/-a	Con otras personas

2.9. Sugerencias para nosotros. Choose three suggestions you would like to use to improve your Spanish and discuss them with your partner. What suggestions do you and your partner both want to follow?

- **¿Tú qué quieres hacer?**
- **Yo quiero** *escribir un diario.*

Exploramos la lengua

Presente: verbos regulares

2.10. Un chat. Read this online chat. What do Laura and Mark want to do?

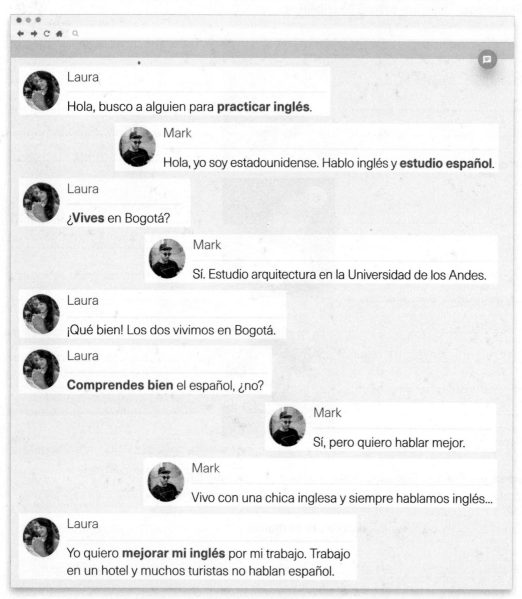

Laura
Hola, busco a alguien para **practicar inglés**.

Mark
Hola, yo soy estadounidense. Hablo inglés y **estudio español**.

Laura
¿**Vives** en Bogotá?

Mark
Sí. Estudio arquitectura en la Universidad de los Andes.

Laura
¡Qué bien! Los dos vivimos en Bogotá.

Laura
Comprendes bien el español, ¿no?

Mark
Sí, pero quiero hablar mejor.

Mark
Vivo con una chica inglesa y siempre hablamos inglés...

Laura
Yo quiero **mejorar mi inglés** por mi trabajo. Trabajo en un hotel y muchos turistas no hablan español.

e **2.11. Verbos regulares.** Underline in the chat the forms of the verbs **hablar**, **comprender**, and **vivir**. Then complete the table.

	HABLAR	**COMPRENDER**	**ESCRIBIR**
(yo)	....	....	....
(tú)	hablas	....	....
(él/ella, usted)	habla	comprende	vive
(nosotros/nosotras)	....	comprendemos	....
(vosotros/vosotras)	habláis	comprendéis	vivís
(ellos/ellas, ustedes)	....	....	viven

2.12. Conjugamos. Now, in your notebook, conjugate the verbs **estudiar**, **aprender**, and **escribir**.

El verbo **querer**

2.13. Actividades para el futuro. Which of the following do you want to do in the future? Choose two.

○ **aprender idiomas**

○ vivir en Colombia

○ **tener amigos** de habla hispana

○ **trabajar en una compañía** española o latinoamericana

○ **ir de vacaciones** a España o a América Latina

○ estudiar en una universidad mexicana

2.14. Comparamos nuestras actividades. Get together with your classmates and compare your answers from activity 2.13. Use the model as a guide.

1. (Yo) Quiero *tener amigos de habla hispana.*
2. Mi compañero/-a *John* quiere *vivir en Colombia.*
3. *Susan* y yo queremos *ir de vacaciones a España y estudiar en una universidad mexicana.*
4. *Kate* y *Michael* quieren *ir de vacaciones a América Latina y aprender idiomas.*

1. (Yo) Quiero ....
2. Mi compañero/-a .... quiere ....
3. .... y yo queremos ....
   ....
4. .... y .... quieren ....
   ....

2.15. El verbo *querer*. Review the sentences in activity 2.14 and underline the different forms of the verb **querer**. Then complete the table.

	QUERER
(yo)	....
(tú)	quieres
(él/ella, usted)	....
(nosotros/nosotras)	....
(vosotros/vosotras)	queréis
(ellos/ellas, ustedes)	....

2.16. Comparamos los verbos. Now compare **querer** to another verb ending in **-er: comprender** (activity 2.11) Are the endings the same? What is different in the verb **querer**?

Exploramos la lengua

Para, por, porque

e **2.17. Razones para aprender español.** Complete the sentences with the options that follow to find out the reason each person has to learn Spanish.

1. Tom estudia español ....

2. Melanie estudia español ....

3. Christina estudia español ....

4. Andrew estudia español ....

5. Rachel estudia español ....

6. Clare estudia español ....

a. para leer literatura hispanoamericana.

b. por su trabajo.

c. para viajar.

d. porque tiene un novio colombiano.

e. para chatear con amigos.

f. porque quiere vivir en Costa Rica.

))) 2.18. Comprobamos. Listen and check your answers from activity 2.17.

2.19. Nuestras razones. Explain why you want to learn Spanish by completing the following sentence using **porque**, **para** and **por**.

Quiero aprender español...

porque ....

para ....

por ....

❶ ¿Necesitas ayuda?

In Spanish, **porque**, **por**, and **para** are used to explain why something is done. **Porque** means "because".
Por is followed by a noun to mean "for the sake of / because of".
Para is followed by a verb in the infinitive to mean "in order to".

Género: nombres y artículos definidos

e **2.20. Completamos la regla.** Pay close attention to the endings of the following nouns, then match the columns to complete the rules.

naturaleza (f)	historia (f)	guitarra (f)
curso (m)	teatro (m)	literatura (f)
música (f)	cine (m)	clase (f)
noche (f)	película (f)	deporte (m)
museo (m)	trabajo (m)	serie (f)

1. Los nombres terminados en -a...   **a.** ... normalmente son masculinos (m).
2. Los nombres terminados en -o...   **b.** ... normalmente son femeninos (f).
3. Los nombres terminados en -e...   **c.** ... son masculinos (m) o femeninos (f).

> **⚙ Estrategia**
>
> You can always check the glossary at the end of the textbook to find the meaning of words, but it is important that you learn how to use dictionaries: they provide more useful and complete information about the words you are trying to learn. For instance, a feminine noun is often indicated by (**f**) and a masculine noun by (**m**).

2.21. Usamos los artículos. Read these dialogs and then complete the table with the correct articles.

1.
● *¿Quieres visitar **el** Museo Nacional de Arte?*
○ *No, quiero ir a **los** museos de Historia y de Antropología.*

2.
● *Quiero ver **la** nueva película de Alfonso Cuarón.*
○ *Sí, yo también, **las** películas de Cuarón son fantásticas.*

> **⚙ Estrategia**
>
> Paying attention to the articles that go with a noun will let you know if it is masculine or feminine. It may be a good idea to memorize nouns along with their coresponding article.

DEFINITE ARTICLES		
	Singular	**Plural**
Masculine	.... muse**o**	.... mus**eos**
Feminine	.... películ**a**	.... películ**as**

Comunicamos

Las imágenes de un país

2.22. Presentamos un país hispano. In pairs, choose a Spanish-speaking country and find images related to the following cultural categories. Create a presentation and share it with the class.

la historia   el arte

la música   la literatura

el cine   la geografía

la naturaleza

Los Andes

LA GEOGRAFÍA

CHILE en imágenes

Gabriela Mistral

LA LITERATURA

El desierto de Atacama

Isabel Allende

Planes para el fin de semana

2.23. Solo/-a o con otras personas. Classify these activities. Which ones do you prefer doing alone and which ones do you prefer doing with other people?

1. leer un libro
2. hacer deporte
3. cocinar
4. ir de compras
5. ir a una exposición
6. ir a un concierto
7. salir de noche
8. tomar fotos
9. pasear
10. jugar videojuegos
11. ver una serie

Solo/-a	Con otras personas

2.24. Compartimos en grupo. In groups of three, share which activities from activity 2.23 you want to do with other people and decide which activities you want to do together this weekend.

• *Este fin de semana, yo quiero pasear, ¿y ustedes?*
○ *¡Yo también!*
■ *Yo, no. Yo quiero...*

2.25. Compartimos con la clase. Share with the class what you and your group want to do. Does anybody want to join you?

Este fin de semana, Matt y yo queremos pasear en Lake Union. Y los tres queremos ir a una exposición en el Seattle Art Museum.

Recomendar ciudades para...

2.26. Elegimos ciudades. Work with a partner and write the name of a city in the United States that you recommend for doing the following activities. Try to name a different city for each activity.

1. hacer deporte:

   ....

2. ir a exposiciones y museos:

   ....

3. salir de noche:

   ....

4. tomar fotos espectaculares:

   ....

5. pasear:

   ....

6. hablar español:

   ....

7. ir a conciertos de música country:

   ....

8. ir de compras:

   ....

⊕ **¿Sabes que...?**

Some U.S. cities and states have Spanish versions for their name.

New York = **Nueva York**
Philadelphia = **Filadelfia**
South Carolina = **Carolina del Sur**

2.27. Elegimos las mejores recomendaciones. Now share your recommendations with the class. As a class, choose the best recommendations and write them on the map.

Para ir a exposiciones, *nosotros recomendamos Nueva York.*

Nueva York: para ir a exposiciones

Ahora podemos...

Decidir qué queremos hacer para aprender español y conocer la cultura hispana

2.28. Interpretación. This web page gives recommendations for learning Spanish. Look at the images and think what the recommendations may be. Write them down using the following verbs.

leer   hacer   ver   ir   hablar   escuchar   escribir   buscar   visitar   practicar

Imagen 1:
- Buscar información en internet
- Visitar páginas web en español

2.29. Comunicación interpersonal. Working in groups, share your lists and decide on the top three activities you want to do in this course to learn Spanish.

- **Yo quiero** *hablar mucho, ver películas en español y leer periódicos y revistas. ¿Y tú?*
- **Yo quiero** *escuchar música.*

2.30. Presentación. Write down your preferences and discuss them with the rest of the class.

En este curso, nosotros queremos...

Video

La niña mariachi

In *La niña mariachi*, we will get to know Yailyn Garcia, a student living with her mother in New York City. Although she was born in New York, Yailyn feels a deep connection to her family's Mexican roots. By studying and performing traditional mariachi music, she is able to combine her passion for music with her love of Mexico.

Pearson MyLab

To find out more about Yailyn and mariachi music, go to MyLab to watch **La niña mariachi** and complete the video activities.

⊕ ¿Sabes que...?

Mariachi music is a style of folkloric music that embodies the spirit of Mexico. Typically a mariachi band is comprised of male and female musicians playing violin, guitar, *guitarrón* (a large acoustic bass guitar), *vihuela* (a five stringed guitar-like instrument), and trumpet. All or some of the musicians sing traditional mariachi songs like *Cielito lindo*, *El rey*, *México lindo y querido*, and others.

⚲ Hacemos conexiones

To get familiar with mariachi culture, search the internet to listen to these songs and find pictures of mariachi bands. Share one interesting fact that you found during your search.

El español y las lenguas originarias en México

DÍA INTERNACIONAL DE LA **LENGUA MATERNA** **21 DE FEBRERO**

MÉXICO MULTILINGÜE **69 LENGUAS NACIONALES**

En México se habla español y cerca de 70 lenguas originarias. De estas, las más importantes son el náhuatl, el ch'ol, el tseltal, el totonaco, el otomí, el tsotsil, el mixteco, el mazateco, el maya y el zapoteco.

El español tiene una posición dominante y cuenta con instituciones como la **Academia Mexicana de la Lengua**. Fundada en el siglo XIX, su objetivo es proteger la lengua española y responder a las preguntas de los hablantes.

El **INALI (Instituto Nacional de Lenguas Indígenas)** promueve la diversidad cultural y lingüística. Su misión es preservar y fortalecer las lenguas originarias. Además, asesora al gobierno mexicano en políticas relacionadas con esta materia.

ANTES DE LEER

2.31. Conocimiento previo. What language or languages do you think are spoken in Mexico?

LECTURA ACTIVA

2.32. Verdadero o falso. Read the text and pay attention to the image.
Then, indicate if these statements are true or false.

	Verdadero	Falso
1. En México existen muchas lenguas nativas.		
2. El náhuatl es la lengua más importante de México.		
3. En México existen instituciones que protegen las lenguas.		
4. El Día de la Lengua Materna solo se celebra en México.		

2.33. Corregimos. Correct the statements from activity 2.32 that are false.

DESPUÉS DE LEER

2.34. Investigamos. Are there any institutions in your country devoted to protecting languages? Research this topic online and share your findings in the class.

Textos escritos: leemos y escribimos

Leemos sobre México

ANTES DE LA LECTURA

2.35. Preparación. What do you know about Mexico? Brainstorm information related to each of the following categories and write it down.

1. Lenguas: ....

2. Turismo: ....

3. Educación: ....

4. Productos: ....

2.36. Comparación. Compare your answers to a classmate's. Are they similar? Have you learned something new about Mexico?

LECTURA ACTIVA

2.37. Lectura. Now read the text and find out more about Mexico. What topic from activity 2.35 relates to each of the facts in the text?

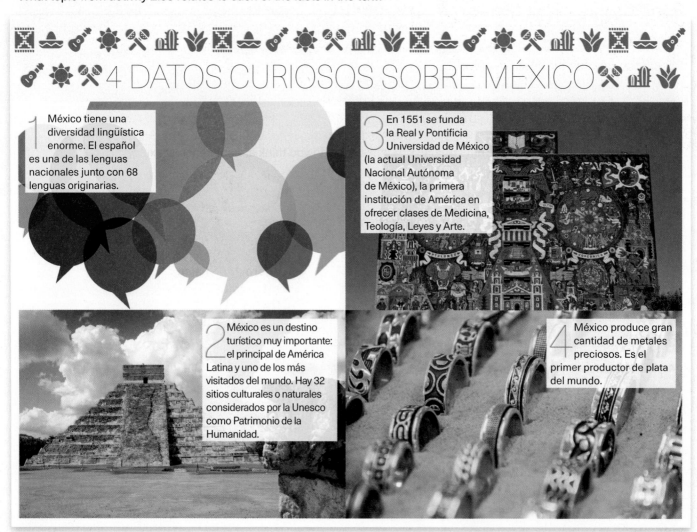

4 DATOS CURIOSOS SOBRE MÉXICO

1 México tiene una diversidad lingüística enorme. El español es una de las lenguas nacionales junto con 68 lenguas originarias.

2 México es un destino turístico muy importante: el principal de América Latina y uno de los más visitados del mundo. Hay 32 sitios culturales o naturales considerados por la Unesco como Patrimonio de la Humanidad.

3 En 1551 se funda la Real y Pontificia Universidad de México (la actual Universidad Nacional Autónoma de México), la primera institución de América en ofrecer clases de Medicina, Teología, Leyes y Arte.

4 México produce gran cantidad de metales preciosos. Es el primer productor de plata del mundo.

2.38. Interpretación. Follow these steps to extract information from the text.

a. First, circle the number of each detail below that is mentioned in the article (not all are included!).
b. Find in the text the information requested and write it down.
c. In pairs, check you answers. Do you have similar ones?

1. Número de lenguas nacionales:

....

2. Número de lugares reconocidos por la Unesco:

....

3. Primera institución universitaria en América:

....

4. Lugar en el *ranking* mundial de producción de plata:

....

Escribimos sobre México y sobre nuestro país

2.39. Reacción personal. Write a personal reaction to specific information provided by the text "4 datos curiosos sobre México". Justify your reaction.

2.40. Comparación. Create a similar fact sheet about your country: "4 datos sobre mi país". Include the answers to the following questions: When was your university founded? How many official languages are spoken in the U.S.? What kind of products are produced in the state you live or are originally from? Include any images to support your information. Then, share it with the rest of the class.

Arkansas es el primer productor de arroz en Estados Unidos.

Recursos lingüísticos

PRESENT: REGULAR VERBS

Remember that in Spanish, verbs are conjugated in three different ways depending on their endings: **-ar** (first conjugation), **-er** (second conjugation) or **-ir** (third conjugation).

Verbs have two parts: the stem and the ending. The stem is the verb without **-ar**, **-er**, **-ir**. The endings of conjugated verbs tell us when the action takes place and who is doing the action.

estudiar → ending
↓
stem

	HABLAR	COMPRENDER	ESCRIBIR
(yo)	habl**o**	comprend**o**	escrib**o**
(tú)	habl**as**	comprend**es**	escrib**es**
(él/ella, usted)	habl**a**	comprend**e**	escrib**e**
(nosotros/nosotras)	habl**amos**	comprend**emos**	escrib**imos**
(vosotros/vosotras)	habl**áis**	comprend**éis**	escrib**ís**
(ellos/ellas, ustedes)	habl**an**	comprend**en**	escrib**en**

THE VERB QUERER

	QUERER	+ INFINITIVE
(yo)	qu**ie**ro	
(tú)	qu**ie**res	
(él/ella, usted)	qu**ie**re	**viajar**.
(nosotros/nosotras)	queremos	**leer** novelas en español.
(vosotros/vosotras)	queréis	**vivir** en España.
(ellos/ellas, ustedes)	qu**ie**ren	

▶ **Querer** is an irregular verb: the letter **e** in the stem changes to **ie** in all forms except **nosotros** and **vosotros**.

▶ When followed by an infinitive (e.g., **hacer**, **estudiar**, **leer**, etc.) **querer** is used to express an intention, that is, something that the person wants or intends to do at some point in the future.

● ¿Qué **quieren hacer** este fin de semana? = What do you want to do this weekend?
○ Yo **quiero hacer** deporte. = I want to play sports.
■ Yo **quiero leer** y **pasear**. = I want to read and go for a walk.

PARA, POR, PORQUE

¿POR QUÉ + CONJUGATED VERB? **¿Por qué** estudias español? = Why do you study Spanish?	**PARA** + INFINITIVE **Para** viajar por Latinoamérica. = In order to travel around Latin America. **POR** + NOUN **Por** mi trabajo. = Because of my job. **PORQUE** + CONJUGATED VERB **Porque** quiero vivir en España. = Because I want to live in Spain.

GENDER: NOUNS AND DEFINITE ARTICLES

	Singular	Plural
Masculine	el museo	los museos
	el curso	los cursos
Feminine	la playa	las playas
	la película	las películas

In general, nouns ending in **-o** are masculine, and those ending in **-a** are feminine. However, there are numerous exceptions: **el idioma**, **el sofá**, **la mano**, **la moto**, etc. Nouns ending in **-e** can be masculine and/or feminine: **la gente**, **el cine**, **el/la estudiante**...

❗ Feminine nouns starting with the stressed **a** sound take the definite article **el** in the singular, even though the noun is feminine: **el a**ula, **el a**gua, etc. (but **las a**ulas, **las a**guas).

PERSONAL PRONOUNS

	Singular	Plural
1st person	yo	nosotros/nosotras
2nd person	tú, usted*	vosotros/vosotras, ustedes*
3rd person	él/ella	ellos/ellas

* **Usted** and **ustedes** take the third person verb forms.

VERBS WITH AND WITHOUT PREPOSITIONS

While most prepositions in Spanish have English equivalents, some are untranslatable or are part of a set expression. For this reason, it helps to focus on the prepositions that frequently accompany certain verbs.

	visitar	la ciudad. **a** mis amigos colombianos.
	estudiar	
	practicar	español.
	aprender	
	hablar	
	hablar	**con** nativos.
	hablar	**de** cine/música/historia...
Quiero	**ir**	**al*** cine. **a** bailar. **de** compras.
	tomar	fotos.
	salir	**con** mis compañeros. **de** noche.
	ver	**a** los amigos. una serie/película.
	hacer	deporte. un intercambio.

* al = a + el

¡Quiero visitar Tegucigalpa!

❗ When the direct object refers to people, it usually takes the preposition **a**:
*Quiero visitar **a** mi hermano.* = I want to visit my brother.

Pronunciamos

Las vocales

In Spanish and in English there are five letters to represent the vowels: **a**, **e**, **i**, **o** and **u**. However, whereas in English they can have different pronunciations (as the **o** in g**o**, d**o**, and g**o**t), in Spanish each of these letters has only one possible pronunciation. Vowels in Spanish are pronounced as single short sounds.

▶ **a** as in f**a**ther   ▶ **e** as in th**e**y   ▶ **i** as in mach**i**ne   ▶ **o** as in l**o**w   ▶ **u** as in S**u**e

 2.41. Pronunciamos. Vowel sounds are sometimes tricky for English speakers, especially when words are similar in English and Spanish. Try and say these pairs of words, noticing the difference in the vowels in each language.

1. Asia   *Asia*
2. Egypt   *Egipto*
3. Ireland   *Irlanda*
4. Uruguay   *Uruguay*
5. London   *Londres*
6. use   *usar*
7. nature   *naturaleza*
8. concert   *concierto*
9. photo   *foto*
10. series   *serie*

2.42. Escuchamos y repetimos. Now listen to the recording of the Spanish words from activity 2.41 and repeat them.

2.43. Pronunciamos. Pronounce these words paying attention to the sound of the vowels in Spanish.

1. mate   agencia   hay
2. me   teatro   Europa
3. isla   país   América
4. muchos   osos   lagos
5. cultural   mundo   Dublín

2.44. Escuchamos y repetimos. Now listen to the recording and repeat.

Vocabulario activo

))) Aprender idiomas *Learning languages*

- **aprender idiomas/lenguas** (el idioma; la lengua) *to learn languages*
- **buscar palabras en el diccionario/en internet** (la palabra; el/la internet) *to look up words in the dictionary/on the internet*
- **chatear con amigos** *to chat with friends*
- **comprender bien una lengua** *to understand a language well*
- **escribir un diario/correos electrónicos/mensajes** (el correo electrónico; el mensaje) *to write a diary/emails/messages*
- **escuchar música latina** (la música) *to listen to Latin music*
- **estudiar en una universidad mexicana/española** *to study at a Mexican/Spanish university*
- **estudiar español/inglés** (el español; el inglés) *to study Spanish/English*
- **hablar con amigos hispanos** *to talk to Hispanic friends*
- **hablar de temas interesantes** (el tema) *to talk about interesting topics*
- **hacer ejercicios de gramática** (el ejercicio) *to do grammar exercises*
- **hacer un intercambio** *to make an exchange*
- **leer libros/periódicos/revistas/novelas** (el libro; el periódico; la revista; la novela) *to read books/newspapers/magazines/novels*
- **leer literatura hispanoamericana/española** (la literatura) *to read Latin-American/Spanish literature*
- **mejorar mi inglés** *to improve my English*
- **practicar español/inglés** *to practice your Spanish/English*
- **practicar la pronunciación** *to practice pronunciation*
- **tener amigos hispanos** (el amigo; la amiga) *to have Hispanic friends*
- **usar internet** *to use the internet*
- **ver películas/series en español** (la película; la serie) *to watch movies/series in Spanish*
- **ver (la) televisión** *to watch TV*

))) Actividades de tiempo libre *Leisure activities*

- **cocinar** *to cook*
- **hacer deporte** (el deporte) *to play sports*
- **ir a un concierto** *to go to a concert*
- **ir a una exposición** *to go to an exhibition*
- **ir de compras** (las compras) *to go shopping*
- **ir de vacaciones** (las vacaciones) *to go on vacation*
- **jugar videojuegos** (el videojuego) *to play videogames*
- **pasear** *to go for a walk*
- **salir de noche** (la noche) *to go out at night*
- **tomar fotos** (la fotografía) *to take pictures*
- **ver a los amigos** *to meet some friends*
- **ver una serie** *to watch a TV series*

))) Palabras relacionadas con la cultura y el patrimonio *Words related to culture and heritage*

- **la arquitectura** *architecture*
- **el arte** *art*
- **la geografía** *geography*
- **la historia** *history*
- **la naturaleza** *nature*

))) Razones para aprender un idioma *Reasons for learning a language*

- **(para) trabajar en una compañía** *(in order) to work in a company*
- **(para) viajar** *(in order) to travel*
- **(para) vivir en (un país)** *(in order) to live in (a country)*
- **(por) su trabajo** (el trabajo) *(for the sake of) his/her job*
- **(porque) tiene un/a novio/-a colombiano/-a** *(because) he/she has a Colombian boyfriend/girlfriend*

))) Expresar una opinión personal *Expressing a personal opinion*

- **Para mí...** *For me (In my opinion)*

))) Preposiciones y conectores *Prepositions and connectors*

- **para** *to, for*
- **por** *for the sake of, because of*
- **porque** *because*

⚙ **Estrategia**

Learning vocabulary in chunks may also help you expand your knowledge of grammar. For instance, when you learn **hablar de temas interesantes**, you are learning one of the ways the preposition **de** is used in Spanish.

Lección

¿Dónde está Toledo?

IN THIS LESSON WE ARE GOING TO

test our knowledge of the Spanish-speaking world

LEARNING OUTCOMES
You will be able to...

• express the existence of people, places, and things

• describe weather

• talk about different kinds of landforms

VOCABULARY

• Information about countries

• Weather

• Geographical terms

LANGUAGE STRUCTURES

• Verbs **ser**, **estar**, **hay**

• Quantifiers: **mucho/-a/-os/-as, muy, mucho**

• The indefinite article (**un/una/ unos/unas**)

• Interrogatives (I): **cuántos/-as, dónde, cómo**

• Interrogatives (II): **qué, cuál/ cuáles**

PRONUNCIATION

• Syllables and diphthongs

CULTURAL CONNECTIONS

• Cities with the same name

Toledo (España).

Primer contacto

3.1. Ciudades que se llaman Santiago. Usa las imágenes y los mapas para relacionar estos datos con las ciudades correctas. En parejas, comparen sus repuestas.

○ Es una ciudad muy antigua.

○ Está en la **costa**.

○ Está en una **isla**.

○ Está en el **norte** del país.

○ Está en el **centro** del país.

○ Está en el **este** del país.

1. Santiago de Compostela (España)

2. Santiago de Chile

3. Santiago de Cuba

3.2. Nuestra ciudad. Compara las ciudades anteriores con el lugar donde vives. ¿En qué son similares y en qué son diferentes?

> *Mi ciudad también está en la costa **oeste**, pero no es muy antigua.*

❶ ¿Necesitas ayuda?

también = *too*
pero = *but*

Comprendemos el vocabulario

Información sobre países

))) 3.3. **Datos sobre Costa Rica.** Lee y escucha la siguiente información sobre este país centroamericano.

e

✿ Estrategia

When you come across words you don't know, looking at "the bigger picture" will help you figure out their meaning. Focus on the meaning of the surrounding words, sentences and paragraphs, and pay attention to the content overall.

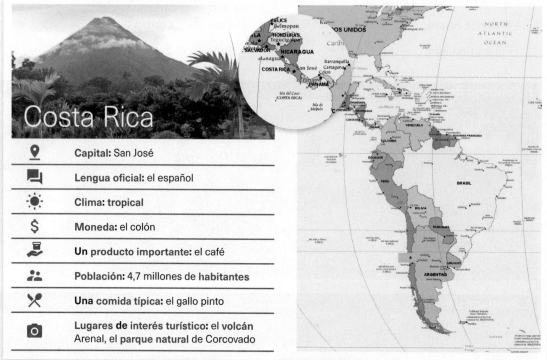

Costa Rica

📍 **Capital:** San José

💬 **Lengua oficial:** el español

☀ **Clima: tropical**

$ **Moneda:** el colón

🤲 **Un producto importante:** el café

👥 **Población:** 4,7 millones de **habitantes**

🍴 **Una comida típica:** el gallo pinto

📷 **Lugares de interés turístico:** el volcán Arenal, el **parque natural** de Corcovado

Más palabras

))) **CLIMA** = *CLIMATE*
(clima) **cálido** = *hot*
(clima) **frío** = *cold*
(clima) **húmedo** = *damp, wet*
(clima) **lluvioso** = *rainy*
(clima) **seco/árido** = *dry*
(clima) **templado** = *temperate, mild*

TEMPERATURA = *TEMPERATURE*
(temperaturas) **altas** = *high*
(temperaturas) **bajas** = *low*
(temperaturas) **extremas** = *extreme*
(temperaturas) **suaves** = *mild*

ESTACIONES = *SEASONS*
invierno = *winter*
otoño = *fall*
primavera = *spring*
verano = *summer*

⊕ ¿Sabes que...?

Celsius (ºC) is the unit used in all the Spanish-speaking countries to measure the temperature.

- 0 ºC = 32 ºF
- 15 ºC = 59 ºF
- 30 ºC = 86 ºF
- 100 ºC = 212 ºF

3.4. Datos sobre mi estado. Completa la ficha con información sobre tu estado. Puedes usar internet.

🗺 **Estado:**

📍 **Capital:**

💬 **Lengua oficial:**

☀ **Clima:**

🤲 **Un producto importante:**

👥 **Población:**

🍴 **Una comida/bebida típica:**

📷 **Lugares de interés turístico:**

3.5. Comparamos datos. Compara tu ficha con la de otra persona. ¿Tienen la misma información?

El tiempo

3.6. El tiempo en España. Lee y escucha la información sobre el tiempo en algunos lugares de España.

1. En Santiago de Compostela **llueve**.

2. En Bilbao **está nublado**.

3. En Huesca **nieva**.

4. En Soria **hace frío**.

5. En Mallorca **hace viento**.

6. En Sevilla **hace sol**.

7. En Cádiz **hace calor**.

> **❶ ¿Necesitas ayuda?**
>
> Note that all weather sentences in Spanish are impersonal. The verbs do not have an actual subject. In English we use the subject pronoun **it**, whereas in Spanish we use the verb in 3rd person singular by itself.

3.7. ¿Qué tiempo hace? Miren las imágenes y, por turnos, describan cómo es el tiempo en estos lugares.

Armenia 9:45 p.m. (Colombia) — 25 °c

Salar de Uyuni 5:15 p.m. (Bolivia) — 11 °c

Cuzco 1:30 p.m. (Perú) — 13 °c

Punta Cana 12:15 p.m. (República Dominicana) — 30 °c

Ushuaia 12:00 p.m. (Argentina) — -5 °c

Guayaquil 6:15 p.m. (Ecuador) — 19 °c

> *En Armenia está nublado y hace calor.*

3.8. El tiempo en nuestra ciudad. ¿Cómo es el tiempo en tu ciudad en las diferentes épocas del año?

> *En el verano hace mucho calor.*

> **💬 Para comunicar**
>
> | En el verano | hace mucho calor/frío... |
> |---|---|
> | En el otoño | las temperaturas son muy altas/bajas... |
> | En el invierno | llueve/nieva mucho/poco. |
> | En la primavera | |

Comprendemos el vocabulario

Geografía

))) **3.9. Océanos y continentes.** Lee y escucha.

océano Pacífico   océano Atlántico   océano Índico

América del Norte   **América del Sur**   **Europa**   **Asia**   **África**   **Oceanía**

))) **3.10. Geografía.** Lee y escucha.

 e

el volcán	**la montaña**	**la cordillera**
el desierto	**el río**	**el lago**
la selva	**el bosque**	**la costa**
la península	**la isla**	**el valle**

))) **3.11. Datos sobre América Latina.** Lee y escucha.

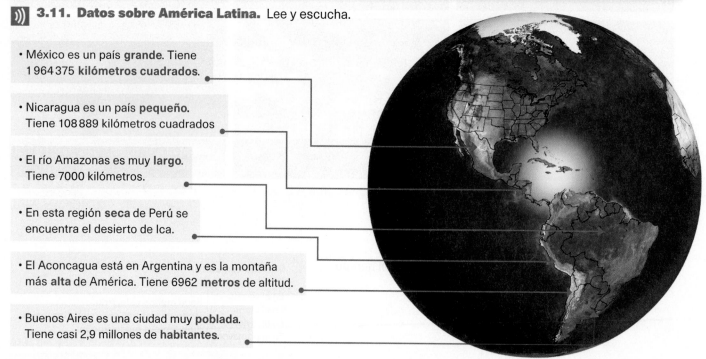

- México es un país **grande**. Tiene 1 964 375 **kilómetros cuadrados**.

- Nicaragua es un país **pequeño**. Tiene 108 889 kilómetros cuadrados

- El río Amazonas es muy **largo**. Tiene 7000 kilómetros.

- En esta región **seca** de Perú se encuentra el desierto de Ica.

- El Aconcagua está en Argentina y es la montaña más **alta** de América. Tiene 6962 **metros** de altitud.

- Buenos Aires es una ciudad muy **poblada**. Tiene casi 2,9 millones de **habitantes**.

))) **3.12. Más datos sobre América Latina.** Escucha estos datos y escribe los adjetivos
e que faltan.

1. El volcán Chimborazo es la montaña más .... de Ecuador.

2. El desierto de Atacama es el lugar más .... del planeta y está en Chile.

3. El lago Maracaibo es el lago más .... de América Latina.

4. Es el país más .... del mundo hispano: México.

5. Son las dos ciudades más .... del mundo hispano: Buenos Aires

y Ciudad de México.

6. El Amazonas es el río más .... del mundo.

7. Uruguay es el país de habla hispana más .... de América del Sur.

e **3.13. Completamos.** Completa las frases con el sustantivo que falta en cada caso.

1. Son los lugares más secos del mundo: los .... de Atacama y del Sáhara.

2. Manhattan es una .... Está en el río Hudson.

3. La .... más alta de Estados Unidos está en Alaska y se llama Denali.

4. El .... Kīlauea está en Hawaii.

5. El .... de la Muerte es un Parque Nacional que está en California.

6. Los grandes .... se encuentran entre Estados Unidos y Canadá y son cinco.

👥 **3.14. Adivinamos.** En parejas, escriban cuatro frases como las de la actividad 3.13 (con un espacio en
blanco). Después, lean las frases a otra pareja. ¿Saben qué palabra falta?

El .... de Napa está en
California y es famoso por los vinos.

🔍 **3.15. Datos sobre nuestro país.** Escribe datos sobre tu país. Usa las estructuras de la actividad 3.12.
Luego puedes leer tus datos en clase y comentarlos con tus compañeros/-as.

Alaska es el estado más grande de Estados Unidos.

---

❶ ¿Necesitas ayuda?

When we compare
people, places or things,
and describe one as
being superior in some
way, we use **el/la/los/
las** (+ noun) + **más** +
adjective (+ **de**).

*El Everest es **la** montaña
más alta **del** mundo.*
= Everest is the highest
mountain in the world.

🌐 ¿Sabes que...?

El Chimborazo is not the
highest mountain in the
world, but at 1.2 miles
higher than Everest, it is
the point farthest away
from the center of the
Earth.

Exploramos la lengua

Los verbos **ser**, **estar** y **hay**

3.16. Un blog de viajes. Lola tiene un blog sobre sus viajes por Latinoamérica. Escribe dónde crees que está ahora: ¿en Guatemala, Argentina o Cuba? ¿En qué información te basas?

Mi viaje por

Lunes, 4 de febrero | 15:50 h

Segunda semana

Aquí todo es bello. Hay unas playas de **arena** negra maravillosas, están en el Pacífico y son increíbles. Hoy estamos en la capital, que está en el centro del país. La gente es muy simpática y todo el mundo es muy amable. La comida también es muy buena: el tamal es el plato más típico, pero hay muchas cosas ricas...

Hace mucho calor y el clima es muy húmedo (llueve por la tarde casi todos los días), pero no importa. Mañana vamos a Tikal para visitar unas ruinas mayas que están en la selva. Dicen que Tikal es muy lindo.

En Tikal hay cinco templos antiguos y también hay palacios, plazas... Fabián y yo queremos visitar una ciudad que se llama Chichicastenango. Allí hay un mercado muy conocido que queremos ver. Y después vamos en autobús a México.

Publicado por: Lola Ordóñez | 0 comentarios

3.17. El verbo *ser* y el verbo *estar*. Lee de nuevo el texto de la actividad 3.16 y clasifica en una tabla las frases que contienen **es/son** y **está/están**. ¿Puedes explicar (en inglés) para qué usamos cada verbo? Luego, confírmalo con la clase.

es/son	está/están
Aquí todo es bello.	

3.18. *Hay*. Observa las frases que contienen **hay**. ¿Qué palabras aparecen después de **hay**? Explica cómo y cuándo usamos el verbo **hay**.

3.19. Usamos *ser*, *estar* y *hay*. Continúa las frases. Usa palabras de la lección u otras relevantes para ti.

1. En mi país **hay** ....
2. En mi país no **hay** ....
3. Mi país **es** ....
4. Mi país **está** ....

5. En mi ciudad **hay** ....
6. En mi ciudad no **hay** ....
7. Mi ciudad **es** ....
8. Mi ciudad **está** ....

Cuantificadores: **mucho/-a/-os/-as**, **muy**, **mucho**

3.20. Datos sobre Argentina. Lee estos datos y subraya qué aspectos de Argentina son más interesantes para ti.

- Es un país **muy variado** con **muchos atractivos**. Los turistas **disfrutan mucho** gracias a esta variedad.
- Buenos Aires, la capital, tiene **muchos lugares** interesantes: la Casa Rosada, la Plaza de Mayo, La Recoleta...
- En el barrio de San Telmo el turista puede ver **muchas actuaciones** de tango.
- La provincia de Mendoza, en el oeste del país, es **muy famosa** por sus vinos.
- Argentina produce **mucha carne** y de **muy buena** calidad.
- Un dato curioso: los argentinos toman **mucho mate**, la bebida nacional.

Yerba mate

3.21. Clasificamos. Clasifica las palabras destacadas en la actividad 3.20.

muy + adjective *muy variado*	**muchos** + plural masculine noun
mucho + singular masculine noun	**muchas** + plural feminine noun
mucha + singular feminine noun	verb + **mucho**

3.22. Buscamos ejemplos. Completa con **muy**, **mucho**, **mucho/-a/-os/-as** y con otra palabra de la lección.

quantifier				other word from the lesson
muchas	playas	montañas	penínsulas	*islas*
	lagos	ríos	bosques	
	comida	costa	arena	
	calor	frío	viento	
	alto	largas	bellos	
other verb				quantifier
	nieva	viajan	toma	

El artículo indefinido: **un**, **una**, **unos**, **unas**

3.23. Completamos la regla. Lee estos diálogos y completa la tabla con los artículos indefinidos.

1
- *En Colombia hay **un** río muy famoso por sus colores.*
- *Sí, el río Caño Cristales. Es precioso.*

2
- *Chile tiene **una** isla con **unas** estatuas muy misteriosas, ¿no?*
- *Sí, es la isla de Pascua y las estatuas se llaman moáis.*

3
- *En Costa Rica hay **unos** parques nacionales espectaculares.*
- *Sí, los parques nacionales de Tortuguero y Corcovado, por ejemplo.*

ARTÍCULOS INDEFINIDOS		
	Singular	**Plural**
Masculino	.... lago	.... ríos
Femenino	.... playa	.... playas

3.24. Usamos el artículo indefinido. Usa estas palabras para escribir frases sobre tu país como las de la actividad 3.23. Luego, juega con tus compañeros/-as, que tienen que adivinar de qué se trata.

montañas	volcanes	río	lagos	cordillera	parque

En Wyoming hay un parque natural muy famoso.

Exploramos la lengua

Interrogativos (I): **cuánto/-a/-os/-as**, **dónde**, **cómo**

3.25. Un concurso sobre México. Responde a las preguntas de este test. Puedes usar internet.

Contesta estas preguntas sobre México y gana un fabuloso viaje a Cancún

CONCURSO MÉXICO LINDO

1.¿Cuántos habitantes tiene el país?
- a. 112 millones.
- b. 57 millones.
- c. 10 millones.

2. ¿Cuántas lenguas oficiales hay?
- a. Ninguna.
- b. Dos. El español y el maya.
- c. Una. El español.

3.¿Dónde está Oaxaca?
- a. En el norte.
- b. En el este.
- c. En el sur.

4. ¿Dónde está la pirámide de Chichén Itzá?
- a. En Baja California.
- b. En Yucatán.
- c. En el Estado de México.

5.¿Cómo es el clima en la costa del Mar Caribe?
- a. Frío.
- b. Tropical y lluvioso.
- c. Seco.

6.¿Cómo se llama la montaña más alta de México?
- a. Pico de Orizaba.
- b. Popocatépetl.
- c. Nevado de Toluca.

3.26. Completamos las reglas. Relaciona las columnas para obtener las reglas.

1. Usamos **dónde**...	**a.** ... para preguntar por la cantidad.
2. Usamos **cuánto/-a/-os/-as**...	**b.** ... para preguntar por el modo.
3. Usamos **cómo**...	**c.** ... para preguntar por el lugar.

3.27. Hacemos preguntas. Completa cada pregunta con la palabra interrogativa apropiada.

1. ¿.......................... personas viven en la isla de Chiloé, en Chile?

2. ¿.......................... días se necesitan para visitar Isla Mujeres, en México?

3. ¿.......................... gente habla náhuatl?

4. ¿.......................... están las islas Galápagos?

5. ¿.......................... es el clima en la isla Suasi, en Perú?

6. ¿.......................... habitantes tiene Argentina?

3.28. Hacemos preguntas para informarnos. Usa los interrogativos **dónde**, **cuánto/-a/-os/-as** y **cómo** para escribir tres preguntas sobre un lugar que aparece en esta unidad y que quieres visitar. Después, busca las respuestas en internet.

SANTIAGO DE CHILE

– ¿Dónde está? Está en el centro de Chile.

– ¿Cómo es el clima? Templado todo el año.

– ¿Cuántos habitantes tiene? 6 millones.

Interrogativos (II): **qué**, **cuál/cuáles**

3.29. Compartimos información. Comparte con el resto de la clase la información de la actividad 3.28 que te parece más interesante.

3.30. *Qué o cuál/cuáles.* Lee estas frases y observa cómo usamos **qué** y cómo usamos **cuál/cuáles**.

- ¿**Cuál** es la bebida más conocida de Cuba?
  ○ El mojito.

- ¿**Qué** es el tequila?
  ○ Una bebida mexicana.

- ¿**Cuáles** son las lenguas oficiales de Perú?
  ○ El español y el quechua.

- ¿**Qué** son las rancheras?
  ○ Una música típica mexicana.

3.31. Comparamos con nuestra lengua. Piensa en cómo dices estas frases en inglés. ¿En todos los casos usas la misma palabra para traducir **qué** o **cuál/cuáles**?

- ¿**Qué** es el son cubano?
- ¿**Cuál** es la moneda de Venezuela?
- ¿**Cuáles** son las playas más lindas de Guatemala?

> ⚙ **Estrategia**
>
> Sometimes there might not be a direct match between Spanish and English words. Translation can help you, but always try to understand how language works.

3.32. Preguntamos con *qué* y *cuál/cuáles.* Completa las frases con **qué**, **cuál** o **cuáles**.

1. • ¿ .... es la capital de Colombia?
   ○ Bogotá.

2. • ¿ .... son las arepas?
   ○ Una comida típica de Colombia y Venezuela.

3. • ¿ .... es el mate?
   ○ Es una infusión que se bebe en Uruguay, Paraguay y Argentina.

4. • ¿ .... es la moneda de Honduras?
   ○ El lempira.

5. • ¿ .... ciudad es llamada "La Gran Manzana"?
   ○ Nueva York.

6. • ¿ .... es el producto más importante de Costa Rica?
   ○ El café.

7. • ¿ .... son los parques naturales más visitados de Estados Unidos?
   ○ El Parque Nacional Great Smoky Mountains, el Gran Cañón del Colorado, Yosemite y Yellowstone.

8. • ¿ .... es el pulque?
   ○ Una bebida típica de México.

Comunicamos

¿Osos en Alaska?

👥 **3.33. Hacemos preguntas.** Por turnos, háganse preguntas para determinar si este mapa es correcto.

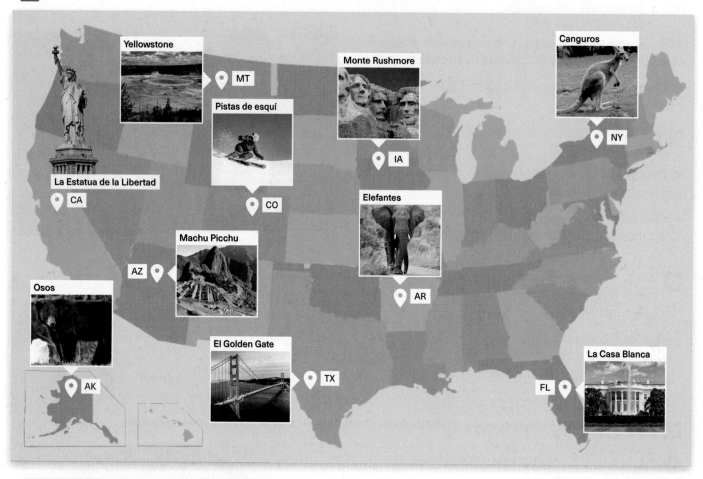

- *El monte Rushmore no está en Iowa, ¿verdad?*
- *No, está en Dakota del Sur.*

- *Hay osos en Alaska, ¿no?*
- *Pues no sé...*

💬 **Para comunicar**

No sé. = *I don't know.*
No lo sé. = *I don't know (it/that).*

👥 **3.34. ¿Qué país es?** Elige cinco de estos países y escribe un dato sobre cada uno sin decir el nombre. Luego léelo en clase. Tus compañeros/-as tienen que adivinar de qué país se trata.

México   Perú   Puerto Rico   Chile   Colombia   Venezuela   Cuba   España

- *Está en Europa.*
- *España.*
- *¡Sí!*

👥 **3.35. Adivinamos el país.** En grupos de cuatro, cada persona piensa en un país. Luego, tomen turnos para hacer preguntas y adivinar de qué país se trata. Pregunten sobre el clima, la naturaleza, la geografía...

- *¿Está en Europa?*
- *No.*

Una semana en Estados Unidos

3.36. Preparamos una conversación. En parejas van a realizar un juego de rol (*role-play*). Lean los roles A y B. Luego, preparen la conversación.

- **Estudiante A:** Eres de un país de América Latina y estás en Estados Unidos para estudiar por un semestre. Quieres conocer mejor el país y haces preguntas a tu compañero/-a estadounidense.
- **Estudiante B:** Un/a estudiante de un país de América Latina pasa un semestre en tu país y necesita información. Te hace preguntas sobre Estados Unidos y tú respondes.

> ⊕ **¿Necesitas ayuda?**
>
> When role-playing, think about these questions:
>
> - What is the context of the situation? Will you use a formal or informal register?
> - How will you start and end the conversation?
> - What vocabulary and grammatical structures from this lesson will you need?

Un país interesante

3.37. Preparamos una ficha. Prepara una ficha con datos sobre un país de América del Sur o América Central.

🗺 **País:**	
📍 **Capital:**	🖐 **Un producto importante:**
💬 **Lenguas oficiales:**	👥 **Población:**
☀ **Clima:**	🍴 **Una comida/bebida típica:**
$ **Moneda:**	📷 **Lugares de interés turístico:**

3.38. Dibujamos un mapa. Dibuja o busca un mapa del país elegido e indica algunos de los datos de la actividad 3.37 (dónde está la capital, los lugares de interés turístico, etc.).

3.39. Presentamos un país. Haz una presentación en clase: lee tu ficha y comenta el mapa. Tus compañeros/-as pueden hacer preguntas.

3.40. Elegimos un país para visitar. Después de todas las presentaciones, ¿qué país quieres visitar?

> *Yo quiero visitar Nicaragua porque quiero ver volcanes.*

Inventa tu país ideal

3.41. Describimos nuestro país ideal. Escribe las características de tu país ideal.

- ¿Cómo se llama tu país y dónde está?
- ¿Cuáles son los productos nacionales más importantes?
- ¿Cuáles son los principales puntos de interés para los turistas?
- ¿Cómo es el clima?
- ¿Cuáles son las características geográficas del país?

3.42. Comparamos. Paseen por el salón y háganse las preguntas de la actividad 3.41 para encontrar puntos en común entre sus países ideales. Luego, por turnos, compartan con todos los puntos en común.

Ahora podemos...

Hacer un concurso sobre países de habla hispana

 3.43. Comunicación interpersonal. La clase se divide en dos equipos. Cada equipo tiene que discutir para preparar ocho tarjetas con preguntas sobre países del mundo hispano.

PAÍSES EN LOS QUE EL ESPAÑOL ES LENGUA OFICIAL O COOFICIAL:

Argentina	El Salvador	Panamá
Bolivia	España	Paraguay
Chile	Guatemala	Perú
Colombia	Guinea Ecuatorial	Puerto Rico
Costa Rica	Honduras	República Dominicana
Cuba	México	Uruguay
Ecuador	Nicaragua	Venezuela

CONCURSO

¿Cuál de estos países es el más poblado?

A. MÉXICO
B. ESPAÑA
C. ARGENTINA

CONCURSO

¿Cuál es la capital de Uruguay?

A. ASUNCIÓN
B. MONTEVIDEO
C. TACUAREMBÓ

CONCURSO
EL MUNDO HISPANO

 3.44. Comunicación interpersonal. Por turnos, cada equipo hace una pregunta. El rival tiene 30 segundos para responder. Cada respuesta correcta vale un punto y gana el equipo que consigue más puntos.

Video

Del mar a tu plato

Maylín Chávez es propietaria de un bar de ostiones en Portland, Oregon, y trabaja con Arnulfo y Luis Carbajal, de la Granja Carbajal de Ostiones, para servir a sus clientes el producto más fresco y delicioso. Para Maylín, es importante colaborar con otros propietarios de negocios de la comunidad hispanohablante y mantener una fuerte conexión con su herencia mexicana.

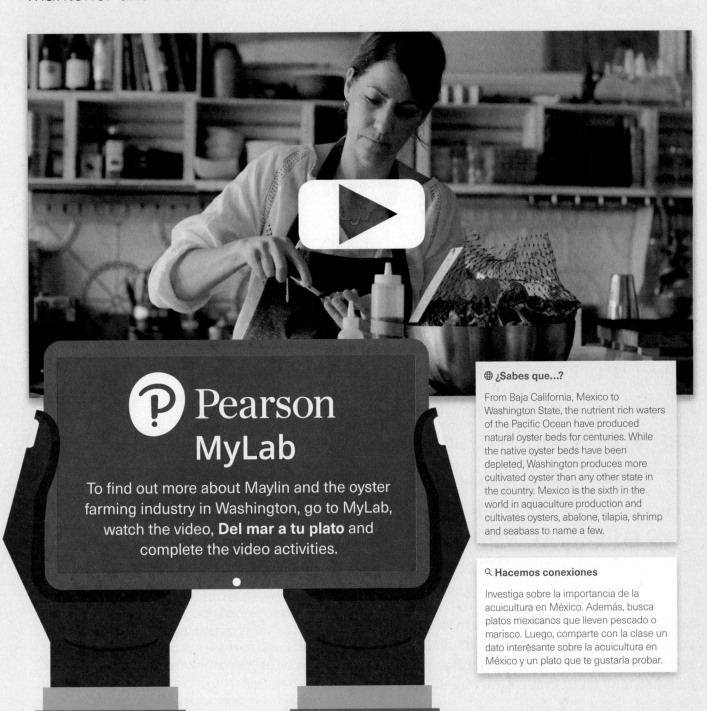

ⓟ Pearson
MyLab

To find out more about Maylin and the oyster farming industry in Washington, go to MyLab, watch the video, **Del mar a tu plato** and complete the video activities.

⊕ ¿Sabes que...?

From Baja California, Mexico to Washington State, the nutrient rich waters of the Pacific Ocean have produced natural oyster beds for centuries. While the native oyster beds have been depleted, Washington produces more cultivated oyster than any other state in the country. Mexico is the sixth in the world in aquaculture production and cultivates oysters, abalone, tilapia, shrimp and seabass to name a few.

🔍 Hacemos conexiones

Investiga sobre la importancia de la acuicultura en México. Además, busca platos mexicanos que lleven pescado o marisco. Luego, comparte con la clase un dato interèsante sobre la acuicultura en México y un plato que te gustaría probar.

Ciudades con el mismo nombre

Toledo
EE. UU.

Habitantes: 287 208

Existen cuatro ciudades en el mundo que se llaman Mérida, cuatro que se llaman Cartagena, seis que se llaman Granada, nueve solo en Estados Unidos que se llaman Madrid...

"Toledo" es uno de los nombres más usados: solo en Estados Unidos hay cinco ciudades con este nombre, dos en Uruguay, una en Filipinas, una en Bolivia... Aquí tenemos dos de ellas.

Fundada en 1833, Toledo es la capital del condado de Lucas, en Ohio, que forma parte de la región de los Grandes Lagos. Entre sus lugares de interés destacan el lago Erie y el Museo de Arte de Toledo, conocido por su exclusiva colección de cristales. Son importantes la industria del vidrio, las fábricas de piezas de automóvil, la construcción naval y la aeronáutica, entre otras. La Universidad de Toledo tiene más de 20 000 estudiantes y es especialmente conocida por su plan de estudios en los campos de la ciencia, la ingeniería y la medicina.

Toledo
España

Habitantes: 83 741

Fundada en el 193 a. C., es la capital de la comunidad autónoma de Castilla-La Mancha, en el interior del país. Por su posición geográfica, en una colina a orillas del río Tajo, Toledo es un lugar estratégico de defensa. Allí viven y han vivido cristianos, judíos y musulmanes, por lo que es conocida como Ciudad de las Tres Culturas. Declarada Patrimonio de la Humanidad en 1986, la ciudad recibe muchos turistas que visitan sus numerosos edificios y monumentos.

TOLEDO

ANTES DE LEER

3.45. Ciudades con el mismo nombre. ¿Conoces ciudades con el mismo nombre en tu país? Si no, busca ejemplos.

LECTURA ACTIVA

3.46. Información sobre Toledo. Escribe a qué Toledo se refieren estas frases de acuerdo con la información de los textos.

1. Es muy antigua.
2. Tiene el reconocimiento de la Unesco.
3. Es una ciudad universitaria.

4. Es una ciudad turística.
5. Es una ciudad industrial.
6. Está cerca de un lago.

DESPUÉS DE LEER

3.47. Investigamos. Busca información en internet sobre otro caso de dos o más ciudades con el mismo nombre y prepara una breve presentación. Puede ser alguna de estas u otra.

- Guadalajara
- Cartagena

- Salamanca
- Pamplona

- Barcelona
- Trujillo

Textos audiovisuales: vemos, escuchamos y presentamos

Vemos un video sobre la Riviera Maya

ANTES DE VER EL VIDEO

3.48. Preparación. Lee estas preguntas y piensa las respuestas. Después, compártelas con otra persona de la clase.

1. ¿Sabes qué son los arrecifes de coral? ¿Sabes dónde hay?
2. ¿Dónde está la Riviera Maya? Ubícala en un mapa. ¿Cómo se llaman las islas que están cerca de la Riviera Maya? ¿Has ido alguna vez?
3. ¿Qué tipo de deportes ofrecen la posibilidad de ver arrecifes coralinos?
4. ¿Sabes que los arrecifes de coral de todo el mundo están en peligro de extinción? ¿Cuál crees que es la causa?

INFORMACIÓN PREVIA Vas a ver un video sobre la Riviera Maya. Primero, ve el video para hacerte una idea general sobre el tema. Después, lee las preguntas de las actividades 3.49. y 3.50 para saber cuál es la tarea y ve de nuevo el video para resolverla.

VEMOS EL VIDEO

3.49. Idea principal. Escribe en inglés un texto corto (2-3 frases) que resuma la información del video.

3.50. Información de apoyo. Para cada uno de los ítems numerados:

- **a.** Señala qué informaciones se mencionan en el video (¡no están todas incluidas!).
- **b.** Escribe en qué minuto y segundo aparecen esas informaciones en el video.
- **c.** Escribe al lado qué dice el video sobre estas cuestiones.

	¿Se menciona?	¿En qué minuto?	Información
1. El segundo arrecife de coral más grande del planeta.			
2. Los países que ocupa.			
3. Número de personas que visitan el arrecife cada año.			
4. El mejor deporte para practicar ahí.			
5. Los dos mejores destinos para experimentar el arrecife.			
6. Las consecuencias del calentamiento global para las tortugas.			

DESPUÉS DE VER EL VIDEO

3.51. Intención del documento. ¿Cuál crees que es el objetivo principal de este video? Responde usando información del video y explica tu respuesta.

3.52. Reacción personal. En inglés, explica tu reacción al video. ¿Qué opinas de la información que proporciona? ¿Qué pensamientos o emociones te provoca?

Presentamos datos interesantes de nuestro país

3.53. Preparación. Antes de empezar, piensa sobre estas cuestiones.

1. ¿Qué aspectos de tu país son más conocidos? ¿Hay aspectos que tú conoces que no son muy conocidos por otras personas?
2. ¿Hay algo de tu país (geografía, lugares, gastronomía, datos curiosos) que te gusta, pero que no mucha gente conoce?

INSTRUCCIONES   Prepara una presentación audiovisual con datos interesantes sobre tu país para publicar en una web de turismo para gente interesada en conocer mejor tu país. Puedes preparar un Power Point y grabarte en video o montar un video con imágenes y tu voz.

3.54. Elaboración. Incluye la siguiente información en tu presentación:

- Un título: "5 datos interesantes sobre [nombre del país]"
- Una breve descripción de cada uno de esos cinco datos sobre tu país (tienes que hablar de cosas que mucha gente no conoce).
- Fotos que acompañen cada descripción.

3.55. Presentación. Hagan sus presentaciones en la clase y elijan los cinco datos más curiosos entre todos los presentados.

El volcán Mauna Kea, en Hawaii, ¡tiene en total 10 000 metros de altitud!

Recursos lingüísticos

THE VERBS SER, ESTAR, AND HAY

In Spanish, there are two different translations for the verb **to be**: **ser** and **estar**. Both verbs have different forms for each subject:

	SER	ESTAR
(yo)	**soy**	**estoy**
(tú)	**eres**	**estás**
(él/ella, usted)	**es**	**está**
(nosotros/nosotras)	**somos**	estamos
(vosotros/vosotras)	**sois**	estáis
(ellos/ellas, ustedes)	**son**	**están**

▸ If we want to define ("What is it?") or to describe something or someone ("What is it like?"), we use the verb **ser**:

*El lempira **es** la moneda de Honduras.* = The lempira is the currency of Honduras.
*Salamanca **es** una ciudad muy linda.* = Salamanca is a very beautiful city.

▸ If we want to tell location (where something or someone is), we use the verb **estar**:

*San Antonio **está** en Texas.* = San Antonio is in Texas.
*Pedro y María **están** en México.* = Pedro and María are in Mexico.

▸ If we talk about the actual existence of a person, a place, an event or a thing, we use **hay** (from the verb **haber**). This form (pronounced like the subject pronoun *I* in English), is always only one word and does not change from singular to plural. It can be either *there is* or *there are* in English:

***Hay** un cine en la calle Reforma.* = There is a movie theater in Reforma street.
*En Buenos Aires **hay** muchas escuelas de tango.* = There are many tango schools in Buenos Aires.

QUANTIFIERS: MUCHO/-A/-OS/-AS, MUCHO, MUY

In Spanish, we use **mucho/-a/-os/-as** followed by a noun. Unlike in English, where quantifiers vary depending on whether the noun following it is countable or uncountable (I have **many** friends, There's not **much** food left), this is not the case in Spanish:
*Tengo **muchos** amigos.* = I have many friends.
*No hay **mucha** comida.* = There's not much food left.

❗ The ending needs to agree with the gender and number of the noun it describes:
*En el sur de Argentina hace much**o** frío.*   *Buenos Aires tiene much**os** lugar**es** turístic**os**.*
*Much**a** gent**e** visita Buenos Aires.*   *En Argentina hay much**as** cos**as** interesant**es**.*

▸ Following a verb, we use **mucho**. **Mucho** never changes, regardless of the subject of the verb. **Mucho** can be translated as *a lot*:

*En Misiones, en el norte de Argentina, llueve **mucho**.* = It rains a lot in Misiones, northern Argentina.

▸ **Muy** is followed by an adjective and can be translated as *very*. **Muy** never changes, regardless of the gender and number of the adjective.

*Patagonia es una región **muy** fría.* = Patagonia is a very cold region.
*Las playas de Costa Rica son **muy** lindas.* = Beaches of Costa Rica are very beautiful.

THE INDEFINITE ARTICLE

We use the indefinite articles **un/una** (**a**, **an** in English) and **unos/unas** to refer to a person, place or thing, when we don't know if it exists, or when we refer to something that is one individual within a category:

*Isla San Luis es **una** isla volcánica.* = Isla San Luis is a volcanic island.

❗ Note that in Spanish the articles agree in number and gender with the noun:

un rí**o** larg**o**   **una** is**la**   **unos** templ**os**   **unas** play**as**

▸ We use **un/una/unos/unas** with **hay** when asking about the existence of a person, place, or thing:

*¿**Hay un** volcán en Lanzarote?* = **Is there a** volcano in Lanzarote?

❗ Note that in Spanish the indefinite article is not combined with **otro/-a/-os/-as**.
*¿**Hay ~~una~~ otra** playa aquí?* = Is there another beach here?

INTERROGATIVES I AND II (QUESTION WORDS)

Just like in English, interrogatives are typically placed at or very near the beginning of a question.
Cuánto/-a/-os/-as (= *how much/many*) have singular, plural, masculine and feminine forms that must agree with the noun they refer to. However, **qué**, **cuál/-es** and **cómo** do not always translate as *what*, *which* and *how*. Read the explanations in the following table:

If we ask...			
about things	**¿Qué** + verb**?**	**What?**	*¿**Qué** comes?* = **What** are you eating?
about a place / thing / person within a limited group or range	**¿Qué** + noun**?** **¿Cuál/cuáles** + noun**?**	**What/which?**	*¿**Qué/cuál** país prefieres?* = **What/which** country do you prefer? *¿**Qué/cuáles** países quieres visitar?* = **What/which** countries do you want to visit?
	¿Cuál/cuáles + verb**?** (Generally speaking, **cuál/ cuáles** suggests choosing from more than one alternative)	**What/which one?** **What/which ones?**	*¿**Cuál** es la capital de Colombia?* = **What**'s the capital of Colombia? *¿**Cuáles** son las ciudades más grandes de España?* = **What/which** are the biggest cities in Spain?
to describe a place / person / thing	**¿Cómo** + ser**?**	**How/what is it like?**	*¿**Cómo** es el clima en Chile?* = **What** is the weather like in Chile?

❗ Question words always have an accent.

❗ Don't forget to add the opening upside-down question mark (**¿**) in Spanish questions.

—*¿Cuál es la moneda de Guatemala?*
—*El quetzal.*

Pronunciamos

Syllables and diphthongs

▶ A syllable is a unit of pronunciation having one vowel sound (with or without surrounding consonants) forming the whole or a part of a word. Spanish words can have from one to more than four syllables, although two and three syllable words are the most common.

▶ In Spanish, syllables tend to end in a vowel whereas in English they often end in a consonant. Look at the word **natural**, which is spelled the same in both languages, and see how syllables break down differently:

English: **nat-u-ral**
Spanish: **na-tu-ral**

▶ Vowel sounds are divided into open (**a**, **e**, **o**) and closed (**i**, **u**). When we have two closed vowels in the same syllable (as in **ciu-dad**) or one closed and one open vowel (as in **tie-nes** or **ai-re**), we have a diphthong.

▶ Whenever there is a closed and open vowel combination and the accent falls on the closed vowel, the syllable is split into two, like in **pa-ís**.

▶ Two open vowels always belong to two different syllables in Spanish, like in **á-re-a**.

3.56. Dividimos las palabras. Separa estas palabras en sílabas e indica si hay algún diptongo.

clima: _cli – ma_

población: _po – bla – ción_

frío: ....

volcán: ....

invierno: ....

lluvioso: ....

parque: ....

viento: ....

calor: ....

Santiago: ....

océano: ....

temperatura: ....

río: ....

bosque: ....

arena: ....

ciudad: ....

oeste: ....

lengua: ....

3.57. Escuchamos y repetimos. Escucha la lista de palabras de la actividad 3.56 y repite.

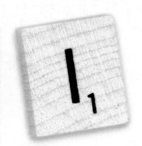

Vocabulario activo

Información sobre países
Information about countries

- **la capital**   *capital*
- **el clima**   *climate*
- **(clima) cálido**   *hot (climate)*
- **(clima) frío**   *cold (climate)*
- **(clima) húmedo**   *damp, wet (climate)*
- **(clima) lluvioso**   *rainy (climate)*
- **(clima) seco / árido**   *dry (climate)*
- **(clima) templado**   *temperate , mild (climate)*
- **(clima) tropical**   *tropical (climate)*
- **la comida típica**   *typical food*
- **los habitantes**   *population*
- **el interés turístico**   *interesting to tourists*
- **la lengua oficial**   *official language*
- **el lugar**   *place*
- **la moneda**   *currency*
- **la población**   *population, inhabitants*
- **el producto importante**   *important product*
- **la temperatura**   *temperature*
- **(temperaturas) altas**   *high (temperatures)*
- **(temperaturas) bajas**   *low (temperatures)*
- **(temperaturas) extremas**   *extreme (temperatures)*
- **(temperaturas) suaves**   *mild (temperatures)*

Puntos cardinales
Cardinal points

- **el centro**   *center*
- **el este**   *east*
- **el norte**   *north*
- **el oeste**   *west*
- **el sur**   *south*

Estaciones
Seasons

- **el invierno**   *winter*
- **el otoño**   *fall*
- **la primavera**   *spring*
- **el verano**   *summer*

El tiempo
Weather

- **está nublado**   *it's cloudy*
- **hace calor**   *it's hot*
- **hace frío**   *it's cold*
- **hace sol**   *it's sunny*
- **hace viento**   *it's windy*
- **llueve**   *it rains*
- **nieva**   *it snows*

Geografía
Geography

- **África**   *Africa*
- **América del Norte**   *North America*
- **América del Sur**   *South America*
- **la arena**   *sand*
- **Asia**   *Asia*
- **el bosque**   *forest*
- **el continente**   *continent*
- **la cordillera**   *mountain range*
- **la costa**   *coast, coastline*
- **el desierto**   *desert*
- **Europa**   *Europe*
- **la isla**   *island*
- **el lago**   *lake*
- **la montaña**   *mountain*
- **Oceanía**   *Oceania*
- **el océano**   *ocean*
- **el océano Atlántico**   *Atlantic Ocean*
- **el océano Índico**   *Indian Ocean*
- **el océano Pacífico**   *Pacific Ocean*
- **el parque nacional**   *national park*
- **el parque natural**   *nature park*
- **la península**   *peninsula*
- **el río**   *river*
- **la selva**   *rain forest, jungle*
- **el valle**   *valley*
- **el volcán**   *volcano*

Adjetivos para describir lugares
Adjectives to describe places

- **alto/-a**   *high*
- **grande**   *big*
- **largo/-a**   *long*
- **pequeño/-a**   *small*
- **poblado/-a**   *populated*
- **seco/-a**   *dry*

Unidades de medida
Units of measure

- **el kilómetro**   *kilometer*
- **los kilómetros cuadrados**   *square kilometer*
- **el metro**   *meter*

⚙ **Estrategia**

Try to connect new words with your own reality and put them to use to talk about what you know.

Lección 4

¿Cuál prefieres?

IN THIS LESSON WE ARE GOING TO

learn to shop in markets

LEARNING OUTCOMES
You will be able to...

- identify objects

- express needs

- shop and ask for clothes, prices, and other items

- talk about preferences

VOCABULARY
- Everyday objects

- Numbers over 100

- Clothing items

- Colors

LANGUAGE STRUCTURES
- Demonstratives (I): **este/-a/-os/-as** and **esto**

- **El/la/los/las** + adjective (to point out)

- **Tener que** + infinitive

- **Cuesta/cuestan**

- Irregular verbs: **ir** and **preferir**

PRONUNCIATION
- Pronouncing numbers

CULTURAL CONNECTIONS
- Colombian handicrafts

Desfile de la diseñadora colombiana Lía Samantha durante el Cali Exposhow.

Primer contacto

4.1. Mercados famosos. Observa esta página web con mercados famosos en el mundo. ¿Dónde puedes comprar estas cosas? Hay varias posibilidades.

1. un **suéter**
2. un **DVD** de Almodóvar
3. un *souvenir*

4. una **novela** de Elena Poniatowska
5. un **disco** de Santana
6. un **teléfono** de los años 60

LOS Mejores Mercados

El Rastro
Para comprar **películas, DVDs...**

Mercado de Otavalo
Para comprar **artesanías**

Green Flea Market
Para comprar **música**

Feria de San Telmo
Para comprar **antigüedades**

Mile High Flea Market
Para comprar **ropa**

Encants Vells
Para comprar **libros**

4.2. De compras en el mercado. ¿Y tú? ¿Compras en mercados? Marca qué cosas compras y coméntalo con tu compañero/-a.

- películas
- **ropa**
- música
- comida
- **artesanías**
- **antigüedades**
- libros
- cómics

- • *Yo, en los **mercados**, **compro** libros y antigüedades.*
- ○ *Yo compro ropa.*

4.3. Los mercados de mi ciudad. ¿Hay mercados en tu ciudad? ¿Qué productos venden?

*En Pasadena hay un mercado muy famoso, el Rose Bowl Flea Market. **Venden** ropa y antigüedades.*

Comprendemos el vocabulario

Objetos para un viaje

 4.4. Objetos para un viaje. Observa, lee y escucha.

1	la ropa interior	9	pasta de dientes	17	el dinero
2	unas gafas de sol	10	una camiseta	18	un jabón
3	un secador de pelo	11	una maleta	19	el champú
4	el pasaporte	12	una chaqueta	20	unas sandalias
5	un libro	13	unos pantalones (cortos)	21	el protector solar
6	un cepillo	14	una toalla de playa	22	las aspirinas
7	un cepillo de dientes	15	un traje de baño	23	el celular
8	una tarjeta de crédito	16	unos zapatos		

💬 La variedad del español

el celular = el móvil (Es)

unos pantalones cortos
= unos shorts (Ar, Cu...)

unas gafas de sol = unos anteojos
de sol (Ar), unos anteojos oscuros
(CR), unos lentes de sol (Cu)

una camiseta
= una playera (Mx, Gu), una remera
(Ar, Ur, Py), una polera (Bo, Ch)

una chaqueta = una chamarra (Mx),
una campera (Ar)

4.5. La maleta de Silvia. Observa las cosas que lleva Silvia en la maleta. ¿Qué conclusiones puedes sacar sobre su viaje? Márcalo y justifica tus respuestas.

- Es un viaje de trabajo.
- Es un viaje de dos días.
- **Va** a un lugar con playa.
- **Va** a un lugar donde hace calor.
- **Va** de viaje a otro país.

*Yo creo que va de viaje a otro país, porque **lleva**...*

4.6. ¿Qué llevamos en la maleta? Cuando haces un viaje corto, ¿llevas las mismas cosas que Silvia? ¿Llevas otras? Coméntalo con tu compañero/-a.

- Yo llevo un libro, pero no llevo secador de pelo.
- Yo llevo la computadora.

> **❶ ¿Necesitas ayuda?**
>
> **Ir** = *to go*
> **Ir de viaje** = *to travel*
>
> **Ir** is an irregular verb.
> **Va** is the **él/ella, usted** form.

Los números a partir de 100

4.7. Aprendemos los números. Este es tu cartón para jugar al bingo. Primero, escribe las cifras en letras.

100	**cien**	1000	**mil**
101	**ciento** uno*/una	2000	dos mil
102	**ciento** dos	...	
...		10 000	diez mil
200	**doscientos/-as**	20 000	veinte mil
300	**trescientos/-as**	...	
400	**cuatrocientos/-as**	100 000	cien mil
500	**quinientos/-as**	200 000	doscientos/-as mil
600	**seiscientos/-as**	...	
700	**setecientos/-as**	1 000 000	**un millón**
800	**ochocientos/-as**	2 000 000	dos **millones**
900	**novecientos/-as**	1 000 000 000	mil millones

* Antes de un sustantivo: ciento **un** dólares.

3 453 276 = tres millones cuatrocientos/-as cincuenta **y** tres mil doscientos/-as setenta **y** seis.

$ 200 *doscientos*	$ 500	£ 300	£ 900
€ 800	£ 400	£ 600	£ 700
£ 500	£ 200 *doscientas*	€ 900	$ 300
£ 800	$ 600	$ 700	€ 400

4.8. Jugamos al bingo. Tu cartón tiene que tener once casillas. Por eso, primero, tienes que anular cinco. Ahora escucha los números y márcalos en tu cartón. Fíjate en el género: ¿dice doscient**os** o doscient**as**?

> **⊕ ¿Sabes que...?**
>
> The euro (€) is the official monetary unit of many of the member states of the European Union (EU), including Spain.
>
> The pound sterling (£) is the monetary unit of the United Kingdom.

Comprendemos el vocabulario

Ropa

⏺⏺ **4.9. Una tienda *online*.** Observa, lee y escucha.

⚙ **Estrategia**

When reading a text in Spanish, try to apply what you already know about familiar formats. For instance, in a web page like this one, there is information we all expect to find, so it's easier to figure out what the words mean.

🌐 **La variedad del español**

los tenis = **los zapatos deportivos** (Ec)

la falda
= **la pollera** (Ar, Ur)

los *jeans*
= **los vaqueros** (Es, Py, Gu, Ur)

el suéter
= **el pulóver** (Ar, Ur, Py), **el saco** (Co), **la chompa** (Pe)

❗ **¿Necesitas ayuda?**

16.90 is read as **dieciséis con noventa** or, more informally, **dieciséis noventa**.

Although a decimal point is recommended, a comma (,) can also be used as a separator.

www.elgancho.dif

EL GANCHO   Tienda   Novedades   Comunidad   **Mi carrito**

Mi carrito

JEANS
COLOR: AZUL OSCURO
TALLA: 38
16.90 USD

TENIS
COLOR: NEGRO
NÚMERO: 39
49.90 USD

CAMISA DE ALGODÓN DE MANGA LARGA
COLOR: VERDE
TALLA: L
19.90 USD

VESTIDO DE TIRANTES
COLOR: ROJO
TALLA: M
35.90 USD

FALDA
COLOR: BLANCO
TALLA: S
26.90 USD

BLUSA DE SEDA SIN MANGAS
COLOR: AZUL CLARO
TALLA: M
15.90 USD

SUÉTER DE LANA
COLOR: GRIS
TALLA: M
26.90 USD

TOTAL: 192.3 USD   COMPRAR

COPIA EL LOOK

GORRO 9,90 USD
BUFANDA 29.90 USD
ABRIGO 89.90 USD
ABRIGO 129.90 USD

También te puede interesar

BOTAS DE PIEL
COLOR: CAFÉ
79.90 USD

BOLSO DE PIEL
COLOR: AMARILLO
35.90 USD

CINTURÓN
COLOR: ANARANJADO
22.90 USD

+ ACCESORIOS

e **4.10. Describimos la ropa.** Observa la página web de la actividad 4.9 y completa el cuadro.

Tipos de camiseta, blusa, camisa o suéter:

.... *de manga corta* ....

Colores:

○ ....o/-a/-os/-as   ● ....o/-a/-os/-as   ● lila/s   ● ..../es

● ....o/-a/-os/-as   ● ....o/-a/-os/-as   ● ....e/s   ● ..../es

● ....o/-a/-os/-as   ● rosa/s   ● ....é/s   ● beige

Talla significa: ....

Lo contrario de claro **es:** ....

e **4.11. El verbo _llevar_.** ¿Qué llevan estas personas? Relaciona las descripciones con las imágenes.

● Lleva unos tenis blancos.

● Lleva una camisa café de manga larga.

● Lleva un vestido azul de tirantes.

A — Valeria

B — Lucas

C — Flavia

> **❶ ¿Necesitas ayuda?**
>
> **llevar** = *to wear*
> *Rosa lleva una chaqueta muy linda.* = Rosa is wearing a very nice jacket.
>
> **llevar** = *to carry*
> *En la maleta llevo un libro.* = I carry a book in my suitcase.

4.12. ¿Qué ropa llevan? Escribe más frases para describir la ropa de las fotos de la actividad 4.11.

Valeria lleva una camiseta blanca de manga corta.

4.13. Hablamos. Comenta con algunos compañeros qué ropa llevan en tu ciudad las siguientes personas.

• los policías / las policías

• los meseros / las meseras

• los hombres de negocios / las mujeres de negocios

> • *Los policías llevan pantalones azules y botas negras.*
> ○ *Sí, y camisa azul.*
> ■ *Y llevan chaqueta.*

Exploramos la lengua

Los demostrativos (I): **este/-a/-os/-as, esto**

e **4.14. Descubrimos los demostrativos.** Lee los diálogos y observa las palabras en negrita. Escribe debajo de cada diálogo a qué prenda de vestir se refieren. Marca también el género y el número de ese sustantivo.

¿Cuáles son más **lindas**?
¿**Estas** o **estas**?

Las verdes.

sustantivo: Sandalias
○ masculino ○ femenino ○ singular ○ plural

¿Cuáles **prefieres**?
¿**Estos** o **estos**?

Los negros.

sustantivo: ....
○ masculino ○ femenino ○ singular ○ plural

¿Cuál es más **barato**?
¿**Este** o **este**?

El gris.

sustantivo: ....
○ masculino ○ femenino ○ singular ○ plural

¿Cuál compro?
¿**Esta** o **esta**?

La azul.

sustantivo: ....
○ masculino ○ femenino ○ singular ○ plural

4.15. Concordancia. Ahora marca en los diálogos de la actividad 4.14 todas las palabras que concuerdan en género y en número con los sustantivos.

Sandalias: ¿Cuáles son más lindas? ¿Estas o estas?

4.16. Usamos los demostrativos. Escribe frases sobre estos productos usando **este/esta/estos/estas** y las palabras siguientes (se pueden repetir).

¿Necesitas ayuda?
barato/-a = *cheap/inexpensive*
caro/-a = *expensive*

original   feo/-a   elegante
lindo/-a   moderno/-a

1   2   3   4   5   6   7

1- Estas sandalias son elegantes.

4.17. Demostrativo neutro. Observa la imagen de la derecha. ¿Qué significa la palabra **esto**? ¿Cuándo crees que usamos esta palabra?

e **4.18. Completamos la regla.** Completa la regla.

1. **Este, esta, estos** and **estas** are used...
2. **Esto** is used...

a. ... to refer to a specific noun.
b. ... to refer to something that the speaker does not want to identify or cannot identify with a specific word.

¿Qué compro para Ángela? ¿Esto o esto?

El/la/los/las + adjetivo

e **4.19. ¿De qué hablan?** Dos personas van de compras. Lee las frases y marca de qué prenda de vestir hablan.

1. La azul es muy pequeña.	2. Los verdes son muy lindos.	3. Las rojas son muy caras.	4. ¡El negro es muy feo!
○ un suéter	○ un traje de baño	○ unos zapatos	○ un traje de baño
○ unas sandalias	○ unas sandalias	○ unas sandalias	○ unas gafas de sol
○ una camiseta	○ unos pantalones	○ un suéter	○ una camiseta

4.20. Otras prendas. Escribe a qué otras prendas de vestir pueden referirse las frases de la actividad 4.19.

1. La azul es muy pequeña.
2. Los verdes son muy lindos.
3. Las rojas son muy caras.
4. ¡El negro es muy feo!

4.21. Respondemos a las preguntas. Observa las imágenes y responde a las preguntas, como en el ejemplo.

1. ¿Qué maleta es más moderna? *La gris.*

2. ¿Qué vestido es más elegante?

3. ¿Qué zapatos son más elegantes?

$12.99 $20.99

4. ¿Qué bufanda es más cara?

5. ¿Qué suéter es más lindo?

$35.95 $65.95

6. ¿Qué sandalias son más baratas?

Exploramos la lengua

Tener que + infinitivo

4.22. El verbo *tener*. ¿En qué frase se expresa una obligación o necesidad? Márcala.

○ Martín tiene 21 años.

○ Para comprar alcohol tienes que tener más de 21 años.

❗ ¿Necesitas ayuda?

English-speaking learners tend to overuse **necesitar** + infinitive because they translate **to need** + infinitve directly. However, **tener que** + infinitive is used in most situations to express that something is required.

4.23. Comparamos con nuestra lengua. ¿Entiendes qué significa **tener que**? ¿Cómo se dice en inglés?

4.24. Conjugamos. Completa las frases con la forma adecuada de **tener que**.

1. Cuando vas a clase de español, ... (tú) llevar el libro y un cuaderno.
2. Si quieren ir a la playa, ... (ustedes) llevar protector solar.
3. Gael y yo queremos alquilar un automóvil. .... (nosotros) llevar la licencia de conducir.
4. Sofía, Mía y Jorge quieren ir de compras. .... (ellos) llevar dinero o una tarjeta de crédito.
5. Quiero ir de viaje al extranjero. .... (yo) llevar el pasaporte.
6. Sebastián quiere ir al gimnasio. .... (él) llevar **ropa deportiva**.

❗ ¿Necesitas ayuda?

TENER

yo	**tengo**
tú	**tienes**
él/ella, usted	**tiene**
nosotros/-as	**tenemos**
vosotros/-as	**tenéis**
ellos/-as, ustedes	**tienen**

Cuesta/cuestan

4.25. Una conversación. Lee este diálogo. ¿Qué situación representa? ¿Para qué sirve el verbo **costar**?

- *Buenos días.*
- *Buenos días.*
- *¿Qué desea?*
- *Un bolígrafo, por favor.*
- *¿De qué color?*
- *Azul.*
- *Mire, aquí tiene estos.*
- *¿Cuánto **cuestan**?*

- *Este **cuesta** 2.80 dólares, y este otro, 3 dólares.*
- *Uy, son muy caros...*
- *También tenemos este. **Cuesta** 80 centavos.*
- *Listo, me llevo este. Gracias.*
- *Muchas gracias.*

❗ ¿Necesitas ayuda?

In this conversation, you can find many expressions that are used for buying something in a store. You are going to practice them on page 86 (Ahora podemos).

4.26. ¿*Cuesta* o *cuestan*? Completa estas preguntas con **cuesta** o **cuestan**.

1. ¿Cuánto .... estos zapatos?
2. Esta camiseta de aquí, ¿cuánto ....?

4.27. Completamos. Una chica va de compras con una amiga. Escucha y anota la información que falta.

Quiere comprar ....

Al final compra .... , que cuesta ....

Verbos irregulares en presente: **ir** y **preferir**

4.28. Trucos. Lee esta entrevista. Marca qué tienes en común con Gustavo Duarte.

ESCAPADA DE FIN DE SEMANA

¿QUÉ LLEVA GUSTAVO DUARTE EN LA MALETA?

Hablamos con el influencer y creador del blog de moda **MR. DUARTE**, *Gustavo Duarte, sobre sus secretos para viajar y hacer la maleta.*

¿Maleta con ruedas o mochila?
En general, maleta con ruedas, pero si <u>voy</u> al campo, <u>prefiero</u> llevar mochila. Es más cómodo.

¿Tenis o zapatos?
Para un viaje de placer, los tenis son la mejor opción. Muchos hombres <u>prefieren</u> llevar zapatos para ir a cenar, salir de noche, etc., pero hay un montón de modelos de tenis urbanos que puedes llevar con *jeans* o con pantalones más elegantes.

¿Cómo <u>prefieres</u> pasar el tiempo, con un libro o con música?
Yo prefiero escuchar música, pero mi pareja <u>prefiere</u> leer. Depende de las preferencias de cada uno…

¿Dinero en efectivo o tarjeta?
Las dos cosas. Siempre llevo mi tarjeta, pero también llevo dinero en efectivo para pagar cosas como un café, el boleto del autobús, etc. Si viajo con mi pareja y <u>vamos</u> a un lugar exótico, <u>preferimos</u> repartir el dinero en efectivo. Uno lleva dólares y el otro, moneda local.

¿Qué prendas llevas siempre en la maleta?
Si <u>vas</u> de viaje de fin de semana y no tienes espacio en la maleta, tienes que **elegir** prendas **cómodas** y versátiles, como unos *jeans*. Yo siempre llevo unos *jeans*. Y una camiseta blanca: el blanco **combina** muy bien con todo.

¿Naturaleza o ciudad? ¿Dónde <u>va</u> Gustavo cuando quiere desconectar?
¿Para desconectar? Naturaleza, sin duda.

● *Yo también prefiero la maleta con ruedas.*
○ *Pues yo prefiero llevar mochila.*

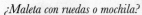

4.29. Conjugamos *ir y preferir*. Completa la tabla con las formas de los verbos **ir** y **preferir** del texto de la actividad 4.28.

	IR	PREFERIR
(yo)	....	....
(tú)	....	....
(él/ella, usted)	....	....
(nosotros/nosotras)	....	....
(vosotros/vosotras)	vais	preferís
(ellos/ellas, ustedes)	van	....

4.30. Comparamos *querer y preferir*. Escribe todas las formas del verbo **querer**.
¿Qué tienen en común los verbos **querer** y **preferir**?

Comunicamos

¿Qué ropa llevar?

4.31. Elegimos ropa. En parejas, elijan las prendas más adecuadas para cada una de estas situaciones.

- un festival de música pop
- una excursión por el campo
- un viaje largo en avión
- una fiesta de cumpleaños en casa de un/a amigo/-a

> • ¿Qué ropa prefieres para ir a un festival de música pop?
> ○ Los jeans, los tenis y la camiseta.

4.32. Nuestra selección. Presenten al resto de la clase las prendas que han elegido para cada situación.

> Para ir a un festival de música pop, los jeans, los tenis y la camiseta blanca de manga corta.

¿Cuánto cuesta?

4.33. El precio justo. Busca en internet un producto que te gusta y que quieres comprar. Muéstraselo a tus compañeros/-as, que tendrán que adivinar cuánto vale.

> • Quiero comprar esta maleta. ¿Cuánto cuesta?
> ○ Ciento cincuenta dólares.
> • Más.
> ■ Doscientos.
> • Menos.

Una semana de viaje

 4.34. Elegimos destino. En grupos, van a pasar una semana en uno de los tres lugares del anuncio de la derecha. ¿Cuál eligen y por qué?

 4.35. ¿Qué vamos a necesitar? Cada persona lleva su ropa. En grupos de tres, piensen en otras cinco cosas que necesitan y que tienen que compartir. Hagan una lista.

> • *Yo creo que tenemos que llevar un mapa.*
> ○ *Sí, es verdad, y un...*

4.36. ¿Qué tenemos que hacer? Ahora tienen que decidir cómo van a conseguir esas cosas. ¿Alguno de ustedes tiene alguna de ellas? ¿Las tienen que comprar?

> • *No tenemos mapa, ¿verdad?*
> ○ *No.*
> • *Pues tenemos que comprar uno.*

Mis cosas de cada día

4.37. Organizamos el vocabulario. Crea un mapa mental como el siguiente con los objetos y prendas que más usas en tu día a día.

4.38. Presentamos y compartimos. Presenta tu mapa mental a otras personas de la clase. ¿Tienen cosas en común?

Ahora podemos...

Comprar y vender en un mercado

4.39. Preparación. Preparen un mercado. Individualmente sigan estos pasos.

a. Elige tres productos para vender (pueden ser de diferente tipo: ropa, accesorios, objetos de clase, etc.).

b. Decide el precio de cada producto.

c. Coloca en la mesa tus productos con el nombre de cada cosa escrito en un papel.

4.40. Comunicación interpersonal. Divídanse en compradores y vendedores, y compren dos cosas para regalar a una persona de la clase. Luego, cambien los papeles.

PARA COMUNICAR

CLIENTES/-AS

Hola / Buenos días / Buenas tardes.

Quiero unos zapatos (para hombre / para mujer).

¿Cuánto cuesta este suéter?
¿Cuánto cuestan estas gafas?

Es un poco caro, ¿no?

¿Tiene/n algo más barato?

(Pues) **me llevo estos** (negros).

(Pues) **me llevo los negros.**

Muchas gracias.

VENDEDORES/-AS

Hola / Buenos días / Buenas tardes.

¿Qué desea/s?

¿De qué color?

Sí, **tenemos estos**.

Gracias a usted. / **Gracias a** ti.

4.41. Presentación. Presenta tus compras y para quién es cada producto.

Estas gafas de sol son para Catherine.

Video

Radio bodega

Vamos a conocer la vida diaria de Geovanny Valdez, propietario de una bodega en la ciudad de Nueva York. Su trabajo le permite tener una buena relación con las personas de su barrio, pero Geovanny también contribuye a la comunidad desde la estación de radio que tiene en el sótano de la bodega.

🅿 Pearson
MyLab

To find out more about Geovanny Valdez and his radio station, go to MyLab to watch **Radio bodega** and complete the video activities.

⊕ ¿Sabes que...?

Hispanics are some of the biggest consumers of radio in the United States, with more than 95% tuning in for about 13 hours per week. The radio formats are as diverse as the population itself, and musical offerings vary by region, but overall the most popular ones feature Mexican and contemporary Latin Caribbean music.

🔍 Hacemos conexiones

Investiga sobre las estaciones de radio en español en tu país:

- ¿Cuáles son las más importantes?
- ¿Hay muchas en tu ciudad o en tu estado?
- ¿Qué tipo de programación tienen?

Colombia protege su herencia

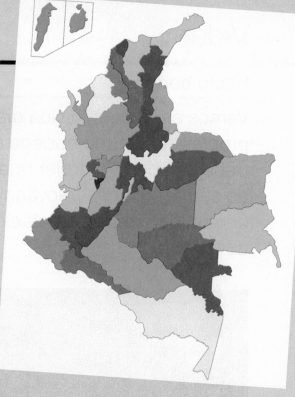

Colombia protege sus artesanías y a sus artesanos con 11 denominaciones de origen. Colombia tiene un patrimonio artesanal único y muy rico. Para protegerlo, existen once denominaciones de origen. ¿Qué significa eso? Que los productos de esas denominaciones pasan estrictos controles de calidad y tienen un sello que lo certifica. De ese modo, los compradores saben que adquieren un producto 100 % artesanal, elaborado con técnicas y materiales tradicionales. Además, así los artesanos protegen su propiedad intelectual contra las copias y, en muchos casos, pueden vender sus artesanías en tiendas especializadas a precios más justos. A continuación, tenemos cuatro ejemplos.

 Tejeduría wayúu: mochilas y otros objetos elaborados en hilo por artesanas de la comunidad Wayúu, en La Guajira.

(2) **Cerámica de Carmen de Viboral:** utensilios, platos, etc. elaborados en cerámica y pintados a mano en Carmen de Viboral, Antioquia.

3 **Sombrero de Suaza, sombrero Aguadeño y sombrero de Sandoná:** elaborados en palma o en fibra de palma por artesanos de Suaza, Aguadas y Sandoná, respectivamente.

4 **La chiva:** "El bus más popular de Colombia", elaborado con arcilla en Pitalito, Huila.

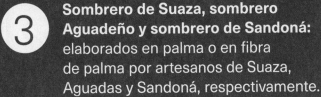

ANTES DE LEER

4.42. Nuestras hipótesis. Antes de leer el artículo, lee el título y observa las imágenes. ¿Cuál crees que es el tema del texto?

LECTURA ACTIVA

4.43. Comprobamos. Lee la introducción y comprueba tus hipótesis de la actividad 4.42.

4.44. Denominación de origen. Explica con tus propias palabras qué es una denominación de origen.

4.45. Interpretamos. ¿Por qué habla el texto de proteger la "propiedad intelectual"?

4.46. Nuestras preferencias. Lee las descripciones de las artesanías. ¿Cuál prefieres? ¿Por qué?

DESPUÉS DE LEER

4.47. Localizamos en el mapa. Ubica en el mapa dónde se hacen los cuatro productos comentados.

4.48. Comparamos con nuestra cultura. En tu país, ¿existe algo similar a las denominaciones de origen? ¿Hay productos como los de este artículo?

Textos escritos: leemos y escribimos

Leemos sobre la industria textil

ANTES DE LA LECTURA

4.49. Interpretación. Observa el texto abajo. ¿De qué tipo de ropa habla?

- nueva
- usada
- vintage

4.50. Comparación. En tu ciudad, ¿dónde puedes comprar este tipo de ropa?

LECTURA ACTIVA

4.51. Lectura. Lee el texto de manera general y selecciona cuál de estas ideas lo resume mejor.

1. Second-hand clothing is a million-dollar business that benefits the planet and allows the consumer to save.
2. There are certain countries that discard a large amount of new clothing and other countries that receive most of the second-hand clothes.
3. Online sites are taking advantage of the increasing number of people who want to buy clothes in a sustainable way.

Ropa de segunda mano, un negocio millonario

El auge del *fast-fashion* tiene como consecuencia un consumo mayor de ropa en el mercado occidental, lo que implica más desechos. De acuerdo con Greenpeace, la industria textil es, después de la petrolera, la segunda más contaminante del mundo.

La ropa de segunda mano representa una alternativa para cuidar el medioambiente y, además de que permite ahorrar, genera ganancias millonarias. Estas son algunas cifras:

• Genera 4300 mdd al año en el mundo.

• Estados Unidos es el proveedor principal de ropa usada. Si calculamos que en un año cada estadounidense desecha 36 kg de ropa, obtenemos 687 mdd al año.

• Canadá, Chile y Guatemala son los principales destinos de ropa usada. México ocupa el sexto lugar (recibe 30 mdd al año en ropa usada).

Beneficios

• Comprar ropa de segunda mano también es un movimiento que propone un consumo consciente y optar por comprar ropa de manera más sustentable. El *slow-fashion* da prioridad al consumo de ropa de segunda mano.

• Es también una alternativa para tener ropa de marca a bajo precio. Prendas de poco uso y en buen estado se pueden encontrar hasta un 75 % más baratas que su precio original.

Sitios como Trendier, una *startup* mexicana, han transformado la compra y venta de prendas de segunda mano por internet de manera fácil y segura: tiene 200 000 usuarios que suben 1000 prendas diariamente y genera 150 transacciones al día.

DESPUÉS DE LEER

4.52. Interpretación. Completa con información del texto.

1. Una de las industrias que más contamina: ....

2. País que genera más ropa usada en el mundo: ....

3. Principales países que reciben ropa usada: ....

4. Un beneficio de comprar ropa usada: ....

5. Sitio en internet donde puedes vender tu ropa usada: ....

4.53. Traducción. Encuentra en el texto la palabra o expresión que significa:

1. waste (párrafo 1)
2. earnings (párrafo 2)
3. millions of dollars (párrafo 3)
4. designer clothes (párrafo 7)
5. clothing items (párrafo 8)

4.54. Comunicación interpersonal. En parejas, conversen a partir de estas preguntas.

1. ¿Qué información sobre la ropa de segunda mano les parece más interesante?
2. ¿Creen que comprar ropa usada tiene aspectos negativos? ¿Cuáles son?
3. ¿Con qué frecuencia compran ropa de segunda mano?
4. ¿Les parece buena idea comprar o poder vender su ropa usada? Comenten los beneficios.

Escribimos sobre el negocio de ropa de segunda mano

4.55. Reacción personal. Crea una infografía para estudiantes universitarios a partir de la información del texto y de las ideas que comentaron en la actividad 4.54. Tienes que usar las ideas más relevantes y condensar la información. Añade información sobre tiendas de ropa de segunda mano que conoces.

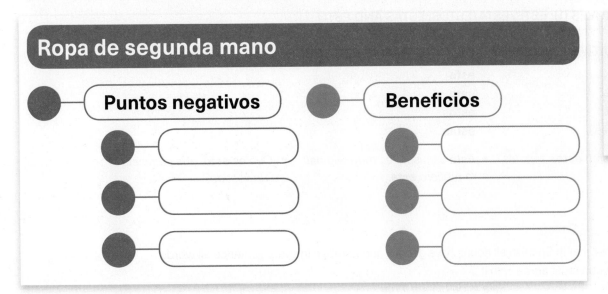

❶ ¿Necesitas ayuda?

An infographic is a combination of images and short, easy-to-understand texts used to present information.

Recursos lingüísticos

NUMBERS OVER 100

100	**cien**	700	**sete**cientos/-as	...	
101	**ciento uno*/una**	800	**ochocientos/-as**	100 000	**cien mil**
102	**ciento dos**	900	**nove**cientos/-as	200 000	**doscientos/-as mil**
...				...	
200	**doscientos/-as**	1000	**mil**	1 000 000	**un millón**
300	**trescientos/-as**	2000	**dos mil**	2 000 000	**dos millones**
400	**cuatrocientos/-as**	...		1 000 000 000	**mil millones**
500	**quinientos/-as**	10 000	**diez mil**		
600	**seiscientos/-as**	20 000	**veinte mil**		

❗ *Before nouns: ciento **un** dólares.

▶ Note that the hundreds have feminine forms. These are needed when the number precedes a feminine word: trescient**as** person**as**, ochocient**as** veinte palabr**as**.

▶ Before nouns: **cien** dólares / **mil** dólares but **un millón de** dólares.

▶ Remember that numbers up to 30 in Spanish are spelled as single words. We use **y** only between the tens and ones place after the number 30:

16: **dieciséis**	32: treinta **y** dos	1930: mil novecientos treinta
30: **treinta**	74: setenta **y** cuatro	1931: mil novecientos treinta **y** uno

❗ Note also that the use of **.** and **,** is different from English. In Spanish, although a space is recommended, the decimal point (**.**) is still commonly used for thousands after ten thousand and millions:
22 015/22.015 (veintidós mil quince), **22 015 000/22.015.000** (veintidós millones quince mil).

❗ The decimal point (**.**) is recommended as a decimal separator, although the comma (**,**) is still used in some countries:
3.5: tres punto cinco = **3,15**: tres coma quince

DEMONSTRATIVES (I): ESTE/ESTA/ESTOS/ESTAS AND ESTO

DEMONSTRATIVE ADJECTIVES	DEMONSTRATIVE PRONOUNS	
este suéter	**este**	
esta camiseta	**esta**	**esto**
estos zapatos	**estos**	
estas sandalias	**estas**	

- ¿Cuánto cuestan **estos** zapatos?
  ○ 50 dólares.
- ¿Y **estos**?
  ○ 75.

- ¡**Esta** camiseta es muy original!
  ○ Yo prefiero **esta**.

- ¿Qué es **esto**: una camiseta o un vestido?

❗ Remember that in Spanish all nouns have gender and number. In every sentence all words refering to the noun must agree with it:

est**e** suéter café
est**os** pantal**es** cort**os**

est**a** fald**a** blanc**a** larg**a**
est**as** camiset**as** roj**as** nuev**as**

EL/LA/LOS/LAS + ADJECTIVE (TO POINT OUT)

In both conversational English and Spanish when we refer to an object according to a characteristic, for example its color, there is no need to repeat the name of the object. Instead, in Spanish we can use the definite article plus the characteristic the same way that we use **the ... one** in English:

- ● *¿Qué falda prefieres?* = What skirt do you prefer?
- ○ **La roja**. = The red one.

! Note that in Spanish the article (**el/la/los/las**) and the adjective need to agree in number and gender with the noun they refer to.

*¿Qué <u>auto</u> usamos: **el** nuev**o** o **el** viej**o**?*	el <u>auto</u> nuevo ▲ **el** nuev**o**
*Luis quiere comprar la <u>camiseta</u> verde, y Julia, **la** amarill**a**.*	la <u>camiseta</u> amarilla ▲ **la** amarill**a**
*Los <u>pantalones</u> más lindos son **los** negr**os**.*	los <u>pantalones</u> negros ▲ **los** negr**os**
*Llevo las <u>sandalias</u> negras y **las** roj**as**.*	las <u>sandalias</u> rojas ▲ **las** roj**as**

TENER QUE + INFINITIVE

Tener can be used in Spanish to express possession (*to have*).
***Tengo** dos celulares.* = I have two cell phones.

▸ To talk about need and obligation (*to have to do something*) use **tener que** + infinitive.

***Tengo que llevar** secador de pelo.* = I have to bring a hair dryer.

	TENER	QUE + INFINITIVE
(yo)	**tengo**	
(tú)	**tienes**	
(él/ella, usted)	**tiene**	**que** + llevar
(nosotros/nosotras)	**tenemos**	
(vosotros/vosotras)	**tenéis**	
(ellos/ellas, ustedes)	**tienen**	

CUESTA/CUESTAN

▸ When **costar** (*to cost*) is followed by a singular noun, it is conjugated in the singular:

*¿Cuánto **cuesta** la chaqueta gris?* = How much does the grey jacket cost?

▸ If it is followed by a plural noun, it is conjugated in the plural:

*Estas gafas de sol **cuestan** 20 dólares.* = These sunglasses cost 20 dollars.

IRREGULAR VERBS: IR AND PREFERIR

	IR	PREFERIR
(yo)	**voy**	prefiero
(tú)	**vas**	prefieres
(él/ella, usted)	**va**	prefiere
(nosotros/nosotras)	**vamos**	preferimos
(vosotros/vosotras)	**vais**	preferís
(ellos/ellas, ustedes)	**van**	prefieren

▸ Remember that verbs in Spanish have a stem (the part of the verb which carries the meaning of the word) and an ending that changes to indicate the person (**yo**, **tú**, **él**...). Irregular verbs are those with spelling changes in the stem, for example **ser** and **querer**.

¿Qué prefieres para ir a clase: tenis o zapatos?

Pronunciamos

Los números

4.56. Escribimos los números en letras. Escribe estos números en letras. Escuchar el audio te puede ayudar a escribir o a comprobar si lo hiciste bien.

1. 28 ....

2. 49 ....

3. 167 ....

4. 715 ....

5. 473 ....

6. 1999 ....

7. 2576 ....

8. 10 089 ....

9. 331 752 ....

10. 5 819 120 ....

4.57. Escuchamos e identificamos. Escucha estos diálogos y marca el número correcto.

1
- Perdone, ¿tiene esta falda en la talla **14 / 40**?
- No, lo siento.
- ¿Y cuánto cuestan estos pantalones?
- **75 / 65** dólares.

2
- Buenas tardes, ¿tienen camisetas de niño de manga corta?
- Sí, ¿de qué talla la necesita?
- De la **2 / 12**.

3
- ¿Cuánto cuesta el vestido negro?
- Son **205 / 250** dólares.

4
- ¿Cuánto cuestan estos tenis?
- Son **15 / 50** dólares.

5
- ¿Es muy caro este abrigo?
- No, solo cuesta **106 / 110** dólares.

4.58. Escuchamos y representamos. Escucha otra vez los diálogos de la actividad 4.57 y represéntalos con tu compañero/-a.

Vocabulario activo

Objetos de uso cotidiano
Everyday objects

- la aspirina   *aspirin*
- el cepillo   *brush*
- el cepillo de dientes   *toothbrush*
- el champú   *shampoo*
- el dinero   *money*
- el dinero en efectivo   *cash*
- el disco   *record*
- el jabón   *soap*
- la maleta   *suitcase*
- la novela   *novel*
- el pasaporte   *passport*
- la pasta de dientes   *toothpaste*
- el protector solar   *sun block*
- la ropa   *clothes*
- el secador de pelo   *hair dryer*
- la tarjeta de crédito   *credit card*
- el teléfono   *telephone*
- la toalla de playa   *beach towel*

Prendas de vestir
Clothing items

- el abrigo   *coat*
- el accesorio   *accessory*
- la blusa   *blouse*
- el bolso   *purse*
- las botas   *boots*
- la bufanda   *scarf*
- la camisa   *shirt*
- la camiseta   *T-shirt*
- la chaqueta   *jacket*
- el cinturón   *belt*
- de manga corta/larga (la manga)   *short/long-sleeve*
- la falda   *skirt*
- las gafas de sol   *sunglasses*
- el gorro   *hat*
- los *jeans*   *jeans*
- los pantalones   *pants, trousers*
- los pantalones cortos   *shorts*
- la ropa deportiva   *sportswear*

- la ropa interior   *underwear*
- las sandalias   *sandals*
- sin mangas   *sleeveless*
- el suéter   *sweater*
- los tenis   *sneakers, tennis shoes*
- el traje de baño   *bathing suit*
- el vestido   *dress*
- los zapatos   *shoes*

Materiales   *Materials*

- el algodón   *cotton*
- la lana   *wool*
- la piel   *leather*
- la seda   *silk*

Colores   *Colors*

- amarillo/-a   *yellow*
- anaranjado/-a   *orange*
- azul   *blue*
- beige   *beige*
- blanco/-a   *white*
- café   *brown*
- claro/-a   *light*
- gris   *grey*
- lila   *purple*
- negro/-a   *black*
- oscuro/-a   *dark*
- rojo/-a   *red*
- rosa   *pink*
- verde   *green*

Ir de compras   *To go shopping*

- la antigüedad   *antique*
- la artesanía   *handicraft*
- combinar   *to combine*
- comprar   *to buy*
- costar (o>ue)   *to cost*
- elegir (e>i)   *to choose*
- el mercado   *flea market*
- preferir (e>ie)   *to prefer*
- la talla   *size*
- vender   *to sell*

Adjetivos para hablar de la ropa   *Adjectives to talk about clothing*

- barato/-a   *cheap*
- caro/-a   *expensive*
- cómodo/-a   *comfortable*
- elegante   *elegant, chic*
- lindo/-a   *beautiful*
- moderno/-a   *modern*
- original   *original*

El verbo llevar   *The verb llevar*

- llevar   *to carry, to wear*

Números a partir de 100
Numbers after 100

- cien   *one hundred*
- ciento uno/-a   *one hundred and one*
- ciento dos   *one hundred and two*
- doscientos/-as   *two hundred*
- trescientos/-as   *three hundred*
- cuatrocientos/-as   *four hundred*
- quinientos/-as   *five hundred*
- seiscientos/-as   *six hundred*
- setecientos/-as   *seven hundred*
- ochocientos/-as   *eight hundred*
- novecientos/-as   *nine hundred*
- mil   *one thousand*
- dos mil   *two thousand*
- diez mil   *ten thousand*
- veinte mil   *twenty thousand*
- cien mil   *one hundred thousand*
- doscientos/-as mil   *two hundred thousand*
- un millón   *one million*
- dos millones   *two million*
- mil millones   *a billion*

⚙ **Estrategia**

Learning the numbers in Spanish can be a little tricky but the good news is that you don't need to memorize them all. Make sure you understand how they work and you'll be able to say any number.

Lección 5

Mis amigos son tus amigos

IN THIS LESSON WE ARE GOING TO

introduce and describe a person

LEARNING OUTCOMES
You will be able to...

- talk about physical descriptions and personality traits

- express and contrast likes and interests

- ask about likes and preferences

VOCABULARY
- Family

- Adjectives of physical appearance

- Adjectives of personality traits

- Music

LANGUAGE STRUCTURES
- The verbs **gustar**, **encantar**, and **interesar**

- **También/tampoco**

- Possessives

- Demonstratives (II): **este**, **ese** and **aquel**

PRONUNCIATION
- The pronunciation of **r/rr**

CULTURE
- The origins of Latin jazz

El dúo de country pop mexicano-estadounidense Ha*Ash durante su gira "100 años contigo" en The Majestic Theatre (Dallas, USA).

Primer contacto

5.1. Las fotos de Marcelo. Mira las fotos de Marcelo y relaciona las palabras de la columna izquierda con su significado (columna derecha). Compara tus respuestas con las de tu compañero/-a.

Marcelo

Con mis amigos Carlos y Adriana.

Con mi padre.

De excursión con mi hermana Viviana.

Con mi sobrina Ana en la playa.

En la montaña con mi hermano.

Con mis compañeros de clase en Dublín.

1. amigo
2. sobrina
3. hermano
4. hermana
5. padre
6. compañeros

a. sister
b. father
c. friend
d. classmates
e. niece
f. brother

5.2. Presentamos a una persona. ¿Cómo se llama tu mejor amigo o amiga? ¿Y tus padres? Busca una foto (en tu teléfono, en una red social, etc.) y presenta a esa persona a la clase.

Esta es *Jen,* **mi mejor amiga**.

Comprendemos el vocabulario

La familia

)))
e
5.3. Un árbol genealógico. Esta es la familia de Juan y de Lucía.

Escucha y lee las frases y completa los cuadros en blanco en el árbol genealógico.

1. Juan es el **esposo** de Lucía.
2. Lucía es la **abuela** de Carla y de Daniel.
3. Carla es la **hija** de Abel y de Luisa.
4. Daniel es el **nieto** de Juan y de Lucía.

5. Juan es el padre de Marcos y de Abel.
6. Marcos es el **tío** de Carla.
7. Daniel es el **primo** de Carla.

 La variedad del español

Padre and **madre** are both used in Latin America and in Spain. However, there are other ways to refer to "father" and "mother": **papá** / **mamá**, **papa** / **mama**, **papi** / **mami**

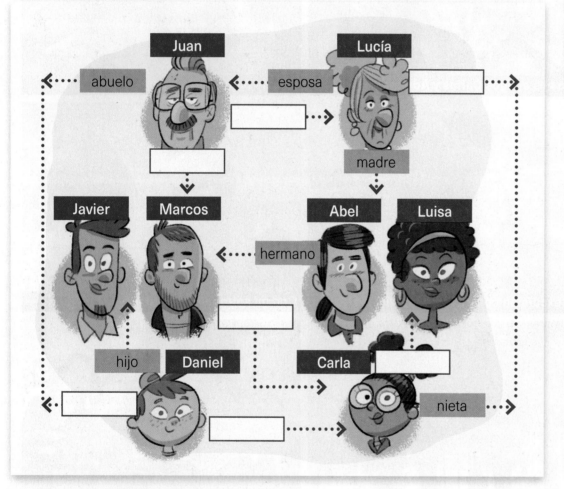

Más palabras

))) **MIEMBROS DE LA FAMILIA =** *FAMILY MEMBERS*

abuelos (abuelo + abuela) = *grandparents (grandfather + grandmother)*

exesposo/-a = *ex-husband, ex-wife*

hermanastro/-a = *stepbrother / stepsister*

hermanos (hermano + hermana) = *siblings*

hijos (hijo + hija) = *children*

medio hermano/-a = *half-brother / half-sister*

nietos (nieto + nieta) = *grandchildren (grandson/-daughter)*

novio/-a = *boyfriend / girlfriend*

padres (padre + madre) = *parents*

la pareja, compañero/-a = *partner*

primos (primo + prima) = *cousins*

prometido/-a = *fiancé/-e*

tíos (tío + tía) = *uncles*

RELACIONES = *RELATIONSHIPS*

estar casado/-a (con alguien) = *to be married (to someone)*

estar divorciado/-a = *to be divorced*

estar separado/-a = *to be separated*

ser/estar soltero/-a = *to be single*

ser/estar viudo/-a = *to be widowed*

ser hijo/-a único/-a = *to be an only child*

e **5.4. La familia de Juan y de Lucía.** Observa el árbol genealógico de la actividad 5.3 y escribe los nombres correctos.

1. Es la esposa de Juan: ....

2. Es la prima de Daniel: ....

3. Es el hermano de Marcos: ....

4. Es el esposo de Luisa: ....

5. Es la madre de Carla: ....

6. Es el tío de Daniel: ....

7. Es el abuelo de Carla y de Daniel: ....

8. Es la madre de Abel: ....

e **5.5. Relaciones de parentesco.** Observa el árbol genealógico de la actividad 5.3 y completa las preguntas con la palabra y el artículo correspondientes.

1
• ¿Cómo se llama .... de Daniel?
○ Carla.

2
• ¿Cómo se llama .... de Marcos?
○ Javier.

3
• ¿Cómo se llaman .... de Carla?
○ Javier y Marcos.

4
• ¿Cómo se llama .... de Daniel?
○ Luisa.

5
• ¿Cómo se llama .... de Abel?
○ Luisa.

6
• ¿Cómo se llaman .... de Juan?
○ Daniel y Carla.

5.6. La familia de Margarita. En parejas, lean las tarjetas y dibujen el árbol genealógico.

Margarita Vidal Méndez
Tiene 69 años.
Es viuda. Tiene una hija que se llama Ana.

Ana Martín Vidal
Tiene 45 años. Es ingeniera. Está casada. No tiene hijos, pero es tía.

Ignacio Álvarez Guzmán
Tiene 41 años. Está casado y tiene una hija.

Carlos Martín Ariza
Tiene 20 años.
Es soltero.
Es hijo único.

Gabriela Álvarez Martín
Tiene 17 años.
Tiene un primo.
Es hija única.

Leonor Martín Vidal
Tiene 38 años.
Tiene pareja. Es la tía de Carlos.

Jorge Martín Vidal
Tiene 47 años. Está divorciado. Tiene dos hermanas.
Tiene un hijo.

Karina Bolívar Hernández
Tiene 49 años. Es médica y está casada con una ingeniera.

Diana Ariza Fisher
Tiene 40 años. Es enfermera. Tiene un hijo con su exesposo.

• Margarita es la madre de Ana, ¿no?
○ Sí. Y Ana está casada con Karina.

Comprendemos el vocabulario

Descripción física

5.7. Describir a una persona. Observa, lee y escucha.

SER 🔊

 rubio/-a

 pelirrojo/-a

 calvo/-a

moreno/-a  castaño/-a

alto/-a = *tall*
bajo/-a = *short*
delgado/-a = *thin*
feo/-a = *ugly*
gordo/-a = *heavy*
guapo/-a = *handsome / beautiful, pretty*

TENER 🔊

 barba

bigote

 perilla

 gafas

 flequillo

- **el pelo...** rubio / negro / castaño / gris / blanco

 largo ≠ corto

 liso ≠ rizado

- **los ojos...** negros / azules / verdes / cafés, claros ≠ oscuros

5.8. Describimos a una persona famosa. Con las palabras de la actividad 5.7, escribe la descripción de tres personas famosas. Introduce una información falsa.

Zoe Saldaña
Tiene el pelo negro y largo. Tiene los ojos cafés.
Es muy alta: mide dos metros.

5.9. Adivinamos la información falsa. Lee tus descripciones en clase. Tus compañeros tienen que decir qué informaciones son falsas.

Zoe Saldaña no es muy alta: mide un metro setenta.

❗ **¿Necesitas ayuda?**

We use the verb **medir** to talk about how tall a person is. It is an irregular verb (**e>i**).

yo	**mido**
tú	**mides**
él/ella, usted	**mide**
nosotros/nosotras	**medimos**
nosotros/vosotras	**medís**
ellos/ellas, ustedes	**miden**

🌐 **¿Sabes que...?**

1.7 m = roughly 5.6 ft.
2 m = roughly 6.5 ft.

For an approximate length in feet, multiply the number of meters by 3.281. Divide feet by 3.281 for length in meters.

Descripción del carácter

 5.10. Tres mensajes. Lee y escucha los mensajes de tres personas en una aplicación de contactos para hacer intercambios lingüísticos. Identifica a la persona de cada fotografía y escribe el nombre.

1

HABLO:
ESPAÑOL

QUIERO PRACTICAR:
INGLÉS, FRANCÉS
Y RUSO

¡Hola! Me llamo Isabel, tengo 26 años y soy de Santiago. Soy una chica **normal**, **agradable** y muy **sociable**. Mis *hobbies* son cocinar, viajar y estar con mis amigos, pero mi pasión es la fotografía.

2

HABLO:
ESPAÑOL

QUIERO PRACTICAR:
INGLÉS, PORTUGUÉS
Y CHINO

Hola, amigos y amigas. Soy una chica argentina, tengo 35 años y me llamo María. Estudio inglés, portugués y chino. Creo que soy una persona **abierta** y **simpática**. ¡Y muy **deportista**! Practico muchos deportes acuáticos: windsurf, kayak...

3

HABLO:
ESPAÑOL

QUIERO PRACTICAR:
INGLÉS Y ALEMÁN

¡Hola desde Monterrey! Me llamo Claudia y tengo 33 años. Estudio inglés y alemán. Soy un poco **tímida**, pero cuando conozco más a las personas, soy muy **divertida** y **habladora**. Mis pasatiempos son el cine y la música. Mi grupo favorito es Imagine Dragons.

....

....

....

Más palabras

 aburrido/-a = *boring*
activo/-a = *active*
amable = *kind*
antipático/-a = *mean, unpleasant*

buena persona = *good person*
cerrado/-a = *closed-minded*
inteligente = *intelligent*
interesante = *interesting*

perezoso/-a = *lazy*
serio/-a = *serious*
tranquilo/-a, calmado/-a = *peaceful, calm*

5.11. Primeras impresiones. ¿Con cuál de las tres chicas de la actividad 5.10 te gustaría hacer un intercambio? ¿Por qué?

> • **A mí, con** *Isabel*, **porque parece** *simpática*.
> ○ **A mí, con** *María*, **porque parece una persona** *muy interesante*.

5.12. El carácter de... En tu opinión, ¿qué carácter tienen que tener estas personas? ¿Cómo no tienen que ser? Completa la tabla.

	Tiene que ser	No tiene que ser
un/a amigo/-a		
un/a compañero/-a de trabajo		
tu pareja		

❗ ¿Necesitas ayuda?

Me gustaría + infinitive = *I would like to (do something)*

❗ ¿Necesitas ayuda?

We use the verb **ser** to talk about features we know about someone's personality:
Paola es tímida. = Paola is shy.
Gustavo es una persona divertida. = Gustavo is a fun person.

We use the verb **parecer** to talk about features we perceive but we are not sure of:
Paola parece tímida. = Paola seems shy.
Gustavo parece una persona divertida. = Gustavo seems like a fun person.

Exploramos la lengua

Los verbos **gustar**, **encantar** e **interesar**

5.13. Preferencias musicales. Cuatro colombianos hablan sobre sus preferencias musicales. Subraya qué cosas tienes en común con ellos.

GUILLERMO. 21 años. Bogotá

¿Qué tipo de música escuchas normalmente?
Escucho mucho **pop latino** y **reguetón**. Y también el vallenato.

¿Escuchas siempre música en español? No, también me interesa el pop-rock en inglés.

¿Tus artistas favoritos?
Me encantan Becky G, J Balvin y Rosalía.

ISABEL. 30 años. Cartagena de Indias

¿Qué tipo de música escuchas normalmente?
Me gustan muchos tipos de música, pero escucho mucha **música electrónica**.

¿Dónde escuchas música?
En el auto, en la casa, en el trabajo... ¡En todas partes!

¿Tu cantante o grupo favorito?
Calvin Harris, Dua Lipa...

MÓNICA. 25 años. Bogotá

¿Qué tipo de música escuchas normalmente?
De todo. Escucho mucha **música independiente**, mucha música electrónica también...

¿Dónde escuchas música?
En la casa, pero también me gusta ir a conciertos.

¿Tu cantante o grupo favorito?
Me gustan mucho Dënver, Caloncho y La Vida Bohème.

SERGIO. 45 años. Cúcuta

¿Qué tipo de música escuchas normalmente?
Música clásica y jazz. ¡Me encanta el jazz!

¿Dónde escuchas música?
En la casa. A mi esposa también le gusta la música y tenemos muchos discos.

¿Y les gusta el mismo tipo de música? Ella prefiere la música soul, a mí me interesan más el jazz y la música clásica.

5.14. *Gustar, encantar e interesar.* Observa en los textos de la actividad 5.13 cómo se usa **gusta/n)**, **encanta/n** e **interesa/n** y marca todas las opciones correctas.

	gusta	gustan	encanta	encantan	interesa	interesan
Con un sustantivo en singular.						
Con un sustantivo en plural o con varios sustantivos.						
Con un verbo en infinitivo.						

5.15. Pronombres. Ahora, completa este cuadro con los pronombres correspondientes.

	PRONOMBRES	
A mí	....	
A ti	te	
A él/ella, usted	....	gusta/n
A nosotros/nosotras	nos	encanta/n
A vosotros/vosotras	os	interesa/n
A ellos/ellas, ustedes	....	

5.16.   Conjugamos. Completa las frases usando los verbos **(no) gustar**, **(no) interesar** y **encantar**.

1. A los jóvenes de mi edad, en general,

.... el jazz.

.... la **ópera**.

.... los **ritmos latinos**.

2. A mis amigos y a mí

.... ir a conciertos.

.... ir a discotecas.

.... los **festivales**.

3. A mí

.... escuchar música por la calle.

.... la **música instrumental**.

.... la música electrónica.

También/tampoco

5.17.   *También/tampoco.* Observa las imágenes. ¿Entiendes las expresiones marcadas en negrita?

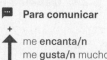 **5.18.   Reaccionamos.** Una chica habla de sus gustos. Escucha las diez frases y reacciona usando **a mí también / a mí tampoco / a mí sí / a mí no**.

5.19.   Nuestros gustos. ¿Te gustan estas cosas? Coméntenlo en parejas.

- cantar
- la música electrónica
- el jazz
- ir a karaokes

- las **canciones** de Lady Gaga
- escuchar música en la **radio**

- los bares con música en **vivo**
- comprar **vinilos**
- ir a conciertos

• No me gusta mucho ir a conciertos, porque hay mucha gente. ¿Y a ti?
○ A mí sí. ¡Me encanta!

Para comunicar

+
↑
me **encanta/n**
me **gusta/n** mucho
me **gusta/n** bastante
no me **gusta/n** mucho
no me **gusta/n** nada
−

5.20.   ¿Coincidimos? ¿Coincides en algo con tu compañero/-a? Escribe frases.

A Patrick le gusta ir a conciertos y a mí también.

Exploramos la lengua

Posesivos

5.21. Un chat. Lee este chat. ¿Prefieres las vacaciones de Teresa o las de Marisa? ¿Por qué?

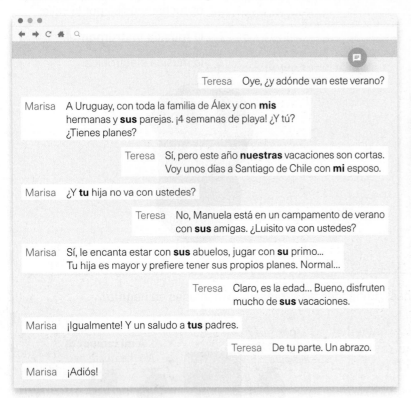

> **Teresa** Oye, ¿y adónde van este verano?
>
> **Marisa** A Uruguay, con toda la familia de Álex y con **mis** hermanas y **sus** parejas. ¡4 semanas de playa! ¿Y tú? ¿Tienes planes?
>
> **Teresa** Sí, pero este año **nuestras** vacaciones son cortas. Voy unos días a Santiago de Chile con **mi** esposo.
>
> **Marisa** ¿Y **tu** hija no va con ustedes?
>
> **Teresa** No, Manuela está en un campamento de verano con **sus** amigas. ¿Luisito va con ustedes?
>
> **Marisa** Sí, le encanta estar con **sus** abuelos, jugar con **su** primo... Tu hija es mayor y prefiere tener sus propios planes. Normal...
>
> **Teresa** Claro, es la edad... Bueno, disfruten mucho de **sus** vacaciones.
>
> **Marisa** ¡Igualmente! Y un saludo a **tus** padres.
>
> **Teresa** De tu parte. Un abrazo.
>
> **Marisa** ¡Adiós!

La Pedrera, Uruguay.

Santiago de Chile, Chile.

5.22. Posesivos. Observa las palabras marcadas en negrita en el chat de 5.21 y completa las tablas.

	Singular	Plural
(yo)	.... esposo **mi** esposa	**mis** hermanos .... hermanas
(tú)	**tu** hijo .... hija	.... hijos **tus** hijas
(él/ella, usted)	.... primo **su** prima	.... abuelos .... abuelas

	Singular	Plural
(nosotros/nosotras)	**nuestro** hijo **nuestra** hija	**nuestros** hijos .... hijas
(vosotros/vosotras)	**vuestro** hijo **vuestra** hija	**vuestros** hijos **vuestras** hijas
(ellos/ellas, ustedes)	**su** padre .... madre	.... amigos .... amigas

5.23. Usamos los posesivos. Completa este correo electrónico con los posesivos adecuados.

Asunto: ¡Saludos!

¡Hola, papás!

¿Qué tal están? Yo estoy muy contenta y (1)....... amigas Marcela y Berenice también. (2)....... compañera de cuarto se llama Samantha. Es muy simpática y está aquí con (3)....... dos hermanos: Jaime y Rodrigo. ¡Las dos tenemos muchas cosas en común! (4)....... cantante favorita también es Taylor Swift y escuchamos (5)....... canciones en (6)....... habitación.

Me gustan todas las actividades aquí, pero (7)....... favoritas son las clases de baile y de windsurf. Y también me gustan todos los profesores, son buenísimos, pero (8)....... profesor favorito es Alberto. (9)....... clases de inglés son muy divertidas.

¿Y cómo están ustedes?

¡Un beso a todos! Manuela

Demostrativos (II): **este**, **ese**, **aquel**

5.24. Demostrativos. Observa las imágenes y lee los diálogos. ¿Entiendes cuándo usamos **este**, **ese** y **aquel**? ¿Cómo expresas lo mismo en tu lengua?

5.25. Recursos para identificar. Para identificar algo o a alguien dentro de un grupo podemos utilizar estas estructuras. Busca en los diálogos de la actividad 5.24. un ejemplo de cada una y escríbelo.

el/la/los/las + adjetivo
el/la/los/las + **de** + nombre
el/la/los/las + **que** + verbo

5.26. Identificamos a unas personas. Escribe frases para identificar a las personas de las imágenes usando las estructuras de la actividad 5.25.

La del vestido largo es Daniela Vega.

5.27. Presentamos a las personas de una fotografía. Busca alguna foto de tus amigos o familia en tu teléfono, en alguna red social, etc. y explica a tus compañeros quién o quiénes aparecen.

Estos son mis compañeros de teatro. La de la camiseta verde es Rose, mi mejor amiga. El de los jeans y las botas es Tony, su novio. Es muy simpático.

Comunicamos

¿Tienes hermanos?

5.28. Nuestra familia. Cuéntale a tu compañero/-a cómo se llaman tus familiares. Tu compañero/-a dibuja tu árbol genealógico.

> • ¿Tienes hermanos?
> ○ Sí, uno. Se llama Dev.
> • ¿Y tu hermano tiene hijos?
> ○ ¡No! Tiene ocho años.

5.29. Hablamos sobre nuestros familiares. Cuenta algo especial de cada miembro de tu familia.

> Mi hermano Dev toca el violín.

¿Cómo es Aaron?

5.30. Observamos y memorizamos. Observa durante un minuto a todas las personas de la clase e intenta memorizar todos los rasgos de su aspecto. Luego, tu profesor va a dividir la clase en dos grupos (uno de espaldas al otro).

5.31. Describimos a los compañeros. Tu profesor/a va a decir el nombre de una persona del grupo contrario. Entre los miembros del grupo tienen que escribir todo lo que recuerden (de su físico y de su ropa).

5.32. Comprobamos y comparamos. Ahora cada grupo lee en voz alta la información que ha recopilado. ¿Qué grupo recuerda más cosas?

> • Aaron tiene los ojos azules.
> ○ Sí, tengo los ojos azules.
> • Y lleva una camisa azul.
> ○ No, llevo una camisa negra.

Es un hombre joven

))) **5.33. Adivinamos.** Escucha a dos personas jugar a adivinar personajes famosos. Intenta adivinar también de quién se trata en cada caso.

))) **5.34. Comprobamos.** Escucha y comprueba.

5.35. Describimos a un personaje famoso. Prepara una descripción de un personaje famoso (real o de ficción). Luego, lee la descripción a tu compañero/-a. ¿Sabe quién es?

> 💬 **Para comunicar**
>
> **un/a niño/-a** = *child*
> **un/a chico/-a** = *boy / girl*
> **un hombre / una mujer joven** = *a young man / woman*
> **un hombre / una mujer mayor** = *an elderly man / woman*
>
> *Tiene 20 años.* = *He / she is 20 years old.*
> *Tiene **unos/aproximadamente** 20 años.* = *He/she is about 20 years old.*

Soy una persona bastante tímida

5.36. Nos describimos. ¿Cómo eres? En una hoja suelta, escribe una descripción de tu personalidad y de las actividades que te gustan.

> 💬 **Para comunicar**
>
> Creo que **soy** una persona **muy / bastante / poco**...
> En mi tiempo libre me encanta...
> Otras cosas que me gusta hacer son... y...
> No me gusta(n) nada...

5.37. Leemos y adivinamos. Tu profesor/a recoge las hojas y las reparte. Cada estudiante debe adivinar de quién es la descripción que tiene. Coméntenlo en grupos.

> *Yo creo que este es Nils porque dice que es muy hablador y le gusta bailar.*

Buscar pareja

5.38. Escribimos un perfil. En parejas van a escribir el perfil de una persona que busca pareja. Propongan a alguien (una persona que conocen o una persona inventada) y conversen sobre cómo es físicamente, cómo es su carácter, qué le gusta hacer y qué tipo de hombre/mujer le gusta.

> • *Mi amigo Aiden está soltero.*
> ○ *¿Ah, sí? ¿Cuántos años tiene?*
> • *Tiene 26 años.*
> ○ *¿Y cómo es físicamente?*
> • *Es alto, tiene los ojos verdes...*

5.39. Escribimos un anuncio. Escriban el anuncio que esa persona envía a una página web de contactos. Luego, cuélguenlo en la pared del salón de clases.

5.40. Una pareja para nuestro perfil. Lean los anuncios que escribieron sus compañeros y busquen alguno que encaje con el que ustedes escribieron.

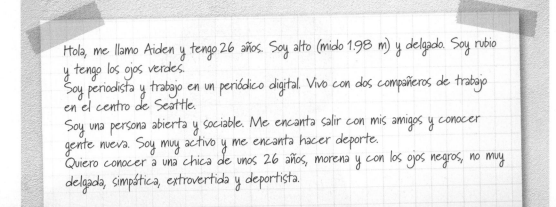

Hola, me llamo Aiden y tengo 26 años. Soy alto (mido 1.98 m) y delgado. Soy rubio y tengo los ojos verdes.
Soy periodista y trabajo en un periódico digital. Vivo con dos compañeros de trabajo en el centro de Seattle.
Soy una persona abierta y sociable. Me encanta salir con mis amigos y conocer gente nueva. Soy muy activo y me encanta hacer deporte.
Quiero conocer a una chica de unos 26 años, morena y con los ojos negros, no muy delgada, simpática, extrovertida y deportista.

Ahora podemos...

Presentar y describir a una persona

5.41. Preparación. Vas a invitar a una persona a clase (un familiar, un amigo o una amiga, etc.). Prepara una descripción de esa persona: su nombre, su relación contigo, su edad, su profesión, sus gustos, etc.

> Persona elegida
> Relación conmigo
> Nacionalidad
> Profesión
> Edad
> Aspecto físico
> Carácter
> Gustos y pasatiempos

5.42. Presentación. Presenta ahora a esa persona al resto de la clase. Tus compañeros tienen que escuchar para elegir a la persona que quieren conocer. También te pueden hacer preguntas.

> • *Mi invitado se llama Tommy, es mi hermano y vive en Minnesota. Tiene 29 años y es ingeniero. Es un chico muy simpático y muy divertido: le gusta viajar y conocer gente nueva. Es estadounidense, como yo, claro. Y es muy deportista: juega fútbol y...*
> ○ *¿Le gusta bailar?*
> • *Sí, mucho.*

5.43. Interpretación. Ahora, cada estudiante debe decidir a qué invitado/-a quiere conocer y explicar por qué.

> *Yo quiero conocer al hermano de Mary, Tommy, porque parece un chico muy divertido y activo. Además, a mí también me gusta bailar.*

Video

Luchadoras de Miami

Esta es la imagen pública de Stella Aldrin, The Wreckening y LiberaShe, tres latinas intrépidas que compiten en la liga de pulseadas femeninas del Sur de Florida (South Florida League of Lady Arm Wrestlers) y recaudan fondos para organizaciones benéficas. En *Luchadoras de Miami* vemos cómo se transforman en sus personajes y qué significa para ellas participar en campeonatos de pulseadas.

P Pearson MyLab

To find out more about these lady arm wrestlers, go to MyLab to watch **Luchadoras de Miami** and complete the video activities.

⊕ ¿Sabes que...?

Sports like soccer, baseball, basketball, boxing, and cycling, to name a few, are widely popular in the Spanish-speaking world. In addition, many countries have their own unique sporting traditions, such as *tejo* in Colombia, *pelota vasca* in northern Spain, *paleta frontón* in Peru, *ecuavóley* in Ecuador, *charrería* in Mexico, and *pato* in Argentina.

⚲ Hacemos conexiones

¿De qué deporte mencionado en **¿Sabes que...?** te gustaría saber más? Elige uno y busca información para hacer una breve presentación en clase.

Los orígenes del jazz latino

En los años 40 surge en Estados Unidos una nueva forma de jazz, el *bebop*, que, en poco tiempo, se fusiona con músicas cubanas. En ese momento nace el jazz afrocubano, conocido como "cubop" (de la unión de las palabras "Cuba" y "bop").

Álbumes más importantes del **jazz afrocubano**

1943
Tanga, de Machito's Afro Cubans, con arreglos de Mario Bauzá.

1948
Manteca, de la Dizzy Gillespie Big Band, con Chano Pozo.

1958
Kenya, de Machito.

1958
Dance manía, de Tito Puente.

Una de las principales figuras de la fusión de estilos y del nacimiento del jazz afrocubano es el músico cubano Francisco Raúl Gutiérrez Grillo, conocido como Machito, que crea la banda Machito y sus Afrocubanos (o Machito and his Afro-cubans). En 1943, con la colaboración de Mario Bauzá (músico, compositor y arreglista también cubano), publica el disco *Tanga*, considerado el primer álbum de jazz afrocubano de la historia.

Músicos cubanos (Machito, Rene Hernández, Mongo Santamaría, Chombo Silva o Cándido Camero) y otros, como Tito Puente, continúan con esta música de fusión en Estados Unidos e incorporan elementos de otros géneros latinoamericanos, como la salsa, el mambo, la samba o la bossa nova. De esta forma surge lo que hoy llamamos "jazz latino".

ANTES DE LEER

🔍 **5.44. ¿Qué sabemos?** ¿Qué sabes del jazz y del *bebop*? Busca información (orígenes y primeras figuras).

LECTURA ACTIVA

5.45. Verdadero o falso. Indica si estas frases son verdaderas o falsas de acuerdo con la información del texto.

1. El Cubop es la música tradicional cubana.
2. Francisco Raúl Gutierrez Grillo es el fundador de la banda Machito y sus Afrocubanos.
3. El jazz afrocubano es el resultado de la fusión entre el jazz más tradicional y la música cubana.
4. El jazz latino surge en Cuba.
5. La fusión del jazz con sonidos latinos tuvo lugar, sobre todo, en países latinoamericanos.

DESPUÉS DE LEER

🔍
e **5.46. Investigamos.** Investiga sobre la importancia del jazz latino en tu país en la actualidad. Puedes buscar qué músicos destacados hay, en qué zonas es más importante, si hay emisoras de radio dedicadas o cualquier otra información que consideres relevante.

Textos audiovisuales: vemos, escuchamos y presentamos

Vemos un video sobre gustos musicales y descripción de personas

ANTES DE VER EL VIDEO

5.47. Preparación. ¿Crees que la música que escucha una persona refleja su edad o cómo es su carácter? ¿Qué dice de ti la música que tú escuchas? Explica tu respuesta.

INFORMACIÓN PREVIA Vas a ver un video en el que unas personas juegan a adivinar la personalidad de otras con base en tres canciones que les gustan. Por ejemplo, Gabriela escucha tres canciones que le gustan a Lucía e intenta adivinar cómo es esta persona, si es hombre o mujer y qué edad tiene. La información que aparece debajo de las personas en la siguiente imagen indica cómo se describe cada uno a sí mismo.

Gabriela, 40 años — Apasionada, Sensible, Simpática
Lucía, 27 años — Extrovertida, Romántica, Seria
Laura, 22 años — Calmada, Sociable, Inteligente
Mariano, 34 años — Tímido, Amable, Tranquilo

VEMOS EL VIDEO

5.48. Opinión. ¿Gabriela y Lucía creen que se puede conocer a alguien por la música que escucha?

5.49. La opinión de Lucía. Escribe qué información cree Lucía que se puede saber gracias a la música.

5.50. ¿Qué dicen mientras escuchan la música? Relaciona estas frases con la persona correspondiente.

	Laura	Mariano	Gabriela	Lucía
1. Dice a qué época pertenece la canción.				
2. Compara al artista con otro similar.				
3. Conoce la canción, el intérprete y el álbum.				
4. Le gusta cómo suena un instrumento.				
5. No conoce al intérprete, pero reconoce la canción.				
6. Le gusta la voz del / de la cantante.				
7. Menciona un género musical que le gusta mucho.				
8. La canción es de un estilo diferente al que a él/ella le gusta.				
9. No reconoce la canción ni el artista.				
10. Menciona a qué estilo pertenece la canción.				
11. Habla sobre el ritmo.				

5.51. Selección de información. Marca las respuestas correctas de los participantes sobre sus compañeros de juego.

Mariano
- sexo
- edad (34 años)
- tímido
- amable
- tranquilo

Laura
- sexo
- edad (22 años)
- calmada
- sociable
- inteligente

Lucía
- sexo
- edad (27 años)
- extrovertida
- romántica
- seria

Gabriela
- sexo
- edad (40 años)
- apasionada
- sensible
- simpática

DESPUÉS DE VER EL VIDEO

5.52. Comparación. ¿Coincides con alguna de las personas del video en los gustos musicales? ¿Y en el carácter?

Presentamos las canciones de los personajes de una película

5.53. Comunicación interpersonal. Van a seleccionar canciones para acompañar algunas escenas en las que aparecen los siguientes personajes de una película. En grupos, decidan una canción para asignar a cada uno. También pueden buscar fotos para cada personaje.

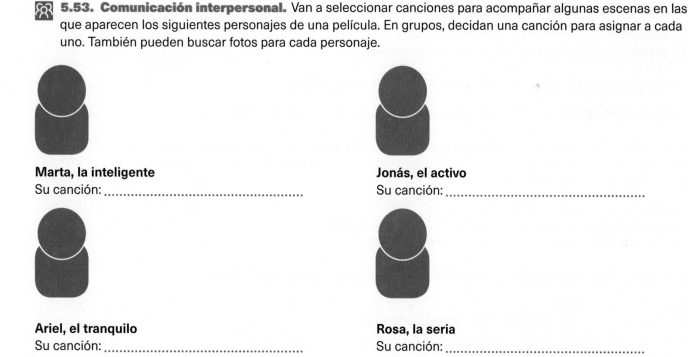

Marta, la inteligente
Su canción: ....

Jonás, el activo
Su canción: ....

Ariel, el tranquilo
Su canción: ....

Rosa, la seria
Su canción: ....

5.54. Presentación. Presenten sus canciones y sus personajes a la clase.

Esta es Marta, la inteligente. Para ella, nosotros proponemos...
Jonás es una persona simpática y le gusta...

Recursos lingüísticos

THE VERBS GUSTAR, ENCANTAR, AND INTERESAR

To express likes and dislikes, in Spanish we use the verbs **gustar** (*to like*) and **encantar** (*to really like, to love*). To talk about things that you find interesting, we use **interesar**. However, these three verbs are 'peculiar' verbs in the sense that they do not work like most verbs.

Whereas in English we follow this pattern:

I	like	going to the cinema.
SUBJECT	VERB	SUBJECT

In Spanish we say:

Me	gusta	ir al cine.
INDIRECT OBJECT PRONOUN	VERB	SUBJECT

▸ Therefore, the subject of the Spanish sentence is not the person who likes something (**yo**), but the thing/person that is liked (**ir al cine**).

▸ It might help you to translate **gustar** as *to appeal (to me, you,...)* or *to be appealing (to me, you,...)*. Bearing in mind that the subject is what is liked, what appeals, the verb will vary according to the number of the subject.

Me gusta el café. = Coffee appeals / is appealing to me.
Me gustan las películas de acción. = Action films appeal / are appealing to me.

▸ Therefore, if **gustar**, **encantar**, and **interesar** are followed by a singular noun or an infinitive verb, they will be conjugated in the singular.

Me encanta esquiar. = I love skiing.
¿Te gusta la música clásica? = Do you like classical music?

▸ And if they are followed by a plural noun, they are conjugated in the plural:

A Clara le encantan las canciones de Lady Gaga. = Clara loves Lady Gaga's songs.

▸ Remember that when we use **gustar**, **encantar**, and **interesar** followed by a noun, we always use an article before the noun, whether it is singular, plural, or uncountable. The article agrees in gender and number with the noun.

Me gusta la música rock. = I like rock music.
No me gustan los festivales de música. = I don't like music festivals.
Me gusta una canción de Rosalía. = I like one song by Rosalía.

▸ However, we do not need the article with a verb or with a name of a place or person.

Nos gusta mucho bailar. = We like to dance.
A mi hermana le encanta Boston. = My sister loves Boston.
A mi hijo le gusta Taylor Swift. = My son likes Taylor Swift.

TAMBIÉN/TAMPOCO

▸ To express agreement with what someone likes, in Spanish we use **a mí también**. If we agree about not liking something, we use **a mí tampoco**. We use **a mí no** and **a mí sí** to express disagreement.

● *Me gusta la ópera.* ☺ = I like opera.
  ○ *A mí también.* ☺ = Me too.
  ■ *A mí no.* ☹ = Not me.

● *No me gusta la ópera.* ☹ = I don't like opera.
  ○ *A mí tampoco.* ☹ = Me neither.
  ■ *A mí sí.* ☺ = I do.

POSSESSIVES

▸ Possessives are the words that we use with a noun to say that a person or thing "belongs" to another.

▸ Like other adjectives in Spanish, possessive adjectives have to agree with the gender and the number of the noun:

	Singular (one thing is possessed)	**Plural (more than one thing is possessed)**
(yo)	**mi** hermano/hermana	**mis** hermanos/hermanas
(tú)	**tu** hermano/hermana	**tus** hermanos/hermanas
(él/ella, usted)	**su** hermano/hermana	**sus** hermanos/hermanas
(nosotros/nosotras)	**nuestro** hermano / **nuestra** hermana	**nuestros** hermanos / **nuestras** hermanas
(vosotros/vosotras)	**vuestro** hermano / **vuestra** hermana	**vuestros** hermanos / **vuestras** hermanas
(ellos/ellas, ustedes)	**su** hermano/hermana	**sus** hermanos/hermanas

!   In Spanish, possessive adjectives agree with what they describe and not with the person who owns the thing:

*Sara vive con **su padre**.* = Sara lives with her father.
*Sara vive con **sus padres**.* = Sara lives with her parents.

DEMONSTRATIVES (II): ESTE, ESE Y AQUEL

▸ Demonstratives are used to indicate how close or how far something is from the speaker, the listener or both.

Near the speaker	Near the listener	Far from both
este	ese	ese/aquel
esta	esa	esa/aquella
estos	esos	esos/aquellos
estas	esas	esas/aquellas

***Este** es Carlos, mi hermano.* = This is Carlos, my brother.
*¿Quién es **ese** chico?* = Who's that guy?
***Aquella** chica es tu hermana, ¿verdad?* = That girl is your sister, right?

▸ In addition to the masculine and feminine forms, gender-neutral forms (**esto**, **eso**, **aquello**) are used to refer to something that the speaker does not want to identify or cannot identify with a word.

● *¿Qué es **eso** que tienes en la mano?* = What's that in your hand?
○ *¿**Esto**? Un regalo para mi madre.* = This? It's a present for my mother.

—*¿Qué flor es esta?*
—*Es un sacuanjoche.*
Es la flor nacional
de Nicaragua.

!   To identify a person or an object, we also can use these structures:

el/la/los/las + adjetivo
el/la/los/las + **de** + nombre
el/la/los/las + **que** + verbo

● *¿Quién es Jorge? ¿El chico alto o **el de la gorra**?* = Who's Jorge? The tall guy or the one with the hat?
○ ***El alto**. **El que lleva** una chaqueta roja.* = The tall one. The one that's wearing a red jacket.

Pronunciamos

La pronunciación de **r/rr**

5.55. Escuchamos y clasificamos. Escucha estas palabras y clasifícalas según el sonido de la **r**.

sobrino   perro   primo   pareja   pelirrojo   rubia   serio   interesante   abierta   perezoso

largo   rock   radio   bailar   mejor   aburrida   hablador   carro   hermana   rizado   rojo

La r vibra una vez	La r vibra más veces
sobrino	perro

5.56. Completamos un cuadro. Ahora, completa el cuadro.

	Vibra una vez	Vibra más veces
1. la **r** a principio de palabra		
2. la doble **r**		
3. la **r** entre dos vocales		
4. la **r** entre una vocal y una consonante		
5. la **r** al final de una sílaba		

5.57. Pronunciamos. Ahora pronuncia tú las palabras de la actividad 5.55.

5.58. Escuchamos y pronunciamos.
Escucha estas frases y, luego, pronúncialas tú.

1. En mi radio siempre quiero rap.
2. Este carro rojo es muy caro.
3. ¿Tu madre es pelirroja?
4. ¿Cuál es tu artista de rock preferido?
5. ¡Pero qué perro más curioso!

> ⚙ **Estrategia**
>
> Recording yourself can help you compare your pronunciation with that of a native speaker so you can work on your specific needs.

Vocabulario activo

))) Familia y amigos
Family and friends

- **el/la abuelo/-a** *grandfather / grandmother*
- **los abuelos** *grandparents*
- **el/la amigo/-a** *friend*
- **el/la compañero/-a** *mate, partner*
- **el/la esposo/-a** *husband / wife*
- **estar casado/-a (con)** *to be married (to)*
- **estar divorciado/-a** *to be divorced*
- **estar separado/-a** *to be separated*
- **el/la exesposo/-a** *ex-husband / ex-wife*
- **el/la hermanastro/-a** *stepbrother / stepsister*
- **el/la hermano/-a** *brother / sister*
- **los hermanos** *siblings*
- **el/la hijo/-a** *son / daughter*
- **los hijos** *children*
- **la madre** *mother*
- **el/la medio/-a hermano/-a** *half-brother / half-sister*
- **el/la mejor amigo/-a** *best friend*
- **el/la nieto/-a** *grandson / granddaughter*
- **los nietos** *grandchildren*
- **el/la novio/-a** *boyfriend / girlfriend*
- **el padre** *father*
- **los padres** *parents*
- **la pareja** *partner*
- **el/la primo/-a** *cousin*
- **los primos** *cousins*
- **el/la prometido/-a** *fiancé/-e*
- **ser/estar soltero/-a** *to be single*
- **ser/estar viudo/-a** *to be widowed*
- **ser hijo/-a único/-a** *to be an only child*
- **el/la sobrino/-a** *nephew / niece*
- **el/la tío/-a** *uncle / aunt*
- **los tíos** *aunt + uncle*

))) Aspecto físico
Physical appearance

- **alto/-a** *tall*
- **bajo/-a** *short*
- **la barba** *beard*
- **el bigote** *mustache*
- **calvo/-a** *bald*
- **castaño/-a** *chestnut-colored*
- **delgado/-a** *thin*
- **feo/-a** *ugly*
- **las gafas** *glasses*
- **gordo/-a** *heavy*
- **guapo/-a** *handsome / beautiful*
- **moreno/-a** *dark-haired / brunette*
- **los ojos** *eyes*

- **pelirrojo/-a** *red-haired*
- **el pelo liso** *straight hair*
- **el pelo rizado** *curly hair*
- **el pelo rubio** *blonde hair*
- **rubio/-a** *blonde*

))) Carácter
Personality traits

- **abierto/-a** *open*
- **aburrido/-a** *boring*
- **activo/-a** *active*
- **agradable** *nice*
- **amable** *kind*
- **antipático/-a** *mean*
- **buena persona** *good person*
- **cerrado/-a** *closed-minded*
- **deportista** *sporty, athletic*
- **divertido/-a** *funny*
- **hablador/a** *talkative, chatty*
- **inteligente** *intelligent, smart*
- **interesante** *interesting*
- **normal** *normal*
- **perezoso/-a** *lazy*
- **serio/-a** *serious*
- **simpático/-a** *likeable, amusing*
- **sociable** *sociable*
- **tímido/-a** *shy*
- **tranquilo/-a, calmado/-a** *calm*

))) Música
Music

- **el/la artista** *artist*
- **la canción** *song*
- **el/la cantante** *singer*
- **el festival** *festival*
- **el grupo** *band*
- **la música clásica** *classic music*
- **la música electrónica** *electronic music*
- **la música en vivo** *live music*
- **la música independiente** *indie music*
- **la música instrumental** *instrumental music*
- **la ópera** *opera*
- **el pop latino** *latin pop*
- **la radio** *radio*
- **el reguetón** *reggaeton*
- **el ritmo latino** *latin rhythm*

⚙ **Estrategia**

Are you good at drawing? It might be a good idea to draw new words to illustrate their meaning and help you remember them better.

Lección

6

Día a día

IN THIS LESSON WE ARE GOING TO
learn about our classmates' routines

LEARNING OUTCOMES
You will be able to...

• talk about habits and personal care

• express frequency

• ask for and tell the time

VOCABULARY

• Days of the week and parts of the day

• Daily routines and activities

• Time expressions

LANGUAGE STRUCTURES

• Reflexive verbs

• Present tense of some irregular verbs

• Sequence expressions: **primero / después / luego, antes/ después de** + infinitive

PRONUNCIATION

• Pronouncing consecutive words

CULTURAL CONNECTIONS

• Unpaid work in Argentina: women and men

Miles de personas utilizan el Teleférico La Paz - El Alto (La Paz, Bolivia) diariamente para ir a trabajar.

Primer contacto

6.1. El momento preferido de la semana. Una revista pregunta a sus lectores cuál es su momento preferido de la semana. Relaciona las respuestas (1-5) con las fotografías (A-E).

¿Cuál es tu momento preferido de la semana?

LIDIA
El lunes y el miércoles a la hora de cenar, porque estoy con mi hija. **1**

MANU
El fin de semana, porque voy a la montaña con mis amigos. **2**

SERGIO
El jueves por la noche, porque toco con mi grupo de música. **3**

BLANCA
Todas las mañanas cuando me levanto hago yoga durante media hora. ¡Me encanta! **4**

ELENA
El domingo por la mañana cuando paseo con mi perro. **5**

A

B

C

D

E

6.2. ¿Coincidimos? Hablen en parejas para saber si tienen cosas en común con las personas de la actividad 6.1. ¿Hacen algunas de esas actividades? ¿Cuándo?

Yo también hago yoga. Los lunes y los miércoles por la noche.

Comprendemos el vocabulario

Actividades y cuidados diarios

))) **6.3. Actividades del día a día.** Observa, lee y escucha.

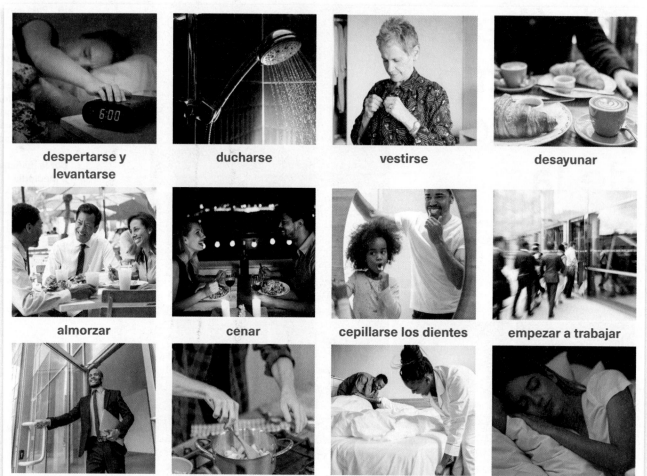

despertarse y levantarse

ducharse

vestirse

desayunar

almorzar

cenar

cepillarse los dientes

empezar a trabajar

salir del trabajo

preparar la comida

hacer la cama

dormir

Más palabras

))) **acostarse** = *to go to bed*
afeitarse = *to shave*
cuidarse = *to maintain your personal appearance, to take care of yourself*
hacer deporte = *to play sports*
ir a clase = *to go to class*
ir a trabajar = *to go to work*

ir al baño = *to go to the bathroom*
maquillarse = *to put on make-up*
ponerse (crema hidratante, perfume...) = *to put on (moisturizer, perfume...)*
regresar a casa = *to return home*
salir de casa = *to leave the house*

⊕ **La variedad del español**

In some Spanish-speaking countries:

de casa = de la casa
a casa = a la casa

6.4. ¿Cuándo lo hacemos? Clasifica en una tabla las actividades de la actividad 6.3: ¿Cuáles haces por la mañana, cuáles por la tarde, cuáles por la noche y cuáles nunca?

Por la mañana	Por la tarde	Por la noche	Nunca (ø)
despertarse y levantarse...			

6.17. Verbos reflexivos. Observa las formas verbales marcadas en negrita en el texto de la actividad 6.16 y completa el cuadro de los verbos reflexivos.

	LEVANTARSE	**DUCHARSE**
(yo)	....	....
(tú)	**te** levantas	**te** duchas
(él/ella, usted)	....	....
(nosotros/nosotras)	....	....
(vosotros/vosotras)	**os** levantáis	**os** ducháis
(ellos/ellas, ustedes)	....	....

6.18. Escribimos un testimonio. Imagina que eres un padre o una madre y escribe un testimonio como los del reportaje de la actividad 6.16. Usa los verbos de las etiquetas.

levantarse   ducharse   secarse el pelo   cepillarse los dientes
afeitarse   maquillarse   desayunar   preparar

6.19. Comparamos. En parejas, compartan sus testimonios. ¿Quién se organiza mejor?

6.20. Preparamos preguntas. Imagina que tienes que compartir apartamento unos meses con una persona de la clase. Prepara preguntas para saber si ustedes dos son compatibles.

1. levantarse / a qué hora

¿A qué hora te levantas?
....

2. ducharse / todos los días

....

3. secarse el pelo / todos los días

....

4. cepillarse los dientes / cuántas veces

....

5. maquillarse / todos los días

....

6. afeitarse / todos los días

....

7. levantarse por la noche / cuántas veces

....

6.21. Entrevistamos a una persona. Por turnos, háganse las preguntas que prepararon en la actividad 6.20 para descubrir si son compatibles para compartir apartamento. Luego, comuniquen el resultado a la clase y digan por qué.

• *¿A qué hora te levantas?*
○ *A las cinco y media de la mañana.*

Exploramos la lengua

Presente de algunos verbos irregulares

6.22. El Día de Reyes. Lee la siguiente historia que ilustra una tradición en algunos países hispanos. ¿Quién la cuenta? ¿Existe algo equivalente en tu cultura?

Unos días antes...
Marta y yo escribimos la carta a los Reyes. Luego, vamos a ver a nuestro rey preferido y le damos la carta. Mi rey preferido es Baltasar, que siempre **se viste** con ropa de muchos colores.

5 de enero, 8:00 – 9:00 p. m
Después de cenar ponemos en el balcón nuestros zapatos y un poco de agua para los camellos. Luego, **nos acostamos**, pero yo no duermo nada...

5 de enero, 11:30 p. m. – 12:15 a. m.
Cuando mis papás **se acuestan**, **salgo** de la habitación y voy al balcón para ver a los Reyes, pero nunca los veo... Al final, vuelvo a la cama y **me acuesto**.

6 de enero, 6:00 a. m.
Por la mañana Marta **se despierta** antes que yo, **sale** al balcón y grita: "¡Miguel, no hay carbón! ¡Hay muchos regalos!" Entonces, mis papás y yo **nos despertamos** y vamos al balcón para abrir los regalos

6 de enero, 6.30 – 9:00 a. m.
Mis papás vuelven a la cama para dormir un poco más y nosotros jugamos con los regalos. Cuando mis papás **se despiertan**, **se visten** y preparan el desayuno.

6 de enero, 4:00 – 6:00 p. m.
Por la tarde, **nos vestimos** bien y **salimos** para la casa de mis tíos para comer la rosca de reyes y tomar un chocolate caliente. Es el mejor día del año

6.23. Verbos irregulares. Observa los verbos en negrita en la actividad 6.22 y completa las tablas.

	ACOSTARSE (o > ue)	DESPERTARSE (e > ie)	VESTIRSE (e > i)	SALIR
(yo)	....	**me** despierto	**me** visto	....
(tú)	**te** acuestas	**te** despiertas	**te** vistes	sales
(él/ella, usted)	**se** acuesta	....	....	....
(nosotros/nosotras)	....	....	....	....
(vosotros/vosotras)	**os** acostáis	**os** despertáis	**os** vestís	salís
(ellos/ellas, ustedes)	....	....	....	salen

6.24. Observamos los verbos. Observa los verbos de la actividad 6.23 y responde a estas preguntas.

1. ¿En qué formas cambia la vocal?
2. ¿En cuáles no?

3. ¿Qué persona cambia en el verbo **salir**? ¿Cómo cambia?

6.25. Escribimos. Escribe la historia desde el punto de vista de los padres. Compara tu versión con la de otra persona de la clase.

Estructuras para secuenciar acciones

6.26. Reaccionamos. Un amigo te dice estas frases. ¿Qué le respondes? Escríbelo.

1. No hago nunca deporte **antes de** ir a la universidad. Yo sí.
2. Nunca veo videos en internet **después de** cenar.
3. Me ducho siempre **antes de** acostarme.
4. Me cepillo los dientes **antes** y **después de** comer.
5. Por las noches, **primero** ceno, **después** me ducho y **luego** leo un poco.

6.27. Antes o después. Escribe frases sobre las afirmaciones de la actividad 6.26 con las que no coincides.

1. Yo muchas veces hago deporte antes de ir a la universidad.

6.28. Nuestro horario. Rellena una tabla horaria con todas las actividades que haces normalmente en un día.

Martes
14

01 a. m.		01 p. m.	
02 a. m.		02 p. m.	
03 a. m.		03 p. m.	
04 a. m.		04 p. m.	
05 a. m.		05 p. m.	
06 a. m.	– me levanto y me ducho	06 p. m.	
07 a. m.		07 p. m.	
08 a. m.	– desayuno	08 p. m.	
09 a. m.		09 p. m.	
10 a. m.		10 p. m.	
11 a. m.		11 p. m.	
12 a. m.		12 p. m.	

6.29. Comparamos nuestros horarios. Compara tu horario con el de otra persona. ¿En qué coinciden?

● Yo me levanto a las seis y me ducho. ¿Y tú?
○ Yo, me levanto a las siete. Y me ducho a las siete y media.

6.30. Un día en la vida de... Escribe un texto corto sobre cómo es el día de una de estas personas. Utiliza los recursos para secuenciar acciones.

una estrella del pop   un/a bombero/-a   el/la presidente/-a de tu país

un/a crítico/-a gastronómico/-a   un/a agricultor/a

6.31. Leemos y adivinamos. Lee el texto a tus compañeros/-as, que tienen que adivinar de quién hablas.

Se levanta a las ocho y media. Se ducha, desayuna y luego toca la guitarra.

Comunicamos

Es una persona muy sana

6.32. Nos ponemos de acuerdo. En parejas, discutan qué hacen y qué no hacen estos tipos de persona.

una persona sana	■ Cosas que hace
	....
	....
	■ Cosas que no hace
	....
	....

una persona fiestera	■ Cosas que hace
	....
	....
	■ Cosas que no hace
	....
	....

una persona intelectual	■ Cosas que hace
	....
	....
	■ Cosas que no hace
	....
	....

una persona casera	■ Cosas que hace
	....
	....
	■ Cosas que no hace
	....
	....

• *Una persona sana hace mucho deporte, por ejemplo.*
○ *Sí, y duerme ocho horas.*

> ❶ **¿Necesitas ayuda?**
>
> **sano/-a** = *healthy*
> **fiestero/-a** = *party-loving*
> **casero/-a** = *homebody*

6.33. Los hábitos de Berta y Natalia. Escucha a unas personas que hablan de Berta y de Natalia. Toma nota de sus hábitos y de qué les gusta.

BERTA RODRIGO, 38 años, taxista.

NATALIA APARICIO, 20 años, estudiante.

6.34. Comparamos nuestras notas. En parejas, comparen sus notas y escuchen de nuevo para completarlas.

• *Dicen que le gusta cocinar, ¿no?*
○ *Sí, creo que sí.*

6.35. ¿Cómo son? ¿Qué adjetivos de la actividad 6.32 describen a Berta y a Natalia?

Dos hermanas

 6.36. Preguntas y respuestas. En parejas (**A/B**), lee tu texto y haz preguntas a tu compañero para encontrar cinco coincidencias en la vida de Sara y Noelia, dos hermanas con vidas diferentes. **A** hace tres preguntas; luego, **B** hace otras tres preguntas y así sucesivamente.

ESTUDIANTE A

Sara

Me levanto a las seis y media de la mañana, me ducho y desayuno. Normalmente veo la televisión cuando desayuno. Luego, a las siete y cuarto, se levantan mis hijos, se visten y preparamos el desayuno. Yo como un poco de fruta (¡es mi desayuno favorito!).
Llevo a mis hijos a la escuela y empiezo a trabajar a las ocho y media. Mis hijos almuerzan en la escuela, y yo en el trabajo. Salgo de trabajar a las cinco y voy a la escuela a buscar a los niños.
Todos los días a las siete voy al gimnasio y me ducho allí otra vez. Cuando llego a casa, ceno con mis hijos y mi esposo sobre las ocho y media. Nunca me acuesto antes de las once.

ESTUDIANTE B

Noelia

Me levanto a las tres de la tarde y me ducho. Me visto y luego desayuno y veo la televisión.
A las cinco voy a clases de inglés porque es muy importante para mi trabajo. Después de las clases, regreso a casa, sobre las siete, como un poco de fruta (¡me encanta la fruta!) y voy al gimnasio una hora. Voy todos los días. No me gusta ducharme allí. Me ducho cuando llego a casa. Luego preparo la cena. Normalmente ceno entre las ocho y las nueve
A las once empiezo a trabajar y salgo del trabajo a las siete de la mañana. Me acuesto entre las siete y media y las ocho.

A: ¿A qué hora se levanta Noelia?
B: A las tres de la tarde.
A: ¿Y qué hace después de levantarse?
B: Primero...

Nuestros momentos preferidos

6.37. Nuestros momentos preferidos. En papeles diferentes, escribe cuatro momentos de la semana que te gustan especialmente. Haz lo mismo con la justificación de por qué te gustan.

el viernes por la tarde

los sábados por la mañana

empieza el fin de semana

duermo mucho

 6.38. Relacionamos y adivinamos. Pongan sus papeles en las mesas y, en parejas, jueguen a conectar los momentos con las justificaciones.

• ¿Te gusta el viernes por la tarde porque empieza el fin de semana?
○ ¡Sí!

Ahora podemos...

Conocer los hábitos de nuestros compañeros y dar premios

6.39. Interpretación. Vamos a entregar estos premios a personas de la clase. Primero, observen las imágenes de los premios y relaciónenlas con lo que representan.

Premio a la...

- persona más sana
- persona más casera
- persona más deportista
- persona más vanidosa
- persona más trabajadora
- persona más intelectual
- persona más dormilona
- persona más fiestera

6.40. Comunicación interpersonal. En parejas, decidan qué premio quieren dar. Después, preparen cuatro o más preguntas para entrevistar a varios compañeros de clase y saber quién ganará el premio.

PREMIO A LA PERSONA MÁS DORMILONA	Jacob	Rachel	Diego
1. ¿Cuántas horas duermes normalmente?	5 o 6.	Unas 9.	6 o 7.
2. ¿...?			
3. ¿...?			
4. ¿...?			

- ¿Cuántas horas duermes normalmente, Jacob?
- Cinco o seis.

6.41. Presentación. Analicen las respuestas y entreguen el premio.

Nosotros entregamos el premio a la persona más dormilona a... ¡Rachel!

Video

Vida de mariposa

En los jardines botánicos de Miami, Sergio Gutiérrez cuida de cientos de mariposas que se crían en el mariposario. En *Vida de mariposa*, Sergio nos muestra que, por corta que sea su existencia, las mariposas pueden impartir lecciones importantes sobre la vida, la belleza y el cambio.

P Pearson MyLab

To find out more about Sergio's work with butterflies, go to MyLab to watch **Vida de mariposa** and complete the video activities.

⊕ **¿Sabes que...?**

Costa Rica's unique geographical position as a land bridge between two continents provided the optimal breeding ground for a flourishing mix of flora and fauna. The country now possesses the highest density of biodiversity on the planet. Over 1,200 different types of butterflies—or ten percent of known butterfly species in the world—reside in Costa Rica.

🔍 **Hacemos conexiones**

Investiga sobre fauna y flora que solo existe o que es muy típica de países de habla hispana. Luego, comparte datos curiosos con la clase.

Trabajo no remunerado en Argentina:
ellas y ellos

A menudo no recordamos que existe
un tipo de trabajo importantísimo:
el trabajo doméstico no remunerado.
Un estudio argentino reciente muestra
las diferencias entre hombres y mujeres
en relación con este tipo de tareas.

El gráfico de abajo muestra que el 86,7 % de las mujeres realizan quehaceres domésticos (lavar y planchar la ropa, preparar las comidas, limpiar la casa, etc.; un 31,3 % de ellas cuidan de personas (niños, enfermos, personas mayores, etc.) y un 19,3 % ayuda a sus hijos en su educación. Los porcentajes para los hombres son claramente inferiores: 50,2 %, 16,8 % y 6,9 %.

Pero las diferencias reales son más dramáticas todavía. Las mujeres que realizan trabajo doméstico no remunerado le dedican 6,4 horas y los hombres, 3 horas menos.

Dos de las consecuencias de esta situación son que muchas mujeres argentinas tienen grandes dificultades para encontrar un trabajo fuera de casa y que, cuando lo tienen, el número total de horas trabajadas es enorme.

Tasas de participación en el trabajo doméstico no remunerado, por sexo

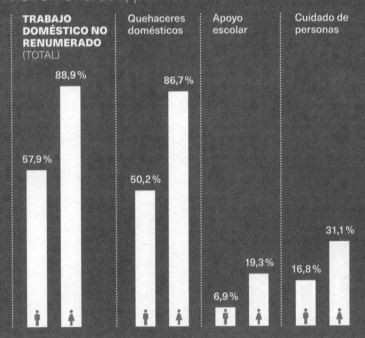

TRABAJO DOMÉSTICO NO RENUMERADO (TOTAL)	Quehaceres domésticos	Apoyo escolar	Cuidado de personas
57,9 % — 88,9 %	50,2 % — 86,7 %	6,9 % — 19,3 %	16,8 % — 31,1 %

ANTES DE LEER

6.42. Hacemos hipótesis. Lee el título del texto (si no entiendes todas las palabras, búscalas en un diccionario en línea) y responde.

1. ¿De qué temas crees que va a tratar el artículo?
2. ¿Qué miembros de las familias crees que hacen más trabajo no remunerado en muchos lugares del mundo?

LECTURA ACTIVA

6.43. Pensamos títulos. Lee el texto y escribe un subtítulo para cada párrafo. Luego, comparen sus propuestas.

DESPUÉS DE LEER

6.44. Consecuencias. El texto menciona dos consecuencias negativas para las mujeres. Piensa otras y coméntalas con la clase.

e 6.45. Comparamos con nuestro país. ¿Crees que la situación en tu país es muy diferente? ¿En qué aspectos?

Textos escritos: leemos y escribimos

Leemos sobre una rutina diaria

ANTES DE LA LECTURA

6.46. Preparación. ¿Qué crees que es lo bueno y lo malo de trabajar desde casa? Márcalo en la tabla.

	Lo bueno	Lo malo
1. No pierdes tiempo en el carro o en el transporte público.		
2. Hay más distracciones.		
3. Puedes ducharte a cualquier hora del día.		
4. Puedes ser más productivo.		
5. Tienes flexibilidad de horario.		

LECTURA ACTIVA

6.47. Lectura. Lee el texto de manera general para tener una idea de cómo es un día típico en la vida de Diego Freniche, un programador que trabaja desde su casa.

Mi rutina

- Me levanto temprano. A las 5:30 o las 6:00. Y me siento en el salón, con el portátil. A esa hora programo: ni correo, ni planificar, ni nada. Programar hasta las 7:30, que es cuando se empieza a despertar la casa.

- De 7:30 a 9:00, dedico el tiempo a estar con mi familia. Hablo con mi esposa. Voy a comprar el pan. Despierto a los niños y preparamos el desayuno. Se visten, los peino y los llevo a la escuela. A las 9:05 suelo llegar a mi casa. Me preparo algo para mantenerme hidratado (un té, manzanilla...) y subo a mi oficina.

- Aquí empiezo el segundo bloque de trabajo. Leo el correo (a las 9:30, luego a las 12:30 y por la tarde a las 16:30). Tengo unas alarmas en un calendario llamado Hábitos. En este segundo bloque hay menos programación y más de otras cosas: preparar presupuestos, responder mensajes, resolver tareas en internet (como mirar el banco, etc.). A las 13:00 paro y, si puedo, salgo a correr media hora. Luego me ducho y voy a buscar a los niños a la escuela. Si no voy a correr, simplemente hago una pausa y sigo hasta las dos menos diez.

- Como en casa de los padres de mi esposa. Los abuelos están con los niños y todos comemos comida de verdad. A las 15:00 estamos de vuelta en casa. Ventajas de vivir en un pueblo pequeño: los desplazamientos son instantáneos.

- Duermo la siesta. Es una siesta de verdad, de cuarenta minutos al menos. Cuando me levanto, me siento muy bien. Me preparo un café y empiezo el último bloque de trabajo del día, de 16:30 a 18:30. A esa hora paro, y hago otras cosas: escribir en mi blog, hacer los deberes con los niños, limpiar la casa, reparar algo...

- Me acuesto temprano (antes de las 23:00). Para empezar bien el siguiente día es importante dejar las tareas preparadas ahora.

Como puedes ver, esta rutina no es la mejor para todo el mundo. Es la que mejor me funciona a mí en este momento de mi vida.

Adaptado de http://blog.freniche.com/2014/02/06/mi-rutina-diaria-de-trabajo/

6.48. Selección de información. Ahora, completa esta tabla con las actividades que hace Diego, según el texto.

Horas	Actividades
5:30-7:30	....
7:30-9:00	....
9:05	....
9:30-13:00	....
13:00-13:50	....
13:50-15:00	....
15:00-15:40	....
16:30-18:30	....
18:30-23:00	....

6.49. Interpretación. Encuentra en el texto la palabra o frase que mejor expresa el significado de estas palabras o frases en inglés.

1. laptop (párrafo 1)
2. real food (párrafo 4)
3. I stop at that time (párrafo 3)
4. take a break (párrafo 3)
5. getting from one place to another really quick (párrafo 4)
6. go to bed early (párrafo 6)

6.50. Selección de información. Escribe en tu cuaderno la información que se pide con base en el texto.

1. Parte de la casa en la que Diego se sienta a programar por la mañana.
2. Cosas que Diego hace para sus hijos.
3. Bebidas que toma mientras trabaja por la mañana.
4. Horas específicas en la que lee el correo electrónico.
5. Lugar donde come con sus hijos.
6. Tiempo para dormir la siesta.
7. Número de bloques de trabajo en un día.
8. Lo más importante para empezar bien el día siguiente.

DESPUÉS DE LEER

6.51. Opinión. Responde a estas preguntas. Luego, comenta tus respuestas con tus compañeros/-as.

1. ¿Cuántas horas dedica Diego a su trabajo? ¿Crees que Diego tiene una rutina productiva? Explica tu respuesta.
2. ¿Qué piensa Diego sobre su rutina diaria? ¿Le gusta? Explica tu respuesta.
3. Con base en la rutina de Diego, identifica qué aspectos de su vida son importantes para él.

Escribimos sobre nuestra rutina

6.52. Reacción personal. ¿Cómo es tu rutina diaria o un día típico de estudio y/o trabajo para ti? Escribe una entrada para un blog titulado "Mi rutina diaria de trabajo y de estudio" donde compartes tus actividades con otros estudiantes universitarios. Recuerda el horario de la actividad 6.28 y sigue estas pautas.

- Usa el texto de la actividad 6.47 como modelo.
- Di si tu rutina funciona bien para ti. Explica por qué.
- Si no funciona bien, identifica qué te gustaría cambiar (por ejemplo, más ejercicio, descansar más, pasar más tiempo con tu familia o amigos, etc.).

Recursos lingüísticos

REFLEXIVE VERBS

	DUCHARSE
(yo)	**me** ducho
(tú)	**te** duchas
(él/ella, usted)	**se** ducha
(nosotros/nosotras)	**nos** duchamos
(vosotros/vosotras)	**os** ducháis
(ellos/ellas, ustedes)	**se** duchan

▶ We often use reflexive verbs in Spanish to describe actions where the subject does the action to him or herself, as in:

*Dorothy **se maquilla**.* = Dorothy puts on makeup.   ***Me lavo** las manos.* = I wash my hands.

▶ The infinitive form of a reflexive verb has **se** attached to the end of it, for example **ducharse** (meaning to shower oneself). When we conjugate a reflexive verb, we place the pronoun (**me**, **te**, **se**, **nos**, **os**, **se**) before the conjugated verb.

*Yo **me ducho** por la noche. (**ducharse**)*

▶ In English, with actions involving parts of the body we use the possessive. In Spanish we use the definite article with body parts since the reflexive verb already indicates that one's own body is receiving the action.

***Me lavo** el pelo.* = I wash my hair.   *Gary **se lava** el pelo.* = Gary washes his hair.

❗ Verbs such as **dormir** or **ir** have a change in meaning if they are used with a reflexive pronoun.

***Duermes** demasiado.* = You sleep too much.   *Siempre **me duermo** en clase.* = I always fall asleep in class.

***Vamos** al cine.* = Let's go to the movies.   ***Nos vamos** de aquí.* = We're leaving/going away.

PRESENT TENSE OF SOME IRREGULAR VERBS

▶ Remember that irregular verbs are those with spelling changes in the stem. In previous lessons we studied the verbs **ser**, **tener**, **ir**, **querer** and **preferir**. Keep in mind that the **nosotros** and the **vosotros** forms do not have these irregularities.

▶ Here are other irregular verbs that have a vowel change (stem-changing verbs) in Spanish:

O > UE	DORMIR	ACOSTARSE	ALMORZAR
(yo)	d**ue**rmo	me ac**ue**sto	alm**ue**rzo
(tú)	d**ue**rmes	te ac**ue**stas	alm**ue**rzas
(él/ella, usted)	d**ue**rme	se ac**ue**sta	alm**ue**rza
(nosotros/nosotras)	dormimos	nos acostamos	almorzamos
(vosotros/vosotras)	dormís	os acostáis	almorzáis
(ellos/ellas, ustedes)	d**ue**rmen	se ac**ue**stan	alm**ue**rzan

E > IE	EMPEZAR	DESPERTARSE
(yo)	emp**ie**zo	me desp**ie**rto
(tú)	emp**ie**zas	te desp**ie**rtas
(él/ella, usted)	emp**ie**za	se desp**ie**rta
(nosotros/nosotras)	empezamos	nos despertamos
(vosotros/vosotras)	empezáis	os despertáis
(ellos/ellas, ustedes)	emp**ie**zan	se desp**ie**rtan

E > I	VESTIRSE
(yo)	me visto
(tú)	te vistes
(él/ella, usted)	se viste
(nosotros/nosotras)	nos vestimos
(vosotros/vosotras)	os vestís
(ellos/ellas, ustedes)	se visten

g in the first person singular (yo)	SALIR	HACER	PONERSE
(yo)	salgo	hago	me pongo
(tú)	sales	haces	te pones
(él/ella, usted)	sale	hace	se pone
(nosotros/nosotras)	salimos	hacemos	nos ponemos
(vosotros/vosotras)	salís	hacéis	os ponéis
(ellos/ellas, ustedes)	salen	hacen	se ponen

! Verbs like **salir**, **hacer**, and **poner(se)** are irregular only in the first person singular.

! In addition to having irregular **yo** forms, verbs like **tener** also have a vowel change (**tengo**, **tienes**, **tiene**, **tenemos**, **tenéis**, **tienen**)

EXPRESSIONS TO SEQUENCE ACTIONS: PRIMERO / DESPUÉS / LUEGO, ANTES/DESPUÉS DE + INFINITIVE

Primero, ...   **Después, ...**   **Luego, ...**

*Yo, **primero**, me ducho y, **después**, me visto. **Luego**, desayuno...* = First, I take a shower and then I get dressed. Then I have breakfast.

DESPUÉS DE + INFINITIVE   **ANTES DE** + INFINITIVE

*Me cepillo los dientes **después de** comer.* = I brush my teeth after eating.
*Me ducho siempre **antes de** desayunar.* = I always take a shower before having breakfast.

! Note that in Spanish actions are expressed with an infinitive after **antes de** and **después de**.

PREPOSITIONS TO TALK ABOUT TIME

a + time	Me levanto **a** las ocho.
por + part of the day*	No trabajo **por** la mañana.
antes/después de	Hago deporte **antes de** cenar.

! *When combining the time with the part of the day, we use the preposition **de** instead of **por**.
*Me levanto a las ocho **de la mañana**.* = I get up at eight in the morning.

Son las seis menos diez de la tarde.

Torre del Reloj. Guayaquil, Ecuador

Pronunciamos

Conectar las palabras

))) **6.53. Escuchamos.** Escucha estas frases, observa la pronunciación
[e] de las letras subrayadas y marca qué escuchas.

1. secars<u>e e</u>l pelo
- ⬤ se-car-se-el-pe-lo
- ⬤ se-car-sel-pe-lo

2. lo<u>s s</u>ábados
- ⬤ lo-sá-ba-dos
- ⬤ los-sá-ba-dos

3. doming<u>o a</u> mediodía
- ⬤ do-min-goa-me-dio-día
- ⬤ do-min-go-a-me-dio-día

4. se maquilla<u>n a</u> menudo
- ⬤ se-ma-qui-llan-a-me-nu-do
- ⬤ se-ma-qui-lla-na-me-nu-do

[e] **6.54. Completamos la regla.** Lee ahora estas recomendaciones y marca la opción correcta en cada caso.

To sound fluent in Spanish, you must pronounce consecutive words properly.
Select the correct completions to formulate the rules:

- when the final letter of a word and the first letter in the next are the same vowel we tend to pronounce them as...
  - ⬤ **one single sound**
  - ⬤ **two independent sounds**

- when the final letter of a word and the first letter in the next are the same consonant we tend to pronounce them as...
  - ⬤ **two independent sounds**
  - ⬤ **one single sound**

- when the final letter of a word is a consonant and the first letter in the next is a vowel we tend to pronounce them...
  - ⬤ **leaving a space between them**
  - ⬤ **together**

- when the final letter of a word is a vowel and the first letter in the next is a different vowel we tend to pronounce them...
  - ⬤ **leaving a space between them**
  - ⬤ **together**

))) **6.55. Detectamos.** Escucha y marca en estas frases qué palabras pronunciamos juntas.

1. ¿Cuidas tu imagen?
2. Me encanta hacer yoga.
3. ¿Te afeitas a menudo?
4. Los sábados salgo a cenar con amigos.
5. Una vez a la semana almuerzo con mis abuelos.
6. Mi hermana se levanta a las seis.
7. Son las ocho y media.
8. Empiezo a trabajar a las siete.
9. Todas las mañanas hago deporte en casa.
10. Siempre me acuesto antes de las once.

))) **6.56. Pronunciamos.** Escucha de nuevo las frases de la actividad 6.55 y pronúncialas en voz alta.
[e]

Vocabulario activo

))) Los días de la semana
Days of the week

- **el domingo** *Sunday*
- **el fin de semana** *weekend*
- **el jueves** *Thursday*
- **el lunes** *Monday*
- **el martes** *Tuesday*
- **el miércoles** *Wednesday*
- **el sábado** *Saturday*
- **el viernes** *Friday*

))) Las partes del día
Parts of the day

- **a mediodía** *at noon*
- **por la mañana** *in the morning*
- **por la noche** *at night*
- **por la tarde** *in the afternoon*

))) Actividades y cuidados diarios
Daily routines and activities

- **acostarse** (o>ue) *to go to sleep/bed*
- **afeitarse** *to shave*
- **almorzar** (o>ue) *to have lunch*
- **cenar** *to have dinner*
- **cepillarse los dientes** *to brush your teeth*
- **cuidar** *to care for*
- **cuidarse** *to maintain your personal appearance, to take care of yourself*
- **desayunar** *to have breakfast*
- **despertarse** (e>ie) *to wake up*
- **dormir** (o>ue) *to sleep*
- **ducharse** *to take a shower*
- **empezar** (e>ie) **a trabajar** *to start to work*
- **hacer deporte** *to play sports*
- **hacer la cama** *to make the bed*
- **ir a clase** *to go to class*
- **ir a la peluquería** *to go to the hair salon*
- **ir al baño** *to go to the bathroom*
- **levantarse** *to wake up*
- **maquillarse** *to put on make-up*
- **ponerse (crema hidratante, perfume...)** *to put on (moisturizer, perfume...)*
- **preparar la comida** *to cook, to prepare a meal*
- **regresar a casa** *to return home*
- **salir de casa** *to leave the house*
- **salir del trabajo** *to leave work*
- **secarse el pelo** *to dry your hair*
- **vestirse** (e>ie) *to get dressed*

))) Preguntar y decir la hora
Asking for and telling the time

- **¿A qué hora...?** *What time...?*
- **las cinco menos cuarto** *it's a quarter to five*
- **las cinco y cuarto** *five fifteen*
- **las cinco y media** *five thirty*
- **en punto** *o'clock*
- **falta un cuarto para las cinco** *it's a quarter to five*
- **¿Qué hora es?** *What time is it?*
- **¿Tiene/s hora/s?** *Do you have the time?*

))) Expresar frecuencia
Expressing frequency

- **a menudo** *often*
- **a veces** *sometimes*
- **casi** *almost*
- **en ocasiones especiales** *in special occasions*
- **normalmente** *normally*
- **nunca** *never*
- **siempre** *always*
- **todos los días** *every day*
- **(tres) veces a la semana** *(three) times a week*
- **(tres) veces al año** *(three) times a year*
- **(tres) veces al día** *(three) times a day*

))) Expresiones de tiempo
Time expression

- **antes de** (+ infinitivo) *before (doing something)*
- **después** *later*
- **después de** (+ infinitivo) *after (doing something)*
- **luego** *later*
- **primero** *first*

⚙ **Estrategia**

Try to categorize words and expressions in different ways so you can create different connections. For instance, try to organize as many words in this lesson as you can in this way: "Things I normally do at home" vs. "Things I normally do somewhere else" or "Things I like" vs. "Things I don't like".

Lección 7

Toda una vida

IN THIS LESSON WE ARE GOING TO

create our life story

LEARNING OUTCOMES
You will be able to...

- talk about past events

- indicate when something happened

VOCABULARY
- Stages in life

- Extraordinary life events

LANGUAGE STRUCTURES
- Forms and uses of the preterit (I)

- Time expressions used with the preterit (I)

PRONUNCIATION
- Pronouncing irregular verbs in the preterit

CULTURAL CONNECTIONS
- Great unknown women in history

Ellen Ochoa, la primera mujer de origen hispano en viajar al espacio.

Primer contacto

7.1. Un reportaje. Observa este fragmento de un reportaje y escribe el nombre de cada persona en el lugar adecuado.

Las primeras #1

Estas mujeres hispanas (algunas famosas, otras casi desconocidas) tienen algo en común: ser las primeras en hacer algo en diferentes disciplinas.

Paola Longoria, mexicana (1989)

Matilde Hidalgo, ecuatoriana (1889-1974)

Rita Moreno, puertorriqueña (1931)

Milka Duno, venezolana (1972)

Gabriela Mistral, chilena (1989 - 1957)

1. .... **fue la primera actriz hispana en** ganar un Óscar (en 1961, por *West Side Story*).

2. .... **fue la primera raquetbolista en** ser número uno ocho años consecutivos.

3. .... **fue la primera mujer en** ganar una Ferrari Challenge Race en Estados Unidos (en 1999).

4. .... **fue la primera escritora hispana en** recibir el Nobel de Literatura (en 1945).

5. .... **fue la primera mujer de Ecuador en** ser doctora en Medicina y **en poder votar**.

7.2. Las primeras personas en... Toma como modelo las frases de la actividad 7.1 y escribe otras sobre personas que también fueron las primeras.

Neil Armstrong fue la primera persona en pisar la Luna.

✿ **Estrategia**

Using new verb forms in phrases and using them right away make them easier to learn:

Ellen Ochoa **fue** *la primera mujer de origen hispano en viajar al espacio.* = Ellen Ochoa was the first woman of Hispanic origin to travel in space.

Comprendemos el vocabulario

Hechos en la vida de una persona

🔊 **7.3. Hechos en la vida de una persona.** Lee y escucha estas palabras y expresiones.

nacer

morir

ir a la escuela
ir a la universidad

dejar los estudios

terminar los estudios
graduarse

irse de casa de los padres

tener hijos

enamorarse

casarse

divorciarse

tener un accidente

enfermarse

pedir un crédito/préstamo para...

empezar a trabajar

quedarse sin trabajo
cambiar de trabajo

retirarse

vivir en otro país

hacer un viaje

aprender a tocar un instrumento
(la guitarra, el piano, el saxofón...)

7.4. Completamos. Completa con palabras y expresiones de la actividad 7.3 (solo puedes poner dos como máximo en cada caso).

1. Es algo que pasa muchas veces en la vida: ....

2. Es algo que solo pasa una vez: ....

3. Es algo que nadie quiere: ....

4. Es algo que normalmente pasa cuando eres joven: ....

5. Es algo que no quiero: ....

7.5. Comparamos. Comparen sus respuestas de la actividad 7.4.

Enamorarse **es algo que pasa muchas veces en la vida, ¿no creen?**

7.6. Una línea del tiempo. En parejas, con el mayor número posible de palabras y expresiones de la actividad 7.3, elaboren una línea del tiempo típica para la vida de una persona. Decidan en qué orden pasan esas cosas.

Para comunicar

¿no crees? / ¿no creen? = *don't you think?*
¿qué crees? / ¿qué creen? = *what do you think?*

nacer — ir a la escuela — morir

• *¿Qué ponemos después de nacer?*
○ *¿Qué te parece si ponemos "enfermarse"? Los niños se enferman mucho.*

Para comunicar

¿Qué ponemos antes/después de...? = *What do we put before/after...?*
¿Qué te parece...? = *How about...?*

7.7. Nuestra línea del tiempo. Cada pareja lee sus líneas del tiempo. Los demás toman nota de las diferencias con sus líneas para comentarlas después.

7.8. En el futuro queremos... Escribe actividades de 7.3 que quieres hacer en el futuro.

¿Necesitas ayuda?

Remember when using reflexive verbs, the pronoun must agree with the subject.

No quiero enfermarme.

Quiero terminar los estudios y, despúes, quiero vivir en otro país.

7.9. Compartimos. Comparte las actividades de 7.8 con un compañero. ¿Tienen cosas en común?

• *¿Qué quieres hacer en el futuro?*
○ *Yo quiero terminar los estudios y, después, quiero vivir en otro país. ¿Y tú?*

Comprendemos el vocabulario

Eventos extraordinarios

🔊 **7.10. Eventos extraordinarios.** Lee y escucha.

grabar un disco

dirigir una película

pintar un cuadro

conocer a una estrella, a un/a presidente/-a...

El limpiaparabrisas, 1903 (Mary Anderson)

inventar (un aparato, una herramienta...)

ganar un premio

batir un récord

publicar un libro

Más palabras

🔊 **cambiar la historia (de la música, del cine...)** = *to change the history (of music, film...)*
descubrir una vacuna / un fármaco = *to discover a vaccine / drug, medicine*
fundar una empresa = *to start a company*

hacerse famoso/-a = *to become famous*
hacerse rico/-a = *to become rich*
luchar por una causa = *to fight for a cause*
ser el/la mejor (en algo) = *to be the best (in something)*
tener éxito = *to succeed*

7.11. Personas y hechos. Busca información en internet sobre cada una de estas personas y escribe qué expresiones de la actividad 7.10 asocias con cada una.

1. Juan José Campanella: ....

2. Nydia Velázquez: ....

3. Javier Sotomayor: ....

4. Julia Álvarez: ....

5. Luis Von Ann: ....

6. Pau Gasol: ....

7. Malala Yousafzai: ....

8. Rosa Parks: ....

9. Marie Curie: ....

10. Stephanie Kwolek: ....

7.12. Un programa de radio. Escucha a estas personas que hablan en un programa de radio y escribe qué cosas extraordinarias quieren hacer.

1 Wendy ....

4 Cristina ....

2 Santiago ....

5 Martín ....

3 Laura ....

7.13. Nuestras vidas. ¿Y tú? ¿Qué cosas extraordinarias quieres hacer? Compártelo con la clase.

Yo quiero ser la mejor guitarrista del mundo y hacerme famosa.

Exploramos la lengua

Forma y usos del pretérito (I)

7.14. Experiencias. Estas personas comparten sus experiencias.
¿Cuál de ellas te parece más interesante? Coméntalo con un/a compañero/-a.

UNA EXPERIENCIA INCREÍBLE

LUCAS
"En 2011 **hice** un viaje de tres meses por África con una mochila y muy poco dinero. **Fueron** los meses más intensos de mi vida y **aprendí** muchas cosas."

ALBERTO
"El año pasado **estudié** seis meses en una universidad de China. **Fue** una experiencia increíble."

LEILA
"Hace unos meses **estuve** en una fiesta... ¡en casa de Camila Cabello!"

ROSA
"Hace unos años **fui** un verano a México. En Guadalajara conocimos a una compañía de circo y **vivimos** con ellos unos meses. Mi amiga después **hizo** un curso en una escuela de circo y ahora es trapecista."

LORENA
"En 2016 **viví** en un barco con un grupo de amigos. **Estuvimos** tres meses en el mar. Luego, **fuimos** a la Polinesia y visitamos muchas islas. **Aprendimos** muchísimo sobre la cultura polinesia."

❶ ¿Necesitas ayuda?

There are different ways to express when an event took place.

en 2011
en abril

hace + amount of time: **hace cinco años** = *five years ago*
hace un mes = *a month ago*
hace unos años = *a few years ago*
hace algunos meses = *a few months ago*

- Para mí, la experiencia más interesante es la de Alberto porque yo también quiero estudiar en otro país.
- Pues para mí, la experiencia de Leila. ¡Me encanta Camila Cabello!

7.15. Conjugamos. Completa los cuadros con las formas en negrita de la actividad 7.14.

VERBOS REGULARES			VERBOS IRREGULARES		
-AR ESTUDIAR	**-ER** APRENDER	**-IR** VIVIR	**IR / SER**	**ESTAR**	**HACER**
....	....	....	....	....	....
estudiaste	aprendiste	viviste	fuiste	estuviste	hiciste
estudió	aprendió	vivió	....	estuvo	....
estudiamos	....	....	....	....	hicimos
estudiasteis	aprendisteis	vivisteis	fuisteis	estuvisteis	hicisteis
estudiaron	aprendieron	vivieron	....	estuvieron	hicieron

7.16. Reflexionamos. Observa las tablas de la actividad 7.15 y responde a estas preguntas.

1. ¿Qué dos conjugaciones tienen las mismas terminaciones en pretérito?
2. En dos casos, la forma es la misma que en presente. ¿Cuáles?

❶ ¿Necesitas ayuda?

In the Recursos lingüísticos section you'll find other examples of irregular verbs in the preterit.

7.17. Experiencias interesantes. ¿Conoces a gente con experiencias interesantes? Escribe algunas frases.

Mi bisabuelo emigró a Estados Unidos hace 100 años y estuvo más de un mes en el barco.

7.18. Investigamos. Busca en internet el nombre de estos famosos e información relacionada con el verbo proporcionado. Luego, escribe frases usando esos verbos, como en el ejemplo.

1. Rodrigo Cortés • **dirigir**

Rodrigo Cortés dirigió en 2010 la película "Buried", protagonizada por Ryan Reynolds.

2. Isabel Allende • **escribir**

....

....

3. Rolando Blackman • **ser el primer latinoamericano**

....

....

4. Penélope Cruz y Javier Bardem • **protagonizar**

....

....

5. Frida Kahlo y Diego Rivera • **casarse**

....

....

6. Guillermo del Toro • **ganar**

....

....

7. Rosario Dawson • **colaborar con una fundación**

....

....

8. Shakira • **fundar**

....

....

7.19. Ser e ir. Escribe la forma apropiada de los verbos **ser** e **ir**. Luego, marca qué verbo es según el contexto.

1. Ellen Ochoa .... la primera mujer de origen latino en viajar al espacio. ○ **ser** ○ **ir**

2. Gael Garcia Bernal .... a Inglaterra para estudiar. ○ **ser** ○ **ir**

3. Octavio Paz .... un escritor mexicano. ○ **ser** ○ **ir**

7.20. Julieta Venegas. Completa los espacios con la forma correcta de los verbos **estar**, **hacer**, **ir** y **ser**.

Julieta Venegas es una cantante de Tijuana, México, que se .... famosa a finales de

los años 90. En 2005, ... a Argentina para trabajar en su disco *Limón y sal*. En 2007,

.... en Los Ángeles para asistir a la ceremonia de los Grammys, ganó el premio

"Mejor disco de pop latino." .... una experiencia increíble para ella.

Exploramos la lengua

Marcadores temporales en pasado (I)

7.21. Un currículum. Lee el currículum de Nieves y completa las frases.

DATOS PERSONALES
Nombre: Nieves
Apellidos: Ruiz Camacho
DNI: 20122810W
Lugar y fecha de nacimiento: Salamanca, 12/06/1985

FORMACIÓN ACADÉMICA
2003 - 2007: Universidad de Salamanca. Grado en Lengua y literatura inglesas.
2006 - 2007: Estudiante Rice University, Houston.
2008 - 2009: Universidad de París-Cluny (Francia). Máster en Traducción.

EXPERIENCIA PROFESIONAL
2006 - 2007: Camarera en diferentes restaurantes de Houston.
2007 - 2009: Profesora de español en París.
2010 - 2011: Traductora en la Editorial Barcana, Barcelona.
2012 - actualidad: Traductora en la ONU, Nueva York.

IDIOMAS
Español: lengua materna.
Inglés: nivel avanzado (C2), oral y escrito.
Francés: nivel avanzado (C2), oral y escrito.
Alemán: nociones básicas (A1).

OTROS DATOS DE INTERÉS
Amplios conocimientos de informática y dominio de programas de edición.
Disponibilidad para viajar.

⊕ **¿Sabes que...?**

Resumes can vary from one culture to another. How does Nieves' resume compare to the ones used in your country?

⊕ **¿Sabes que...?**

DNI stands for "Documento Nacional de Identidad". This card is required in Spain after age fourteen for identification purposes.

⊕ **¿Sabes que...?**

The terms A1 and C2 correspond to the European standards for grading language proficiency. They are known as the *Common European Framework of Reference for Languages* (CEFR) and include levels A1 (beginner), A2, B1, B2, C1 and C2 (proficient).

1. Estudió en la Universidad de Salamanca **de** .... **a** ....

2. Llegó a Houston en 2006 y **al** .... **siguiente** volvió a Salamanca.

3. Trabajó como profesora de español **durante** .... años.

4. Empezó la carrera en 2003 y .... años **después** la terminó.

5. Terminó un máster en Traducción **hace** .... años.

6. Trabajó como traductora en una editorial de Barcelona **hasta** ....

7. Trabaja como traductora de la ONU **desde** ....

❗ **¿Necesitas ayuda?**

Desde expresses **since** in the following case. Note that the verb is used in the present:

*Vivo aquí **desde** 2018.* = I have been living here since 2018.

7.22. Completamos. Completa las frases con las palabras destacadas en la actividad 7.21.

1. Gabriela Mistral publicó su primera obra en 1922 y, 23 años ...., en 1945, ganó el premio Nobel.

2. Barack Obama fue presidente de los Estados Unidos .... 2008 .... 2016.

3. Frida Kahlo murió .... más de 60 años.

4. El cocinero José Andrés trabaja en los EE. UU. .... 1991.

5. Ernest Hemingway trabajó como periodista en España .... los años de la guerra civil.

6. Kat Von D nació en México en 1982 y vivió en ese país .... 1986, cuando se fue a California.

7. Lupita Nyong'o nació en México en 1983 y .... año .... se fue a vivir a Kenia con su familia.

7.23. Una historia de amor. Completa esta historia con las expresiones que faltan.

un mes más tarde   una semana después   poco tiempo después

durante ese tiempo   en 2016

03/05/2014

El 3 de mayo de 2014 Guillermo conoció a Rosa en una discoteca. Se enamoraron a primera vista.

10/05/2014

.... , la llamó, fueron al cine y cenaron juntos.

10/06/2014

Empezaron a salir y

.... , pasaron un fin de semana en la playa y decidieron irse a vivir juntos.

09/08/2014

.... , Guillermo tuvo un accidente y estuvo dos años en coma en un hospital.

2014-2016

.... , en el hospital, Rosa conoció al doctor Urquijo, el médico de Guillermo.

ENERO 2016

.... , Guillermo se despertó. Vio a Beatriz, una amiga de Rosa, y se enamoró de ella.

7.24. El final de la historia. ¿Qué pasó después? En parejas, escriban el final de la historia.

....
....
....
....
....
....
....
....

10/06/2017

2018

Comunicamos

El "Che"

7.25. ¿Qué sabemos? ¿Qué saben de Ernesto Guevara, una de las figuras más conocidas del mundo hispano? En parejas, marquen cuáles de estos datos creen que son verdad.

- Nació en Cuba.
- Estudió Medicina y trabajó como médico.
- Conoció a Fidel Castro en México.
- No aceptó nunca cargos políticos en el gobierno de Castro.
- Participó en movimientos revolucionarios de diferentes países de América Latina y África.
- Murió a los 60 años en un accidente de tráfico.
- En 2004, el actor Gael García Bernal protagonizó una película sobre su juventud.

> • ¿Tú crees que nació en Cuba?
> ○ No sé, no estoy segura, pero...

> 💬 **Para comunicar**
>
> No estoy seguro/-a = *I'm not sure.*

7.26. La biografía del Che. Lean ahora esta biografía del "Che" Guevara y comprueben sus hipótesis.

El Che Guevara

Ernesto Guevara, más conocido como "Che" Guevara o "El Che", nació en Rosario, Argentina, en 1928. Con 9 años se fue con su familia a Buenos Aires y unos años después se fue a vivir a Alta Gracia (cerca de Córdoba).

En 1952 hizo un viaje por algunos países de América Latina: Chile, Bolivia, Perú y Colombia. El contacto directo con la difícil realidad social de la zona fue una experiencia determinante para sus ideas revolucionarias. La película *Diarios de motocicleta*, protagonizada por el actor mexicano Gael García Bernal en 2004, narra ese viaje.

En 1953, cuando terminó sus estudios de Medicina, se fue a Centroamérica y apoyó los movimientos revolucionarios de Guatemala y Costa Rica.

En 1955 trabajó de médico en México. Allí conoció a Fidel Castro y durante diez años la vida del "Che" estuvo totalmente dedicada a Cuba: participó en la Revolución, obtuvo la nacionalidad cubana, fue comandante del ejército y fue dos veces ministro.

En 1965 abandonó su trabajo en Cuba y se dedicó de nuevo a la lucha activa, primero en África y luego en Sudamérica. Murió en Bolivia en 1967, asesinado por el ejército boliviano.

7.27. Investigamos sobre Ernesto Guevara. Elijan una etapa de la vida del "Che" Guevara y busquen más información sobre lo que hizo en ese periodo. Luego, preséntenla en la clase.

Personas extraordinarias de nuestro país

7.28. Proponemos nombres. En parejas, propongan una o varias personas con las que pueden asociar cada una de las siguientes afirmaciones. Luego, compartan sus propuestas con la clase.

1. Luchó por los derechos de los afroamericanos en los años 60.
2. Inventó cosas relacionadas con la tecnología.
3. Cambió la historia de la música en el siglo XXI.

7.29. Los diez de Estados Unidos. Preparen frases como las de la actividad 7.28 sobre personas destacadas de la historia de los Estados Unidos. Entre todos, elijan a las diez personas más destacadas.

El juego de los errores históricos

 7.30. Detectamos y corregimos. En cada una de estas tarjetas hay una información falsa. En parejas, encuéntrenla y corríjanla (pueden usar internet).

Cine

- Halle Berry fue la primera mujer afroamericana que ganó un Óscar a la mejor actriz.

- Leonardo DiCaprio ganó un Óscar por *El renacido*, película del mexicano Alejandro González Iñárritu.

- *Lincoln* ganó el Óscar a la mejor película en 2013.

Historia

- Cristóbal Colón llegó a América en su primer viaje en 1492.

- Kennedy murió asesinado en el año 1963.

- La Primera Guerra Mundial terminó en 1920.

Deportes

- Manu Ginóbili, jugador argentino de los San Antonio Spurs, se retiró en 2015.

- En las olimpiadas de Londres de 2012 Usain Bolt batió el récord olímpico en los 100 metros lisos.

- Con 21 años, el jugador de golf Tiger Woods ganó el Major en 1997.

Música

- Los Beatles fueron a Estados Unidos por primera vez en 1964.

- *Despacito*, la canción de Luis Fonsi, no tuvo mucho éxito en Estados Unidos.

- Mozart empezó su *Réquiem* en 1791, pero no lo terminó.

7.31. Creamos tarjetas. Ahora preparen cuatro tarjetas como las anteriores sobre cine, historia, música y deportes. Una información de cada tarjeta tiene que ser falsa.

7.32. Jugamos. En grupos, lean sus frases. ¿Quién encuentra más informaciones falsas?

Lugares importantes en la vida de Verónica

7.33. Verónica en el mundo. Verónica es un chica argentina que vive en España. Escucha lo que cuenta sobre su vida. ¿Qué hizo en cada uno de estos lugares? Toma notas en tu cuaderno.

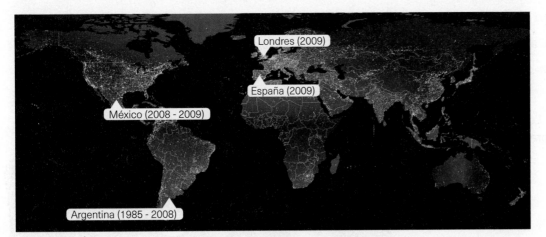

Londres (2009)
España (2009)
México (2008 - 2009)
Argentina (1985 - 2008)

7.34. Tres lugares importantes para nosotros. Escribe los nombres de los tres lugares más importantes de tu vida y, luego, explícale a un compañero por qué son importantes para ti.

> *Los tres lugares más importantes de mi vida son Tucson, porque es donde nací; San Francisco, porque es donde estudié, y Jacksonville, porque es donde conocí a mi mejor amiga.*

Ahora podemos...

Escribir una biografía

7.35. Comunicación interpersonal. Estamos en el año 2045 y tienes que escribir la biografía de una persona de la clase. Primero, prepara las preguntas que vas a hacer para investigar sobre su pasado, sobre sus intereses y sobre los proyectos que tiene en la vida.

> ¿Cuándo naciste?
>
> ¿Cuándo terminaste tus estudios?
>
> ¿Cuál es tu trabajo ideal?
>
> ¿Quieres tener hijos?
>
> ...

7.36. Preparación. Ahora hazle la entrevista a una persona de la clase.

> ● ¿Cuándo naciste?
> ○ En 1990.
> ● ¿Cuándo terminaste tus estudios?
> ○ En 2012.
> ● ¿Cuál es tu trabajo ideal?
> ○ Fotógrafo de famosos.
> ● ¿Quieres tener hijos?

7.37. Preparación. Ahora vas a escribir la biografía de tu compañero. Considera los cambios que puede haber en los próximos años (políticos, tecnológicos, sociales, etc.).

> Nathan nació en Connecticut en 1990. Terminó sus estudios de Periodismo en 2012. Después estudió Fotografía y en 2018 empezó a trabajar para "Vanity Fair" como fotógrafo.
>
> En 2020 conoció a Kirsten Stewart en una fiesta en casa de Lady Gaga. Se enamoraron y un año después tuvieron un hijo.

7.38. Presentación. Lee la biografía a los demás. Puedes acompañar la presentación con una historia ilustrada de su vida.

Video

Alegría Peruanx

Connie Chavez nació en Lima, Perú, y ahora vive en la ciudad de Nueva York. A través de su proyecto multimedia "Alegría Peruanx", Chavez usa el activismo visual para crear un sentimiento de comunidad en los peruanos que viven en Estados Unidos y para dar representación y voz a personas que, por fin, tienen la oportunidad de explorar el complejo y diverso patrimonio peruano.

Pearson MyLab

To find out more about Connie Chavez and her visual activism, go to MyLab to watch **Alegría Peruanx** and complete the video activities.

⊕ ¿Sabes que...?

Some of the first Peruvians to emigrate to the United States came as laborers during the California Gold Rush in 1849.

⚲ Hacemos conexiones

Investiga sobre la emigración peruana a Estados Unidos. ¿Llegaron en momentos concretos de la Historia? ¿En qué estados están más presentes? ¿Hay personajes famosos peruanos o descendientes de peruanos?

Grandes desconocidas

La historia no siempre reconoce –o no reconoce a tiempo– la aportación de las mujeres. Y, en ocasiones, el reconocimiento oficial llega, pero sus nombres no son conocidos.

Mi tía, un amiguito y yo (1942), María Izquierdo.

María Izquierdo

(San Juan de los Lagos, 1902 — Ciudad de México, 1955) fue una gran figura del muralismo mexicano. Internacionalmente, Frida Kahlo eclipsa a otras artistas mexicanas, pero María Izquierdo fue la primera pintora en exponer su obra fuera de México. Izquierdo denunció la hegemonía masculina en el arte mexicano de su época, hegemonía que tuvo consecuencias negativas en su carrera. "Es delito ser mujer y tener talento", dijo en 1953. En 2012 el gobierno mexicano la nombró Mujer ilustre.

Erika Ender

(Ciudad de Panamá, Panamá, 1974) es la compositora del superéxito *Despacito* (con Luis Fonsi y Daddy Yankee), pero su nombre no es tan conocido como el de los dos cantantes.

Celia Sánchez -Ramos

(Zaragoza, España, 1959) inventó un sistema de seguridad biométrico que permite verificar la identidad de una persona gracias al reconocimiento por córnea. En 2009 recibió el Premio a la Mejor Inventora Internacional, que concede la ONU.

ANTES DE LEER

7.39. Nuestras hipótesis. Lee el título del texto. ¿De qué te imaginas que va a hablar?

LECTURA ACTIVA

7.40. ¿Estamos de acuerdo? Lee la introducción del texto. ¿Estás de acuerdo? Justifica tu respuesta.

7.41. Relacionamos. De acuerdo con la información de los textos, ¿con qué mujeres relacionas estas afirmaciones?

1. Fue reconocida internacionalmente hace algunos años.
2. Tuvo problemas por ser mujer.

DESPUÉS DE LEER

7.42. Investigamos y presentamos. Busca ejemplos de mujeres poco conocidas en tu país, pero que aportaron mucho a la historia. Haz una breve presentación en clase.

Textos audiovisuales: vemos, escuchamos y presentamos

Vemos un video sobre Gabriela Mistral

ANTES DE DE VER EL VIDEO

INFORMACIÓN PREVIA   Vas a ver un video ilustrado con imágenes sobre Gabriela Mistral, una poeta, diplomática y pedagoga.

7.43. Preparación. Ve el video sin sonido y fíjate en las imágenes. ¿Qué información sobre Gabriela Mistral puedes saber ya (información personal, cosas que hizo, etc.)? Escríbela.

VEMOS EL VIDEO

7.44. Comprensión. Ve el video hasta el minuto 0:58 y responde a estas preguntas.

1. ¿Qué familiares de Gabriela Mistral se mencionan en este fragmento del video?
¿Qué se dice sobre ellos?
2. El video menciona un libro que marcó la infancia de Gabriela Mistral.
¿De qué libro se trata y de qué forma influyó en su obra?

7.45. Datos sobre las obras. Ve el resto del video y escribe en qué año se publicaron estas obras. ¿Se dice algo más de alguna de ellas? Toma notas.

Título de la obra	Año de publicación	Otras informaciones
Desolación		
Lectura para mujeres		
Tala		
Lagar		

7.46. Datos sobre la escritora. Toma nota de las cosas que hizo Gabriela Mistral en cada uno de estos lugares.

Chile:

....

....

....

....

....

....

....

México:

....

....

....

....

....

....

....

Brasil:

....

....

....

....

....

....

....

Estados Unidos:

....

....

....

....

....

....

....

DESPUÉS DE VER EL VIDEO

7.47. Comprensión. Gabriela Mistral fue poeta, diplomática y pedagoga.
Justifica con información del video el uso de estas tres palabras.

Presentamos la biografía de un personaje célebre

7.48. Búsqueda de información. Busca datos sobre la vida de un personaje célebre que te interese.

7.49. Preparación. Prepara una presentación animada para ilustrar los datos que tienes.
Puedes hacer dibujos o recopilar imágenes de internet.

7.50. Presentación. Hagan sus presentaciones en la clase. Pueden hablar frente
a sus compañeros o hacerlo mediante alguna plataforma o recurso digital.

Recursos lingüísticos

FORMS AND USES OF THE PRETERIT (I)

The preterit is used to describe actions that took place and were completed in the past.

REGULAR VERBS

	HABLAR	BEBER	ESCRIBIR
(yo)	hablé	bebí	escribí
(tú)	hablaste	bebiste	escribiste
(él/ella, usted)	habló	bebió	escribió
(nosotros/nosotras)	hablamos	bebimos	escribimos
(vosotros/vosotras)	hablasteis	bebisteis	bebimos
(ellos/ellas, ustedes)	hablaron	bebieron	escribieron

IRREGULAR VERBS

Stem changes: e > i, o > u

▸ Some **-ir** verbs stem change from **e** to **i** and **o** to **u** in the third person singular and plural of the preterit. This occurs in **-ir** verbs like **pedir** and **dormir** and is true for all **-ir** verbs that stem change in the present (**e > ie, e > i, o > ue**). Remember that unlike in the present, this change only occurs in the él, ella, usted, ellos, ellas, ustedes forms of the preterit.

	PEDIR	MORIR
(yo)	pedí	morí
(tú)	pediste	moriste
(él/ella, usted)	pidió	murió
(nosotros/nosotras)	pedimos	morimos
(vosotros/vosotras)	pedisteis	moristeis
(ellos/ellas, ustedes)	pidieron	murieron

Spelling changes

▸ Verbs ending in **-car**, **-gar**, **-guar**, and **-zar** have spelling changes in the yo form of the preterit. These changes are made to maintain correct spelling and pronunciation of the verb. See the examples below:

practi**car** → practi**qué** = I practiced
lle**gar** → lle**gué** = I arrived

averi**guar** → averi**güé** = I found out
almor**zar** → almor**cé** = I had lunch

Verbs with irregular stems

▸ The following verbs have irregular stems and use special endings regardless of whether they end in **-ar**, **-er**, or **-ir**.

estar → **estuv-**	querer → **quis-**		-e
			-iste
hacer → **hic-/hiz-**	tener → **tuv-**		-o
		+	-imos
poder → **pud-**	venir → **vin-**		-isteis
poner → **pus-**			-ieron

▸ When a verb is irregular, verbs derived from it have the same irregular stem.

componer → **compus-**   deshacer → **deshic-/deshiz-**   obtener → **obtuv-**

❗ * Verbs like **decir** and **traer** follow the rule above except for the 3rd person plural (ellos/ellas, ustedes): decir → **dij-**, traer → **traj-**. This applies to other verbs with stems ending in **-j**.

*Wendy y Pilar **dijeron** que les gusta mucho el jazz.* = Wendy and Pilar said that they like jazz very much.
*Luis y Marisol **trajeron** a sus hijos a la fiesta.* = Luis y Marisol brought their children to the party.

Verbs ir and ser

▸ The verbs **ir** and **ser** have the same form in the preterit.

	IR/SER
(yo)	**fui**
(tú)	**fuiste**
(él/ella, usted)	**fue**
(nosotros/nosotras)	**fuimos**
(vosotros/vosotras)	**fuisteis**
(ellos/ellas, ustedes)	**fueron**

TIME EXPRESSIONS USED WITH THE PRETERIT (I)

SEQUENCING EVENTS IN THE PAST

*Se casaron en 1997 y **tres años después / más tarde** se divorciaron.* = They married in 1997 and three years later, they divorced.
*Se graduó en mayo y **al mes siguiente** encontró trabajo.* = He graduated in May and the following month he found a job.

TALKING ABOUT DURATION OF TIME (II)

Use **desde, desde hace, hasta, de... a**, and **durante** to express an action taking place over a period of time.

*Vivo en Santander **desde febrero / desde hace unos meses**.* = I've been living in Santander since February. (since a point in time) / for a few months. (for a period of time)
*Estuve en casa de Alfredo **hasta las seis de la tarde**.* = I was at Alfredo's house until six o'clock in the evening.
*Trabajé en un periódico **de 1996 a 1998 / del 96 al 98**.* = I worked at the newspaper from 1996 to 1998. (from '96 to '98)
*Trabajé como periodista **durante dos años**.* = I worked as a journalist for two years.

❗ Note that **desde** and **desde hace** can be used with the present tense form of the verb.

Durante las primeras décadas del siglo XIX Simón Bolívar luchó por la independencia de los países de Suramérica.

Pronunciamos

El pretérito: los cambios ortográficos y la primera y tercera personas

7.51. Escuchamos. Escucha. ¿Se pronuncian igual las letras destacadas del infinitivo y del pretérito?

INFINITIVO	PRETÉRITO
1. lle**g**ar	lle**gu**é
2. empe**z**ar	empe**c**é
3. bus**c**ar	bus**qu**é
4. averi**gu**ar	averi**gü**é

7.52. Escribimos, escuchamos y comprobamos. Ahora escribe las formas del pretérito de estos infinitivos. Luego, pronúncialas y comprueba con el audio que lo haces bien.

1. Jugar (1ª persona del pretérito) ....

2. Utilizar (1ª persona del pretérito) ....

3. Hacer (3ª persona del pretérito) ....

4. Marcar (1ª persona del pretérito) ....

5. Rechazar (1ª persona del pretérito) ....

7.53. La sílaba tónica. Escucha cómo se pronuncian estas formas del pretérito y marca cuál es su sílaba tónica. Luego, marca la opción correcta en cada regla.

estudié   estuve   tuve   comí   vine   nació   quiso   dijo   escribió

En la primera y en la tercera persona del singular de los verbos regulares, la sílaba tónica es la...

○ penúltima

○ última

En la primera y en la tercera persona del singular de los verbos irregulares, la sílaba tónica es la...

○ penúltima

○ última

7.54. Pronunciamos. Pronuncia tú ahora las formas del pretérito de la actividad 7.53.

Vocabulario activo

Hechos en la vida de una persona
Events in a person's life

- **aprender a tocar un instrumento** *to learn to play an instrument*
- **cambiar de trabajo** *to switch jobs*
- **casarse** *to get married*
- **dejar los estudios** *drop out of school/university*
- **divorciarse** *to get divorced*
- **empezar a trabajar** *to get your first job*
- **enamorarse** *to fall in love*
- **enfermarse** *to get sick /to become ill*
- **graduarse** *to graduate*
- **hacer un viaje** *to travel*
- **ir a la escuela** *to go to school*
- **ir a la universidad** *to go to the university*
- **morir** *to die*
- **nacer** *to be born*
- **pedir un crédito / un préstamo para...** *to ask for a loan to...*
- **poder votar** *to be able to vote*
- **quedarse sin trabajo** *to lose your job*
- **retirarse** *to retire*
- **ser doctor/a en** *to have a PhD in*
- **tener hijos** *to have children*
- **tener un accidente** *to have an accident*
- **terminar los estudios** *to graduate*
- **vivir en otro país** *to live in another country*

Hechos extraordinarios en la vida de una persona
Extraordinary events in the life of a person

- **batir un récord** *to break a record*
- **cambiar la historia (de la música, del cine...)** *to change the history (of music, film...)*
- **conocer a (una estrella, un/a presidente/-a...)** *to meet (a movie star, a president...)*
- **descubrir (una vacuna / un fármaco...)** *to discover (a vaccine/medication...)*
- **dirigir una película** *to direct a movie*
- **fundar una empresa** *to start a company*
- **ganar un Óscar** *to win an Oscar*
- **ganar un premio** *to win an award*
- **grabar un disco** *to record an album*
- **hacerse famoso/-a** *to become famous*
- **hacerse rico/-a** *to become rich*
- **inventar (un aparato, una herramienta...)** *to invent (a device, a tool...)*
- **luchar por una causa** *to fight for a cause*
- **pintar un cuadro** *to paint a painting*
- **publicar un libro** *to publish a book*
- **recibir el premio Nobel** *to receive a Nobel prize*
- **ser el/la mejor (en algo)** *to be the best (in something)*
- **ser el/la primero/-a en** (+ infinitivo) *to be the first to (+ infinitive)*
- **ser número uno** *to be number one*
- **tener éxito** *to be succesful*

> ⚙ **Estrategia**
>
> Begin to take note of words and phrases that can have different meanings. You will discover, for example, that **quedarse sin** can be used to express both "to lose" and "to run out of" in English.

Lección

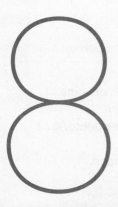

El barrio ideal

IN THIS LESSON WE ARE GOING TO

imagine and describe our ideal neighborhood

LEARNING OUTCOMES
You will be able to...

- describe towns, neighborhoods, and cities

- talk about what we like most about a place

- ask for and give directions

VOCABULARY

- Services and places to go in a city

- Adjectives and expressions to describe a neighborhood or a city

- Expressions for giving information about location, an exact address, and identifying city places

LANGUAGE STRUCTURES

- Expressing quantity (how much or how many of something)

- Asking for and giving information about location

- Prepositions of place: **a, en, de, desde, hasta, por**

PRONUNCIATION

- Word stress and written accent

CULTURAL CONNECTIONS

- The most beautiful neighborhoods in Latin America

Ciudad de Panamá (Panamá).

Primer contacto

8.1. Granada. Observa la foto de Granada, en Nicaragua. ¿Cómo te parece que es?

- linda
- fea

- **antigua**
- nueva

- tranquila
- agradable

- **rica**
- **pobre**

Parece un lugar tranquilo, ¿no?

8.2. De dónde venimos. Elige una de las palabras de la actividad 8.1 para describir el lugar de donde eres. Compártelo con la clase.

Yo soy de Austin. Para mí, es una ciudad muy agradable.

Comprendemos el vocabulario

Servicios y lugares de las ciudades

))) **8.3. Un barrio.** Lee, observa y escucha. ¿Te gustaría vivir en este barrio?

e

1 **un centro comercial**

2 **un hospital**

3 **un restaurante**

4 **un supermercado**

5 **una oficina de correos**

6 **una plaza**

7 **un estacionamiento**

8 **una farmacia**

9 **un cajero automático**

10 **una biblioteca**

11 **un gimnasio**

12 **un bar**

13 **una tienda de ropa**

14 **una escuela**

15 **un parque**

16 **una zona peatonal**

17 **una estación de metro**

18 **una parada de autobús**

Más palabras

))) **un apartamento** = *apartment*
una avenida (avda.) = *avenue*
un banco = *bank*
un bloque de apartamentos = *apartment building*
una calle (c., c/, cl.) = *street (St.)*
el casco antiguo = *old (part of) town*
una cuadra = *block*
un edificio = *building*

una iglesia = *church*
una librería = *bookstore*
una mezquita = *mosque*
un paseo (p.º) = *promenade*
un rascacielos = *high-rise, skyscraper*
una sinagoga = *synagogue*
una vivienda = *home*
zonas verdes = *green zones*

La variedad del español

estacionamiento = *parking* (Es)

apartamento = departamento (Ar, Bo, Ch, Mx, Py, Pe), **piso** (Es)

metro = tren (CR, Cu, Ec, Pa, PR), **tren eléctrico** (Pe), **subte** (Ar, Ur)

8.4. Servicios y lugares. Escribe el nombre de los lugares de las imágenes.

1. .... 2. .... 3. .... 4. .... 5. .... 6. ....

8.5. ¿Hay? Clasifica en una tabla qué servicios y lugares de la lista de la actividad 8.3 hay o no hay donde tú vives.

Hay	No hay
un centro comercial	

8.6. Lugares. Escribe a qué lugares vas para hacer estas cosas. En algunos casos hay más de una opción posible.

1. Para comprar comida: ....

2. Para comprar un libro: ....

3. Para comprar medicamentos: ....

4. Para comprar unos pantalones: ....

5. Para estar con amigos: ....

6. Para pasear: ....

7. Para hacer deporte: ....

8. Para estacionar el auto: ....

9. Para estudiar: ....

8.7. En una semana. Marca a qué lugares vas durante una semana normal en tu vida.

- gimnasio
- biblioteca
- iglesia/sinagoga/mezquita
- restaurante
- bar
- parque
- centro comercial
- escuela/universidad
- supermercado
- tienda de ropa
- parada de autobús

8.8. Compartimos. En parejas, hablen de con qué frecuencia van a los lugares de la actividad 8.7 y qué hacen allí.

Yo voy todas las mañanas al gimnasio para hacer yoga.

Comprendemos el vocabulario

Describir un barrio

))) **8.9. Tres barrios.** Escucha y lee las descripciones de tres barrios de Madrid.

⚙ **Estrategia**

Remember you are not expected to understand all the new vocabulary in context. When in doubt, look it up!

BARRIOS EMBLEMÁTICOS *de* **Madrid**

Madrid

LAVAPIÉS

Lavapiés está en el centro de Madrid. Es un barrio **bohemio**, antiguo, un poco **sucio** y **con pocas comodidades**, pero **animado** y **con mucho encanto**. Las calles son **angostas** y hay muchos bares. En general, no es un barrio caro y por eso muchos artistas y jóvenes viven aquí. En este barrio **histórico** viven también muchos inmigrantes y gente mayor. En Lavapiés hay bastantes corralas, bloques de apartamentos pequeños con un jardín interior comunitario.

Chamberí es un barrio **céntrico**, elegante y **limpio**. En la actualidad es uno de los barrios **residenciales** más caros de Madrid, con **amplias** calles y apartamentos grandes en edificios de principios del siglo xx. Tiene zonas peatonales y muchos **servicios**; hay **tiendas de lujo** y gimnasios, cines... También hay muchas cafeterías y restaurantes. Es un barrio **alegre** y **con mucha vida**, aunque un poco **ruidoso**. Es uno de los mejores barrios de Madrid para ir a cenar y salir de noche.

CHAMBERÍ

VALLECAS

Vallecas es un **barrio obrero** muy tranquilo y agradable. Hay muchos edificios de viviendas construidos en los años 60 y 70. En este barrio hay mercados, varias escuelas, muchas tiendas... Es un barrio **alejado del centro** de la ciudad, pero **está bien comunicado**. Tiene parques grandes y varios centros comerciales. Aquí vive mucha gente venida de otros lugares de España en los años 60.

))) **8.10. El barrio de Fernando.** Escucha a Fernando. ¿Vive en Lavapiés, Chamberí o Vallecas? ¿Por qué?

e **8.11. Opuestos.** En los textos de la actividad 8.9, ¿qué palabras o expresiones son opuestas a las siguientes?

1. moderno: ....

4. céntrico: ....

2. tranquilo: ....

5. limpio: ....

3. rico: ....

6. angostas: ....

8.12. Barrios y ciudades. ¿Conoces algún barrio o ciudad con estas características? Escribe los nombres.

1. Es una ciudad moderna y antigua a la vez. ....

2. Es muy caro/-a. ....

3. Tiene mucha vida, tanto de día como de noche. ....

4. Es un barrio histórico, con algunos monumentos. ....

5. Es un barrio bohemio: viven artistas y hay galerías de arte. ....

6. Es un barrio muy tranquilo y agradable. ....

7. Está mal comunicado. ....

8. Tiene mucho encanto. ....

9. Hay tiendas de lujo. ....

10. Es un barrio residencial. ....

> ❶ **¿Necesitas ayuda?**
>
> When describing a place, **tener** is used to say the facilities or amenities a place has:
>
> *¿Tu barrio **tiene** buenas tiendas?*
>
> *Este barrio **tiene** muchos museos.*

e **8.13. Completamos.** Completa estas frases con la palabra o expresión que falta.

con mucha vida	ruidoso/-a	tiendas de lujo	bien comunicado/-a

mal comunicado/-a	caro/-a	antiguo/-a

1. No duermo bien en mi casa, mi calle es muy ....

2. Mi barrio está ....: hay dos estaciones de metro y seis líneas de autobús.

3. Es un barrio muy ....: todas las tiendas de lujo están ahí.

4. Mi barrio es el más .... de la ciudad. Las casas son del siglo XVIII.

5. Mi barrio me encanta; siempre hay gente en la calle, es un barrio ....

6. El problema de mi apartamento es que está .... Necesito más de una hora para ir al trabajo.

7. Es un barrio caro; hay .... y restaurantes exclusivos.

Q **8.14. Investigamos.** Busca en internet imágenes de Lavapiés, Chamberí y Vallecas que ilustren lo que se describe en los textos de la actividad 8.9.

8.15. Compartimos. Muestra las imágenes al resto de la clase y cuenta qué se puede ver en ellas.

Esta es una foto de las calles angostas de Lavapiés.

Exploramos la lengua

Cuantificadores

8.16. Nuestro barrio. ¿Cómo es tu barrio? Marca con una cruz (**X**) la información que sea verdad.

- Mi barrio tiene **bastante** ambiente.
- Mi barrio no tiene **nada de** vida.
- En mi barrio hay **muchos** restaurantes.
- En mi barrio hay **pocas** zonas verdes.
- En mi barrio hay **demasiados** automóviles.
- En mi barrio hay **varias** escuelas.
- En mi barrio **no** hay **ninguna** iglesia.
- Las casas en mi barrio cuestan **demasiado** dinero.
- En mi barrio hay **poco** tráfico.
- En mi barrio hay **mucha contaminación**.
- En mi barrio hay **bastantes** tiendas.
- En mi barrio hay **un poco de** ruido.
- En mi barrio hay **algunas** plazas.

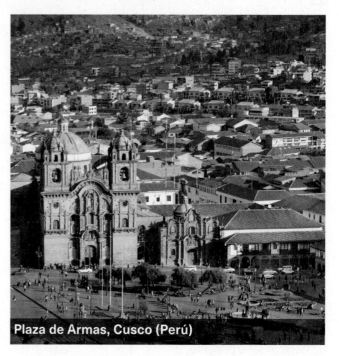

Plaza de Armas, Cusco (Perú)

e 8.17. Buscamos ejemplos. Completa el cuadro con los cuantificadores y sustantivos de la actividad 8.16.

SINGULAR		PLURAL	
Masculino	**Femenino**	**Masculino**	**Femenino**
nada de ambiente	*nada de vida*	**pocos** restaurantes	....
ningún banco	....	**algunos** mercados	....
....	**poca** vida	**varios** hospitales	....
....	**un poco de** contaminación	**bastantes** automóviles	....
algún templo	**alguna** iglesia	....	**demasiadas** viviendas
....	**bastante** vida	....	**muchas** plazas
mucho tráfico	....		
....	**demasiada** contaminación		

e **8.18. Completamos.** Elige en cada caso la opción correcta para completar las reglas.

1. bastante/s...	**a.** ... tiene la misma forma para el masculino y para el femenino.
	b. ... tiene formas distintas para el masculino y para el femenino.
2. poco/-a/s, bastante/s, mucho/-a/s, demasiado/-a/s...	**a.** ... acompaña a sustantivos incontables en singular (tráfico, contaminación...) y contables en plural (museos, casas...).
	b. ... acompaña solo a sustantivos incontables.
3. nada de / un poco de...	**a.** ... acompaña a sustantivos incontables en singular (tráfico, contaminación...) y contables en plural (museos, casas...).
	b. ... acompaña solo a sustantivos incontables.

e **8.19. Cuantificadores.** Completa estas frases en tu cuaderno con todas las opciones posibles. En algunos casos solo hay una respuesta.

1. En este barrio hay *pocos / algunos / varios / bastantes / demasiados / muchos* restaurantes.

2. En el barrio de Julia no hay .... restaurante.

3. El barrio de mis padres tiene .... plazas.

4. Tu barrio no tiene .... vida.

5. En este barrio no hay .... escuela.

6. En ese barrio hay .... tráfico.

7. En mi barrio hay .... contaminación.

8. ¿En tu barrio hay .... supermercado?

8.20. Un barrio para cada cosa. Piensa en las características de un barrio ideal para hacer estas cosas.

• Para ir de compras: *tiene un centro comercial, hay muchas...*

• Para vivir tranquilo: ....

• Para vivir con niños pequeños: ....

• Para estudiantes: ....

8.21. Nuestro barrio. Piensa en tu barrio y completa las ideas siguientes.

Mi barrio es un barrio ideal...

para ....

porque ....

para ....

porque ....

si te gusta/n ....

porque ....

---

❶ ¿Necesitas ayuda?

Countable nouns refer to things that can be counted with numbers (in English, **many** is used with these nouns). Uncountable nouns refer to things like qualities, abstract ideas, or objects that cannot be counted (liquids, powders...). Uncountable nouns are generally used in singular (in English, **much** is used with these nouns).

❶ ¿Necesitas ayuda?

Remember that in Spanish **para** is used to express a purpose; whereas **porque** is used to express a reason.

Para is followed by an infinitive verb.

*Este es mi barrio preferido **para** salir.*

Para is followed by a noun to express the beneficiary of an action.

*Este barrio es ideal **para** estudiantes.*

Porque introduces a clause that explains the reason why.

*Mi barrio es turístico **porque** tiene muchos monumentos.*

Exploramos la lengua

Pedir y dar información sobre la ubicación

8.22. Indicaciones. En estas conversaciones, cuatro personas preguntan cómo llegar a diferentes lugares. Relaciona las indicaciones que les dan con los planos.

1
- *Disculpe, ¿sabe si hay alguna farmacia por aquí?*
- *Sí, a ver... En la segunda calle **a la derecha**. Está justo **en la esquina**.*

2
- *Disculpa, ¿sabes si el hospital está por aquí **cerca**?*
- *¿El hospital? Sí, mira: Sigues **derecho** y está al final de esta calle, **al lado de** la universidad.*

3
- *Disculpa, ¿sabes si hay una estación de metro cerca?*
- *Cerca, no. Hay una, pero está un poco **lejos**, a unos diez minutos de aquí.*

4
- *Disculpe, ¿la biblioteca está en esta calle?*
- *Sí, pero al final. Sigues derecho hasta la plaza y está en la misma plaza, **a la izquierda**.*

❶ ¿Necesitas ayuda?

In Spanish, when asking any information to people you do not know, you need to decide whether a formal (**usted**) or an informal (**tú**) address is required.

💬 Para comunicar

To get someone's attention, we use:
disculpe/perdone (formal)
disculpa/perdona (informal)

If we are not sure if the person will know the answer, we use:
¿Sabe/sabes si...? = *Do you know if...?*

e 8.23. Ubicación, dirección y distancia. Observa las expresiones que están en negrita en los diálogos de la actividad 8.22. Expresan ubicación, dirección o distancia. Úsalas para escribir dónde está la casa.

a la izquierda

)) 8.24. Representamos. Escuchen los diálogos de la actividad 8.22 y represéntenlos.

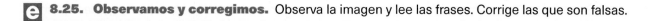

e **8.25. Observamos y corregimos.** Observa la imagen y lee las frases. Corrige las que son falsas.

1. El cine está a la izquierda de la escuela.
2. La estación de metro está al lado del restaurante.
3. El museo está lejos del restaurante.
4. El cine está en una esquina.
5. El metro está a la derecha del banco.
6. El mercado está en la avenida de América.

8.26. Pedir y dar información sobre la ubicación. En parejas, observen de nuevo la imagen de la actividad 8.25 e imaginen que están en la puerta de la escuela. Por turnos, háganse estas preguntas. Su compañero/-a les responde.

1. ¿Hay alguna farmacia por aquí cerca?
2. Perdone, ¿sabe dónde está el hospital?
3. Perdona, ¿el museo está muy lejos de aquí?
4. ¿Sabe si hay un banco cerca de aquí?
5. ¿En este barrio no hay ningún restaurante?
6. Perdona, ¿sabes dónde está la estación de metro?
7. Disculpe, ¿la plaza de Bolívar?
8. Perdone, ¿la biblioteca está cerca de aquí?
9. ¿Sabe si hay algún mercado por aquí?
10. Disculpa, ¿la avenida de América está por aquí cerca?

• *¿Hay alguna farmacia por aquí cerca?*
○ *Cerca, no... Lo siento.*

Comunicamos

Ciudades con encanto

8.27. Tres ciudades. Tres personas nos hablan de su ciudad. ¿En cuál de estas ciudades te gustaría vivir? ¿Por qué? Coméntenlo en pequeños grupos.

ME ENCANTA MI CIUDAD

BUENOS AIRES (ARGENTINA)

Aquí se vive muy bien. Buenos Aires es una ciudad alegre, con mucha vida y llena de contrastes: modernos rascacielos en Puerto Madero, casas de colores en La Boca o arquitectura colonial de estilo francés en el barrio de La Recoleta. Hay muchos monumentos y lugares para visitar, como la Casa Rosada, la Plaza de Mayo o el mercado de San Telmo. También hay muchos lugares para comer bien y salir al teatro o a bailar.

Mis recomendaciones: una visita por las librerías de la ciudad, especialmente la librería Ateneo Grand Splendid.

JULIÁN CABALLERO

SANTIAGO (CHILE)

Santiago está muy bien situada: a una hora y media del mar y a una hora y media de las montañas. También es una ciudad bien comunicada, con una buena red de metro y de autobuses. Uno de los lugares que más me gusta de Santiago es el cerro San Cristóbal, un mirador natural con una vista increíble. También hay edificios muy bonitos, como la catedral, el palacio de La Moneda o el castillo Hidalgo, en el cerro Santa Lucía. Además, tiene buen tiempo todo el año.

Mis recomendaciones: disfrutar de la vida nocturna de los barrios de Lastarria y Bellavista.

ESTHER RUIZ

MONTEVIDEO (URUGUAY)

Montevideo es una ciudad tranquila. Tiene un casco antiguo muy lindo, con monumentos y lugares de interés turístico, como el palacio Salvo en Plaza Independencia, el Cabildo o el teatro Solís. Dos de mis lugares favoritos de la ciudad son la peatonal Sarandí, la principal calle peatonal de la ciudad vieja, y la rambla, una avenida que conecta la ciudad con playas y poblaciones cercanas. También hay muchos restaurantes donde se come muy bien.

Mis recomendaciones: un paseo gastronómico por el mercado del puerto para probar comidas típicas. Es un lugar con mucho ambiente nocturno.

NICOLÁS IGLESIAS

> Me gustaría vivir en Buenos Aires porque tiene mucha vida y para mí eso es importante...

> ❶ **¿Necesitas ayuda?**
> Remember: **Me gustaría** + infinitive = *I would like to (do something)*

8.28. Más sobre... Vas a escuchar una conversación entre dos amigas. ¿De cuál de las tres ciudades hablan? ¿Qué más dicen sobre ella?

8.29. Elegimos una ciudad e investigamos. Busca en internet más información (población, dónde está, etc.) sobre una de las tres ciudades de la actividad 8.27 y expónsela a tus compañeros/-as.

Compartimos lugares interesantes

 8.30. Lugares interesantes. Piensa en lugares interesantes de tu ciudad (una tienda, un restaurante, etc.). Luego, con un mapa, cuenta a tus compañeros/-as dónde están.

> • *Yo voy mucho a un club que se llama Ritmo latino. Ponen música en español todos los viernes y no es muy caro. Está en el puerto.*
> ○ *Pues en mi barrio hay una tienda de productos ecológicos muy buena. Está muy cerca de...*

Nuestra ciudad

 8.31. Creamos un mapa mental. En grupos, creen un mapa mental sobre la ciudad en la que están.

 8.32. Presentamos nuestro mapa mental. Presenten su mapa mental al resto de la clase. En cada nueva presentación, tomen nota de la información nueva.

 8.33. Lo bueno y lo malo. ¿Cuáles son los puntos fuertes de su ciudad? ¿Qué cosas negativas tiene? Coméntenlo entre todos a partir de la información de los mapas que crearon.

Ahora podemos...

Imaginar y describir un barrio ideal

8.34. Nuestro barrio ideal. En grupos van a imaginar su barrio ideal. Primero, completen esta ficha.

Cómo se llama: ....

Dónde está: ....

Cómo es: ....

Qué hay: ....

8.35. Presentamos nuestro barrio ideal. Ahora dibujen un plano para explicar al resto de la clase cómo es ese barrio. Los demás pueden hacer preguntas.

> **Para comunicar**
>
> Nuestro barrio...
>
> **es...**
> **muy** tranquilo
> **bastante** agradable
>
> **está...**
> **cerca de** la playa
> **lejos de** la montaña
> **en** el centro
> **al lado de** un río
>
> **En** nuestro barrio **hay...**
> **mucho/-a** tráfico
> **bastante** gente
> **poco/-a** ambiente
>
> **muchos/-as** parques
> **bastantes** plazas
> **varios/-as** escuelas
> **algunos/-as** bares
>
> **es** un barrio...
> con encanto
> bien comunicado
> moderno
>
> **En** nuestro barrio **no hay...**
> **ningún** parque
> **ninguna** iglesia
> bares **ni** restaurantes

> *Nuestro barrio se llama Marina Linda y está al lado del mar, a 20 kilómetros de Malibú, en California. Es un barrio muy lindo. En Marina Linda hay muchos restaurantes...*

8.36. Decidimos cuál es el mejor barrio. Entre todos, van a decidir cuál es el mejor barrio de todos.

> *Yo elijo el barrio Marina Linda, porque tiene muchos bares y restaurantes. **Lo que más me gusta** de este barrio es que está al lado del mar.*

Video

La ciudad mágica

Aunque conoce más de 30 países, la bloguera y viajera Elizabeth Garcia siempre descubre cosas nuevas en Miami, su ciudad natal. En *La ciudad mágica*, esta joven con herencia hondureña y cubana nos muestra los lugares más multiculturales de la ciudad.

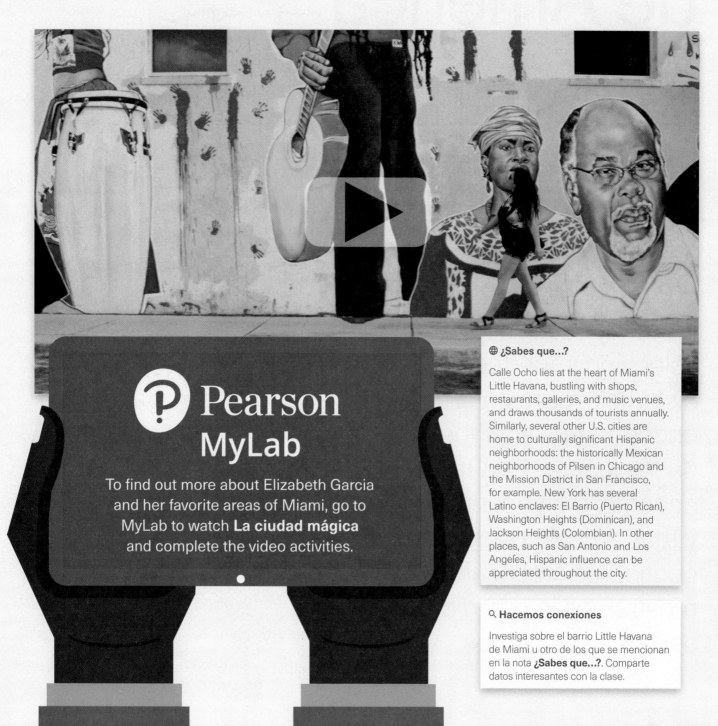

Pearson MyLab

To find out more about Elizabeth Garcia and her favorite areas of Miami, go to MyLab to watch **La ciudad mágica** and complete the video activities.

⊕ ¿Sabes que...?

Calle Ocho lies at the heart of Miami's Little Havana, bustling with shops, restaurants, galleries, and music venues, and draws thousands of tourists annually. Similarly, several other U.S. cities are home to culturally significant Hispanic neighborhoods: the historically Mexican neighborhoods of Pilsen in Chicago and the Mission District in San Francisco, for example. New York has several Latino enclaves: El Barrio (Puerto Rican), Washington Heights (Dominican), and Jackson Heights (Colombian). In other places, such as San Antonio and Los Angeles, Hispanic influence can be appreciated throughout the city.

⌕ Hacemos conexiones

Investiga sobre el barrio Little Havana de Miami u otro de los que se mencionan en la nota **¿Sabes que...?**. Comparte datos interesantes con la clase.

Los barrios más bonitos de América Latina

La revista *Condé Nast Traveler* publicó recientemente una lista de los barrios más bonitos de América Latina. Como todas las listas, es una selección imperfecta y discutible, pero en ella encontramos algunos de los lugares con más encanto, más bohemios y más auténticos del continente americano. Aquí mostramos lo que dice de seis de esos barrios.

La Candelaria
Bogotá, Colombia

Un barrio de poetas

Uno de los barrios con más encanto de América Latina está en Bogotá: La Candelaria, un *collage* de casas de colores que ocupan el centro histórico de la capital colombiana. La Candelaria tiene mucha vida: hay cafés bohemios, galerías de arte, centros culturales...

Puerto Madero
Buenos Aires, Argentina

El barrio más joven de Buenos Aires

Puerto Madero, sobre el Río de la Plata, es uno de los 48 barrios de Buenos Aires y uno de los más valorados por turistas y por gente local. Es un barrio con mucho ambiente, con numerosos bares, restaurantes, discotecas y boutiques. Sus calles llevan el nombre de mujeres importantes de la historia de Argentina.

La Habana Vieja
La Habana, Cuba

La esencia de Cuba
La Habana Vieja es la zona más antigua de la capital cubana. Este histórico barrio está lleno de angostas callejuelas de piedra que nos llevan a edificios coloniales, barrocos y *art déco*.

Miraflores
Lima, Perú

El pulmón de la ciudad
Miraflores es el barrio más *fashion* de la ciudad de Lima. Con unas espectaculares vistas al océano, aquí descubrimos las tiendas más caras de la ciudad, buenos restaurantes y muchas zonas verdes y parques. El más representativo es el parque del Amor.

Coyoacán
Ciudad de México

Cultura, arte y música
Al sur de Ciudad de México está Coyoacán. En este barrio bohemio encontramos buenos cafés, librerías, restaurantes y unas fiestas populares muy vistosas. Una visita obligada: La Casa Azul - Museo de Frida Kahlo.

Diez barrios más

Barranco (Lima, Perú): un barrio muy bohemio; **Bellavista** (Santiago de Chile): gastronomía y diversión; **Barrio del SoFo** (San Juan, Puerto Rico): barrio de *flea markets*; **San Telmo** (Buenos Aires, Argentina): mítico y colonial; **La Boca** (Buenos Aires, Argentina): el más bohemio de la ciudad; **El Malecón** (La Habana, Cuba): atardeceres con música cubana; **Nuevo Polanco**: el barrio de moda de Ciudad de México; **Ciudad Vieja** (Montevideo, Uruguay): un barrio renovado; **Casco Viejo** (Ciudad de Panamá, Panamá): casitas coloniales y ambiente *hipster*; **Zona Colonial** (Santo Domingo, Rep. Dominicana): el origen del Nuevo Mundo.

ANTES DE LEER

8.37. Ciudades turísticas. ¿Qué ciudades de América Latina son un destino turístico popular? ¿Conoces alguna?

LECTURA ACTIVA

8.38. Opinamos. Lee la introducción. ¿Qué opinas tú sobre las listas y los *rankings*? ¿Crees que son útiles?

8.39. Situamos en un mapa. Sitúa en un mapa las cinco ciudades que se muestran.

8.40. Leemos y observamos. Identifica en las fotografías elementos mencionados en los textos.

8.41. Nuestros intereses. Señala en los textos qué características y lugares consideras más atractivos cuando visitas una ciudad. Luego, coméntalo con tus compañeros/-as.

- *Cuando viajo, me gusta ir a museos, pero las tiendas, por ejemplo, no me interesan nada.*
- *A mí tampoco. A mí me interesan los barrios históricos...*

8.42. Otros barrios. Lee los nombres de los otros diez barrios de la lista. ¿Qué barrio te parece más atractivo? ¿Cuál menos? ¿Por qué?

DESPUÉS DE LEER

 8.43. Barrios de nuestro país. En grupo, preparen su lista de los cinco barrios más bonitos de su país.

Textos escritos: leemos y escribimos

Leemos sobre un fenómeno mundial

ANTES DE LA LECTURA

8.44. Preparación. ¿Sabes qué es la **gentrificación**? Selecciona la definición que crees es la correcta.

1. Es un cambio que ocurre en un barrio obrero para mejorar las condiciones de vida, pero tiene como consecuencia hacer más cara la renta y los servicios. Como resultado, las personas que viven ahí tienen que mudarse a otro barrio más barato. El barrio, entonces, se vuelve un barrio para personas con más dinero.
2. Es un cambio que ocurre en un barrio rico en el centro de la ciudad y que se vuelve ruidoso, sucio y peligroso con el tiempo. Como resultado, las personas que viven ahí tienen que mudarse a un barrio más seguro pero alejado del centro y en la periferia de la ciudad. El barrio, entonces, se vuelve un barrio con pocas comodidades y con malos servicios.

LECTURA ACTIVA

8.45. Lectura. Lee este artículo para informarte sobre la gentrificación y comprobar tu respuesta de la actividad 8.44.

Gentrificación: ¿Qué es y cómo afecta a la vida de la ciudad?
Por: yaencontre

Los barrios cambian con el tiempo, y muchas veces los propios gobiernos propician estos cambios para mejorar la calidad de vida. El problema es que a veces se revaloriza y encarece de una manera insostenible para los vecinos.

Cuando se habla de la vida en las ciudades y de cómo está evolucionando, muchas veces aparece la palabra gentrificación. Es uno de los cambios a los que se enfrentan las grandes urbes, y, a medida que pasa el tiempo, se intensifica. Aunque algunos la consideran positiva, la mayoría sigue viéndola como un problema para los vecinos.

Qué es la gentrificación
El término gentrificación hace referencia al proceso de revalorización de un barrio donde normalmente viven personas de clase obrera que se ven desplazadas por población de mayor nivel adquisitivo.

Algunos consideran este fenómeno como algo positivo porque revaloriza las zonas. Pero la parte negativa afecta a los residentes originarios de la zona. Todo se encarece: los apartamentos, los locales, los alquileres... incluso los bares y tiendas. Eso hace que muchos tengan que irse de su barrio de toda la vida por no poder afrontar el precio.

Lo que hace este proceso es trasladar gran parte de la vida de las zonas céntricas a las periféricas, donde la vida es más barata. Sí es cierto que si se hace de manera controlada, puede ser bueno para los propios vecinos, pues en muchas ocasiones lo que se intenta es apartar lo negativo del barrio y culturizarlo. En algunos casos, por ejemplo, llevan universidades y centros culturales a zonas conflictivas para darles más vida y mejorar el ambiente.

Por tanto, se puede considerar bueno para una ciudad si se hace para evitar que haya zonas consideradas malas o peligrosas. Pero si lo que se pretende es atraer a gente de mayor nivel adquisitivo, el resultado es que los vecinos de siempre tienen que abandonar su lugar natural de residencia.

Fuente del texto: https://www.yaencontre.com/noticias/vivienda/gentrificacion-que-es/

8.46. Idea principal. Observa la fotografía, lee el título y lee otra vez los dos primeros párrafos. ¿Qué idea quieren transmitir?

1. Las ciudades evolucionan con el tiempo y las consecuencias son negativas.

2. Las ciudades cambian con el tiempo y las consecuencias son positivas y negativas.

3. La gentrificación es un cambio positivo para la gente en las grandes ciudades.

8.47. Interpretación. Dos conceptos clave en este artículo son **revalorizar** y **encarecer** (aparecen en los párrafos 1 a 4). Lee de nuevo los párrafos donde aparecen y con base en el significado de **revalorizar** y **encarecer** y el argumento del texto, ¿qué interpretación tiene la frase "**se revaloriza el barrio**"?

1. El barrio cambia de valor: pasa a ser más caro.

2. El barrio cambia de valor: pasa a ser menos caro.

8.48. Selección de información. Lee el resto del artículo y escribe en tu cuaderno la respuesta a estas preguntas.

1. ¿Qué cosas se encarecen como resultado de la gentrificación?
2. ¿Qué aspecto positivo tiene la gentrificación si se hace de manera controlada?
3. ¿Qué consecuencia de la gentrificación afecta negativamente a la vida de las personas que viven en un barrio?

DESPUÉS DE LEER

8.49. Reacción. Usando información específica del texto, escribe tu reacción personal sobre cómo afecta la gentrificación a las ciudades.

En mi opinión, la gentrificación tiene más efectos positivos que negativos porque...
En mi opinión la gentrificación tiene más efectos negativos que positivos porque...

Creamos una infografía sobre la gentrificación

8.50. Infografía. Tienes que crear una infografía para un sitio web donde explicas qué es la gentrificación y sus consecuencias. Usa la información del texto "Gentrificación: ¿Qué es y cómo afecta a la vida de la ciudad?" y con tus propias palabras debes:

- Explicar qué es la gentrificación.
- Hablar de los aspectos positivos.
- Hablar de los aspectos negativos.
- Explicar las consecuencias si no es controlada.
- Incluir algunas imágenes para facilitar la comprensión.
- Incluir la fuente de información (es decir, el nombre del artículo que leíste y dónde se puede encontrar).

> **❶ ¿Necesitas ayuda?**
>
> Remember that an infographic is a combination of images and short, easy-to-understand texts used to present information.

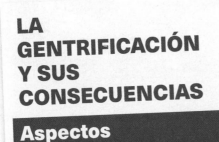

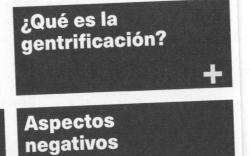

Recursos lingüísticos

EXPRESSING QUANTITY (HOW MUCH OR HOW MANY OF SOMETHING)

QUANTIFIERS + UNCOUNTABLE NOUNS

demasiado ruido / **demasiada** gente = *too much noise / too many people*
mucho ruido / **mucha** gente = *a lot of noise / a lot of people*
bastante ruido / gente = *quite a lot of noise / quite a lof of people*
un poco de ruido / gente = *a little noise / a few people*
poco ruido / **poca** gente = *little noise / few people*
nada de ruido / gente = *no noise / no people*

QUANTIFIERS + COUNTABLE NOUNS

demasiados restaurantes / **demasiadas** tiendas = *too many restaurants/stores*
muchos restaurantes / **muchas** tiendas = *many restaurants/stores*
bastantes restaurantes/tiendas = *enough restaurants/stores*
varios restaurantes / **varias** tiendas = *various restaurants/stores*
pocos restaurantes / **pocas** tiendas = *few restaurants/stores*
algún restaurante / **alguna** tienda / **algunos** restaurantes / **algunas** tiendas = *some restaurants/stores*
ningún restaurante / **ninguna** tienda = *no restaurants/stores*

▶ Remember that to say **a** and **some** we use **un**, **uno/-a** (singular), and **unos/-as** (plural). **Un** is used for a masculine singular noun when it appears before the actual noun. However, when it replaces the noun, it takes the full form **uno** and in English it is translated as **one**.

● *Disculpe, ¿hay **un** estacionamiento por aquí cerca?* = Excuse me, is there a parking garage near here?
○ *¿Un estacionamiento? Sí, al final de esta calle hay **uno**.* = Yes, there is one at the end of this street.

▶ When asking questions, **un** can become **algún** (masculine) or **alguna** (feminine) in Spanish:

*Perdone, ¿sabe si hay **alguna** tienda en esta calle?* = Excuse me, do you know if is there a store on this street?

▶ When the answer (or the question) is negative, we use **ningún/-a** to say that there isn't any:

*No, creo que no hay **ningún** parque por aquí.* = No, I don´t think there is a (any) park near here.
*No, creo que no hay **ninguna** farmacia por aquí.* = No, I don´t think there is a (any) pharmacy near here.

▶ In the same way that **un** becames **uno** when replacing the noun it refers to, **algún** and **ningún** become **alguno** and **ninguno**:

● *En mi barrio no hay ningún hospital, ¿en tu barrio hay **alguno**?*
○ *No, no hay **ninguno**.*

Zona Colonial es un barrio de Santo Domingo con mucha vida.

ASKING FOR AND GIVING INFORMATION ABOUT LOCATION

In Spanish, when asking for directions (as well as when asking for any other information to people you do not know), you need to be aware of the formal and informal ways of addressing people.

*Disculp**a**, ¿**sabes** si hay una parada de autobús por aquí cerca? (informal)*	= Excuse me, do you know if there is a bus stop near here?
*Perdon**e**, ¿**sabe** si hay una parada de autobús por aquí cerca? (formal)*	

Está a	unos 20 minutos **a pie / en metro / en auto**. = *by foot/subway/car*
	(unos) 200 metros **de aquí**. = *from here*
Está	muy **lejos**. = *very far*
	bastante **lejos**. = *rather far*
	un poco **lejos**. = *a little far*
	bastante **cerca**. = *rather close*
	muy **cerca**. = *very close*
	aquí al lado. = *close by here*
	aquí mismo. = *right here*

- *¿La universidad está **muy lejos de aquí**?* = Is the university very far from here?
- *No. **Está aquí al lado. A cinco minutos a pie**.* = No. It's close by here. Five minutes by foot (A five-minute walk).

Todo derecho/recto = *all straight*	**En** la esquina = *on/at the corner*
A la derecha (de...) = *on the right (of)*	**En** la plaza... = *in/at the square*
A la izquierda (de...) = *on the left (of)*	**En** la calle... = *on the street*
Al lado (de...) = *next to*	**En** la avenida... = *on the avenue*
Al final de la calle = *at the end of the street*	**En** el paseo... = *on the promenade*
La primera / la segunda... (calle) a la derecha/izquierda... = *the first/second street on the right/left*	

PREPOSITIONS OF PLACE: A, EN, DE, DESDE, HASTA, POR

a	direction	Vamos **a** Asunción.
	distance	Loja está **a** 55 kilómetros de aquí.
en	location	Godoy Cruz está **en** la provincia de Mendoza.
	means of transportation	Vamos **en** auto.
de	origin	Venimos **de** la universidad.
	position with reference to another point	Caracas está lejos **de** Lima.
desde	starting point	Vengo a pie **desde** el centro.
hasta	point of arrival	Podemos ir en metro **hasta** el centro.
por	movement within a space	Me gusta pasear **por** la playa.
	movement through a space	Hay un gato que siempre entra **por** la ventana.

Pronunciamos

Palabras agudas, llanas y esdrújulas

8.51. Escuchamos. Escucha estas palabras. ¿Qué sílaba es más prominente: la antepenúltima (1), la penúltima (2) o la última (3)? Clasifícalas.

típico · ciudad · dólar · café · isla · interés · importante · capital · concurso · lugar

Tucumán · moneda · calor · Galápagos · población · México · simpática · húmedo · después

autobús · también · allí · infusión · Pacífico · América · región · Perú · kilómetro

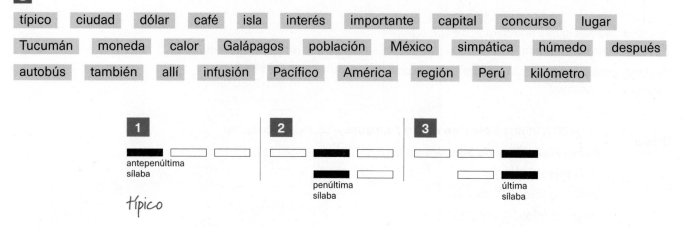

8.52. Entendemos las reglas. Lee estas reglas y asegúrate de que las entiendes con la ayuda de tus compañeros/-as y de tu profesor/a.

> **1** Words with the accent on the third-from-last syllable are always written with an accent over the vowel to indicate the stress. These words are referred to as **esdrújulas**.
>
> **2** Words with the accent on the next-to-last syllable are written with an accent when they do not end in **-n**, **-s**, or a **vowel**. These words are referred to as **llanas**.
>
> **3** Words with the accent on the last syllable are written with an accent over the vowel when they end in **-n**, **-s**, or a **vowel**. These words are referred to as **agudas**.

8.53. Escuchamos y pronunciamos. Escucha de nuevo las palabras de la actividad 8.51 y pronúncialas poniendo atención a la sílaba fuerte.

8.54. Buscamos ejemplos. Busca otros ejemplos en el libro y clasifícalos en una tabla.

1 (esdrújulas)	2 (llanas)	3 (agudas)

8.55. Pronunciamos. Ahora lee en voz alta las palabras que encontraste en la actividad 8.54. Presta especial atención a la pronunciación de la sílaba fuerte.

Vocabulario activo

Describir ciudades, barrios y países
Describing towns, neighborhoods and cities

- **alegre** *lively*
- **alejado/-a del centro** *away from the city center*
- **amplio/-a** *wide*
- **angosto/-a** *narrow*
- **animado/-a** *bustling*
- **antiguo/-a** *old, ancient*
- **el barrio obrero** *working-class neighborhood*
- **el barrio residencial** *residential neighborhood*
- **bohemio/-a** *bohemian*
- **céntrico/-a** *central*
- **con mucha vida** (la vida) *very lively*
- **con mucho encanto** (el encanto) *very charming*
- **con pocas comodidades** (la comodidad) *with few amenities*
- **la contaminación** *pollution*
- **está bien/mal comunicado/-a** *to have easy/ difficult access to other areas (easy access to public transportation)*
- **histórico/-a** *historic*
- **limpio/-a** *clean*
- **pobre** *poor*
- **rico/-a** *rich*
- **ruidoso/-a** *noisy*
- **los servicios** *services*
- **sucio/-a** *dirty*

Servicios y lugares de las ciudades
Services and places to go in a city

- **el apartamento** *apartment*
- **la avenida** *avenue*
- **el banco** *bank*
- **el bar** *pub*
- **la biblioteca** *library*
- **el bloque de apartamentos** *apartment building*
- **el cajero automático** *ATM*
- **la calle** *street*
- **el casco antiguo** *old (part of) town*
- **el centro comercial** *mall*
- **la cuadra** *block*
- **el edificio** *building*
- **la escuela** *school*
- **la estación de metro** (el metro) *metro station*
- **el estacionamiento** *parking lot, parking garage*
- **la farmacia** *pharmacy*
- **el gimnasio** *gym*
- **el hospital** *hospital*
- **la iglesia** *church*
- **la librería** *bookstore*
- **la mezquita** *mosque*
- **la oficina de correos** (el correo) *post office*
- **la parada de autobús** (el autobús) *bus stop*
- **el parque** *park*
- **el paseo** *promenade*
- **la plaza** *square*
- **el rascacielos** *high rise, skyscraper*
- **el restaurante** *restaurant*
- **la sinagoga** *synagogue*
- **el supermercado** *supermarket*
- **la tienda de lujo** (el lujo) *luxury store (boutique)*
- **la tienda de ropa** *clothing store*
- **la vivienda** *home*
- **la zona peatonal** *pedestrian zone*
- **las zonas verdes** *green zones*

⚙ **Estrategia**

Do you like to travel? Would you like to visit a Spanish-speaking country? It might be a good idea to start creating your own travel guide. Select places or cities you would like to visit and take notes in Spanish about them.

Lección

Como en casa

IN THIS LESSON WE ARE GOING TO

design a place to live

LEARNING OUTCOMES
You will be able to…

- express likes and dislikes

- describe a house

- locate objects in a room

VOCABULARY

- Types of housing

- Parts of a house

- Furniture and decorative articles

- Shapes, styles, and materials

LANGUAGE STRUCTURES

- Prepositions and adverbs of place: **sin, con, debajo, encima, detrás, delante…**

- Comparatives

PRONUNCIATION

- Pronouncing letters **c/qu/z, r/rr,** and **j/g**

CULTURAL CONNECTIONS

- Famous house museums: Pablo Neruda, Frida Kahlo, Simón Bolívar

Patio de una vivienda particular en Córdoba (España).

Primer contacto

9.1. Tipos de vivienda. Observen estos anuncios de viviendas en México. ¿Qué casa prefieren? ¿Por qué? Coméntenlo en parejas.

- El **condominio**
- La **casa**

- El departamento
- La **villa**

- *A mí, me gusta la villa en Mérida, porque es muy grande.*
- *Pues yo prefiero el departamento, porque...*

Se vende casa en Puerto Vallarta (Jalisco). 180 m². Precio: $280,000.00.

Se vende villa en Mérida, (Yucatán). 650 m². Precio: $985,000.00.

Se vende condominio en Puerto Vallarta (Jalisco). 304 m². Precio: $599,000.00.

Se vende departamento en Monterrey (Nuevo León). 63 m². Precio: $109,000.00.

9.2. ¿Dónde vives? ¿En qué tipo de casa vives ahora? Coméntalo con la clase.

Yo vivo en un departamento con otros estudiantes.

Comprendemos el vocabulario

Partes y características de la casa

))) **9.3. Anuncios de viviendas.** Lee y escucha estos anuncios de viviendas.

CASA
¡GRAN OPORTUNIDAD!
$3500/mes

Casa de nueva construcción.
367 m² y 250 de jardín.
**Dos plantas + garaje
doble. Antesala, cuarto de
estudio, 3 baños, lavadero,
cocina, sala-comedor de
60 m², terraza de 40 m²,
5 habitaciones, sala de
juegos. Con calefacción
y aire acondicionado.
Ventanas de aluminio en
toda la casa.**

OTRAS OFERTAS

Ático de 85 m² **en perfecto estado**. 2 terrazas (una de 20 m²).
3 habitaciones, cocina totalmente **equipada**, baño. $1200/mes.

Estudio de 40 m². **Sin amueblar. Elevador. Bien ubicado** y muy
luminoso. 1 habitación. Edificio antiguo, **céntrico** y con encanto.
Terraza **con vista**. $500/mes.

Apartamento **amueblado** de 80 m² **a cinco minutos de** la playa. Sala-
comedor, 2 habitaciones, **cocina americana, balcón** con fantástica
vista. $850/mes.

Apartamento de 110 m². Muy bien comunicado. Muy tranquilo. **Buena
distribución**: 3 habitaciones, 2 baños, **amplia sala, comedor** y balcón.
Espacioso y con mucho sol. **Listo para entrar a vivir.** $1300/mes.

Apartamento de 60 m², a 5 minutos del mar, 2 habitaciones, 1 baño,
1 sala-comedor de 16 m². $600/mes.

⚙ **Estrategia**

Remember you are not
expected to know all the
new vocabulary in context.
When in doubt, look it up!

❗ **¿Necesitas ayuda?**

1 square meter = 10.76
square feet

40 square meters = 430.55
square feet

🌐 **La variedad del español**

habitación = dormitorio,
cuarto, recámara (Mx).

9.4. Las partes de la casa. Lee de nuevo el primer anuncio e identifica algunas partes de la casa.

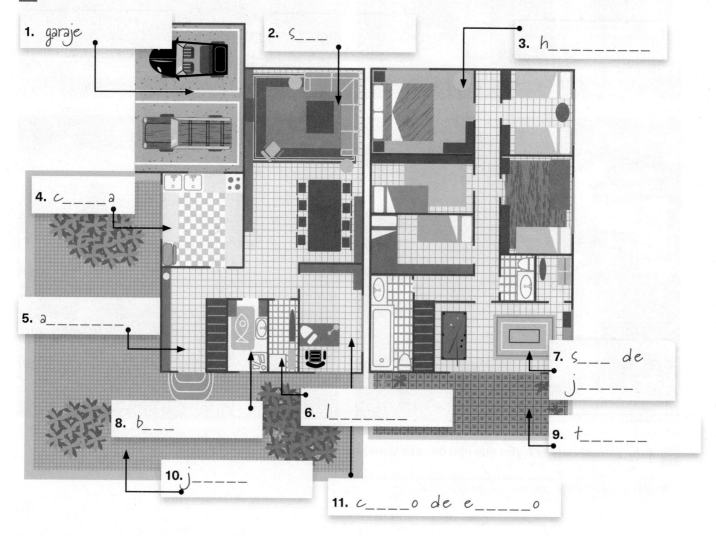

1. garaje
2. s___
3. h_____
4. c_____a
5. a_____
6. l_____
7. s___ de j_____
8. b___
9. t_____
10. j_____
11. c____o de e_____o

e **9.5. La palabra adecuada.** Completa las frases con la palabra adecuada.

1. En esta parte de mi casa, duermo. Es mi ....

2. Estaciono mi auto en esta parte de mi casa. Es mi ....

3. Para subir al piso 10 de mi edificio uso el ....

4. Mi abuela no vive en una casa. Ella vive en un .... en un edificio.

5. Mi cocina tiene mucha luz. Es muy ....

9.6. ¿Qué es? Ahora escribe frases como las de la actividad 9.5: describe una parte o característica de una casa y otra persona tiene que adivinar qué palabra falta.

9.7. La mejor vivienda para… Lee de nuevo el apartado "Otras ofertas" en los anuncios de la actividad 9.3. ¿Cuál de las viviendas crees que es más adecuada para estas personas? Coméntalo con otra persona de la clase.

LAURA CAPDEVILA (40):
psicóloga
ÁLVARO PÉREZ (43):
director de una empresa
HIJOS: 2 (6 y 4 años)
AFICIONES: bicicleta, tenis, pasear
NIVEL ADQUISITIVO: alto
OTROS: Laura trabaja en casa

CARLOS DOMÍNGUEZ (39):
profesor de inglés
MIGUEL RUIZ (37): músico
HIJOS: 1 (9 meses)
AFICIONES: cine, museos, nadar
NIVEL ADQUISITIVO: medio
OTROS: tienen un perro

RAÚL TORRES (23):
repartidor de pizzas
HIJOS: no
AFICIONES: pescar, básquetbol
NIVEL ADQUISITIVO: medio-bajo
OTROS: tiene dos gatos y
un perro pequeño

- *Para Laura y Álvaro, el ático.*
○ *No sé, tienen dos hijos y...*

9.8. La casa de Julián. Julián habla con Sara de su nueva casa. Escucha y completa las frases.

La casa de Julián...

- es ....
....

- está ....
....

- tiene ....
....

9.9. Lo que más nos gusta. Cuenta a otra persona qué tres cosas de la casa de Julián te gustan más.

Comprendemos el vocabulario

Muebles, formas, estilos y materiales

))) **9.10. En la casa.** Observa, lee y escucha.

e

1. la planta
2. la lámpara de pie **negra**
3. la pared **azul**
4. la lámpara de techo **negra de metal**
5. la mesa de madera **para ocho personas**
6. las sillas **de madera en varios colores**

7. la cama doble
8. el sofá de tela *beige* **de tres plazas**
9. los cojines **en varios colores**
10. el jarrón **negro** de cerámica
11. la mesa de centro **redonda de vidrio y madera**
12. la alfombra **de colores**
13. el piso **de madera**

⊕ **La variedad del español**

librero = **biblioteca** (Ch, Ar, Co, Ve...), **estante** (Bo, Cu...), **librera** (ES), **estantería** (Es, Ur), **librería** (Es, Pe)

tina = **bañera** (Es), **bañadera** (Cu, Ar)

regadera = **ducha** (Es)

lavadora = **lavarropa** (Ar, Ur)

alfombra = **tapete** (Mx)

Más palabras

))) **MUEBLES Y ELECTRODOMÉSTICOS** = *FURNITURE AND APPLIANCES*

el clóset = *closet*
el escritorio = *desk*
el espejo = *mirror*
la lavadora = *washing machine*
el lavaplatos = *dishwasher*
el librero = *bookcase*
la mesita de noche = *nightstand*
el microondas = *microwave oven*

el refrigerador = *refrigerator*
la regadera = *shower*
la secadora = *dryer*
el sillón = *armchair*
la tina = *bathtub*

CARACTERÍSTICAS = *CHARACTERISTICS*

acogedor/a = *cozy*
cómodo/-a = *comfortable*
cuadrado/-a = *square*
de estilo industrial/minimalista... = *industrial/minimalist... style*
frío/-a = *cool*
de piel = *(made of) leather*

9.11. Comparamos. ¿Cuáles de las cosas de la actividad 9.10 tienes en el lugar donde vives o en casa de tu familia? Escribe frases comparándolas.

En mi casa tengo una alfombra, pero es negra.

e **9.12. ¿De qué material es?** Escribe de qué material son estos muebles. Se pueden repetir.

| de madera | de tela | de vidrio | de piel | de metal | de plástico | de cerámica |

1. El cojín es de...

9.13. Escuchamos. Marta y Sebastián hablan sobre la vivienda de la actividad 9.10. Marca quién hace cada valoración.

	Marta	Sebastián
1. No me gusta nada el color de las paredes.		
2. El sofá parece cómodo.		
3. Me encanta la lámpara de estilo industrial.		
4. Es acogedor y muy luminoso.		
5. Para mí, es demasiado moderno.		
6. Me parece un poco frío.		
7. Me gustan las sillas en varios colores.		

9.14. Opinamos. En parejas, observen el apartamento de la actividad 9.10 y expresen su opinión sobre el ambiente, los muebles y la decoración.

• *Es muy moderno. A mí me gusta mucho.*
○ *A mí, no. Para mí, es un poco frío.*
• *¿Y qué te parecen los muebles?*
○ *El sofá me encanta. Es grande, moderno y parece cómodo.*

💬 **Para comunicar**

Think about other adjectives you've learned that you can use to describe a room and its furniture. Here are a few:

elegante	**original**
moderno/-a	**lindo/-a**
clásico/-a	**feo/-a**

Exploramos la lengua

Preposiciones y adverbios de lugar

e **9.15. Dos salas.** Observa estas dos salas y la localización de los objetos y muebles. Luego, completa las frases con la expresión más conveniente.

1. Hay una silla **encima de** la mesa.

2. La lámpara está **a la derecha del** sofá.

3. **Entre** la ventana y el televisor hay un librero.

4. Hay un cuadro en la pared, **detrás del** televisor.

5. El televisor está **enfrente del** sofá:

1. Hay una alfombra **debajo del** sofá.

2. La lámpara está **al lado de** la ventana.

3. **En el centro de** la sala hay una mesa de centro.

4. Hay un libro en el piso, **delante del** televisor.

5. El librero está **a la izquierda del** televisor.

En la sala A...

- Hay dos cojines .... sofá.

- Hay revistas en el piso, ... sofá.

- .... mesa hay una alfombra.

En la sala B...

- Hay una silla .... mesa de centro.

- Hay una planta .... lámpara y el televisor.

- Hay un libro .... computadora.

> ❶ **¿Necesitas ayuda?**
>
> **De + el = del**

9.16. Cada cosa en su lugar. En parejas, di frases a tu compañero/-a sobre la localización de los objetos en las salas de la actividad 9.15. Él/ella tiene que adivinar si se trata de la sala A o de la sala B.

> • *El librero está al lado de la ventana.*
> ○ *¡La sala A!*

9.17. Escuchamos e identificamos. Escucha la descripción de esta habitación y escribe las tres cosas que no se corresponden con la imagen.

> 1. La lámpara no está..., está...

9.18. Nuestro salón de clases. Describe tu salón de clases. Escribe, al menos, cuatro frases.

> Hay una ventana al lado de la puerta.

9.19. ¿Dónde está? En grupos, uno esconde un objeto en el salón de clases (por ejemplo, un bolígrafo). Los demás hacen preguntas para averiguar dónde está.

> 💬 **Para comunicar**
>
> **Frío/caliente** = *cold/hot (in a game play)*

> • *¿Está al lado de la computadora?*
> ○ *Caliente...*

Exploramos la lengua

Comparativos

9.20. Un foro. Lee este foro de hispanos que buscan apartamento en otros países. Escribe si los aspectos que comentan son parecidos o diferentes en tu campus, ciudad o país.

BUSCO APARTAMENTO

¿Quieres vivir en el extranjero? ¿Necesitas consejos para encontrar apartamento?
Escribe tus preguntas en este foro.

Elena: Soy mexicana y voy a estudiar en la Binghamton University. ¿Alguien vive en Binghamton? ¿Qué me recomiendan: un departamento o una residencia de estudiantes?

Comentarios (3)

Álex: Hola, Elena. Binghamton es una ciudad de estudiantes y es fácil encontrar apartamento. Las rentas no son **tan** caras **como** en otras ciudades de Estados Unidos.

Inma: Sí, pero una residencia universitaria es también una buena opción. Es **más** barata **que** un apartamento y te diviertes **más** porque conoces a **más** gente. **No** tienes **tanto** espacio **como** en un apartamento, pero las habitaciones no están mal...

Nadia: Los estudiantes en Estados Unidos tienen **más** ayudas **que** en México y no gastan **tanto** en cosas **como** la comida, por ejemplo, porque comer en el campus es muy barato.

Jorge: Hola desde Costa Rica. Encontré un trabajo en Buenos Aires. Me voy el mes que viene y busco apartamento. ¿Qué tengo que saber?

Comentarios (2)

Diego: Hola, Jorge. En Buenos Aires, la electricidad y el agua nunca están incluidas en el alquiler. Y en Costa Rica hay **menos** meses de frío **que** aquí, así que mejor si el apartamento tiene calefacción.

Gerardo: Te recomiendo buscar apartamento en el Gran Buenos Aires. Son zonas **menos** conocidas **que** Capital Federal, pero las rentas cuestan **menos**.

> *En mi campus los estudiantes normalmente viven en...*

9.21. Clasificamos. Observa las estructuras que están marcadas en negrita en los textos de la actividad 9.20. Todas sirven para comparar. Clasifícalas en el cuadro.

	Comparar adjetivos	Comparar sustantivos	Comparar verbos
Superioridad	**Más** + adjetivo (+ **que**) *Más barato que...*	**Más** + nombre (+ **que**)	Verbo + **más** (**que**)
Inferioridad	**Menos** + adjetivo (+ **que**)	**Menos** + nombre (+ **que**)	Verbo + **menos** (**que**)
	No + **tan** + adjetivo (+ **como**)	**No** + **tanto/-a/-os/-as** + nombre (+ **como**)	**No** + verbo + **tanto** (**como**)

9.22. Comparamos las casas. Escribe frases comparando las casas de tu ciudad con las de otro lugar que conoces. En clase, compártelas con otra persona.

> *En Nueva York, los edificios son más altos que en mi ciudad.*

9.23. Comparamos edificios y ciudades. Lee estos datos y escribe el máximo de comparaciones posibles.

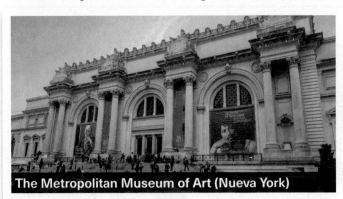

The Metropolitan Museum of Art (Nueva York)

- Abrió en 1879.
- Tiene más de 2 millones de obras.
- Es el 3.er museo más visitado del mundo.

Museo del Prado (Madrid)

- Abrió en 1819.
- Tiene más de 20 000 obras.
- Es el 18.º museo más visitado del mundo.

Teatro Colón (Argentina)

- Abrió en 1908.
- Tiene 2487 localidades.
- Tiene 28 metros de altura.

Palacio de Bellas Artes (Ciudad de México)

- Abrió en 1934.
- Tiene 1677 localidades.
- Tiene 42 metros de altura.

Nueva York

- Se fundó en 1624.
- Tiene 1214 km^2.
- Tiene unos 8 500 000 habitantes.
- Llueve 1300 litros por m^2 al año.
- La temperatura media anual es de 13 °C.

Ciudad de México

- Se fundó en 1325.
- Tiene 1495 km^2.
- Tiene unos 8 900 000 habitantes.
- Llueve 850 litros por m^2 al año.
- La temperatura media anual es de 17 °C.

 9.24. Más comparaciones. Escribe frases comparativas sobre...

| dos museos | dos estadios | dos teatros | dos monumentos | dos templos | dos ciudades |

Comunicamos

Cosas imprescindibles en una casa

👥 **9.25. Imprescindibles.** En parejas, discutan qué cinco cosas de las siguientes consideran imprescindibles para vivir.

> • *Para mí, es imprescindible el refrigerador.*
> ○ *Sí, y también la cama, ¿no?*
> • *Sí, claro, la cama también es importante.*

👥 **9.26. Colocamos nuestros imprescindibles.** Discutan en qué partes de la casa quieren colocar sus cinco cosas imprescindibles.

> • *¿Colocamos la mesa en la cocina?*
> ○ *¿Y si la ponemos en la sala?*

💬 **Para comunicar**

¿Y si ponemos la mesa en la cocina?
¿Qué te parece si ponemos la mesa en la cocina?
¿Por qué no ponemos la mesa aquí?

Dos viviendas

🔍 **9.27. Comparamos dos viviendas.** Busca en un portal inmobiliario de tu país dos viviendas bien diferentes. Escribe dónde están, cuál es el precio y cuáles son sus características principales.

Vivienda 1 ....

....

....

....

Vivienda 2 ....

....

....

....

9.28. Presentamos. Presenta las dos viviendas a tus compañeros. Después, di cuál te gusta más y por qué.

> *Prefiero la vivienda 2 porque tiene terraza, es más grande y tiene más habitaciones.*

Nuestros lugares favoritos de la casa

 9.29. ¿Dónde...? Escribe en qué lugar de la casa haces estas actividades. Luego, coméntalo con otra persona.

- estudiar
- escuchar música
- vestirte
- leer
- usar la computadora
- estar con tus amigos
- hacer la tarea
- ver televisión
- maquillarte/afeitarte
- reunirte con la familia
- relajarte
- desayunar

> ● *Yo normalmente estudio en mi habitación. ¿Y tú?*
> ○ *Depende. A veces en mi habitación y a veces en la sala.*

9.30. Sus lugares favoritos. Escucha a estas cuatro personas y toma nota de sus lugares favoritos de la casa y de las actividades que hacen en ellos.

	1. Jorge	2. Isabella	3. Pedro	4. Carolina
Lugar/es favorito/s				
Actividades				

9.31. Nuestro lugar favorito de la casa. ¿Qué lugar de tu casa prefieres? ¿Por qué? Coméntenlo en grupos.

> ● *Mi lugar favorito es la cocina, porque me encanta cocinar.*
> ○ *Para mí es el jardín, porque me gusta jugar ahí con mi perro.*

Hacemos el plano de nuestras habitaciones

9.32. Dos planos. Prepara dos planos de tu habitación en dos hojas de papel diferentes. El plano **A** debe incluir el contorno, la puerta y varios de tus objetos o muebles; el plano **B** debe incluir solo el el contorno y la puerta.

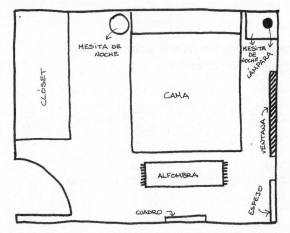

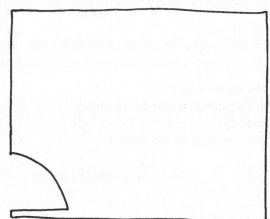

9.33. Nuestra habitación. En parejas, entréguense los planos **B** y por turnos, cuéntense qué cosas (muebles, objetos, etc.) tienen y dónde están. La otra persona dibuja.

> *A la izquierda de la puerta hay un clóset.*

9.34. Comparamos. Luego, comprueben si los planos que dibujaron son similares a sus planos **A**.

Ahora podemos...

Describir una casa ideal

9.35. Elegimos. En parejas, van a diseñar viviendas para un tipo específico de personas. Elijan uno de estos.

Parejas jóvenes

Retirados

Familias numerosas

Artistas

Estudiantes

Otros

9.36. La vivienda ideal para... Decidan cuáles pueden ser las características de una vivienda ideal para estas personas.

> • *Yo creo que una vivienda para estudiantes tiene que ser céntrica y estar bien comunicada.*
> ○ *Sí, y tener cerca restaurantes baratos y tiendas.*
> • *Y tiene que ser barata.*

💬 **Para comunicar**

Ser	céntrica / no muy cara / espaciosa un chalé / un ático
Estar	en el centro / cerca de la playa
Tener	mucho espacio / hospitales cerca...

9.37. Preparamos una presentación. Preparen una presentación para sus compañeros. Pueden acompañarla con fotos o dibujos. Incluyan la siguiente información:

- Perfil de los inquilinos
- Dónde están situadas las viviendas
- Precio
- Características de las viviendas

9.38. Escribimos un anuncio. Escriban un anuncio publicitario para anunciar su proyecto.

> Edificio La ola
> Estudios económicos ideales para estudiantes. 35 m². Totalmente amueblados. Calefacción y aire acondicionado. A un minuto de la biblioteca. Wifi gratis en todo el edificio...

Video

Casita pequeña

Entramos en la casa de Lucas Cumming en Portland, Oregon. Lucas, integrante del movimiento Casa pequeña, valora los beneficios económicos y medioambientales de vivir en un espacio muy reducido y está orgulloso de saber que él mismo construyó la casa con materiales reciclados.

Pearson MyLab

To find out more about Lucas Cummings and his tiny house, go to MyLab to watch **Casita pequeña** and complete the video activities.

⊕ ¿Sabes que…?

One of the most famous microhomes in the world, *Casa Tiny*, is located near the coastal town of Puerto Escondido in Oaxaca, Mexico. Architect Aranza de Ariño created the house when she was just 25 years old and still a student in Mexico City. The home's minimalist design, executed solely in sleek concrete and *parota*, a local wood, was inspired by Henry David Thoreau's *Walden*. Casa Tiny does indeed live up to the source material: the home is entirely surrounded by dense vegetation, and when its unique windows and doors are open, guests can hear the waves of the nearby Pacific Ocean.

⚲ Hacemos conexiones

Investiga sobre el movimiento Casa pequeña y su presencia en diferentes países de habla hispana. Comparte con la clase información e imágenes curiosas.

Casas

Nuestra casa es parte de nosotros y refleja nuestros gustos y nuestra vida. Por eso, algunas casas donde vivieron personas conocidas ahora son lugares de especial interés. Estas son las casas de tres personajes históricos convertidas en museos.

únicas

1. CASA MUSEO DE PABLO NERUDA

Esta fue la casa preferida de Neruda (Premio Nobel de Literatura en 1963) en Chile. En ella escribió parte de su obra literaria y en ella murió. Está en Isla Negra (Chile), al lado del mar, y tiene una vista espectacular. Tiene forma de barco y es de piedra y de madera. Pablo Neruda compró la casa en 1937.

2. LA CASA AZUL

En esta casa nació, vivió y murió la pintora mexicana Frida Kahlo. Está en Coyoacán, uno de los barrios más antiguos de Ciudad de México. Tiene más de 800 m² y está pintada de azul. Tiene grandes ventanas y en el centro hay un lindo jardín. Actualmente es uno de los museos más visitados de México.

3. QUINTA DE SIMÓN BOLÍVAR

La casa, de finales del siglo XVII, fue un regalo del nuevo gobierno independiente de Colombia para Simón Bolívar por su contribución a la lucha por la independencia. Bolívar utilizó la casa como residencia de verano entre 1820 y 1830. Antes de ser un museo, el espacio se utilizó como cervecería, hospital y escuela.

Hay muchas otras casas museo en países de habla hispana

Casa museo de Che Guevara (Alta Gracia, Argentina)
Casa museo Carlos Gardel (Buenos Aires, Argentina)

Casa natal de Cervantes (Alcalá de Henares, España)
Casa museo Hemingway (La Habana, Cuba)

Casa Borges (Adrogué, Argentina)
Casa museo Hermanas Mirabal (Tenares, República Dominicana)

Casa museo de Juana de Ibarbourou (Melo, Uruguay)
Museo Archivo Rubén Darío (León, Nicaragua)

ANTES DE LEER

🔍 **9.39. Investigamos.** Investiga en qué lugares vivieron Pablo Neruda, Frida Kahlo y Simón Bolívar.

LECTURA ACTIVA

9.40. Tres casas. Ahora lee la información sobre las tres casas. ¿Cuál de ellas quieres visitar? ¿Por qué?

👥 **9.41. Relacionamos textos e imágenes.** En parejas, comenten con cuál de las tres casas museo relacionan estas imágenes. Expliquen su respuesta.

DESPUÉS DE LEER

🔍 **9.42. Presentamos una casa.** Elige otra casa museo (de la lista o de tu país) y preséntala.

👥 **9.43. La casa de...** Comenten si les gustaría visitar la casa de algún personaje histórico de su país. Expliquen sus respuestas.

Textos audiovisuales: vemos, escuchamos y presentamos

Vemos un video sobre arquitectura boliviana

ANTES DE VER EL VIDEO

INFORMACIÓN PREVIA Freddy Mamani es un arquitecto boliviano. Sus edificios, modernos e innovadores, se llaman *cholets* y están inspirados en la arquitectura del Imperio tiwanaku (1500 a. C. - 1000 d. C.). El canal de televisión chileno Iquique Televisión grabó un reportaje sobre Mamani y le hizo una entrevista donde habla de su trabajo.

9.44. Preparación. Observa estas tres imágenes. ¿Qué crees que son? Relaciona cada una con su descripción.

 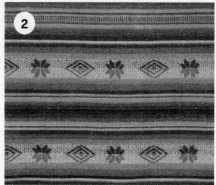 

- Aguayo aimara (pieza textil).
- Sitio arqueológico Tiwanaku.
- Bandera wiphala (bandera de los pueblos andinos).

VEMOS EL VIDEO

9.45. Primer visionado. Ve el video para confirmar tus respuestas y para tener una idea general de qué se trata.

9.46. Colores, formas y figuras. Ve el video desde el principio al minuto 0:24 y responde.

1. ¿Qué colores, formas geométricas y figuras ves?
2. Compara el edificio con las formas y figuras aimara. ¿Hay características similares?

9.47. Propósito. Del minuto 0:24 a 1:12 explica el propósito de su arquitectura: recuperar una identidad milenaria. ¿Cómo recupera esa arquitectura? Selecciona las opciones que menciona.

- Usa líneas y trazos geométricos de las ruinas de Tiwanaku.
- Usa materiales de construcción similares a las ruinas de Tiwanaku.
- Usa los colores de la bandera wiphala.

9.48. El Alto. Ve el segmento del minuto 1:12 al minuto 2:14 y contesta las preguntas.

1. ¿El Alto es la ciudad más poblada de Bolivia? Explica.
2. ¿Cuántos habitantes tiene?

9.49. Características de los edificios. Ve el video del minuto 2:14 al minuto 2:28 para saber cómo son las casas que hace Mamani. Completa con la información que falta.

"Casas de varios .... que –nos señala–, están dirigidas a los estratos más ....

del .... indígena .... Dentro de ellas se puede apreciar instalaciones que grafican

la .... de los .... más acomodados."

9.50. Conclusión. Ve el final de reportaje y selecciona la conclusión más apropiada.

◯ La arquitectura de Freddy Mamani fue muy criticada en el mundo.

◯ Las casas y edificios de Freddy Mamani son para la gente de pocos recursos económicos.

◯ La arquitectura de Freddy Mamani crea una nueva identidad arquitectónica basada en la identidad aimara.

◯ Los novedosos diseños de la arquitectura de Freddy Mamani todavía no son reconocidos por los expertos.

DESPUÉS DE VER EL VIDEO

9.51. Reacción personal. Responde estas preguntas.

1. ¿Te gusta la arquitectura de Mamani? Explica por qué sí o por qué no.
2. En tu opinión, ¿qué valores representan los edificios y los diseños de Mamani? ¿Qué cosas importantes se reflejan en su diseño?
3. ¿Qué imágenes o información te pareció más sorprendente en este reportaje?

Presentamos un edificio inspirado en pueblos nativos americanos

9.52. Elaboración. Diseña un edificio o una casa inspirada en los pueblos nativos americanos. Sigue estos pasos.

• Haz una pequeña investigación sobre productos y elementos artísticos de las culturas nativas americanas. Busca imágenes de esculturas, diseños textiles u objetos de la vida cotidiana.
• Piensa cómo puedes incorporar algunas características de esos elementos artísticos para diseñar tu edificio o casa.
• Ahora dibuja: usa el color, las figuras y las formas de este arte en tu diseño.

9.53. Presentación. Prepara un video o una presentación para mostrar tu diseño a la clase.

• ¿Qué es?
• ¿Qué características tiene?
• ¿En qué es similar a las características del arte nativo americano?
• ¿Cuál es su funcionalidad: es una vivienda, un lugar para eventos sociales...?

Recursos lingüísticos

PREPOSITIONS AND ADVERBS OF PLACE

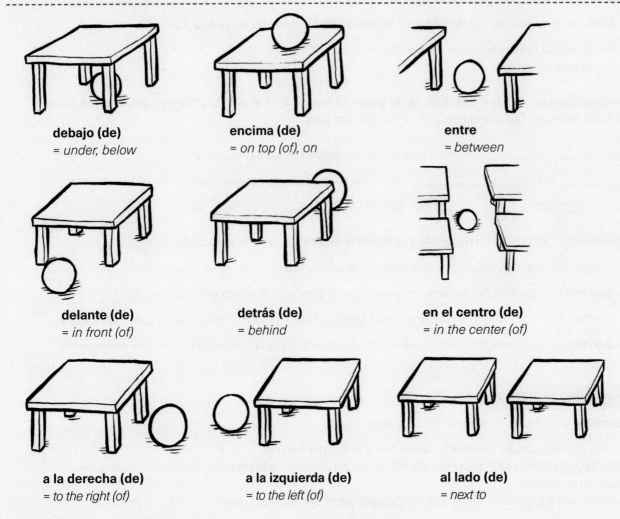

debajo (de)
= *under, below*

encima (de)
= *on top (of), on*

entre
= *between*

delante (de)
= *in front (of)*

detrás (de)
= *behind*

en el centro (de)
= *in the center (of)*

a la derecha (de)
= *to the right (of)*

a la izquierda (de)
= *to the left (of)*

al lado (de)
= *next to*

La mesa está **en el centro de** *la habitación.* = The table is in the center of the room.
¿Te gusta el sofá aquí, **entre** *los dos sillones?* = Do you like the sofa here, between the two armchairs?

▶ We can use prepositions and adverbs of place without **de** when the reference point is not mentioned.

¿Dónde ponemos el cuadro: **a la derecha de** *la ventana o* **a la izquierda**? = Where should we put the painting, to the right of the window or to the left?

❗ Remember: **de + el = del**

COMPARATIVES OF INEQUALITY (MORE)

WITH NOUNS	Ciudad de México tiene **más** <u>habitantes</u> **que** Guadalajara. = *Mexico City has more inhabitants than Guadalajara.*
WITH ADJECTIVES	Ciudad de México es **más** <u>grande</u> **que** Guadalajara. = *Mexico City is larger than Guadalajara.*
WITH VERBS	En Ciudad de México la gente <u>sale</u> **más que** en Guadalajara. = *In Mexico City people go out more than in Guadalajara.*

> ❗ Irregular forms: más bueno/-a → **mejor** = *better*
> más malo/-a → **peor** = *worse*

COMPARATIVES OF EQUALITY (AS MUCH AS, AS MANY AS)

WITH NOUNS

Esta casa tiene	**tanto** <u>espacio</u> **tanta** <u>luz</u> **tantos** <u>balcones</u> **tantas** <u>habitaciones</u>	**como** la otra.

This house has as much space/light as the other one.

This house has as many balconies/rooms as the other one.

> ❗ **Tanto** needs to agree with the noun it modifies: tant**o**/-**a**/-**os**/-**as**.

WITH ADJECTIVES

Aquí las casas son **tan** <u>caras</u> **como** en Bogotá.   *Here the houses are as expensive as in Bogotá.*

> ❗ **Tan** never changes, even if the adjective after it is singular or plural.

WITH VERBS

Aquí la gente <u>sale</u> **tanto como** en tu ciudad.   *Here people go out as much as in your city.*
Estas sillas me <u>gustan</u> **tanto como** las otras.   *I like these chairs as much as the other ones.*

> ❗ **Tanto** never changes, even if the verb form changes.

COMPARATIVES OF INEQUALITY (LESS)

WITH NOUNS

Mi casa tiene **menos** <u>balcones</u> **que** esta.   *My house has fewer balconies than this one.*

Esta casa no tiene	**tanto** <u>espacio</u> **tanta** <u>luz</u> **tantos** <u>balcones</u> **tantas** <u>habitaciones</u>	**como** la otra.

This house doesn't have as much space/light as the other one.

This house doesn't have as many balconies/rooms as the other one.

WITH ADJECTIVES

Esta casa es **menos** <u>luminosa</u> **que** la otra.   *This house is less bright than the other one.*
Aquí las casas no son **tan** <u>caras</u> **como** en mi ciudad.   *Here the houses are not as expensive as the ones in my city.*

WITH VERBS

Aquí la gente <u>sale</u> **menos que** en España.   *Here people go out less than in Spain.*
Aquí la gente **no** <u>sale</u> **tanto como** en España.   *Here people don't go out as much as in Spain.*

Pronunciamos

Los sonidos de **c/qu/z**, **r/rr**, **j/g**

e **9.54. Clasificamos.** Clasifica estas palabras según el sonido de las letras marcadas en negrita.

al**qu**ilar	**g**usto	**c**éntri**c**o
cuadrado	**c**entro	**j**ardín
lib**r**ero	e**qu**ipado	ga**r**aje
regadera	**j**arrón	espe**j**o
cocina	co**j**ín	**g**ente
habita**ción**	**c**uadro	made**r**a
refri**g**erador	afue**r**a	ho**g**ar
bal**c**ón	**r**uidoso	**c**erámica
te**rr**aza	ba**r**ata	os**c**uro
aco**g**edor	pe**qu**eña	**r**edondo
clásico	**g**astar	

Como **c**asa	Como pe**rr**o	Como **j**amón

Como **c**ine	Como pe**r**o	Como **g**ato

9.55. Escuchamos y comprobamos. Escucha y comprueba.

9.56. Escuchamos y repetimos. Escucha y repite.

e

Vocabulario activo

))) Tipos de casa   *Types of housing*
- **el ático**   *attic, loft, penthouse*
- **la casa**   *house*
- **el condominio**   *condominium*
- **el estudio**   *studio*
- **la villa**   *villa, vacation property*

))) Partes de la casa   *Parts of a house*
- **la antesala**   *(entrance) hall*
- **el balcón**   *balcony*
- **el baño**   *bathroom*
- **la cocina**   *kitchen*
- **la cocina americana**   *open-floor kitchen*
- **el comedor**   *dining room*
- **el cuarto de estudio**   *studying room*
- **el elevador**   *elevator*
- **el garaje**   *garage*
- **la habitación**   *room, bedroom*
- **el jardín**   *garden, yard*
- **el lavadero**   *laundry room*
- **la planta**   *story, level*
- **la sala-comedor**   *living-dining room*
- **la sala de juegos** (el juego)   *game room, playroom*
- **la terraza**   *terrace*
- **la ventana**   *window*

))) Características de una casa   *Features of the house*
- **a cinco minutos de...**   *five minutes from*
- **acogedor/a**   *cozy*
- **el aire acondicionado**   *air conditioner*
- **amplio/-a**   *spacious*
- **amueblado/-a**   *furnished*
- **sin amueblar**   *unfurnished*
- **bien ubicado/-a**   *well located*
- **buena/mala distribución**   *good/bad distribution*
- **la calefacción**   *heating*
- **céntrico/-a**   *central*
- **cómodo/-a**   *comfortable*
- **de nueva construcción**   *new construction*
- **en perfecto estado** (el estado)   *in perfect condition*
- **equipado/-a**   *equipped*
- **espacioso/-a**   *spacious, roomy*
- **frío/-a**   *cool (not warm)*
- **listo/-a para entrar a vivir**   *move-in ready*
- **luminoso/-a**   *bright*
- **con vista**   *with views*

))) Muebles, electrodomésticos y artículos de decoración   *Furniture, appliances, and decorative articles*
- **la alfombra**   *carpet*
- **la cama (doble)**   *(double) bed*
- **el clóset**   *closet*
- **el cojín**   *cushion*
- **el escritorio**   *desk*
- **el espejo**   *mirror*
- **el jarrón**   *vase*
- **la lámpara de pie**   *floor lamp*
- **la lámpara de techo** (el techo)   *ceiling light*
- **la lavadora**   *washing machine*
- **el lavaplatos**   *dishwasher*
- **el librero**   *bookcase*
- **la mesa**   *table*
- **la mesa de centro**   *coffee table*
- **la mesita de noche**   *nightstand*
- **el microondas**   *microwave oven*
- **la pared**   *wall*
- **el piso**   *floor*
- **la planta**   *plant*
- **el refrigerador**   *refrigerator*
- **la regadera**   *shower*
- **la silla**   *chair*
- **el sillón**   *armchair*
- **el sofá**   *sofa, couch*
- **la tina**   *bathtub*

))) Formas, estilos y materiales   *Shapes, styles, and materials*
- **cuadrado/-a**   *square*
- **de cerámica**   *(made of) ceramic*
- **de colores**   *colored*
- **de estilo industrial/minimalista** (el estilo)   *industrial/minimalist style*
- **de madera**   *(made of) wood*
- **de metal**   *(made of) metal*
- **de piel**   *(made of) leather*
- **de tela**   *(made of) cloth*
- **de vidrio**   *(made of) glass*
- **en varios colores**   *in various colors*
- **redondo/-a**   *round*

> ⚙ **Estrategia**
>
> This might be a good time to fill your house with stickers with the Spanish words to name everything you've learned in this lesson!

Lección 10

Guía del ocio

IN THIS LESSON WE ARE GOING TO

organize a weekend of activities for a group of tourists

LEARNING OUTCOMES
You will be able to...

- talk about leisure activities

- talk about intentions and projects

VOCABULARY

- Events and practical information

- Places to go and things to do

LANGUAGE STRUCTURES

- **Ir a** / **pensar** + infinitive

- Temporal markers to talk about the future (I)

- Conditional clauses (I): **si** + present

- Expressing conditions with **depende**

PRONUNCIATION

- The sounds /k/ and /s/: **c, k, qu, z**

CULTURAL CONNECTIONS

- Latin entertainment in New York

Fans de Boca Juniors en el Estadio Alberto J. Armando (La Bombonera). Buenos Aires (Argentina).

Primer contacto

10.1. Cinco eventos. Relaciona cada evento con la imagen correspondiente.

1. un **espectáculo de circo**
2. un concierto
3. una exposición
4. una **obra de teatro**
5. un festival

⚙ **Estrategia**

When working with authentic texts like the ones on this page, remember to read them as you would in your own language. Let the design and the way the information is presented help you understand the message. Focus also on to key words.

A

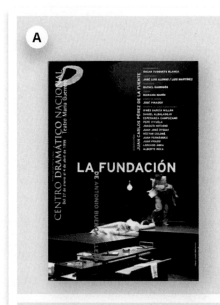

C

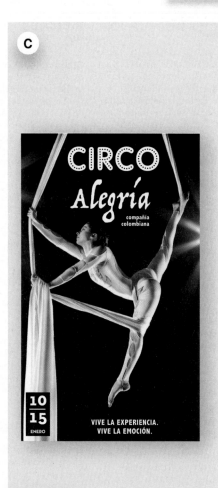

D

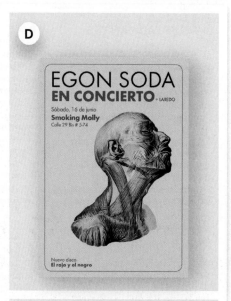

B

E

10.2. Nos gusta. ¿A qué evento te gustaría ir? ¿Por qué? Coméntalo con otra persona de la clase.

A mí me gustaría ir al concierto. Me gusta mucho la música en vivo.

10.3. Eventos en nuestra ciudad. ¿Hay eventos como los de 10.1 en el lugar donde viven? Comenten dónde, cuándo y con qué frecuencia. Si no hay, comenten por qué creen que es así.

Aquí hay muchas exposiciones. Yo conozco algunos lugares que organizan exposiciones durante todo el año.

Comprendemos el vocabulario

Eventos e información práctica

10.4. Guía de entretenimiento. Lee y escucha este fragmento de una guía de entretenimiento de Bogotá. Elige una opción de ocio que te interesa y otra que no te interesa nada.

Qué hacer hoy en Bogotá

CAFÉS Y RESTAURANTES

Andrés Carne de Res. Calle 3 Nº 11A-56. ⏱ (1) 8612233. Restaurante temático para comer bien, rumbear y tomar un coctel. Ambiente único y **actuaciones en vivo**. Se puede **reservar**. Dispone de menú especial para grupos. **Precio promedio:** $36 700-$98 900. **Horario:** de miércoles a domingo de 12 m. a 12 a.m. (miércoles y domingos) / 2 a.m. (jueves) / 3 p.m. (viernes y sábados).
www.andrescarnederes.com

La Puerta Falsa. Calle 11 Nº 6-50. ⏱ (1) 2865091. **Local de comida tradicional y dulces. Abierto** desde 1816, sirve los tamales más famosos de la ciudad, además de otros platos típicos de la zona. Precio promedio: $2500-$15 000. Abierto todos los días de 7 a.m. a 10 p.m.
www.restaurantelapuertafalsa.inf.travel

Mini-mal. Transversal 4 Bis Nº 57 - 52. ⏱ (1) 3475464. Cocina contemporánea colombiana elaborada con productos autóctonos. Ambiente relajado y familiar. **Buena relación calidad-precio. Servicio** excepcional. De lunes a jueves, abierto de 12:30 p.m. a 3 p.m. y de 7 p.m. a 10 p.m. (jueves hasta las 11 p.m.). Viernes y sábados de 12:30 p.m. a 11 p.m. Domingos **cerrado**.
www.mini-mal.org

CLUBES NOCTURNOS

Theatron. Calle 58 Nº 10-18. ⏱ 310 3040689. Complejo de bares, discotecas y clubes nocturnos. En total, dieciséis salas con atmósferas y estilos musicales diferentes. También organizan **eventos. Cover:** $55 000 y **barra libre** hasta las 2 p.m. Horario: jueves de 9 p.m. a 3 p.m.; viernes y sábado de 9 p.m. a 5 p.m.; de domingo a miércoles, cerrado.
www.theatron.co

MUSEOS

Museo del Oro. Carrera 8 Nº 15-88. ⏱ (1) 3432222. Uno de los museos más fascinantes de Suramérica, con más de 55 000 piezas de oro y otros materiales del periodo precolombino de la actual Colombia. Horario de 9 a.m. a 6 p.m. de martes a sábado. Domingos de 10 a.m. a 4 p.m. Cerrado todos los lunes. **Entrada general** $4000. Domingos, **entrada gratuita**.
www.banrepcultural.org

Museo Santa Clara. Carrera 8 Nº 8-91. ⏱ (1) 3376762. Edificio barroco de los siglos XVII y XVIII. Gran colección de **obras de arte** de los siglos XVII, XVIII, XIX y XX. Abierto de 9 a.m. a 5:00 p.m. de martes a viernes. Sábados y domingos de 10 a.m. a 4 p.m. Lunes cerrado. Entrada general: $4000. **Entrada reducida para estudiantes** ($3000) y niños ($2000). **Gratis para estudiantes de colegios y universidades públicas.** Domingos, entrada gratuita.
www.museocolonial.gov.co

CINES

Cinemanía. Carrera 14 Nº 93A - 85. ⏱ (1) 6550265. Hasta la 1 p.m. (películas infantiles): $4000. Lunes, miércoles y jueves antes de las 5 p.m.: $13 000; después de las 5 p.m.: $15 000. Martes, todas las **funciones**: $13 000. Viernes después de las 5 p.m.: $20 000. Sábados, domingos y **festivos** antes de las 2 p.m.: $15 000; después de las 2 p.m.: $20 000.
Ciclo Cine italiano
La gran belleza.
Función: 5 p.m.
Bienvenidos al sur.
Función: 9 p.m.
Vencer.
Función: 7 p.m.
Todas las películas con **subtítulos** en español.

Gran Estación. Avenida Calle 26 Nº 62 - 47 Centro comercial Gran Estación. ⏱ (1) 4042463. Valor de la **boleta**: de lunes a jueves antes de las 2:59 p.m. $6000; después de las 3 p.m.: $14 000. Miércoles: $7000 todas las funciones. Viernes a domingos y festivos: $20 000.
El Grinch. (**Público general**)
2D - Doblada. Funciones: 11:40 a.m. | 1:55 p.m. | 4:10 p.m.
La pequeña traviesa.
(**Apta para menores**)
2D - Doblada. Funciones: 11:10 a.m. | 1:30 p.m. | 3:50 p.m.
Familia al instante.
2D - Doblada. Funciones: 12:20 p.m. | 3:05 p.m. | 5:50 p.m.
2D - Subtitulada: 8:35 p.m.

🌐 La variedad del español

la boleta (Co) = **el boleto** (AmL), **la entrada** (Es).

❗ ¿Necesitas ayuda?

1 USD = 3158 Colombian pesos (COP)

20 000 COP = 6.33 USD

Más palabras

el campeonato = *championship*
la comida rápida = *fast food*
la conferencia = *conference, lecture*
el espectáculo de baile/danza = *dance show*

el espectáculo de magia = *magic show*
el estreno = *premiere*
el partido = *game, match (sports)*

e **10.5. Relacionamos.** Marca con qué lugares relacionas las palabras o expresiones de la izquierda.

	Cafés y restaurantes	Clubes nocturnos	Museos	Cines
1. Actuaciones en vivo				
2. Reservar				
3. Comida tradicional				
4. Buena relación calidad-precio				
5. Servicio				
6. Cover				
7. Entrada general				
8. Entrada reducida				
9. Obra de arte				
10. Función				
11. Barra libre				
12. Con subtítulos / subtitulada				
13. Público general				
14. Doblada				

10.6. Consultamos la guía. En parejas, consulten la página de la guía de entretenimiento de Bogotá (actividad 10.4) y decidan cuál es el mejor lugar para estas personas.

1. Sofía y Vicente quieren salir a bailar.
2. Carlos y Antonella quieren ir a un museo, pero no tienen dinero.
3. Samuel quiere ir al cine a ver una película en español.
4. Es la 1 de la tarde de un sábado y Emiliano y Salomé quieren cenar.
5. Matías quiere ir al cine con su sobrino de 8 años.
6. Danilo quiere escuchar música en vivo.
7. Irene quiere organizar un espectáculo de baile.
8. Fernanda y Pablo quieren ver obras de arte de la época precolombina.

> • *Para salir a bailar, Sofía y Vicente pueden ir a Andrés Carne de Res.*
> ○ *O también pueden ir a...*

Comprendemos el vocabulario

Actividades de tiempo libre

 10.7. Actividades de tiempo libre. Lee y escucha.

jugar

| juegos de mesa | ajedrez
póker | boliche | un partido de \| beisbol
voleibol |

ir

al estadio
al teatro
a la bolera
a una fiesta
a una inauguración

de viaje
de excursión

a clases de \| dibujo
canto
defensa
personal

> ❗ **¿Necesitas ayuda?**
>
> It is very common to use **salir / ir a** + infinitive to say you are going out to do something.
>
> *Ayer salí a bailar.* = Yesterday I went out dancing.
>
> *Todos los martes voy a hacer surf.* = Every Tuesday I go out surfing.

hacer un curso de \| cocina
escritura
creativa

hacer/ practicar surf
natación
meditación
artes marciales

hacer/ organizar un pícnic
una barbacoa
una fiesta

participar en una carrera
una competición
una maratón

Más palabras

 bucear = *to scuba dive*
correr = *to run, to jog*
escalar = *to scale, to climb*
hacer/practicar senderismo = *to hike*
no hacer nada = *to do nothing*
pasar el día con la familia / (los) amigos = *to spend the day with the family / with friends*

pasar el día en la casa / en la playa = *to spend the day at home / at the beach*
pescar = *to fish*
quedarse en casa = *to stay at home*
relajarse = *to relax*
tomar algo = *to have a drink*
tomar el sol = *to sunbathe*

e **10.8. Clasificamos.** Escribe tres actividades de tiempo libre de la actividad 10.7 para cada categoría.

Actividades deportivas	Actividades artísticas	Actividades sociales	Actividades intelectuales
bucear			

10.9. ¿Qué haces en...? En parejas, digan qué actividades pueden hacer en cada uno de estos lugares.

la casa   la playa   el gimnasio   el parque   el mar/océano   el campus

• *En la casa, podemos jugar juegos de mesa y jugar póker o ajedrez.*
○ *Sí, y también organizar una barbacoa o una fiesta.*

10.10. ¿Con quién? Marca con quién haces normalmente estas actividades.

	Solo/-a	Con tu pareja	Con amigos	Con tu familia
Ir a la bolera				
Hacer senderismo				
Jugar juegos de mesa				
Jugar videojuegos				
Jugar un partido				
Ir al cine				
Ir al gimnasio				
Relajarte				
Ir a una fiesta				
Organizar una barbacoa				
Tomar algo				

10.11. Compartimos. Comenten en grupos con quién hacen las actividades de 10.10. ¿Hacen todas las actividades con las mismas personas?

• *Yo voy a la bolera con mis amigos.*
○ *Sí, yo también.*

10.12. Actividades favoritas. Escribe las actividades de ocio favoritas de cuatro personas que conoces. Compártelo con personas de la clase y busquen cosas en común.

• *A mi madre le gusta correr, jugar boliche y el canto.*
○ *¡A mi hermano también le gusta el canto!*

Exploramos la lengua

Hablar de planes e intenciones: **ir a** / **pensar** + infinitivo

10.13. Un mensaje. Viviana está de vacaciones y les envía un mensaje a sus padres. ¿Dónde crees que está? ¿En qué te basas?

> ¡Hola, familia!
> Después de unos días de playa en Varadero, ya estamos en La Habana. ¡Es increíble! Vamos a quedarnos aquí hasta el día 10. Conocimos a unos chicos y mañana nos van a mostrar La Habana Vieja. Y este fin de semana vamos a ir a la Isla de la Juventud. Suena bien, ¿no? Mami, este viaje me hizo reflexionar y tengo que decirte una cosa: el año que viene pienso continuar en la universidad.
> ¡Un beso a todos!

10.14. Los planes de Viviana. Lee de nuevo el mensaje de la actividad 10.13 y escribe las frases que usa Viviana para presentar sus planes e intenciones.

> Vamos a quedarnos aquí hasta el día 10.

10.15. Planes e intenciones. Completa la tabla con las formas verbales de los verbos **pensar** e **ir** que aparecen en el mensaje de la actividad 10.13. Luego, en parejas, completen la conjugación de los dos verbos.

	PENSAR	IR + A	+ INFINITIVO
(yo)	....	.... a	
(tú)	....	.... a	
(él/ella, usted)	....	.... a	**mostrar**
(nosotros/nosotras)	....	.... a	**comer**
(vosotros/vosotras)	....	vais a	**ir**
(ellos/ellas, ustedes)	....	.... a	

> **❗ ¿Necesitas ayuda?**
>
> **Pensar** is a stem-changing verb in the present tense (**e > ie**). It's conjugated like the verb **empezar**.

10.16. ¿Qué planes tienen? En parejas (**A/B**), pregunten a su compañero/-a para completar su tabla.

Estudiante A	
¿Quién?	**¿Qué piensa / va a hacer?**
Jimena	....
César y Leticia	organizar una barbacoa con amigos
Gustavo	....
Luna	salir a pescar con su abuelo
Rosa y Aitana	....
Isaac	ir a la playa y tomar el sol

Estudiante B	
¿Quién?	**¿Qué piensa / va a hacer?**
Jimena	ir al estadio para ver un partido
César y Leticia	....
Gustavo	hacer meditación todos los días
Luna	....
Rosa y Aitana	hacer senderismo
Isaac	....

10.17. Viaje a Cuba. Estas son algunas actividades que se pueden hacer en La Habana. Imagina que estás de vacaciones unos días en la ciudad y elige cuatro cosas que vas a hacer allí. Después, escribe frases.

- ir al teatro
- pasear por el Malecón
- visitar el Museo de Bellas Artes
- probar comidas y bebidas típicas

- montar en un "almendrón"
- tomar clases de baile
- ir a la playa
- visitar la catedral

> Voy a pasear por el Malecón.

El Malecón

10.18. Nuestros planes en Cuba. Cuenta a una persona de la clase tus planes en Cuba. ¿Van a hacer las mismas cosas?

10.19. De vacaciones. Elijan un destino de vacaciones que les guste a los dos y piensen en las actividades que quieren hacer allí. Después, cuenten sus vacaciones a otra pareja. ¿Tienen planes en común? ¿Quién va a pasar las vacaciones más divertidas?

"Almendrón"

Marcadores temporales para hablar del futuro

10.20. Hablar del futuro. Todos estos marcadores temporales pueden referirse al futuro. Ordénalos cronológicamente. Imagina que son las 12:30 p.m.

- **mañana**
- *1* **esta tarde**
- **pasado mañana**

- **dentro de dos años**
- **el mes que viene**
- **el próximo año**

- **el 31 de diciembre**
- **esta noche**
- **en verano**

10.21. Los planes de Paula. Hoy es el día 20 de mayo. Mira la agenda y el pasaje de avión de Paula y escribe cuáles son sus planes. Usa los siguientes marcadores temporales.

| mañana | pasado mañana | este sábado |

| el domingo | el martes que viene |

| el próximo fin de semana | dentro de tres meses |

> Pasado mañana, Paula piensa ir a...

10.22. Nuestros planes. Y tú, ¿tienes planes para los próximos meses? Piensa en tus estudios, en tu trabajo, en tus vacaciones... Escríbelos y, luego, habla con tus compañeros/-as.

> *Este verano voy a hacer un curso de danza. ¿Y tú?*

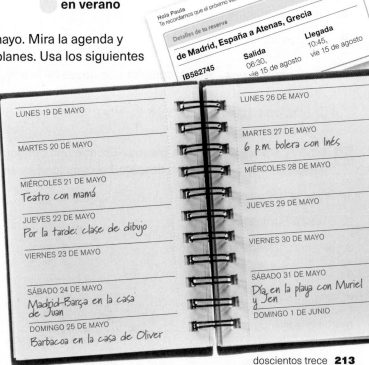

Hola Paula
Te recordamos que el próximo viernes 15/08 sale tu vuelo con destino Atenas

Detalles de tu reserva

de Madrid, España a Atenas, Grecia

	Salida	Llegada
IB582745	06:30, vie 15 de agosto	10:45, vie 15 de agosto

LUNES 19 DE MAYO

MARTES 20 DE MAYO

MIÉRCOLES 21 DE MAYO
Teatro con mamá

JUEVES 22 DE MAYO
Por la tarde: clase de dibujo

VIERNES 23 DE MAYO

SÁBADO 24 DE MAYO
Madrid-Barça en la casa de Juan

DOMINGO 25 DE MAYO
Barbacoa en la casa de Oliver

LUNES 26 DE MAYO

MARTES 27 DE MAYO
6 p.m. bolera con Inés

MIÉRCOLES 28 DE MAYO

JUEVES 29 DE MAYO

VIERNES 30 DE MAYO

SÁBADO 31 DE MAYO
Día en la playa con Muriel y Jen

DOMINGO 1 DE JUNIO

Exploramos la lengua

Frases condicionales (I): **si** + presente

10.23. Si tengo tiempo. Lee estas frases y marca con cuáles te identificas.

- **Si** por las tardes **tengo** tiempo libre, voy a correr.

- **Si** esta tarde **tengo** tiempo libre, voy a ir al gimnasio.

- **Si** este fin de semana **hace** mal tiempo, voy a quedarme en casa.

- **Si** no **puedo** dormir, me levanto y hago meditación.

- **Si hace** buen tiempo, los fines de semana me gusta organizar barbacoas.

- **Si** algún día **gano** mucho dinero, pienso pasar un año en el Caribe.

e 10.24. Completamos la regla. Elige la opción correcta para completar la regla.

Usamos **si** + presente...

- ...para expresar condiciones referidas al presente.
- ...para expresar condiciones referidas al presente o al futuro.

e 10.25. ¿Presente o futuro? Marca si estas partes de frases condicionales se refieren al presente o al futuro.

	Presente	Futuro
1. ... voy a comprar una casa.		
2. ... siempre llevo protector solar.		
3. ... voy a organizar una fiesta.		
4. ... voy a ir al estadio.		
5. ... me gusta salir a caminar por la ciudad.		
6. ... no voy a pasar el examen.		
7. ... voy a pasar el día en la playa.		
8. ... voy a quedarme en casa.		
9. ... veo películas o series.		

10.26. Condiciones. Ahora, completa las frases de la actividad 10.25 de manera lógica.

Si ahorro mucho dinero, voy a comprar una casa.

10.27. Continuamos las frases. Escribe una continuación lógica para estas frases. Luego, habla con otra persona para descubrir si coinciden en algo.

1. Si mañana llueve, ...

2. Si voy a Europa en verano, ...

3. Si tengo el fin de semana libre, ...

4. Si esta noche quiero relajarme, ...

5. Si quiero divertirme, ...

6. Si no duermo bastante, ...

Expresar condiciones: **depende de / depende de si**

e **10.28. Depende.** Observa las imágenes y lee estas conversaciones. Después, completa la regla.

1 • ¿Van a ir de vacaciones a Japón?
  ○ No sé, **depende del** dinero.

2 • ¿Van a ir a la playa el domingo?
  ○ **Depende de si** hace buen tiempo.

Para expresar una condición, podemos usar:

.... + sustantivo

.... + verbo en presente de indicativo

)))) **10.29. Escucha y completa.** Escucha los diálogos y completa la oración de forma correcta y gramaticalmente apropiada.

1. El viaje de Marta depende de si tiene ....

2. Ir de campamento con Juan y Luis depende del ....

3. Ir al cine depende de la ....

4. La celebración de cumpleaños depende de si sus padres ....

10.30. ¿De qué depende? Imagina que te hacen estas preguntas. Escribe tus respuestas.

1 • ¿Vas a hacer algún viaje al extranjero este año?

  ○ No sé, depende ....

2 • ¿Qué vas a hacer este fin de semana?

  ○ No sé, depende ....

3 • ¿Vas a ir al cine esta semana?

  ○ No sé, depende ....

4 • ¿Cómo vas a celebrar tu cumpleaños?

  ○ No sé, depende ....

Comunicamos

Un local con buena música

10.31. Lugares. Piensa en lugares de la ciudad o la región donde vives y completa el cuadro.

	Nombre	¿Dónde está?
1. Un local con buena música	*Sounds*	*cerca del puerto*
2. Un lugar para organizar una barbacoa		
3. Un lugar para hacer deporte		
4. Una tienda de ropa linda y barata		
5. Un cine con restaurante		
6. Una bolera		
7. Un estadio de beisbol		

10.32. Recomendamos lugares. Ahora, coméntalo con tus compañeros/-as.

> • *Yo conozco un local con buena música. Se llama "Sounds".*
> *¿Saben cuál es?*
> ○ *No, ¿dónde está?*
> • *Está cerca del puerto.*

> ❗ **¿Necesitas ayuda?**
> The verb **conocer** is irregular in the present **yo** form:
> **yo conozco**

10.33. Nuestros descubrimientos. ¿Descubriste algo nuevo? Decide qué lugares te interesan, a cuáles quieres ir y cuándo. Cuéntaselo a la clase.

> *Creo que voy a ir a "Sounds" este fin de semana. Grace dice que la música es muy buena.*

> ❗ **¿Necesitas ayuda?**
> The verb **decir** is irregular in the present tense:
> | yo | **digo** |
> | tú | **dices** |
> | él/ella, usted | **dice** |
> | ellos/ellas, ustedes | **dicen** |

Soñar es gratis

10.34. Nuestro negocio ideal. En parejas, imaginen su negocio ideal: un restaurante, una discoteca, una galería de arte, etc. Decidan cuáles son sus características.

- Qué es y cómo se llama
- Dónde está y cómo llegar
- Información útil: horario, precio medio, etc.
- Qué cosas o actividades hay
- Otras características

10.35. Presentamos nuestro negocio. Ahora van a explicar a sus compañeros/-as cómo es su negocio. Escriban el nombre de su negocio en el pizarrón y, luego, comenten a cuáles les gustaría ir.

Programa cultural

 10.36. Programa de actividades. Imaginen que su escuela ofrece estas actividades para el próximo semestre. ¿Qué tres actividades creen que van a ser más populares? Coméntenlo en grupos.

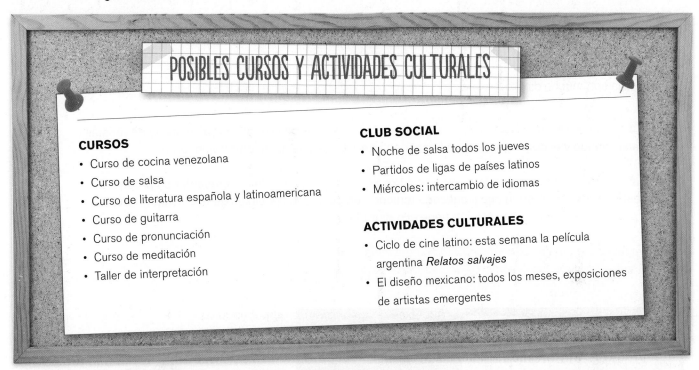

POSIBLES CURSOS Y ACTIVIDADES CULTURALES

CURSOS

- Curso de cocina venezolana
- Curso de salsa
- Curso de literatura española y latinoamericana
- Curso de guitarra
- Curso de pronunciación
- Curso de meditación
- Taller de interpretación

CLUB SOCIAL

- Noche de salsa todos los jueves
- Partidos de ligas de países latinos
- Miércoles: intercambio de idiomas

ACTIVIDADES CULTURALES

- Ciclo de cine latino: esta semana la película argentina *Relatos salvajes*
- El diseño mexicano: todos los meses, exposiciones de artistas emergentes

- *Yo creo que mucha gente quiere aprender a tocar la guitarra.*
- *Pues yo creo que va a ser más popular el intercambio de idiomas. A mucha gente le interesa aprender idiomas.*

10.37. Nuestras preferencias. Pongan en común con el resto de la clase las tres actividades seleccionadas.

10.38. Nuestras propuestas. En grupos, creen el programa de actividades para el semestre que viene. Propongan las cinco actividades ideales para los estudiantes de su clase.

La vida de los estudiantes en nuestro país

10.39. Estudiantes preguntan. Lean y contesten estas preguntas de unos estudiantes latinos sobre la vida en su universidad. Luego pongan sus respuestas en común con la clase y comprueben si están de acuerdo.

1. ¿Los fines de semana los estudiantes regresan a sus casas?
2. ¿Los profesores salen a tomar algo con los estudiantes después de clase?
3. ¿Los estudiantes desayunan, almuerzan y cenan en el campus?
4. ¿Es posible practicar deportes en el campus?
5. ¿Todos los estudiantes estudian y trabajan?
6. ¿Es mejor vivir en el campus o en otro lugar?
7. ¿Todos los estudiantes tienen que hablar con un consejero?
8. ¿Hay centros de ayuda para estudiantes?
9. ¿Es muy importante pertenecer a una fraternidad de hombres o de mujeres?

- *Yo creo que muchos estudiantes sí regresan a sus casas los fines de semana, pero depende de si viven cerca, de si tienen que trabajar...*
- *Sí, pero muchos estudiantes se quedan también.*

Ahora podemos...

Organizar un fin de semana de actividades para un grupo de turistas

10.40. Elegimos grupo. En grupos, imaginen que son guías turísticos y que deben preparar actividades para un sábado y un domingo en la ciudad donde están. Primero, elijan uno de estos grupos.

- 35 estudiantes de 18 años
- una pareja de luna de miel
- un grupo de niños de 10 a 14 años
- un grupo de retirados
- una familia con mucho dinero

10.41. Programamos actividades. Ahora programen seis actividades para su grupo de turistas para el sábado y el domingo. Pueden buscar en internet o en guías de entretenimiento.

10.42. Presentamos nuestros planes para el fin de semana. Van a presentar su propuesta al resto de la clase. Tienen que justificarla teniendo en cuenta los posibles gustos de su grupo, los precios, los horarios, etc. ¿Quién tiene el mejor plan?

> Nuestro fin de semana es para un grupo de estudiantes.
> El sábado por la mañana vamos a ir al Discovery Green...

Sábado por la mañana: paseo por el parque Discovery Green.

Sábado por la tarde: visita al Centro Espacial Houston.

Domingo: distrito de los museos. Visita al Museo de Bellas Artes y al Museo de Arte Contemporáneo.

Video

Poder Nocturno vs. AeroBoy

En este video, Poder Nocturno defiende su título de campeón de la lucha libre de Texas en un combate contra AeroBoy. Para Poder Nocturno el deporte está muy relacionado con su herencia mexicana y su identidad personal.

⊕ **¿Sabes que...?**

Lucha libre (literally, "free fight") is enormously popular throughout Mexico and in Mexican-American communities in the United States. Most matches pit a *técnico* (or "good" character) against a *rudo* ("bad guy"). One of the most famous *luchadores* of all time is the legendary El Santo, who won numerous championships, starred in films, and became a cultural icon and folk hero during his 50-year career. His son, El Hijo del Santo, carries on the family's professional legacy.

🔍 **Hacemos conexiones**

Busca información sobre la lucha libre mexicana y selecciona cinco curiosidades para compartir en la clase.

ⓟ **Pearson**
MyLab

To find out more about *lucha libre*, go to MyLab to watch **Poder Nocturno vs. AeroBoy** and complete the video activities.

Por la mañana
visitar el Museo del Barrio

QUÉ ÉS

Es un referente cultural en la ciudad de Nueva York. Se trata de un museo de arte latinoamericano y su objetivo es promover la cultura latinoamericana y su influencia en Nueva York.

UBICACIÓN

1230 5th Ave. (82th St., en pleno Spanish Harlem).

QUÉ SE PUEDE VER

La colección permanente tiene más de 6500 piezas de arte caribeño y latino e incluye objetos precolombinos, artesanías, esculturas, dibujos, fotografía, films documentales y videos.

Y ADEMÁS...

El museo también tiene una cafetería, que sirve cocina mexicana y latinoamericana, y un precioso teatro. Además, en La Tienda se pueden comprar *souvenirs* realizados por artistas de América Latina a buenos precios.

A la hora del almuerzo
una clase en DanceSports

QUÉ ÉS

Es el salón de baile y escuela de ritmos latinos más grande de la ciudad.

UBICACIÓN

22 W 34th St.

QUÉ SE PUEDE HACER

Esta escuela ofrece cada semana 80 clases de bailes latinos de todos los estilos y niveles. De 12 a 2 horas ofrece la posibilidad de ir a una *party class* y bailar ritmos latinos con la supervisión de los profesores de la escuela.

Y ADEMÁS...

Durante la *party class*, se puede comer una ensalada o empanadas argentinas.

Un día de entretenimiento latino en Nueva York

Por la tarde
El New York Latino Film Festival

Por la noche
Cenar en el restaurante Ofrenda

QUÉ ÉS

Es el festival de cine latino más importante de EE. UU. y se celebra desde 1999.

UBICACIÓN

Salas de cine AMC Empire 25 (234 W 42nd St.) y Julia De Burgos Performance and Arts Center (1680 Lexington Ave.).

QUÉ SE PUEDE VER

Una selección de largometrajes (provenientes de Chile, México, Colombia, Cuba, España, Estados Unidos, etc.), estrenos mundiales, documentales y numerosos cortometrajes.

Y ADEMÁS…

Durante el festival, que se celebra cada año en agosto, se organizan actividades como foros y conferencias sobre el futuro del cine latino.

QUÉ ÉS

La crítica lo considera uno de los mejores restaurantes mexicanos de la ciudad de Nueva York. Ofrece comida casera a buenos precios.

UBICACIÓN

113 7th Ave South.

QUÉ SE PUEDE COMER

Deliciosa cocina casera mexicana. Entradas típicas como el guacamole o las quesadillas, tacos de varios tipos y platos fuertes como el mole poblano o chiles rellenos de carne o pescado.

Y ADEMÁS…

También hacen deliciosos cocteles.

ANTES DE LEER

10.43. Un sitio para… Marca en cuáles de estos lugares puedes hacer estas actividades. Luego, discútelo con otras personas de la clase.

	Un museo	Una escuela de baile	Un festival de cine	Un restaurante
Tomar un coctel				
Comer empanadas argentinas				
Comer comida mexicana				
Ver estrenos de películas				
Comprar artesanías				
Bailar ritmos latinos				
Asistir a una conferencia				

LECTURA ACTIVA

10.44. Leemos. Lee el texto. ¿En cuál de los cuatro lugares puedes hacer las actividades de 10.43?

10.45. Elegimos. Imagina que solo puedes elegir una de las ofertas de entretenimiento. ¿Cuál eliges y por qué?

DESPUÉS DE LEER

e **10.46. Proponemos opciones de entretenimiento.** Describe dos opciones de entretenimiento latino en tu ciudad o en alguna otra. Luego, preséntalas.

Textos escritos: leemos y escribimos

Leemos sobre los beneficios de escuchar música

INFORMACIÓN PREVIA Un estudio sobre los pasatiempos de la Generación Z (las personas que nacieron a partir del año 1994) indica que la música es el pasatiempo más practicado en los jóvenes, más que estar en las redes sociales o ver televisión.

10.47. La música y nosotros. ¿Es importante la música en tu vida? ¿Cuántas horas de música escuchas al día? ¿Qué tipo de música escuchas?

10.48. Efectos de la música. Marca qué efectos tiene la música en ti. Luego, da ejemplos concretos de canciones o músicas que te provocan esos efectos.

- Me hace bailar.
- Me relaja.
- Me ayuda a concentrarme.
- Me pone de buen humor.
- Me ayuda a dormir.
- Me da energía.

LECTURA ACTIVA

10.49. Lectura. Lee la infografía de forma general y observa las imágenes para obtener las ideas principales. Después, marca cuáles de estos beneficios tiene escuchar música.

- Ayuda a dormir.
- Facilita la digestión.
- Es bueno para los dientes y para la salud de la boca.
- Mejora la memoria a largo plazo.
- Previene problemas cardiovasculares.
- Ayuda a expresar nuestras emociones.
- Ayuda a perder peso.
- Fomenta el hábito de la lectura, especialmente entre los jóvenes.

¿Para qué es bueno escuchar música?

Para su salud mental
Porque le ayuda a combatir la depresión, la ansiedad y la demencia.

Para su felicidad
Porque estimula la producción de hormonas que generan alegría y optimismo, como la dopamina o la endorfina.

Para su placer
Porque activa el cerebro de la misma manera que cuando uno siente la satisfacción de comer u otros placeres.

Para su éxito académico
Porque el entrenamiento musical se relaciona con habilidades cognitivas, como el lenguaje. Eso mejora el rendimiento académico.

Para conciliar el sueño
Porque escuchar música antes de acostarse ayuda a quedarse dormido y proporciona un sueño más profundo y reparador.

Para expresar sus sentimientos
Porque la música permite exteriorizar sentimientos e impulsos reprimidos.

10.50. Comprobación. Compara con un/a compañero/-a tus respuestas de la actividad 10.48. Justifiquen su respuesta con frases o fragmentos del texto.

10.51. Interpretación. Lee la explicación de cada beneficio y encuentra en el texto las palabras que mejor expresan el significado de las palabras en inglés de la lista. Después lee el texto otra vez para entenderlo mejor.

1. to fight
2. joy
3. brain
4. school performance
5. to fall sleep
6. deep
7. it allows

10.52. Selección de información. Ahora, contesta las preguntas.

1. ¿Qué relación tiene escuchar música con la comida y otros placeres?
2. ¿Qué relación tiene escuchar música con la dopamina o la endorfina y por qué nos sentimos contentos cuando la escuchamos?
3. ¿Qué relación tiene aprender música con el rendimiento académico?

DESPUÉS DE LEER

10.53. Opinión. Responde estas preguntas.

1. ¿Hay algo que no sabías sobre los beneficios de escuchar música y que aprendiste en la infografía? ¿Qué te pareció lo más sorprendente?
2. ¿Has experimentado alguno de estos beneficios? ¿Cuál? Explica tu respuesta.
3. ¿Crees que cualquier tipo de música (rock, reguetón, etc.) puede ayudar a combatir el insomnio? ¿O crees que solo cierto tipo de música es mejor para poder dormir bien? Explica tu respuesta.

Creamos una infografía sobre los beneficios de un pasatiempo

10.54. Reacción personal. Sigue estas pautas para crear una infografía sobre un pasatiempo que aprendiste en esta lección u otro que tú haces.

- Haz una lista de cinco o seis posibles beneficios (observa el ejemplo).
- Escribe una pequeña explicación de cada beneficio.
- Selecciona una imagen y crea una infografía para compartirla con tu instructor/a y tus compañeros/-as.

Beneficios de cocinar

- Te alimentas de manera más saludable.
- Tienes más energía.
- Ahorras dinero.
- Te permite compartir buenos momentos con la gente que quieres.
- Relaja y es desestresante.
- Aprendes sobre otras culturas y tradiciones.

Recursos lingüísticos

IR A / PENSAR + INFINITIVE

▸ To talk about what you are going to do use **ir a** followed by an infinitive.

	IR	+ A	+ INFINITIVE
(yo)	**voy**		
(tú)	**vas**		
(él/ella, usted)	**va**		enseñar
(nosotros/nosotras)	**vamos**	**a**	comer
(vosotros/vosotras)	**vais**		ir
(ellos/ellas, ustedes)	**van**		

- ¿Qué **vas a hacer** el sábado por la noche? = What are you going to do Saturday night?
- **Voy a ir** a la casa de Pedro. = I'm going to Pedro's house.

▸ To talk about what we are planning to do we use **pensar** + infinitive.

	PENSAR	+ INFINITIVE
(yo)	**pienso**	
(tú)	**piensas**	
(él/ella, usted)	**piensa**	enseñar
(nosotros/nosotras)	**pensamos**	comer
(vosotros/vosotras)	**pensáis**	ir
(ellos/ellas, ustedes)	**piensan**	

Este fin de semana **pienso quedarme** *en casa y* **ver** *series todo el tiempo.* = This weekend I'm planning to stay home and watch shows online.

❗ In both these structures only the verbs **ir** and **pensar** are conjugated according to the person doing the action. The infinitive does not change.

❗ To talk about projects and intentions that are firm or have already been decided, we can also use the present tense.
Mañana **cenamos** *en la casa de Marta.* = Tomorrow we are having dinner at Marta's house.
El año que viene **termino** *la universidad.* = Next year I'm graduating from college.

TEMPORAL MARKERS TO TALK ABOUT THE FUTURE

Temporal markers refer to when things happen.

mañana = *tomorrow*
pasado mañana = *the day after tomorrow*

▸ Words like **hoy**, **por la tarde**, **el jueves**, **el fin de semana**, **en agosto**, **en el invierno**, etc. can also be used to refer to the future.

Hoy voy a salir a bailar. = Today I'm going to go out dancing.
En el invierno *pienso hacer un curso de natación.* = In the winter I'm planning to take a swim class.

ESTE/ESTA + POINT IN TIME

esta tarde/noche/semana... = *this afternoon / tonight / this week...*
este jueves/viernes/sábado/fin de semana... = *this Thursday/Friday/Saturday/weekend...*

DENTRO DE + A PERIOD OF TIME

dentro de un año / dos meses / tres semanas... = *in a year / two months / three weeks...*

POINT IN TIME + QUE VIENE

el lunes/mes/año... **que viene** = *next Monday/month/year...*

EL/LA PRÓXIMO/-A + POINT IN TIME

el próximo día/lunes/mes/año/verano = *next day/Monday/month/year/summer*
la próxima clase/sesión/primavera = *next class/session/spring*

CONDITIONAL CLAUSES (I): SI + PRESENT TENSE

▶ To express conditions referring to actions that habitually occur in the present, we use:

si + present tense

*Normalmente voy al trabajo, pero **si llueve**, voy en autobús.* = Normally I walk to work, but if it rains, I
go by bus.

▶ When the conditions refer to the future, we use **ir a / pensar** + infinitive:

*Si mañana llueve, **voy a ir** al trabajo en autobús.* = If it rains tomorrow, I'm going to go to work by bus.
*Si mañana llueve, **pienso ir** al trabajo en autobús.* = If it rains tomorrow, I'm planning to go to work by bus.

EXPRESSING CONDITIONS: DEPENDE DE / DEPENDE DE SI

Condtions can also be expressed using phrases meaning "depending on".

depende de + noun

• *¿Vas a ir a la fiesta de cumpleaños de Gabriela?* = Are you going to go to Gabriela's birthday party?
○ *No sé... **Depende de** mi trabajo.* = I don't know. It depends on work.

depende de si + present tense

• *¿A qué hora vas a salir del trabajo?* = What time are you leaving work?
○ *No sé... **Depende de si** termino el informe.* = I don't know... It depends on if/whether I finish the report.

¿Qué vas a hacer este fin de semana?

Depende. Si hay nieve, vamos a ir a esquiar, pero si no, vamos a quedarnos aquí.

Pronunciamos

Los sonidos /k/ y /s/: **c**, **k**, **qu**, **z**

10.55. Escuchamos y clasificamos. Un mismo sonido se puede escribir con letras diferentes. Escucha estas palabras y clasifícalas según su sonido: /k/, como en **casa**, o /s/, como en **cinco**.

discoteca	tranquilo	querer
excursión	ocio	precio
coctel	bucear	hacer
cerrado	escalar	que
zumba	pícnic	parque
organizar	correr	karaoke
exposición	quedarse	

/k/	/s/

10.56. Completamos la regla. Observa la clasificación de las palabras de la actividad 10.55 y completa la regla.

sonido /k/

- Se escribe **c** antes de **a**, ... y ....

  También se escribe **c** en posición final de sílaba.

- Se escribe **qu** antes de las vocales .... e ....

- Se escribe .... en algunas palabras procedentes de otras lenguas.

sonido /s/

- Se escribe **z** delante de .... o y ....

  También se escribe **z** en posición final de sílaba y en posición final de ....

- Se escribe **c** antes de las vocales .... e ....

> ⊕ **La variedad del español**
>
> Remember that in some parts of Spain, the letters **c** and **z** are pronounced like the **th** in *nothing* in the following cases:
>
> - **c** before **e** and **i**: **cerrado, cinco**
> - **z** before **a, o, u** or a consonant: **organizar, zona, zumba, puzle**

10.57. Escuchamos y repetimos. Escucha y repite.

1. En este restaurante sirven comida tradicional colombiana y el servicio es excepcional.
2. Vamos a hacer un pícnic en un parque tranquilo.
3. La discoteca cierra a las 10.
4. ¿Quieres ir al cine o prefieres quedarte en casa?
5. Mis aficiones son bucear, pescar y bailar zumba.

Vocabulario activo

))) **Eventos e información práctica**
Events and practical information

- **abierto** *open*
- **la actuación en vivo** *live performance*
- **la barra libre** *open bar*
- **la boleta** *ticket*
- **buena relación calidad-precio** *good value for the money*
- **el campeonato** *championship*
- **cerrado** *closed*
- **la comida rápida** *fast food*
- **la comida tradicional** *traditional food*
- **la conferencia** *conference, lecture*
- **la cover** *ticket*
- **doblado/-a** *dubbed*
- **la entrada** *ticket*
- **la entrada general** *general admission*
- **la entrada gratuita** *free admission*
- **la entrada reducida** *reduced ticket price*
- **el espectáculo** *show*
- **el espectáculo de baile/danza** (el baile, la danza) *dance performance*
- **el espectáculo de circo** (el circo) *circus show*
- **el espectáculo de magia** (la magia) *magic show*
- **el estreno** *premiere*
- **el evento** *event*
- **el (día) festivo** *holiday*
- **la función** *showing*
- **gratis** *free*
- **el horario** *schedule*
- **el local** *local*
- **la obra de arte** *work of art*
- **la obra de teatro** *play*
- **el partido** *game, match (sports)*
- **el precio promedio** *average price*
- **público general** *suitable for general public / all audiences*
- **reservar** *to book/reserve*
- **el servicio** *service*
- **subtitulado/-a** *subtitled*
- **con subtítulos** (el subtítulo) *with subtitles*

))) **Actividades de tiempo libre** *Leisure activities*

- **bucear** *to scuba dive*
- **correr** *to run, to jog*
- **escalar** *to scale, to climb*
- **hacer/practicar artes marciales** (las artes marciales) *to do martial arts*
- **hacer/practicar meditación** (la meditación) *to meditate*
- **hacer/practicar natación** (la natación) *to swim*
- **hacer/practicar senderismo** (el senderismo) *to hike*
- **hacer/practicar surf** (el surf) *to surf*
- **hacer un curso de cocina / escritura creativa** *to take a cooking/creative writing class*
- **hacer/organizar un pícnic** *to have/organize a picnic*
- **hacer/organizar una barbacoa** *to have/organize a barbecue*
- **hacer/organizar una fiesta** *to have/organize a party*
- **ir a clases de canto / dibujo / defensa personal** *to go to singing / drawing / self defense lessons*
- **ir a la bolera** *to go bowling*
- **ir al estadio** *to go to the stadium*
- **ir al teatro** *to go to the theater*
- **ir a una fiesta** *to go to a party*
- **ir a una inauguración** *to go to an opening*
- **ir de excursión** *to go on a trip*
- **ir de viaje** *to go traveling*
- **jugar ajedrez** *to play chess*
- **jugar boliche** *to bowl*
- **jugar juegos de mesa** *to play board games*
- **jugar póker** *to play poker*
- **jugar un partido de beisbol/voleibol** *to play a baseball/volleyball game*
- **no hacer nada** *to do nothing*
- **participar en una carrera/competición/maratón** *to participate in a race/cempetition/marathon*
- **pasar el día con la familia/(los) amigos** *to spend the day with the family/friends*
- **pasar el día en casa / la playa** *to spend the day at home / the beach*
- **pescar** *to fish*
- **quedarse en casa** *to stay at home*
- **relajarse** *to relax*
- **tomar algo** *to have a drink*
- **tomar el sol** *to sunbathe*

> ⚙ **Estrategia**
>
> For those words that are not presented as part of an expression or phrase, try to combine them with other words as you might in English. Then check yourself using online dictionaries, language forums, search engines, etc. to see if the combination also works in Spanish.

Lección 11

No como carne

IN THIS LESSON WE ARE GOING TO

prepare a menu for a class party

LEARNING OUTCOMES
You will be able to...

- talk about food preferences

- explain how to prepare a dish

VOCABULARY

- Foods

- Packaging, weights, and measures

- Food preparation

- Kitchen utensils

LANGUAGE STRUCTURES

- Impersonal expressions (I): using **se**

- Impersonal expressions (II): other forms

- Direct object (DO) pronouns (I)

- Connectors: **pero**, **además**

PRONUNCIATION

- Pronunciation of the letters **z/c**, **j**, and **ll/y**

CULTURAL CONNECTIONS

- Four of the best Hispanic-American chefs in the world

El chef Enrique Olvera en el Food Network & Cooking Channel South Beach Wine & Food Festival (Miami, Florida)

Primer contacto

11.1. ¿Qué cenan? Unas personas cuentan qué cenan normalmente. ¿Te identificas con alguna de ellas?

1 Compro algo para cenar rápido: muchas veces una **arepa**.

2 Cenamos algo fácil: normalmente una **ensalada**.

3 Normalmente ceno **verdura**. Y, a veces, también **queso**.

4 Casi nunca cenamos. A veces, si tenemos hambre, comemos algo ligero: un **yogur**...

5 Cenamos dos platos: una **sopa** o verdura y **carne**.

Yo normalmente también ceno algo ligero, una ensalada o un yogur.

Comprendemos el vocabulario

Alimentos

))) 11.2. A granel. Estas son las ofertas de la semana de una tienda de México. Observa, lee y escucha.

e

DESPENSA A GRANEL

NOSOTROS   CONTACTO   🔍

OFERTAS ▼   frutas y **verduras** | cereales y harinas | frutos secos y **semillas** | lácteos | aceites y vinagres | hierbas y especias | legumbres

tomate
MXN 25/k

cebolla
MXN 21/k

papa
MXN 24,5/k

aguacate
MXN 44/k

limón
MXN 18/k

naranja
MXN 21/k

chile serrano
MXN 416/k

manzana
MXN 30,5/k

yuca
MXN 21,6/100 g

elote
MXN 130/unidad

frijoles
MXN 1038/k

arroz integral
MXN 69/k

leche fresca
MXN 46/l

ajo
MXN 31/100 g

galletas de avena
MXN 92/100 g

azúcar integral
MXN 55/k

harina de maíz
MXN 45/k

cacahuates
MXN 85/500 g

Más palabras

))) CARNE Y PESCADO= *MEAT AND FISH*
- **el atún** = *tuna*
- **el cerdo** = *pork*
- **el embutido** = *cold meat*
- **el jamón** = *ham*
- **el marisco** = *shellfish*
- **el pavo** = *turkey*
- **el pollo** = *chicken*
- **la res** = *beef*

VERDURAS Y VEGETALES = *GREENS AND VEGETABLES*
- **la calabacita** = *zucchini*
- **la lechuga** = *lettuce*
- **el pimiento** = *pepper*
- **la zanahoria** = *carrot*

BEBIDAS = *BEVERAGES*
- **el agua** = *water*
- **el agua con gas** = *sparkling water*
- **el café** = *coffee*
- **el jugo** = *juice*
- **el refresco** = *soda, soft drink*
- **el té** = *tea*
- **el vino** = *wine*

FRUTAS = *FRUITS*
- **la banana** = *banana*
- **el durazno** = *peach*
- **la fresa** = *strawberry*
- **la pera** = *pear*
- **la piña** = *pineapple*
- **la uva** = *grape*

OTROS = *OTHER*
- **el aceite de oliva** = *olive oil*
- **la barra energética** = *energy bar*
- **el chocolate** = *chocolate*
- **el helado** = *ice cream*
- **el huevo** = *egg*
- **la jalea** = *jelly*
- **la miel** = *honey*
- **la mostaza** = *mustard*
- **el pan** = *bread*
- **la sal** = *salt*
- **la salsa** = *sauce*
- **la torta** = *cake*

> 🌐 **La variedad del español**
>
> The names for food vary across Spanish-speaking countries and even in different regions of the same country. For instance, **cacahuate** is **maní** in many countries and **cacahuete** in Spain. **Frijoles** is **habichuelas** in Puerto Rico and República Dominicana, **poroto** in at least five countries and **alubias** or **judías** in Spain. **Patatas** is used in Spain instead of **papas**.

11.3. ¿Todos los días? ¿Con qué frecuencia consumes los productos de la actividad 11.2? Clasifícalos.

Todos los días	A menudo	De vez en cuando	Nunca o casi nunca

11.4. Comentamos nuestros hábitos. En parejas, comenten si consumen los productos de la actividad 11.2 con la misma frecuencia.

> ● *Yo casi nunca como fruta. No me gusta mucho. ¿Y tú?*
> ○ *Yo sí, me gusta mucho. Pero nunca como fresas, soy alérgico.*

💬 **Para comunicar**

ser alérgico/-a (a) = *to be allergic (to)*
tener alergia a = *to have an allergy to*

Soy alérgico a las fresas.
Tengo alergia a las fresas.

11.5. Las comidas de mañana. Piensa qué vas a comer mañana y escribe la lista de la compra.

Mis comidas de mañana	Mi lista de la compra
Desayuno: Almuerzo: Cena:	

11.6. ¿Qué llevan? Escucha y escribe en tu cuaderno qué ingredientes llevan estos platos típicos de Hispanoamérica.

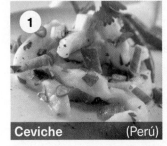
Ceviche (Perú)

Bolón de verde (Ecuador)

Bandeja paisa (Colombia)

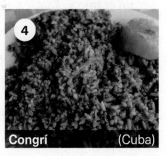
Congrí (Cuba)

11.7. Queremos probar... ¿Cuál de los platos de la actividad 11.6 te gustaría probar? ¿Por qué? Coméntenlo entre todos para saber cuál es el plato más popular en la clase.

> *A mí me gustaría probar el ceviche porque me encanta el pescado y casi nunca como.*

❗ **¿Necesitas ayuda?**

probar = *to try*

11.8. Dos platos típicos. Piensa en dos platos típicos de tu país. Anota cómo se llaman y qué llevan.

Plato:
....

Lleva:
....
....

Plato:
....

Lleva:
....
....

❗ **¿Necesitas ayuda?**

Do you remember that the verb **llevar** means "to carry" or "to wear"? Note that it can also be used to tell the ingredients in a dish.

¿Qué lleva la sopa? = What is in the soup?

¿La ensalada lleva queso? = Does the salad have cheese?

Comprendemos el vocabulario

Empaques, pesos y medidas

 11.9. Empaques, pesos y medidas. Lee y escucha.

una lata de atún

una docena de huevos

un paquete de arroz

una caja de chocolates

un frasco de jalea

una bolsa de papitas

un cartón de leche

una botella de agua

un pedazo de queso

una loncha de jamón

Más palabras

 una cucharada = *tablespoon*
una cucharadita = *teaspoon*
un gramo = *gram*
un kilo = *kilo*

un litro = *liter*
por peso = *by weight*
un poco de = *a little bit of*
una taza = *cup*

> **❶ ¿Necesitas ayuda?**
> 1 onza (ounce) = 28,35 g
> 1 libra (pound) = 453,6 g

11.10. ¿Por peso o por unidades? Escribe cómo compras estos alimentos normalmente.

en cartones   en bolsas   en botellas   en latas   en frascos   en paquetes   en cajas   por peso

• el arroz: *en paquetes o por peso*

• la harina:

• la pasta:

• las galletas:

• los cereales:

• los frutos secos:

• la leche:

• las especias y hierbas aromáticas:

• el queso:

• el jugo:

11.11. Una bolsa de... Completa cada unidad de medida o empaque con tres alimentos diferentes a los de la actividad 11.10.

1. Una bolsa de ....

2. Una lata de ....

3. Una loncha de ....

4. Una taza de ....

9. Un frasco de ....

5. Un paquete de ....

6. Un kilo de ....

7. Un litro de ....

8. Un cartón de ....

Elaboración de platos y utensilios de cocina

 11.12. Lavar, pelar y cortar. Lee y escucha.

Tacos de pollo al horno

- **Echar** un poco de aceite de oliva en **una sartén** y **poner a fuego medio**.
- **Picar** media cebolla y **saltear** 2-3 minutos.
- **Lavar, pelar** y **cortar** tres tomates grandes en pedazos pequeños y **reservar**.
- **Trocear** 250 g de pollo y **agregar** el tomate y el pollo a la sartén. **Remover** bien.
- **Añadir** 100 g de jalapeños y 25 g de condimento para tacos.
- **Tapar** y cocinar durante 5-8 minutos **a fuego lento, mezclar** bien y **retirar**.
- **Colocar** unas 10 tortillas de maíz en una **bandeja de horno**.
- **Rellenar** las tortillas con una cucharada de frijoles negros y la mezcla de cebolla, tomate y pollo.
- **Rallar** queso y echar por encima de las tortillas.
- **Hornear** los tacos unos 10-12 minutos.
- **Sacar** del horno y **servir** con lechuga, más queso, etc.

Más palabras

 ELABORACIÓN = *PREPARATION*

aplastar = *to crush*
asar = *to roast*
batir = *to whip*
calentar = *to heat*
cocer = *to boil, to cook*
exprimir = *to squeeze*
freír = *to fry*

hacer a la plancha = *to grill*
moler = *to grind*
quitar = *to remove*
triturar = *to blend*

UTENSILIOS DE COCINA = *KITCHEN UTENSILS*
la cacerola = *saucepan*
la cuchara = *spoon*

el cuchillo = *knife*
el horno = *oven*
la olla = *pot*
el tenedor = *fork*
el vaso = *glass*

> ⚙ **Estrategia**
>
> Recognizing word families will help you build your vocabulary.
>
> **freír** **frito** *(fried)*
> **asar** **asado** *(roasted)*
> **moler** **molido** *(ground)*

e **11.13. Acciones.** Escribe el verbo correspondiente en cada caso. Usa el vocabulario de la receta y de Más palabras.

 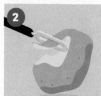    

11.14. Para cocinar. Escribe qué objetos necesitamos para hacer estas cosas. Hay más de una opción posible.

1. Para freír: ....
2. Para cortar: ....
3. Para cocer: ....
4. Para calentar: ....

5. Para asar: ....
6. Para beber: ....
7. Para tomar sopa: ....

Exploramos la lengua

Expresar impersonalidad (I): oraciones con **se**

e **11.15. La receta del guacamole.** Lee la receta y escribe a qué se refieren los verbos en negrita.

Ingredientes para 6 personas

- dos aguacates
- un tomate
- 1/2 cebolla
- un diente de ajo

- uno o dos chiles
- un poco de jugo de limón
- sal
- nachos

Preparación

Se pelan los aguacates, **se colocan** en un recipiente y, con un tenedor, **se aplastan** hasta obtener un puré. **Se pela** el tomate, **se quitan** las semillas, **se corta** en pedazos pequeños y **se añade** al puré de aguacate. Luego, **se pican** la cebolla, el ajo y los chiles y **se agregan** a la mezcla junto con el jugo de limón y la sal (al gusto). **Se sirve** con nachos.

1. Se pelan: los aguacates
2. Se colocan:
3. Se aplastan:
4. Se pela:
5. Se quitan:

6. Se corta:
7. Se añade:
8. Se pican:
9. Se agregan:
10. Se sirve:

11.16. Completamos la regla. Observa los verbos de la actividad 11.15 y relaciona para obtener la regla.

1. Se usa la tercera persona del singular con...	**a.** ... sustantivos en singular.
2. Se usa la tercera persona del plural con...	**b.** ... sustantivos en plural o varios sustantivos en singular.

11.17. Se producen vinos. Transforma estas frases usando **se** + 3ª persona, como en el ejemplo.

1. La provincia de Mendoza, en Argentina, produce vinos.

> En la provincia de Mendoza, en Argentina, se producen vinos.

2. Los restaurantes de la zona de Salta sirven unas empanadas riquísimas.
3. Los mexicanos cocinan con mucho picante.
4. Los argentinos, los uruguayos y los paraguayos toman mucho mate.
5. En la Patagonia elaboran la cerveza Patagonia.
6. Los peruanos comen mucho pescado y marisco.

11.18. ¿Qué se hace? Escribe qué cosas se hacen en algún lugar que conoces bien.

> En Napa, California, se producen vinos muy buenos.

11.19. Las papas se lavan. Escribe qué se hace normalmente con estos productos.

| las papas | las naranjas | el arroz | el pescado |
| la carne | los huevos | la leche | las fresas |

> Las papas se lavan y se pelan. Y se fríen, se asan o se cuecen.

❗ ¿Necesitas ayuda?

Cocer, moler, calentar, and **servir** are stem-changing verbs: **se cuece, se muele, se calienta, se sirve...**

FREÍR

yo	**frío**
tú	**fríes**
él/ella, usted	**fríe**
nosotros/-as	**freímos**
vosotros/-as	**freís**
ellos/-as, ustedes	**fríen**

Expresar impersonalidad (II): otras estructuras

11.20. Costumbres gastronómicas. Lee los textos e identifica a qué país se refiere cada persona: ¿Estados Unidos, China o Italia?

¿Qué y cómo come la gente?

Tres personas nos hablan de costumbres gastronómicas de los países donde fueron a vivir hace algunos años.

"Se come con palillos y a todas horas del día. La gente come mucho parada, en la calle, en sitios de comida rápida. ¡Ah! Y hay que comer rápido. A veces, en 10 o 15 minutos."

Gerardo

"Aquí es normal comer pasta una o dos veces al día. La pasta está riquísima, especialmente cuando la hacen en la casa. También se toma mucho café, incluso por la noche, antes de acostarse. Y no es raro tomar helado en el invierno; el helado aquí está riquísimo."

Aileen

"Cuando vas a un restaurante, tienes que dejar propina, por lo menos un 20%; si no lo haces, te miran mal. En los sitios de comida rápida no funciona así, ahí hay que pagar justo lo que cuesta la comida. También es sorprendente la cantidad: ¡sirven mucha comida!"

Ayana

11.21. Expresar impersonalidad. En estas frases de los textos de la actividad 11.20 hay recursos que sirven para expresar impersonalidad. ¿Cómo expresas lo mismo en tu lengua?

1. **Se come** con palillos.
2. **La gente come** mucho parada.
3. Ahí **es normal comer** pasta una o dos veces al día.
4. Y **no es raro tomar** helado en invierno.
5. Cuando **vas** a un restaurante, **tienes que** dejar propina.
6. Ahí [en los sitios de comida rápida] **hay que** pagar justo lo que cuesta la comida.
7. **Sirven** mucha comida.

> ⚙ **Estrategia**
>
> Comparing Spanish to your language will help you discover if both languages work the same. Thus, you'll realize that translating literally does not always work. You will also learn more about your own language and how you comunicate.

"Se come con palillos" en inglés se puede expresar con "People eat with chopsticks", ¿no?

11.22. Nuestras costumbres. Escribe frases sobre las costumbres de tu país usando estas ideas.

la hora de la cena   el desayuno fuerte o ligero   costumbres en los restaurantes

comprar comida preparada o fresca   consumo de pescado, carne y leche

almorzar en el trabajo   número de comidas en un día   comer con la familia

> 💬 **Para comunicar**
>
> Es...
> **normal** + infinitivo
> **habitual** + infinitivo
> **frecuente** + infinitivo
> **raro** + infinitivo

En Estados Unidos es raro cenar después de las 9 p.m.

11.23. Comparamos. En parejas, comparen sus frases de la actividad 11.22. ¿Coinciden?

Exploramos la lengua

Pronombres Personales de Objeto Directo (OD)

11.24. Las empanadas de Florián. Florián es un gran cocinero y su hija Marisa, que ahora vive sola, le pide consejos. Escucha la conversación y contesta estas preguntas.

1. ¿Qué ingredientes llevan las empanadas?
2. ¿Cuál es el truco de Florián para hacer las empanadas?
3. ¿Qué decide Marisa hacer al final?

11.25. Lo, la, los, las. Observa los pronombres de objeto directo (OD) **lo**, **las**, **los** y **las** marcados en negrita y señala a qué sustantivo se refieren en cada caso.

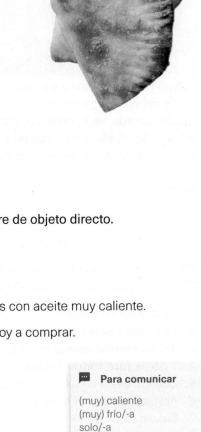

1. Picas la carne y **la** reservas. ....

2. Limpias los tomates, **los** pelas y **los** trituras. ....

3. Rallas el queso y **lo** agregas a la mezcla. ....

4. Rellenas las empanadas y **las** cierras. ....

11.26. Pronombres de objeto directo. Completa el cuadro con los pronombres de objeto directo.

PRONOMBRES PERSONALES DE OBJETO DIRECTO		
	Singular	**Plural**
Masculino	....	....
Femenino	....	....

11.27. Usamos los pronombres. Completa estas frases con un pronombre de objeto directo.

1. Hoy las verduras tienen un sabor diferente. .... hice con especias.

2. ¡Qué pan tan rico! ¿.................... hiciste tú?

3. Para hacer patacón con hogao, cortas un plátano en pedazos y .... fríes con aceite muy caliente.

4. No tengo tiempo para hacer una torta de cumpleaños para Javier. .... voy a comprar.

11.28. ¿Cómo lo tomas? Escribe cómo tomas estas comidas y bebidas, como en el ejemplo.

cereales	hamburguesas	pizza	papas fritas

café	té	leche	refrescos	agua

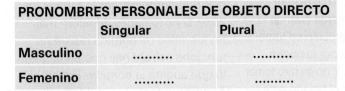

Yo, el café, lo tomo solo y sin azúcar. / Yo, café, no tomo nunca.

11.29. ¿Coincidimos? En parejas, comparen cómo toman las comidas y bebidas de la actividad 11.28. ¿Coinciden?

- ¿Cómo tomas tú el café?
- Yo no tomo nunca café. No me gusta. ¿Y tú?
- Yo lo tomo solo y sin azúcar.

> **··· Para comunicar**
>
> (muy) caliente
> (muy) frío/-a
> solo/-a
> No tomo nunca.
>
> con/sin | leche
> | limón
> | gas
> | hielo
> | azúcar
> | sal
> | kétchup
> | mostaza
> | carne
> | queso
> | lechuga
> | cebolla
> | ...

11.30. ¿En la alacena o en el refrigerador? Skyler fue al supermercado. Identifica los productos que compró y di dónde los guardó: en la alacena o en el refrigerador.

el aceite
los huevos
las papitas
las manzanas
el café
el pescado
la carne
la leche
la jalea
el queso
los ajos
las zanahorias
los yogures
la miel
las galletas
los tomates

El aceite, lo guardó en la alacena.
Los huevos, los guardó en el refrigerador.

Conectores: **pero**, **además**

11.31. Dos supermercados. Lee estas frases. Las palabras destacadas son conectores. ¿Cuál se utiliza para presentar un argumento opuesto al anterior? ¿Cuál para presentar un argumento que refuerza otro?

**Este supermercado es muy bueno y,
además, no es muy caro.**

**Este supermercado es muy bueno,
pero es muy caro.**

e 11.32. Además o pero. Escribe la opción más lógica en cada una de estas frases: **además** o **pero**.

1. La sopa está rica, ... le falta un poco de sal, ¿no crees?

2. Al lado de mi casa hay un supermercado muy barato. .... está abierto hasta las doce de la noche.

3. Me encanta el café, ... el médico me recomendó reducir el consumo.

4. Prueba estas galletas. Están muy ricas y, ..., son muy ligeras.

5. Normalmente como postre, ... hoy no quiero.

Comunicamos

Consejos para una dieta sana

11.33. Consejos. Lee los consejos que dan en una campaña de salud. Marca los que normalmente sigues.

SE ACONSEJA
EL CONSUMO FRECUENTE DE:

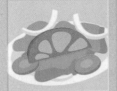     

| Verduras crudas (en ensalada) o al vapor | Papas cocidas o al vapor | Carne blanca (pollo, pavo, etc.) a la plancha o al horno | Pescado blanco y pescado azul crudo, a la plancha o al horno | Productos lácteos y huevos cocidos | Cereales integrales (arroz, pan, pasta, etc.). Frutas y frutos secos |

NO SE ACONSEJA
EL CONSUMO FRECUENTE DE:

  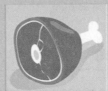

| Alimentos fritos • papas fritas • pescado frito | Comida preparada • pizzas • platos de pasta preparados | Dulces y tortas | Carne roja | Embutidos (chorizo, jamón, etc.) |

 11.34. Nuestros hábitos. Comenta con otra persona de la clase cuáles de los consejos de la actividad 11.33 sigues y cuéntale cómo te alimentas.

- Yo no como carne roja. No me gusta.
- Yo sí como carne roja; normalmente la como a la plancha.

11.35. Comer sano. ¿Crees que en tu país se come sano? ¿Por qué? Coméntenlo en grupos.

- Yo creo que no mucho, porque hay que comer pan integral y la gente normalmente come pan blanco.
- Sí, y no se come mucho pescado...

Para comunicar

El pescado **lo** como...	cocid**o**/-**a**/-**os**/-**as**
La carne **la** como...	frit**o**/-**a**/-**os**/-**as**
Los huevos **los** como...	asad**o**/-**a**/-**os**/-**as**
Las papas **las** como	crud**o**/-**a**/-**os**/-**as**
	a la plancha
	al horno/vapor

La dieta de Silvia

11.36. Una dieta para mantenerse en forma. ¿Qué cosas de la lista creen que come una preparadora física para mantenerse en forma? ¿Cuáles no?

- verdura
- *sushi*
- marisco
- fruta
- pescado
- tortas
- chocolate
- hamburguesas
- pan integral
- pasta

11.37. La dieta de Silvia. Escucha a una preparadora física y comprueba tus hipótesis de la actividad 11.36. Escribe en la tabla qué come y qué no come.

Come	No come

11.38. Comentamos algunas dietas. ¿Siguen o conocen alguna dieta? Expliquen a sus compañeros/-as en qué consiste.

> ● *Yo hice una vez la dieta Atkins. Tienes que comer solo proteína.*
> ○ *¿Solo?*
> ● *Al principio, sí.*

Para comunicar

Hay que...	
No hay que...	comer/beber/tomar...
Tienes que...	
No tienes que	

Una comida familiar

11.39. Una comida familiar. Antonio cuenta cómo es una comida familiar en su casa. Escucha y toma nota de lo que dice.

11.40. Encuentros y reuniones familiares. ¿Se parecen las reuniones familiares de Antonio a las reuniones familiares en tu entorno (tu ciudad, tu comunidad, tu familia...)? Coméntenlo en grupos.

> ● *Aquí también se hacen comidas al aire libre cuando hace buen tiempo.*
> ○ *Sí, es habitual hacer barbacoas y...*

11.41. ¿Cómo se celebra? En grupos, piensen en una fiesta que se celebra en su entorno (ciudad, comunidad, familia...) y preparen una presentación. Tengan en cuenta estas cuestiones.

- ¿Qué fiesta es?
- ¿Se celebra en un día o época específica del año?
- ¿Hay un lugar específico donde se celebra? ¿Cuál?
- ¿Quién se reúne en esta celebración?
- ¿Qué se hace?
- ¿Qué se come?
- ¿Durante cuánto tiempo se celebra?

Ahora podemos...

Organizar una cena de la clase

 11.42. Platos para un menú. Van a preparar una cena. En parejas, piensen un plato para cada categoría. Pueden combinar platos de todo el mundo con platos hispanos.

- entrada fría
- entrada caliente
- plato fuerte
- postre

 11.43. Los ingredientes. Investiguen y escriban cómo se preparan y qué ingredientes llevan los platos que pensaron en la actividad 11.42.

 11.44. Presentamos nuestros platos. Presenten sus platos a los demás. Ellos les van a hacer preguntas sobre los ingredientes y la preparación.

> - *Nosotros queremos preparar tembleque, un postre típico de Puerto Rico. Se hace con leche de coco, azúcar...*
> - *¿Lleva harina?*
> - *Sí, lleva harina de maíz.*
> - *¿Es fácil de hacer?*

> 💬 **Para comunicar**
>
> **¿Es fácil/difícil de hacer?** = *Is it easy/hard to do or to make?*

11.45. Elegimos el menú. Entre todos, elijan los platos que gustan a la mayoría (dos platos por cada categoría y la bebida). Tengan en cuenta los gustos, alergias e intolerancias de todas las personas de la clase.

MENÚ

ENTRADA FRÍA
Ensalada de tomate y queso fresco
Guacamole con nachos

ENTRADA CALIENTE
Jalapeños rellenos de queso
Macarrones con queso

PLATO FUERTE
Pescado al horno con verduras asadas
Carne a la plancha con papas fritas

POSTRE
Tembleque
Suspiro limeño

BEBIDA
Agua y refrescos

 11.46. La lista de la compra. Ahora, tienen que hacer la lista de la compra. Tengan en cuenta cuántas personas van a la cena.

> - *Tenemos que comprar leche de coco. Dos latas es suficiente, ¿no?*
> - *No sé, somos diecisiete...*

> 💬 **Para comunicar**
>
> **¿Es suficiente?** = *Is it enough?*
> **No tenemos (suficiente/s)...**
> **Necesitamos (más)...**
> **Tenemos que comprar...**
> **Hay que comprar...**

Las recetas de mi abuela

Alma Medina dice que sus recetas familiares son el legado que deja para sus hijos y nietos. Su receta secreta de panes con pollo, un plato tradicional salvadoreño, forma parte de la familia desde hace generaciones y ahora, en *Las recetas de mi abuela*, Alma pasa su legado a la siguiente generación.

Pearson MyLab

To find out more about Alma and her family recipes, go to MyLab to watch **Las recetas de mi abuela** and complete the video activities.

⊕ ¿Sabes que...?

Foods from Spanish-speaking countries make their way on to the dinner plates of everyday Americans. For most Americans, *tacos* are about as exotic as pizza. *Salsa* consistently beats out ketchup as the most popular condiment in the U.S., and in towns across the country, you can easily find restaurants serving *arroz con pollo* or Salvadoran *pupusas*. The influence of foods from Central and South America, Mexico, and the Caribbean on American cuisine is so strong that in 2017, the United States Post office issued Delicioso stamps featuring images of *ceviche*, *tamales*, *sancocho*, *chile relleno*, *flan* and *empanadas*.

🔍 Hacemos conexiones

Investiga sobre la presencia de la comida de países donde se habla español en los Estados Unidos y sobre cómo la cocina americana refleja la influencia de ese tipo de comida.

Sabor hispano:

4 de los mejores chefs hispanos del mundo

José Ramón Andrés Puerta, de origen español y nacionalizado estadounidense en 2013, es un chef reconocido internacionalmente por su cocina y por sus labores humanitarias. En 2012 y en 2018, la revista *Times* lo incluyó en la lista de las 100 personas más influyentes del mundo. José Andrés vive en Estados Unidos y tiene varios restaurantes en diferentes ciudades del país, como Washington, Las Vegas, Los Ángeles o Miami.

Después del terremoto en Haití, en 2010, fundó la ONG World Central Kitchen para dar alimentos a los afectados por catástrofes naturales. En Puerto Rico, tras el paso del huracán María, el chef español y su equipo repartieron más de tres millones de raciones de comida.

Daniela Soto-Innes nació en México, pero se fue a vivir a Estados Unidos a los 12 años.

A los 15, empezó a trabajar como cocinera profesional. Soto-Innes es la jefa de cocina del restaurante Cosme, en Nueva York, propiedad del chef mexicano Enrique Olvera.

En 2015 ganó el StarChefs Rising Stars Award y, un año más tarde, la Fundación James Beard la nombró "Rising Star Chef".

En 2017 abrió el restaurante Atla con el chef Olvera en el NoHo neoyorquino, un restaurante de cocina mexicana saludable y ligera. El nombre "Atla" viene del náhuatl *atl-tlachinolli*, que significa 'la unión entre el agua y el fuego'.

Richard Sandoval es uno de los chefs mexicanos más reconocidos. Estudió en The Culinary Institute of America de Nueva York, donde abrió sus primeros restaurantes, Savann y Savann Est, y, más tarde, el famoso Maya, que fusiona la gastronomía tradicional mexicana con la cocina moderna.

Cocinero, asesor gastronómico, autor de libros de cocina y personaje televisivo, el chef Sandoval dirige el grupo de restaurantes RS Hospitality.

En 2017 The World's 50 Best nombró a Leonor Espinosa mejor cocinera de Latinoamérica.

Leonor Espinosa de La Ossa nació en Bogotá, Colombia. Su restaurante Leo es un referente de la gastronomía colombiana: usa productos locales y recupera recetas nativas. En 2007, la revista *Condé Nast Traveler* lo incluyó en la lista de los 82 mejores del mundo –y entre los cinco de América Latina–.

En 2017 ganó la segunda edición del Basque Culinary World Prize con su proyecto Funleo, una fundación que reivindica el saber ancestral de las comunidades de su país, especialmente las indígenas y afrocolombianas.

ANTES DE LEER

11.47. Chefs. ¿Conoces algún/a chef hispano/-a? ¿Qué sabes de él/ella (cómo se llama, de dónde es...)?

11.48. Características. ¿Qué define a un/a gran chef? Marca las características más importantes según tu opinión.

Un/a gran chef...

- ⬤ hace labores humanitarias.
- ⬤ tiene muchos restaurantes.
- ⬤ prepara comida saludable.
- ⬤ prepara comida diferente.
- ⬤ tiene muchos premios.
- ⬤ usa productos locales.
- ⬤ escribe libros de cocina.
- ⬤ tiene un programa de televisión.

LECTURA ACTIVA

11.49. ¿Quién es? Lee el texto sobre los cuatro chefs y di con quién o quiénes relacionas estas informaciones.

1. Tiene restaurantes en varias ciudades de EE. UU.
2. Tiene un restaurante en Manhattan con otro chef.
3. Ganó dos premios para los chefs principiantes.
4. Es el/la mejor cocinero/-a de Latinoamérica.
5. Combina dos tipos de gastronomía.
6. Escribe libros de recetas.
7. Quiso alimentar a la gente afectada por catástrofes naturales.
8. Tiene uno de los mejores restaurantes del mundo.

11.50. Intercambiamos opiniones. Para ti, ¿cuál es el más interesante de los cuatro? ¿Y el que hace un trabajo más importante? ¿Por qué? Coméntalo con otras personas de la clase.

DESPUÉS DE LEER

11.51. Queremos probar... En grupos, comenten de qué chef les gustaría probar la comida. Justifiquen su respuesta. Pueden usar internet para consultar la carta de sus restaurantes.

Textos audiovisuales: vemos, escuchamos y presentamos

Vemos un video de cómo se prepara un plato típico mexicano

11.52. Preparación. ¿Qué platos mexicanos conoces? ¿Qué ingredientes llevan?

INFORMACIÓN PREVIA Vas a ver un video en el que una persona explica cómo se preparan las calabacitas con crema, una receta típica de México, y habla de algunas características de la gastronomía y costumbres mexicanas.

VEMOS EL VIDEO

11.53. Ingredientes. Ve hasta el minuto 00:40 y escribe qué ingredientes lleva el plato.

11.54. Cantidades. Ve de nuevo el mismo fragmento y escribe las cantidades que se mencionan de los ingredientes que anotaste en la actividad 11.53.

11.55. Utensilios. Ve ahora hasta el minuto 1:00 y di qué tres utensilios se mencionan en el video.

11.56. Características del plato. Ve de nuevo desde el principio hasta el minuto 1:00 y responde.

1. ¿De qué parte de México es típica esta receta?
2. ¿Qué tipo de plato es: una entrada, un plato fuerte, un postre...?
3. ¿En qué momento del día se suele comer?

11.57. Comprensión. Continúa viendo el video hasta el minuto 2:09 y, después, realiza estas actividades.

1. Marca, en cada caso, qué ingrediente se corta más pequeño.

❶ 	❷ 	❸
a. la cebolla **b.** los tomates	**a.** los tomates **b.** las calabacitas	**a.** la cebolla **b.** los chiles

2. Di tres características sobre los chiles en general que se mencionan en el video.
3. ¿Cómo es el chile serrano según el video? Escríbelo.

11.58. Fiesta en casa. Ve el video desde el minuto 2:12 hasta 3:02. Completa la información.

1. Cuando celebran una fiesta en la casa de César, preparan ....
2. Un taco es ....

11.59. Procedencia. Termina de ver el video y escribe en la columna correcta los alimentos que menciona César según el origen que tienen.

Origen americano	Origen europeo

11.60. Elaboración de la receta. Ve el video completo y ordena los pasos de la receta.

a. Se ralla el queso.
b. Se pone aceite en la cacerola.
c. Se agregan los tomates.
d. Se agrega la sal y la crema de leche.
e. Se pican las verduras en diferentes tamaños.
f. Se calientan unas tortillas y se hacen tacos.

g. Se remueven los ingredientes y se dejan cocinar de 10 a 15 minutos.
h. Se cubre.
i. Se agregan las calabacitas.
j. Se agregan la cebolla y los chiles.

1	2	3	4	5	6	7	8	9	10
e								f	

DESPUÉS DE VER EL VIDEO

11.61. Reacción. Piensa y contesta.

1. En el video, César dice que la receta de calabacitas con crema es versátil. ¿A ti te parece que lo es? ¿Por qué?
2. ¿Te parece que las calabacitas con crema es un plato completo? Justifica tu respuesta.
3. ¿Qué te parece la opción de comer este plato por la mañana, por la tarde o por la noche? ¿Hay algún plato en tu cultura, o en alguna que conozcas, que también se come a cualquier hora del día? Habla con tus compañeros/-as.

Presentamos un plato que nos gusta

11.62. Presentación. Vas a crear un video de unos 4-5 minutos para presentar un plato (puede ser algo típico de tu país o región) y animar a la gente del mundo hispano a probarlo. Piensa en algo sencillo. Sigue estos pasos.

- Primero, escribe el guion del video. Debes incluir una descripción del plato y datos que te parezcan interesantes o relevantes: ¿hay ingredientes que no son muy conocidos? ¿De dónde vienen? ¿Se come como entrada, como plato fuerte, como postre, como *snack*...?
- Haz una lista de todos los ingredientes y las cantidades. Después, escribe los pasos de la receta.
- Revisa tu guion. Recuerda que la audiencia son personas del mundo hispano.
- Piensa en el lugar donde vas a cocinar y grabar tu video. ¿Necesitas ayuda para grabarlo?
- Consigue los ingredientes para tu plato y déjalos listos para preparar la receta.
- Graba tu video.

11.63. Comparte el video con la clase. ¿Cuál es el plato más fácil de preparar? ¿Y el más versátil?

Recursos lingüísticos

IMPERSONAL EXPRESSIONS (I): USING SE

In impersonal sentences the subject or person doing the action is either unknown or not relevant. In Spanish there are various ways to highlight and focus on what is done rather than who does it. One way is by using the structure **se** + verb in the third person. The verb always agrees with the noun it refers to:

se + third person singular (without a noun)

*En mi casa **se cena** a las ocho y media.*

se + third person singular + singular noun

*En Perú **se come** mucho pescado.*

se + third person plural + plural noun

*En Venezuela **se toman** muchos jugos.*

echar	**se echa/n**	reservar	**se reserva/n**	rellenar	**se rellena/n**	batir	**se bate/n**
poner	**se pone/n**	trocear	**se trocea/n**	rallar	**se ralla/n**	triturar	**se tritura/n**
picar	**se pica/n**	agregar	**se agrega/n**	hornear	**se hornea/n**	exprimir	**se exprime/n**
añadir	**se añade/n**	remover	**se remueve/n**	freír	**se fríe/n**	moler	**se muele/n**
saltear	**se saltea/n**	tapar	**se tapa/n**	cocer	**se cuece/n**	aplastar	**se aplasta/n**
lavar	**se lava/n**	mezclar	**se mezcla/n**	calentar	**se calienta/n**	quitar	**se quita/n**
pelar	**se pela/n**	retirar	**se retira/n**	asar	**se asa/n**	servir	**se sirve/n**
cortar	**se corta/n**	colocar	**se coloca/n**	hacer	**se hace/n**		

❗ We do not use the impersonal **se** with verbs like **gustar**, **encantar**, **interesar**, or with reflexive verbs:
~~En México se gusta comer picante.~~ > *A los mexicanos les gusta comer picante.*
~~En España se acuesta tarde.~~ > *En España la gente se acuesta tarde.*

IMPERSONAL EXPRESSIONS (II): OTHER FORMS

Impersonal constructions can also be expressed:

▶ with a generic noun:
*A la **gente** le gusta mucho la comida mexicana.* = People like Mexican food a lot.

▶ using the **tú** form of the verb:
*Pon**es** aceite en una sartén y ech**as** la cebolla y el ajo.* = You put oil in the pan and put in the onions and garlic.

▶ usando la 3ª persona del plural:
*En Colombia **producen** un café excelente.* = In Colombia they produce excellent coffee.

▶ with the construction **(no) es normal/habitual/frecuente/raro** + infinitive:
*En Venezuela **es habitual** desayunar arepas.* = It's common in Venezuela to have arepas for breakfast.

▶ with **hay que** + infinitive:
*En los restaurantes de Estados Unidos **hay que** dejar, al menos, un 15 % de propina.* = In the United States restaurants you (impersonal) have to leave a tip of at least 15 %.

DIRECT OBJECT (DO) PRONOUNS (I)

Direct object pronouns take the place of nouns when it is clear what is being talked about, and are used to avoid repeating the noun:

	Singular	Plural
Masculine	lo	los
Feminine	la	las

- *¿Dónde está el queso?* = Where's the cheese?
- ○ ***Lo** guardé en el refrigerador.* = I put it in the refrigerator.

- *¿Dónde compras la fruta?* = Where do you buy fruit?
- ○ *Normalmente **la** compro en el mercado.* = Normally, I buy it at the market.

- *¡Compraste muchos plátanos!* = You bought so many plantains!
- ○ *Sí, **los** compré para preparar plátanos calados, un plato colombiano.*
  = Yes, I bought them to make platanos calados, a Colombian dish.

- *¿Preparaste tú las enchiladas?* = Did you make the enchiladas?
- ○ *Sí, **las** hice ayer. ¿Están ricas?* = Yes, I made them yesterday. Are they tasty?

▶ Remember that every noun is masculine or feminine and singular or plural. The direct object pronoun must reflect the gender and the number of the noun it replaces.

▶ We also use direct object pronouns when the direct object goes before the verb:

*El pescado **lo** preparé yo, pero <u>la torta</u> **la** compré.* = The fish, I prepared, but the cake, I bought.

❗ The direct object pronoun always comes before a conjugated verb.

❗ We do not use pronouns when the direct object goes with no determinant (article, possessive or demonstrative):
- *¿Esta sopa lleva Ø cebolla?*
- ○ *No, no Ø lleva.*

Este postre se llama "suspiro limeño". Siempre lo preparo en ocasiones especiales.

CONNECTORS: PERO, ADEMÁS

Sentence connectors are used to to combine sentences and express relationships between the ideas.

▶ **Pero** connects two sentences that contrast or contradict each other.

*Es un restaurante muy lindo, **pero** la comida es horrible.* = It's a very nice restaurant, but the food is horrible.

▶ **Además** adds new information to what has already been stated.

*Es un restaurante muy lindo y, **además,** los meseros son muy amables.* = It's a very nice restaurant and, moreover, the waiters are very nice.

Pronunciamos

La z y la c; la j; la ll y la y

En toda Hispanoamérica, las consonantes z y c (antes de e e i) se pronuncian como una s. Esto pasa también en las Islas Canarias y en algunas zonas del sur de España; mientras que en el resto de España, estas consonantes se pronuncian como la th de *nothing* en inglés.

La letra j también se pronuncia de forma diferente en España y en Hispanoamérica. En casi toda la península la pronunciación es fuerte, mientras que en toda Hispanoamérica tiene una pronunciación más suave, más similar a la h de *hotel* en inglés.

En español, la y y la ll se pronuncian de la misma manera; es decir, que **maya** y **malla** se pronuncian igual. En la mayoría de países se pronuncian como la y de *yes* en inglés, pero en Argentina y Uruguay se pronuncian como la sh de *she* en inglés.

11.64. Escuchamos y comparamos. Escucha, compara la pronunciación de c y z y marca de dónde son las personas que hablan.

	Salamanca (España)	Bogotá (Colombia)
1. Hay que comprar arroz, cereales, manzanas y azúcar.		
2. Necesito la receta para hacer el ceviche.		
3. Las hamburguesas llevan carne de cerdo, zanahoria cocida y especias.		
4. A veces como dulces, pero no muy a menudo.		

11.65. Escuchamos y comparamos. Observa ahora la pronunciación de la letra j en estas frases y marca de dónde son las personas que hablan en cada caso.

	Madrid (España)	San Salvador (El Salvador)
1. La bandeja paisa lleva frijoles rojos, ¿verdad?		
2. Quiero un jugo de naranja, por favor.		
3. Esta jalea de frutos rojos está riquísima.		
4. El jamón y el ajo no me gustan. ¿Y a ti?		

11.66. Escuchamos y comparamos. Haz lo mismo con la pronunciación de y y ll. ¿De dónde son las personas que hablan? Márcalo.

	Medellín (Colombia)	Montevideo (Uruguay)
1. No sé comer con palillos. Prefiero tenedor y cuchillo.		
2. Siempre desayuno un yogur con galletas.		
3. El chivito es un plato típico uruguayo.		
4. ¿La sopa lleva pollo?		

11.67. Leemos, escuchamos y comparamos. Lee en voz alta las frases de las actividades 11.64, 11.65 y 11.66 y, luego, escúchalas de nuevo. ¿A qué pronunciación se parece más la tuya en cada caso?

Vocabulario activo

Alimentos *Foods*

- el aceite (de oliva) *olive oil*
- el agua *water*
- el agua con gas *sparkling water*
- el aguacate *avocado*
- el ajo *garlic*
- el arroz (integral) *(brown) rice*
- el atún *tuna*
- la avena *oats*
- el/la azúcar *sugar*
- la banana *banana*
- la barra energética *energy bar*
- el cacahuate *peanut*
- el café *coffee*
- la calabacita *zucchini*
- la carne *meat*
- la cebolla *onion*
- el cerdo *pork*
- el cereal *cereal, grain*
- el chile serrano *serrano chili*
- el chocolate *chocolate*
- el durazno *peach*
- el elote *corn on the cob*
- el embutido *cold meat*
- la ensalada *salad*
- la especia *spice*
- la fresa *strawberry*
- el frijol *bean*
- la fruta *fruit*
- el fruto seco *nut*
- la galleta *cookie*
- la harina *flour*
- el helado *ice cream*
- la hierba aromática *aromatic herb*
- el huevo *egg*
- la jalea *jelly*
- el jamón *ham*
- el jugo *juice*
- el lácteo *dairy*
- la leche *milk*
- la lechuga *lettuce*
- la legumbre *legume*
- el limón *lemon*
- el maíz *corn*
- la manzana *apple*
- el marisco *shellfish*
- la miel *honey*
- la mostaza *mustard*
- la naranja *orange*
- el pan *bread*
- la papa *potato*
- la pasta *pasta*
- el pavo *turkey*
- la pera *pear*
- el pescado *fish*
- el pimiento *pepper*
- la piña *pineapple*
- el pollo *chicken*
- el queso *cheese*
- el refresco *soda, soft drink*
- la res *veal, beef*
- la sal *salt*
- la salsa *sauce*
- la sopa *soup*
- el té *tea*
- el tomate *tomato*
- la torta *cake*
- la uva *grape*
- la verdura *vegetable*
- el vinagre *vinegar*
- el vino *wine*
- el yogur *yogurt*
- la yuca *yuca, manioc*
- la zanahoria *carrot*

Empaques y recipientes
Packaging and containers

- la bolsa *bag*
- la botella *bottle*
- la caja *box*
- el cartón *carton*
- el frasco *jar*
- la lata *can*
- el paquete *packet*

Pesos y medidas
Weights and measures

- la cucharada *tablespoon*
- la cucharadita *teaspoon*
- la docena *dozen*
- el gramo *gram*
- el kilo *kilo*
- el litro *liter*
- la loncha *slice*
- el pedazo *piece, chunk, bit*
- una pizca de *a pinch of*
- un poco de *a little bit of*
- por peso *by weight*
- por unidades *by units*
- la taza *cup*

Utensilios de cocina
Kitchen utensils

- la bandeja de horno *baking sheet*
- la cacerola *saucepan*
- la cuchara *spoon*
- el cuchillo *knife*
- el horno *oven*
- la olla *pot*
- la sartén *frying pan*
- el tenedor *fork*
- el vaso *glass*

Elaboración de platos
How to prepare a dish

- a fuego lento *at low heat*
- a fuego medio *at medium heat*
- agregar *to add*
- añadir *to add*
- aplastar *to crush*
- asar *to roast*
- batir *to whip*
- calentar (e>ie) *to heat*
- cocer (o>ue) *to cook*
- colocar *to place*
- cortar *to cut*
- echar *to pour*
- exprimir *to squeeze*
- freír (e>i) *to fry*
- hacer a la plancha *to grill*
- hornear *to bake, to roast*
- lavar *to wash*
- mezclar *to mix, to blend*
- moler (o>ue) *to grind*
- pelar *to peel*
- picar *to chop*
- poner *to put*
- quitar *to remove*
- rallar *to grate*
- rellenar *to fill, to stuff*
- remover (o>ue) *to stir*
- reservar *to save*
- retirar *to move away*
- sacar *remove*
- saltear *to sauté, to stir-fry*
- servir (e>i) *to serve*
- tapar *to cover*
- triturar *to blend*
- trocear *to dice*

Lección

12

Acción y aventuras

IN THIS LESSON WE ARE GOING TO

create our own movie plot

LEARNING OUTCOMES
You will be able to...

- talk about movies and television

- summarize the plot of a book, a series, or a movie

- tell stories

VOCABULARY

- Movies and television shows

- Elements and parts of a film

- TV and movie genres

LANGUAGE STRUCTURES

- Connectors: **porque, como, sin embargo, aunque,** and **pero**

- Pronouns: direct object (II), indirect object (I) and double object pronouns (I)

PRONUNCIATION

- The sounds of **p, t,** and **ca/co/cu**

CULTURAL CONNECTIONS

- TV shows in Spanish on Netflix

El director Alfonso Cuarón y las actrices Yalitza Aparicio y Marina de Tavira en el estreno de la película *Roma.*

Primer contacto

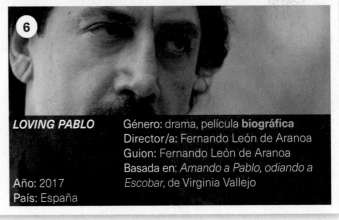

12.1. Adaptaciones cinematográficas. Lee las fichas de estas adaptaciones cinematográficas de novelas de autores y autoras latinos. ¿Conoces las películas o las novelas? Coméntalo con otras personas de la clase.

1

COMO AGUA PARA CHOCOLATE

Año: 1992
País: México

Género: **drama romántico**
Director/a: Alfonso Arau
Guion: Laura Esquivel
Basada en: *Como agua para chocolate*, de Laura Esquivel

2

BLOW-UP. DESEO DE UNA MAÑANA DE VERANO
Año: 1966
País: Reino Unido

Género: intriga
Director/a: Michelangelo Antonioni
Guion: Tonino Guerra, Michelangelo Antonioni
Basada en: "Las babas del diablo", de Julio Cortázar

3

EL AMOR EN LOS TIEMPOS DEL CÓLERA
Año: 2007
País: Estados Unidos

Género: drama romántico
Director/a: Mike Newell
Guion: Ronald Harwood
Basada en: *El amor en los tiempos del cólera*, de Gabriel García Márquez

4

EL SECRETO DE SUS OJOS

Año: 2009
País: Argentina

Género: **intriga**
Director/a: Juan José Campanella
Guion: Eduardo Sacheri, Juan José Campanella
Basada en: *La pregunta de sus ojos*, de Eduardo Sacheri

5

LA CASA DE LOS ESPÍRITUS

Año: 1993
País: Estados Unidos

Género: drama romántico
Director/a: Bille August
Guion: Bille August
Basada en: *La casa de los espíritus*, de Isabel Allende

6

LOVING PABLO

Año: 2017
País: España

Género: drama, película **biográfica**
Director/a: Fernando León de Aranoa
Guion: Fernando León de Aranoa
Basada en: *Amando a Pablo, odiando a Escobar*, de Virginia Vallejo

- **Yo vi** *"Como agua para chocolate"* **hace** años.
- **Yo leí**...

12.2. ¿Qué sabemos? Comenten qué otras películas, series, novelas, directores o actores conocen de países donde se habla español.

- **Yo conozco** algunas películas de Cuarón, como *"Gravity"* o *"Hijos de los hombres"*.
- Pues yo conozco a Sofía Vergara. Es una actriz colombiana.
- ¿Y conocen alguna serie?
- ¡Sí! *"La casa de papel"*. Aquí se llama *"Money Heist"*. ¡Me encanta! Creo que es española...

Comprendemos el vocabulario

Cine

))) **12.3. Roma.** Escucha y lee.

ROMA
★★★★★

Director/a: Alfonso Cuarón
Reparto: Yalitza Aparicio, Marina de Tavira, Marco Graf, Diego Cortina, Carlos Peralta, Daniela Demesa, Nancy García García
Título original: *Roma*
País: México
Duración: 135 min.
Año: 2018
Fecha de estreno: 05-12-2018
Género: Drama
Color o en B/N: B/N
Guion: Alfonso Cuarón
Fotografía: Alfonso Cuarón, Galo Olivares
Sinopsis: Cleo es una joven trabajadora del hogar de una familia que vive en la Colonia Roma, un barrio de clase media de Ciudad de México. [...] Cuarón se inspira en su propia infancia para pintar un retrato realista y emotivo de los conflictos domésticos y las jerarquías sociales durante la agitación política de la década de 1970.

Más palabras

))) **GÉNEROS** = *GENRES*
una comedia = *comedy*
una comedia romántica = *rom-com*
un documental = *documentary*
un drama = *drama*
un musical = *musical*
una película
- **bélica** = *war*
- **de amor / romántica** = *romance*
- **de acción** = *action*
- **de animación** = *animated*
- **de aventuras** = *adventure*
- **de ciencia ficción** = *science fiction*
- **de terror** = *horror, chiller*
- **de superhéroes** = *superhero*
- **del oeste** = *western*
- **fantástica** = *fantasy*
- **futurista** = *futuristic*
- **histórica** = *historical*
- **policiaca** = *crime thriller*

ELEMENTOS DE LAS PELÍCULAS/SERIES =
ELEMENTS OF MOVIES/SERIES
el actor / la actriz = *actor, actress*
el argumento / la trama = *plot*
la banda sonora = *soundtrack*
el cortometraje = *short film*
la escena = *scene*
el final = *ending*
el/la guionista = *scriptwriter*
interpretar = *to play a role, to act*
el largometraje = *feature film*
el papel = *role, part*
el personaje = *character*
el/la protagonista = *main character*
protagonizar = *to star in*
el reparto = *cast*

⊕ **¿Sabes que...?**

In Spanish-speaking countries, movie titles are often translated from the originals. In some cases, the translations are literal as in *Hijos de los hombres* (*Children of Men*). In others, the titles are changed to make them more relevant or attractive to audiences as for example:

Sleepless in Seatle = *Sintonía de amor* (Ar, Co, Mx), *Algo para recordar* (Es)

There Will Be Blood = *Petróleo sangriento* (Ar, Co, Mx), *Pozos de ambición* (Es)

Note also that translations can vary from country to country.

12.4. Géneros. ¿Con qué géneros cinematográficos asocias estas cosas? Coméntalo con otra persona.

unos binoculares	una nave espacial	un anillo	una placa de policía	unas botas de vaquero	unas esposas	un monstruo
pruebas	un caballo	un juicio		una investigación		un payaso
un coche deportivo	un casamiento	un tesoro	la magia	sangre		

- *Yo relaciono los binoculares con las películas de acción.*
- *Sí, y también con las bélicas.*

12.5. Criterios para valorar una película. ¿Qué aspectos son más importantes para ti para valorar una película? Ordénalos de más (1) a menos (8).

⚪ el género	⚪ el reparto	⚪ la trama	⚪ la duración
⚪ el/la director/a	⚪ la banda sonora	⚪ los personajes	⚪ la fotografía

12.6. Compartimos opiniones. Ahora, coméntalo con otra persona de la clase. ¿Coinciden?

- *Para mí, lo más importante es la trama.*
- *Pues, para mí, el género, porque hay algunos que no me gustan, como el terror.*

12.7. Preparamos un test. En parejas, preparen un test de cinco o seis preguntas sobre cine, como en el ejemplo. Anoten también las respuestas.

1. ¿Quién es la actriz protagonista de "Hereditary"? (Toni Collette)
2. ¿Qué personaje interpreta Scarlett Johansson en "Los Vengadores"? (Viuda negra)
3. ¿Cuál fue la primera película que ganó el Óscar a la mejor película de animación? (Shrek)
...

12.8. Hacemos el test. Hagan el test a otra pareja. ¿Qué pareja sabe más de cine?

Comprendemos el vocabulario

Contar el argumento de un libro, una serie o una película

12.9. Una telenovela. Escucha a dos personas hablando de una telenovela colombo-estadounidense y marca las opciones correctas.

La reina del sur

- **Trata sobre...**
  - ◯ una familia aristocrática.
  - ◯ un caso de corrupción política.
  - ◯ el narcotráfico.

- **La serie cuenta la historia de...**
  - ◯ un grupo de políticos corruptos que cometen un crimen e intentan encubrirlo.
  - ◯ una mujer que pasa de ser la novia ingenua de una narco mexicano a dominar el negocio del tráfico de drogas.
  - ◯ una mujer que renuncia a su herencia para vivir su sueño de viajar y ayudar a los más necesitados.

- **Salen...**
  - ◯ personajes populares interpretándose a sí mismos.
  - ◯ actores mexicanos y españoles.
  - ◯ actores y actrices de teatro.

- **La actriz que hace el papel protagonista es...**
  - ◯ muy mala.
  - ◯ muy famosa.
  - ◯ española.

- **Está ambientada en...**
  - ◯ México y Colombia.
  - ◯ una época y un lugar imaginarios.
  - ◯ México y España, principalmente.

- **Vale/n la pena, sobre todo...**
  - ◯ la primera temporada.
  - ◯ la interpretación de la protagonista.
  - ◯ los primeros episodios.

> **⊕ ¿Sabes que...?**
>
> *La reina del sur* is a soap opera based on the novel by the same name written by Arturo Pérez-Reverte. The series was first broadcast in 2011 and was the most watched premiere episode in Telemundo's history.
>
> In 2016, USA Network premiered *Queen of the South*, an adaptation of *La reina del Sur*.

12.10. Una serie. Piensa en una serie exitosa, actual o no, y escribe cinco frases usando algunas de las expresiones de la actividad 12.9.

> Está ambientada en Nueva York en los años 50-60.

12.11. Adivinamos. Ahora, lean sus frases al resto de la clase sin decir qué serie es. ¿Quién necesita menos pistas para adivinarlo?

- ● *Está ambientada en Nueva York en los años 50-60.*
- ○ *¡"Mad Men"!*
- ● *¡No! Salen Rachel Brosnahan y Alex Borstein.*
- ○ *¡"La maravillosa Sra. Maisel"!*
- ● *¡Sí!*

Léxico de la televisión

12.12. Programación televisiva. Esta semana, en algunos canales de televisión españoles, puedes ver estos programas. ¿Qué tipo de programas son? Lee y escucha. Luego, coméntalo con otras personas.

ESTA SEMANA RECOMENDAMOS...

SALVADOS
Domingo, a las 21:30 h | La Sexta

Esta semana, **entrevista** al periodista y escritor Arturo Pérez-Reverte sobre la actitud de los españoles ante la crisis y del "miedo de los españoles al cambio".

CORAZÓN
De lunes a viernes, a las 14:30 h | La 1

Anne Igartiburu y Carolina Casado presentan este espacio, con información sobre la vida de los famosos, **noticias** sobre eventos sociales y **reportajes** sobre el mundo de la moda.

SABER Y GANAR
De lunes a domingo, a las 15:45 h | La 2

El **concurso** más veterano de la historia de la televisión en España. Cada día los **concursantes** ponen a prueba sus conocimientos y tratan de responder a preguntas de ámbito general para continuar en el programa siguiente y ganar más dinero.

EL DOCUMENTAL DE LA 2: MARÍA Y YO
Viernes, a las 22 h | La 2

Esta semana, documental sobre el autismo: la historia de Miguel Gallardo, autor del cómic *María y yo*, y su hija autista.

INFORME SEMANAL
Sábado, a las 23:30 h | La 1

"Revolución verde" – Un equipo de Informe Semanal habla con los líderes de la "generación del plástico", con la física e investigadora del clima Yolanda Luna y con el codirector del *Informe de Naciones Unidas sobre Economía Sostenible*, el británico Nick Robins.

EL MINISTERIO DEL TIEMPO
Lunes, a las 22:30 h | La 1

Los protagonistas hacen viajes en el tiempo para solucionar contratiempos y evitar cambios en la historia de España. En el episodio de esta semana, tienen que asegurarse de que el arquitecto Antoni Gaudí acepta el encargo de construir la Sagrada Familia.

FÚTBOL: EL CLÁSICO
Sábado, a las 21:00 h | La 1

Partido de liga entre el Fútbol Club Barcelona y el Real Madrid en el Santiago Bernabéu. Es la primera vez que se enfrentan esta temporada.

un programa de	humor	**un programa musical**	**una retransmisión deportiva**
	entrevistas	**dibujos animados**	**un magacín**
	actualidad	un documental	una película
	preguntas y respuestas	**un informativo**	una serie

- *"Salvados" es un programa de entrevistas, ¿no?*
- *Sí. Y parece que "Corazón" es un programa de...*

12.13. Nuestro programa favorito. Escribe cómo se llama tu programa favorito, qué tipo de programa es y por qué te gusta.

> Mi programa favorito se llama "La teoría del Big Bang". Es una serie. Me encanta porque es una comedia muy divertida.

12.14. Programas de éxito. Comenten en parejas qué programas tienen éxito en su país y si a ustedes les gustan.

- *Aquí todo el mundo ve "Jeopardy!".*
- *Sí, pero a mí no me gusta, porque...*

Exploramos la lengua

Conectores: **porque**, **como**, **sin embargo**, **aunque** y **pero**

12.15. Cuatro películas argentinas. Lee las sinopsis de estas películas y observa los carteles. ¿Te gustaría ver alguna? ¿Por qué? Escríbelo y luego compártelo con tus compañeros/-as. ¿Coinciden?

LAS MEJORES PELÍCULAS DEL CINE ARGENTINO

El secreto de sus ojos (2009), J. J. Campanella

Benjamín Espósito, un agente judicial retirado, empieza a recordar un caso de asesinato que investigó años atrás **porque** quiere escribir una novela. Revivir esa historia le trae recuerdos muy duros. **Sin embargo**, gracias a eso, Espósito vuelve a ver a Irene, la mujer de la que estuvo enamorado hace años.

La historia oficial (1985), Luis Puenzo

Durante la dictadura militar argentina, Alicia, una profesora de Historia, y su marido, un empresario, adoptan a una niña llamada Gaby. **Aunque** al principio Alicia no sospecha nada, varios acontecimientos la llevan a descubrir que Gaby es hija de "desaparecidos" y a cuestionar "la historia oficial".

Esperando la carroza (1985), Alejandro Doria

Mamá Cora vive con su hijo Jorge y su nuera Susana. **Como** tienen problemas económicos y la relación entre las dos mujeres no es muy buena, Susana no quiere que viva con ellos. Un día, en una reunión familiar, se discute sobre el futuro de Mamá Cora. **Pero** todo cambia cuando se enteran de que otra mujer mayor se ha suicidado.

Elsa & Fred (2005), Marcos Carnevale

Alfredo es un hombre serio y responsable, que queda viudo y se muda a un apartamento más pequeño. Allí conoce a Elsa, su vecina, una mujer anciana, **pero** llena de vitalidad y con una imaginación desbordante. Elsa le demuestra que el tiempo que le queda es precioso y debe disfrutarlo.

> ⊕ **¿Sabes que...?**
>
> During the military dictatorship in Argentina (1976-1983), the term **desaparecidos** was used to refer to people who were arrested and imprisoned in secret detention centers where they were tortured and in many cases, killed for their political views.

e **12.16. Completamos la regla.** Observa los conectores en negrita de las sinopsis de la actividad 12.15 y relaciona para obtener la regla.

1. **Como** y **porque** sirven para...   **a.** ... expresar la causa de un acontecimiento.
2. **Pero**, **sin embargo** y **aunque** sirven para...   **b.** ... expresar un contraste entre ideas.

e **12.17. Sinopsis.** Marca el conector adecuado en cada sinopsis.

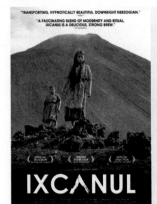

Ixcanul
(2015), Jayro Bustamante

María es una joven maya cakchiquel de 17 años que está enamorada de Pepe, un chico que trabaja en los cultivos de café. **Como / Porque / Sin embargo**, sus padres la obligan a casarse con el encargado de la finca en la que trabaja su padre, **pero/ aunque/porque** es la única forma de mantener el empleo del padre y la casa donde viven. María va a intentar cambiar su destino.

El abrazo de la serpiente
(2016), Ciro Guerra

El chamán Karamakate, último superviviente de su tribu, es el protagonista de dos historias que suceden en el mismo espacio, la selva amazónica colombiana, **aunque/porque/como** con más de 30 años de diferencia. En la primera, un explorador alemán le pide ayuda para encontrar yakruna, una planta sagrada. En la segunda es un explorador americano quien busca la planta. Karamakate se adentra en la selva para ayudar a los exploradores. **Sin embargo / Porque / Como**, con los años y debido al negocio del caucho, el paisaje es muy distinto.

Fresa y chocolate
(1993), Tomás Gutiérrez Alea y Juan Carlos Tabío

La película cuenta la relación de amistad entre dos hombres en La Habana de finales de los años 70. David es un estudiante de Sociología en la Universidad de La Habana, idealista y muy fiel al régimen comunista. **Aunque / Sin embargo / Como**, Diego es un artista culto y homosexual, que sufre la homofobia del régimen de Castro. **Pero/Como/Aunque** son diferentes en muchos aspectos, entre ellos surge una profunda y bonita amistad.

12.18. Conectores. Continúa estas frases de forma lógica.

1.
  a. Aunque Clara es actriz, *trabaja de mesera en un restaurante.* ....

  b. Como Clara es actriz, ...

2.
  a. Pedro no ve la televisión **porque** ....

  b. Pedro no ve la televisión, **pero** ....

3.
  a. Diana ve muchas películas en español. **Sin embargo**, ...

  b. Como Diana ve muchas películas en español, ...

Exploramos la lengua

Pronombres: objeto directo (II), objeto indirecto (I) y combinación (I)

e **12.19. Una novela.** Lee el argumento de esta novela de la escritora colombiana Laura Restrepo y ordena los hechos del 1 al 5.

Delirio
El realismo mágico de Laura Restrepo

Aguilar regresa a su casa después de pasar unos días fuera, en un viaje de negocios. A su llegada, un hombre desconocido **lo** llama y <u>le</u> dice que su esposa Agustina está en una habitación de hotel y que debe ir a recoger**la**. Aguilar, sorprendido, **lo** hace: va a buscar**la**, pero **la** encuentra completamente enloquecida.

Como Aguilar no sabe qué <u>le</u> pasó a su esposa en su ausencia y nadie se lo cuenta, decide comenzar a investigar el pasado de Agustina y contacta con la tía de esta y con personas de su infancia y de su juventud. Aguilar **las** visita y <u>les</u> pregunta sobre el pasado de Agustina y de su familia. Parece que la vida de Agustina está llena de secretos y Aguilar no va a parar hasta descubrir**los**.

○ Aguilar decide investigar el pasado de su esposa.

○ Va a un hotel a recoger a su esposa.

○ Se va de viaje de negocios.

○ Recibe la llamada de un desconocido.

○ Habla con la tía de Agustina.

> ⊕ **¿Sabes que...?**
>
> **Realismo mágico**, known as magical or magic realism in English, is a literary movement associated primarily with mid-twentieth century Latin American writers. It incorporates elements that defy logic but seem normal to the characters in the story.

e **12.20. Pronombres de OD y de OI.** Escribe a qué se refieren los pronombres de objeto directo (OD), marcados en **negrita** en el texto de la actividad 12.19, y los pronombres de objeto indirecto (OI), subrayados en el texto.

1. un hombre desconocido **lo** llama → *Aguilar*

2. debe ir a recoger**la** → ....

3. **lo** hace → ....

4. va a buscar**la** → ....

5. **la** encuentra completamente enloquecida → ....

6. Aguilar **las** visita → ....

7. no va a parar hasta descubrir**los** → ....

8. <u>le</u> dice que su esposa está en una habitación de hotel → ....

9. no sabe qué <u>le</u> pasó → ....

10. <u>les</u> pregunta sobre el pasado de Agustina → ....

e **12.21. Completamos.** Ahora, completa las tablas con los pronombres de OD y de OI de la actividad 12.19.

PRONOMBRES DE OD			
	Masculino	**Femenino**	**Neutro**
Singular	....	....	
Plural	....	....	....

PRONOMBRES DE OI	
	Masculino / Femenino
Singular	....
Plural	....

> **!** **¿Necesitas ayuda?**
>
> Remember only nouns have gender (masculine or feminine). The neuter pronoun is used to replace concepts, actions, ideas, or statements that have no gender.

12.22. ¿A quién se refiere? Ahora, escribe a quién se refiere el pronombre **se** en esta frase.

> Nadie **se** lo cuenta.

e **12.23. ¿Objeto directo u objeto indirecto?** Indica si las partes subrayadas son un OD o un OI.

1. Decir <u>algo</u> <u>a alguien</u>.
         OD   OI
2. Conocer <u>a alguien</u>.
3. Abandonar <u>a alguien</u>.
4. Pedir <u>algo</u> <u>a alguien</u>.
5. Dar <u>algo</u> <u>a alguien</u>.

6. Ver <u>a alguien</u>.
7. Ver <u>algo</u>.
8. Robar <u>algo</u> <u>a alguien</u>.
9. Querer <u>a alguien</u>.

12.24. ¿Antes o después? Lee esta frase y observa la posición del pronombre **la**. Luego, relaciona para obtener la regla.

> Va a buscar**la**, pero **la** encuentra completamente enloquecida.

1. Con un verbo conjugado, el pronombre va...
2. Con un infinitivo, el pronombre va...

a. ... antes del verbo, separado de este.
b. ... después del verbo, formando una sola palabra.

e **12.25. Usamos los pronombres.** Este es el argumento de la novela *El amor en tiempos del cólera*, de Gabriel García Márquez. Escribe los fragmentos en negrita usando pronombres.

Florentino Ariza se enamora de Fermina Daza (1) cuando **ve a Fermina Daza** en su casa, en Cartagena de Indias. Desde ese día, (2) **escribe** cartas de amor **a Fermina Daza**. Ella (3) **lee las cartas** y poco a poco se enamora de él. Sin embargo, el padre de Fermina se opone a esta relación y (4) **envía a Fermina** lejos de Cartagena de Indias para (5) **alejar a Fermina** de Florentino. Pasa el tiempo y Fermina se casa con el doctor Juvenal Urbino. Sin embargo, Florentino sigue enamorado de ella. Muchos años después, cuando el marido de Fermina muere, Florentino (6) **va a ver a Fermina** para (7) **declarar a Fermina** su amor y (8) **decir a Fermina** que está dispuesto a casarse con ella. Ella (9) **rechaza a Florentino**, pero él no se rinde y (10) **empieza a enviarle** cartas **a Fermina** hasta que ella accede a (11) **ver a Florentino**. Así empieza una relación de amistad entre ellos. Un día deciden hacer un viaje en barco por el río Magdalena. Es allí cuando, 53 años después, pueden estar finalmente juntos.

1. cuando la ve

Comunicamos

Géneros de cine

12.26. Creamos un mapa mental. En parejas o pequeños grupos creen un mapa mental sobre un género de cine: una película policiaca, de superhéroes, de animación, de ciencia ficción, un drama...

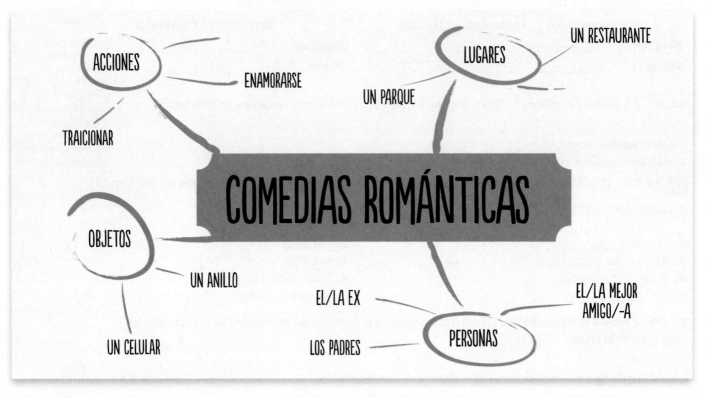

12.27. Presentamos nuestro mapa mental. Presenten su mapa mental al resto de la clase. En cada nueva presentación, tomen nota de la información nueva.

12.28. ¿Qué tienen en común? ¿Qué elementos son muy comunes en las películas de un mismo género? Coméntenlo entre todos. Piensen en el tipo de música, en la iluminación, en la trama, en los tipos de personajes, etc.

- *Las películas de amor normalmente tienen siempre un final feliz.*
- ○ *Sí, y además siempre hay una escena con el primer beso.*

Adivina, adivinanza

12.29. Tres títulos. En grupos. Cada grupo piensa en tres títulos de películas, series o novelas. Tienen que ser muy conocidos.

12.30. Tres argumentos. Preparen tres tarjetas con el argumento de las obras que pensaron en la actividad 12.29.

12.31. Adivinamos. Lean sus tarjetas a otro grupo. Si adivinan de qué obra se trata, ganan un punto. Si no, no se suma ningún punto.

ADIVINA, ADIVINANZA

Cine

Es una película musical ambientada en Los Ángeles. Los protagonistas, Mia, una aspirante a actriz, y Sebastian, un pianista de *jazz*, se conocen y se enamoran.

Las mejores de la historia

 12.32. Las mejores. Según una encuesta a los lectores de una revista, estas son las mejores películas de la historia por géneros. ¿Las conoces? ¿Estás de acuerdo? Coméntalo con otras personas de la clase.

LAS MEJORES PELÍCULAS POR GÉNERO

CASABLANCA

Año: 1942
Director: Michael Curtiz
Reparto: Humphrey Bogart, Ingrid Bergman, Paul Henreid

De amor

INDIANA JONES Y LA ÚLTIMA CRUZADA

Año: 1989
Director: Steven Spielberg
Reparto: Harrison Ford, Sean Connery

De aventuras

KILL BILL (VOL. 1 y VOL. 2)

Año: 2003, 2004
Director: Quentin Tarantino
Reparto: Uma Thurman, David Carradine

De acción

BLADE RUNNER

Año: 1982
Director: Ridley Scott
Reparto: Harrison Ford, Rutger Hauer, Sean Young

De ciencia ficción

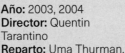

EL REY LEÓN

Año: 1994
Director: Roger Allers, Rob Minkoff
Reparto (voces): Matthew Broderick, Jeremy Irons, James Earl Jones

De animación

EL RESPLANDOR

Año: 1980
Director: Stanley Kubrick
Reparto: Jack Nicholson, Shelley Duvall, Danny Lloyd

De terror

EL SILENCIO DE LOS CORDEROS

Año: 1991
Director: Jonathan Demme
Reparto: Jodie Foster, Anthony Hopkins, Scott Glenn

De intriga

SIN PERDÓN

Año: 1992
Director: Clint Eastwood
Reparto: Clint Eastwood, Gene Hackman, Morgan Freeman

Del oeste

- *Para mí, la mejor película de amor es "Love Actually" porque cuenta historias muy diferentes.*
- *Pues yo estoy de acuerdo con el artículo: "Casablanca" es un clásico. Los actores son muy buenos y el guion también. Además, está ambientada en un lugar exótico y eso me gusta.*

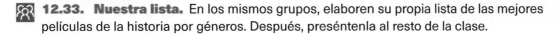

12.33. Nuestra lista. En los mismos grupos, elaboren su propia lista de las mejores películas de la historia por géneros. Después, preséntenla al resto de la clase.

Ahora podemos...

Escribir la sinopsis de una película

12.34. Elegimos. Imaginen que van a hacer una película. En parejas, elijan uno de los títulos que aparecen dentro de la claqueta (u otro) y preparen un resumen de la historia que debe incluir información sobre:

- El/la protagonista y los personajes principales.
- El lugar o lugares donde ocurre la historia.
- El argumento.

- P. S. TE ODIO
- 2056: ODISEA EN LA UNIVERSIDAD
- LOCA ESCUELA DE ESPAÑOL III
- MEDIANOCHE EN BUENOS AIRES
- BLA BLA LAND
- TODO SOBRE MI GATO

> ● ¿Te gusta alguno de estos títulos?
> ○ No sé. ¿Qué te parece "P. S. Te odio"?
> ● Sí, listo. Me gusta. ¿Y qué tipo de película puede ser?
> ○ ¿Una comedia de acción? Es la historia de una pareja que...

12.35. Producimos. Para la producción de la película, tienen que decidir los siguientes puntos.

- Qué actores y actrices necesitan.
- En qué localizaciones van a grabar las escenas.
- Quién es el director o la directora.
- Qué música van a elegir para la banda sonora.

12.36. Presentamos. Ahora presenten su película al resto de la clase.

> ● Les vamos a presentar una comedia de acción
>   y aventuras que se titula "P. S. Te odio".
> ○ Va de una pareja, Dylan y Camila, que...

💬 **Para comunicar**

La película **se titula**...
Está ambientada en...
El / la protagonista es...
Va de / trata de...
La historia pasa/ocurre en...

Video

Improvisando

Raiza Licea se mudó de Miami a Los Ángeles hace varios años y descubrió una pasión por el teatro de improvisación. Formó parte del grupo Improvisos Peligrosos con sus amigos Tony Rodríguez, Óscar Montoya y Carlos Santos. Juntos decidieron crear un programa de variedades formado solamente por hispanos y con actuaciones en español e inglés.

Ⓟ Pearson MyLab

To find out more about Raiza Licea and the other members of her improv group, go to MyLab to watch **Improvisando** and complete the video activities.

⊕ ¿Sabes que...?

The Spanish language is becoming commonplace in mainstream American entertainment. In Disney Pixar's *Coco*, the writers and directors went to great lengths to incorporate culturally-correct content, as well as Spanish phrases and songs, into the movie. Phil Lord, one of the main writers and producer of *Spider-Man: Into the Spider-Verse*, grew up in Miami, where hearing Spanish everyday was normal. For Lord, it was important for cultural authenticity not to use subtitles when the main character and others in his Brooklyn community speak Spanish. And in music, "crossover" artists have long been popular in the U.S.

⚲ Hacemos conexiones

Investiga sobre artistas de Estados Unidos que usan el español o la mezcla del español con el inglés. Comparte la información en la clase.

En Netflix y en español

Estas son cuatro de las series en español que se pueden encontrar en el catálogo del gigante del entretenimiento.

Pasión de gavilanes.
Colombia

Considerada como una de las mejores teleseries colombianas de todos los tiempos, la historia de amor y venganza entre los hermanos Reyes y las hermanas Elizondo es un éxito en los países que se emite. Todo empieza cuando Bernardo Elizondo, esposo y padre de tres jóvenes, se enamora de la hija menor del clan Reyes, Libia. Bernardo decide luchar por ella, pero tiene un sospechoso accidente y muere. Libia, embarazada de Bernardo, va a la casa de Bernardo Elizondo, pero la viuda y sus hijas la humillan. Desesperada por el trágico final de su amante, Libia se suicida. Los hermanos Reyes deciden vengarse de la familia Elizondo, pero se enamoran de las hermanas Elizondo.

El marginal.
Argentina

Drama carcelario que cuenta la historia de Miguel Palacios, un expolicía que se infiltra en una prisión con una identidad falsa para investigar el secuestro de la hija de un juez. Después de liberar a la joven, Palacios es traicionado y se queda en la cárcel como un prisionero más. Sin ayuda, Miguel se da cuenta de que solo puede hacer una cosa para recuperar su vida y su identidad: escapar.

La niña.
Colombia

Cuenta la historia de Belky, una joven que de niña es reclutada por la guerrilla colombiana. La joven logra salir de este ambiente de violencia y comienza una nueva vida: decide estudiar la carrera de Medicina para ejercer como médico. Pero nada es tan fácil como parece: Belky, además de estudiar, debe trabajar en un *call center* y sus antiguos compañeros de la guerrilla van tras ella.

Jenni Rivera, mariposa de barrio. México

Bioserie que narra la vida de la artista mexicana Jenni Rivera a partir de algunos testimonios e imágenes reales de la cantante y que revela sus secretos más íntimos, desde su complicado camino para convertirse en estrella, pasando por abusos y traiciones, hasta su trágico accidente aéreo en el que perdió la vida en el 2012. Basada en gran parte en su libro autobiográfico *Inquebrantable: Mi Historia, a mi manera*, que fue escrito antes de su muerte, la serie revela cómo Jenni vivió su embarazo prematuro y cómo soportó por años los abusos de su marido.

ANTES DE LEER

12.37. Series en español. ¿Conoces series en español? ¿Alguna es famosa en tu país?

LECTURA ACTIVA

12.38. Sinopsis. Lee las sinopsis de las series. ¿Cuál te gustaría ver? ¿Por qué?

12.39. Un subtítulo. Piensa un subtítulo para cada serie. Después, compártelo con otras personas de la clase y justifica el subtítulo que elegiste.

DESPUÉS DE LEER

 12.40. Vemos escenas. En parejas, busquen escenas de las series y véanlas. ¿Todavía te gustaría ver la serie que elegiste en la actividad 12.38? ¿Por qué?

 12.41. Comparamos. En grupos, comenten si encuentran similitudes entre estas series y otras que ustedes conocen.

Textos escritos: leemos y escribimos

Leemos sobre "días internacionales"

INFORMACIÓN PREVIA Las Naciones Unidas, conformadas por 193 Estados miembros, debaten sobre los problemas del mundo en el siglo XXI: la paz, la seguridad, el cambio climático, el desarrollo sostenible, los derechos humanos, el terrorismo o la igualdad de género. Con el fin de promover los objetivos de la organización, las Naciones Unidas proponen "días internacionales" y los aprueban por medio de una resolución. El texto que vas a leer es una resolución para tener un día internacional de la televisión y explica por qué es importante tener ese día.

12.42. Investigación. Busca cuándo se celebran estos días internacionales.

1. Día Mundial contra el Cáncer   **2.** Día Internacional de la Mujer   **3.** Día Mundial de los Océanos

12.43. Preparación. ¿Crees que es importante tener un Día Internacional de la Televisión? ¿Por qué? ¿De qué formas tú crees que la televisión contribuye a la paz o a los derechos humanos o la igualdad de género?

LECTURA ACTIVA

12.44. Lectura. Lee la resolución para informarte sobre el Día Internacional de la Televisión.

Reafirmando su compromiso con los principios de la Carta de las Naciones Unidas y con los principios de la libertad de información, así como con los principios de independencia, pluralismo y diversidad de los medios de comunicación,

Subrayando que las comunicaciones se han convertido en una de las cuestiones internacionales básicas de hoy día, no solo por su importancia para la economía mundial, sino también por sus repercusiones para el desarrollo social y cultural,

Reconociendo la influencia cada vez mayor que la televisión tiene sobre el proceso de adopción de decisiones al señalar a la atención mundial los conflictos y amenazas para la paz y seguridad, así como el papel que puede desempeñar centrando la atención en otras cuestiones importantes, incluidas las cuestiones económicas y sociales,

Subrayando que se pide cada vez con más frecuencia a las Naciones Unidas que aborden los principales problemas que afectan a la humanidad, y que la televisión, como uno de los medios de comunicación más poderosos de hoy día, podría desempeñar una función exponiendo estos problemas al mundo,

Tomando nota con satisfacción de la celebración en la Sede los días 21 y 22 de noviembre de 1996 del primer Foro Mundial de la Televisión, en el que se reunieron figuras destacadas de los medios de comunicación bajo los auspicios de las Naciones Unidas para discutir la importancia creciente de la televisión en el mundo actual en evolución y para considerar la forma en que podrían intensificar su cooperación mutua,

1. Decide proclamar el 21 de noviembre Día Mundial de la Televisión, en conmemoración de la fecha en que se celebró el primer Foro Mundial de la Televisión;

2. Invita a todos los Estados Miembros a que observen el Día Mundial de la Televisión promoviendo intercambios mundiales de programas de televisión centrados, en particular, en cuestiones como la paz, la seguridad, el desarrollo económico y social y la promoción del intercambio cultural;

3. Pide al Secretario General que señale la presente resolución a la atención de todos los gobiernos y de las organizaciones no gubernamentales interesadas.

88a. sesión plenaria
17 de diciembre de 1996

fuente: https://undocs.org/es/A/RES/51/205

12.45. Interpretación. Encuentra en el texto las palabras que mejor expresan el significado de las palabras en inglés de la lista.

1. powerful

2. growing

3. development

4. Non-governmental organizations

12.46. Selección de información. Ahora contesta las preguntas con base en el texto.

1. ¿De qué diferentes maneras es importante la televisión?

2. ¿Por qué se escogió el 21 de noviembre como Día Mundial de la Televisión?

3. ¿Qué propone hacer la resolución en el Día Mundial de la Televisión?

DESPUÉS DE LEER

12.47. Opinión. ¿Es similar tu respuesta a la actividad 12.43 a las razones que da la resolución? Explica tu respuesta.

Escribimos un artículo sobre un día internacional

12.48. Reacción personal. Prepara un artículo para presentar un día internacional. Sigue estos pasos.

1. Consulta en internet la lista de días internacionales y selecciona uno de especial interés para ti.

2. Da respuesta a estas preguntas:

• ¿Qué día se celebra?

• ¿Por qué ese día?

• ¿Qué justifica la existencia de ese día internacional?

3. Aporta ejemplos de cómo se celebra ese día en tu país y en diferentes países de habla hispana. Puedes acompañar la información de fotografías o videos.

Sede de las Naciones Unidas en Manhattan.

Recursos lingüísticos

PRONOUNS: DIRECT OBJECT (II), INDIRECT OBJECT (I) AND DOUBLE OBJECT PRONOUNS (I)

▶ Remember, to avoid repeating elements that have already been mentioned, we use direct and indirect object pronouns.

DIRECT OBJECT (II)

	Singular	Plural	Neutro
Masculine	lo	los	lo
Feminine	la	las	

▶ The direct object is the person or thing receiving the action from the verb.

● *¿Qué sabes del último libro de Laura Restrepo?* = What do you know about Laura Restrepo's last book?
○ *No **lo** he leído, pero dicen que está muy bien.* = I haven't read it, but they say it's good.

● *Rosa me recomendó* Roma*, la última película de Cuarón.* = Rosa recommended *Roma*, Cuarón's last film.
○ *Sí, a mí también. **La** voy a ver este fin de semana.* = Yes, I'm going to see it this weekend.

● *El año pasado leí los libros de Harry Potter.* = Last year, I read the Harry Potter books.
○ *¿**Los** leíste todos?* = You read them all?

● *Me encantan las películas de Almodóvar.* = I love Almodóvar's movies.
○ *A mí también. Ya **las** vi todas.* = Me, too. I saw them all.

▶ We need to use pronouns when the direct object is mentioned before the verb.

*Al protagonista de la novela **lo** condenan por un crimen que no cometió.* = The main character is found guilty of a crime he didn't commit. Literally: The main character, they found him guilty of a crime he didn't commit. (The Spanish pronoun **lo** would correspond to **him** in the example)

*En la película, la historia **la** cuenta una abuela.* = In the movie, the story is told by the grandmother.

▶ The direct object pronoun **lo** can also replace an entire sentence or part of a conversation.

● *¿Sabes que Penélope Cruz y Javier Bardem son pareja?* = Do you know that Penélope Cruz and Javier Bardem are a couple?
○ *Sí, **lo** sé. Y tienen dos hijos, ¿no?* = Yes, I know that (it). They have two children, right?

▶ The pronoun **lo** can also be substituted for actions expressed by **ser**, **estar**, and **parecer**.

● *La película* La forma del agua *es muy buena.* = The movie *The Shape of Water* is very good.
○ *Para mí no **lo** es. Es la película de Guillermo del Toro que menos me gusta.* = Not for me. It's Guillermo del Toro's movie I like the least.

INDIRECT OBJECT (I)

Singular	Plural
le	les

▶ The indirect object is the person (and less frequently, the thing) to whom or for whom the action is being done.

● *¿Marcos sabe que estás aquí?* = Does Marcos know you are here?
○ *No, no **le** dije nada todavía.* = No, I haven't told him yet.

- ¿Qué hiciste ayer? = What did you do yesterday?
- Fui a la casa de <u>mis padres</u> y **les** llevé un regalo. = I went to my parents' house and brought them a gift.

▸ Indirect object pronouns are often used even when the element they refer to is present in the sentence.

¿Qué **le** has comprado <u>a Madison</u> por su cumpleaños? = What did you buy Madison for her birthday?
Todas las noches **les** leo un cuento <u>a mis hijos</u>. = Every night I read my kids a bedtime story.

DOUBLE OBJECT PRONOUNS (I)

▸ When the indirect object pronouns (**le**, **les**) are combined with direct object pronouns, **le** and **les** change to **se**.

- ¿**Le** contaste a alguien <u>nuestro secreto</u>? = Did you tell anyone our secret?
- No, no **se** <u>lo</u> conté a nadie. = No, I didn't tell (it to) anyone.

- ¿**Les** dijiste a papá y mamá <u>que nos vamos</u>? = Did you tell Dad and Mom that we are leaving?
- No. ¿**Se** <u>lo</u> puedes decir tú? = No. Can you tell (it to) them?

🛈 Remember that the direct object pronoun always comes before a conjugated verb. However, this is not the case when pronouns are used with infinitives, gerunds (present participles), and verbs in the command form (imperative). In those cases, the pronouns are attached to the verb forms.

- ¿Qué van a hacer con sus libros? = What are you going to do with your books?
- Yo, **guardar**<u>los</u>. = I'm keeping them.
- Yo, **dár**<u>selos</u> a mi hermana. = I'm giving them to my sister.

CONNECTORS

▸ We use transitional phrases or connectors to organize a story.

▸ Use these connectors to explain the reason or cause of an event:

como
porque

Como Aguilar no sabe qué le pasó a su esposa, decide investigar su pasado. = Since Aguilar doesn't know what happened to his wife, he decides to investigate her past.
Aguilar decide investigar el pasado de su esposa **porque** no sabe qué le pasó. = Aguilar decides to investigate his wife's past because he doesn't know what happened to her.

▸ Use these connectors to contrast ideas:

pero
sin embargo
aunque

El padre de la protagonista se opone a su relación con Tomás, **pero** ellos se ven en secreto. = The main character's father is opposed to her relationship with Tomás, but they continue to see each other secretly.
El padre de la protagonista se opone a su relación con Tomás, **sin embargo** ellos se ven en secreto. = The main character's father is opposed to her relationship with Tomás, nonetheless they continue to see each other secretly.
Aunque el padre de la protagonista se opone a su relación con Tomás, ellos se ven en secreto. = Even though the main character's father is opposed to her relationship with Tomás, they continue to see each other secretly.

Pronunciamos

Los sonidos de p, t y ca/co/cu

12.49. Leemos y grabamos. Lee en voz alta estas palabras y grábate.

título   comedia   terror   policiaca   documental   contar

director   bélica   fantástico   papel   concurso   cartel

12.50. Leemos, escuchamos y comparamos. Lee la explicación y escucha cómo pronuncia un nativo las palabras de la actividad 12.49. ¿Notas diferencia en la pronunciación de los sonidos de **p, t** y **ca, co, cu**?

▶ In English, the sounds **p**, **t**, and **k** are pronounced with a strong puff of breath. This is not the case in Spanish.

⚙ **Estrategia**

To improve your pronunciation, keep the following tips in mind:

• Pay attention to how your lips, tongue, and mouth move. When you speak, how you open and close your mouth affects your pronunciation. Use a mirror to practice.

• Remember that words are composed of syllables. If you focus on each syllable, it will be easier to pronounce the whole word. Don't forget to put more emphasis on the pronunciation of the stressed syllable of each word.

• Record yourself. You can make a voice or a video recording. In this way, you will be able to detect errors and correct them.

12.51. Practicamos. Lee de nuevo en voz alta las palabras de la actividad 12.49. Mientras lo haces, coloca la palma de tu mano a unos centímetros de la boca. Si notas el aire en la palma de la mano, relaja la pronunciación.

12.52. Escuchamos y repetimos. Escucha estas palabras de la lección y repite.

protagonista   reportaje   entrevista   programa   concursante   histórico   aventuras   tratar

retransmisión   intriga   actualidad   estreno   futurista   cortometraje   presentar   personaje

12.53. Escribimos y practicamos. Elige algunas palabras de las actividades 12.49 y 12.52 y escribe frases. Luego, léelas en voz alta prestando atención a la pronunciación de los sonidos de **p, t** y **ca, co, cu**.

El director y la protagonista del cortometraje "Madre" cuentan en una entrevista su experiencia en la ceremonia de los Óscar.

Vocabulario activo

)) Cine *Film*

- **el actor / la actriz** *actor/actress*
- **el argumento** *plot*
- **la banda sonora** *soundtrack*
- **el cortometraje** *short film*
- **el/la director/a** *director*
- **la duración** *length*
- **el episodio** *episode*
- **la escena** *scene*
- **la fecha de estreno** *premiere date*
- **el final** *ending*
- **el género** *genre*
- **el guion** *script*
- **el/la guionista** *scriptwriter*
- **interpretar** *to play a role, to act*
- **el largometraje** *feature film*
- **el papel** *role, part*
- **el personaje** *character*
- **el/la protagonista** *main character*
- **protagonizar** *to have the leading role*
- **el reparto** *cast*
- **la sinopsis** *synopsis*
- **la temporada** *season*
- **el título** *title*
- **la trama** *plot, storyline*

)) Hablar de las características de una obra *Talking about movies and series*

- **contar** (o>ue) *to tell*
- **estar ambientado/-a en** *to be set in*
- **estar basado/-a en** *to be based on*
- **hacer el papel (de)** *to play the role (of)*
- **salir** *to appear*
- **valer la pena** *to be worthwhile*
- **tratar de** *to be about*

)) Géneros *Genres*

- **de acción** *action*
- **de amor** *love*
- **de animación** *animated*
- **de aventuras** *adventure*
- **una película bélica** *war movie*
- **biográfico/-a** *biopic*
- **de ciencia ficción** *science fiction (sci-fi)*
- **la comedia** *comedy*
- **la comedia romántica** *rom-com*
- **el documental** *documentary*
- **el drama** *drama*
- **fantástico/-a** (una película, un cortometraje...) *fantasy (movie, short film...)*
- **futurista** *futuristic*
- **histórico/-a** *historical*
- **de intriga** *intrigue*
- **el musical** *musical*
- **del oeste** *western*
- **policiaco/-a** *crime thriller*
- **romántico/-a** *romantic*
- **de superhéroes** *superhero*
- **de terror** *horror, chiller*

)) Vocabulario relacionado con los medios de comunicación *Vocabulary related to media*

- **la actualidad** *current affairs*
- **el/la concursante** *contestant*
- **el concurso** *contest*
- **los dibujos animados** *cartoons*
- **la entrevista** *interview*
- **el informativo** *the news*
- **el magacín** *magazine*
- **la noticia** *news*
- **el programa** *program*
- **el programa musical** *music program*
- **el reportaje** *article, report*
- **la retransmisión deportiva** *sports broadcast*

⚙ **Estrategia**

Who doesn't love movies? When you find a topic that you like, try to create opportunities to practice what you've learned with others that share similar interests. In this case, you can use social networks to talk in Spanish about movies you like.

Lección
13

Antes y ahora

IN THIS LESSON WE ARE GOING TO

decide which period in history was the most interesting

LEARNING OUTCOMES
You will be able to...

- talk about habits, customs, and circumstances in the past

- situate actions in the past and in the present

VOCABULARY
- Landmarks and inventions
- Socio-economic data

LANGUAGE STRUCTURES
- The imperfect tense
- Temporal markers for present and past
- **Cuando** + imperfect tense
- **Ya no / todavía** + present tense

PRONUNCIATION
- Pronunciation of **ia** and **ía**

CULTURAL CONNECTIONS
- The Mayan civilization

Estudio del escritor Pablo Neruda en su casa en Atlántida, una ciudad-balneario cerca de Montevideo, Uruguay.

Primer contacto

13.1. Los años... En grupos, ¿qué cosas (productos, personajes famosos, géneros musicales, etc.) relacionan con cada una de estas épocas? Justifíquenlo.

- los años 20
- los años 40
- los años 50
- los años 60
- los años 80
- los años 90

Rosa Parks sentada en el autobús, Montgomery, Alabama, 1956.

La Segunda Guerra Mundial

MARTIN LUTHER KING JR.

TUPAC & BIGGIE

La Gran Depresión

La llegada del hombre a la Luna

The Beatles

BILL CLINTON

El asesinato de John Lennon

Los primeros videojuegos

MOVIMIENTO HIPPIE

Andy Warhol delante de una de sus obras.

El *apartheid* en Sudáfrica

John F. Kennedy

El juicio a O.J. Simpson

NELSON MANDELA

La guerra de Vietnam

MARILYN MONROE

Nelson Mandela, presidente de Sudáfrica entre 1994 y 1998.

- Yo relaciono el apartheid en Sudáfrica con los años 90 porque fue cuando terminó.
- Sí, y a principios de los años 90 Nelson Mandela salió de prisión.

▬ **Para comunicar**
You can place an event in a given time using:
a principios/mediados/finales de los (años) 50/60...
en los (años) 60/70...

Comprendemos el vocabulario

Hitos e inventos

13.2. **Hitos e inventos.** Escucha y lee.

el descubrimiento

del fuego

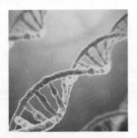

del ADN

de la electricidad

de la penicilina y otros medicamentos

la invención

de la rueda

de la imprenta

del avión

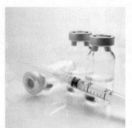

de las vacunas

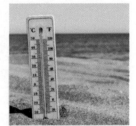

del termómetro

del telescopio

del microscopio

del papel

de la pólvora

la aparición

del turismo

del dinero

de la escritura

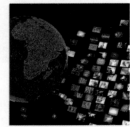

del petróleo

de los medios de comunicación

13.3. Clasificamos las palabras. Escribe en la tabla las palabras de la actividad 13.2 que relacionas con cada uno de estos ámbitos. Luego, compara tu tabla con la de otra persona.

La salud	La ecología	El entretenimiento y la comunicación	La tecnología
El ADN			

13.4. Utilidades. Escribe qué descubrimientos o inventos de la actividad 13.2 permiten hacer estas cosas.

1. Consumir alimentos cocinados y protegerse del frío.
2. Observar objetos que están lejos.
3. Medir la temperatura.
4. Desplazarse largas distancias en poco tiempo.
5. Prevenir y tratar determinadas enfermedades
6. Ampliar cosas muy pequeñas para verlas en detalle.
7. Escribir, dibujar, envolver cosas...
8. Reproducir textos e imágenes sobre papel, tela u otros materiales.

1. El fuego y la electricidad

13.5. Inventos. Busca información en internet sobre los inventos de la actividad 13.2 y prepara una ficha como la del ejemplo para cada uno.

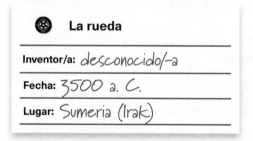

La rueda

Inventor/a: desconocido/-a

Fecha: 3500 a. C.

Lugar: Sumeria (Irak)

❶ ¿Necesitas ayuda?

a. C. (antes de Cristo) = *B.C.*
d. C. (después de Cristo) = *A.D.*
siglo = *century*

13.6. Cronología de los inventos. Sitúa los inventos de la actividad 13.5 en una línea temporal. Indica la fecha en la que se inventaron. Luego, en parejas, comparen sus líneas temporales.

1903: ...

3500 a. C.: la rueda

Comprendemos el vocabulario

Datos socioeconómicos

))) **13.7.** **¿Siglo xv o siglo xxi?** Escucha y lee la información. Marca qué frases corresponden al Imperio
e incaico y cuáles a Estados Unidos. Busca información en internet si lo necesitas.

Imperio incaico, siglo xv.

Estados Unidos, siglo xxi.

A   B

1. El **sistema político** es una **democracia** presidencialista.

2. La **forma de gobierno** es una **monarquía absoluta**.

3. Es un **imperio** de dos millones de kilómetros cuadrados.

4. Es un país de más de nueve millones de kilómetros cuadrados.

5. **Existe** la **esclavitud**: las personas sin **libertad** son los yanakuna, los **esclavos** de la **nobleza**, y los
   pinakuna, los **prisioneros** de **guerra**.

6. Hay numerosos problemas de **medioambiente**, como la contaminación de las aguas y del aire.

7. Hay una **red de caminos** de 30 000 km llamada Qhapaq Ñan (camino del rey).

8. La **actividad económica** principal es la **agricultura**.

9. La **base de la alimentación** son la papa, el maíz y la carne de alpaca.

10. La **esperanza de vida** es de 79 años.

11. La **industria** del entretenimiento es muy importante: todos los días millones de personas van al cine,
    escuchan la radio, ven televisión, etc.

12. La **medicina** está muy vinculada a la naturaleza, las creencias y la **religión**.

13. La **red de transporte** es impresionante: cientos de aeropuertos, miles de kilómetros de autopistas,
    una importante red ferroviaria.

14. La tecnología está muy presente en todos los ámbitos: la **educación**, el entretenimiento, la información, etc.

15. Las mujeres no tienen los mismos **derechos** que los hombres: el **poder político** y **económico** están
    totalmente en manos de los hombres.

16. Las principales **causas de muerte** son los **problemas cardiovasculares**, **enfermedades** como el
    cáncer y los accidentes de varios tipos.

17. Las mujeres se encargan de las **labores del hogar**, de **cuidar** a sus hijos, de **fabricar** la ropa de la
    familia y de ayudar en el campo.

ⓔ 13.8. Definiciones. ¿A qué palabras de la actividad 13.7 corresponden estas definiciones?

1. Forma de gobierno que se basa en el **poder** total de una sola persona.
2. Ciencia que estudia las enfermedades de las personas.
3. Organización política, normalmente dirigida por un emperador o emperatriz, en la que un estado extiende su poder a otros.
4. Forma de gobierno basada en el derecho de las personas a elegir a sus gobernantes.
5. Actividades para trabajar la tierra y obtener productos vegetales.
6. De media, años que vive una población determinada.
7. Actividad técnica para transformar materias en productos.

> **❶ ¿Necesitas ayuda?**
>
> **de media** = *average*

13.9. Relacionamos. Relaciona los elementos de cada columna para formar expresiones.

1. la esperanza
2. la red
3. las labores
4. cuidar
5. la actividad
6. los problemas

a. de transporte
b. cardiovasculares
c. a los hijos
d. económica
e. de vida
f. del hogar

ⓔ 13.10. Completamos. Completa estas frases con las palabras de la actividad 13.9.

1. Medellín tiene una moderna ....: el metro, el tranvía, el metroplús, el metrocable, autobuses y taxis permiten moverse con facilidad por la ciudad.

2. Costa Rica es el país de América Latina con la .... más alta de todo el continente: 80,98 años.

3. Los malos hábitos en la alimentación causan muchos ....

4. La **desigualdad** entre mujeres y hombres todavía existe cuando hablamos de .... Los hombres cocinan menos, limpian menos...

5. La .... de El Salvador se basa principalmente en la agricultura y los **servicios**.

> **⊕ ¿Sabes que...?**
>
> Medellin's subway or *metro*, inaugurated in 1995, is the first mass transit system constructed in Colombia. In addition, Medellin has a cable car system called the "metrocable" that is used for mass transit, the first of its kind. The public transportation system in Medellin is considered to be one of the best in the world.

13.11. En nuestro entorno. Piensa en tu comunidad o en tu estado y responde estas preguntas.

1. ¿Cómo es la red de transporte?

....

2. ¿Cuál es la actividad económica principal?

....

3. ¿Ves ejemplos de **igualdad** o desigualdad entre hombres y mujeres? ¿Cuáles?

....

4. ¿Hay lugares para practicar diferentes religiones?

....

5. ¿Qué enfermedades afectan más a las personas?

....

6. ¿En qué ámbitos está presente la tecnología? Pon algunos ejemplos.

....

Exploramos la lengua

El imperfecto

13.12. La España de los años 50. Elisa está mirando unas fotos con su abuela, que tiene más de 90 años. Localiza en las imágenes elementos que mencionan en su conversación.

- Abuela, ¿qué es esta foto?
- Es una foto de la frontera con Francia, en los años 50.
- ¿Y eso que lleva la mujer? ¿Es un pan?
- Sí, en los años 50 en España **había** poca comida y algunas personas que **vivían** cerca de Francia **pasaban** la frontera para comprar pan.
- ¡Qué me dices!
- Y aquí la escena parece simpática, pero antes las cosas **eran** muy difíciles. Por ejemplo, las mujeres no podíamos tener un pasaporte propio y no **teníamos** derecho a viajar al extranjero sin el permiso de nuestro padre o nuestro marido.
- ¡Qué horror!
- Sí, horrible.

- ¿Y este sitio tan bonito?
- Mi universidad: Salamanca.
- ¿Salamanca? ¿**Vivías** allí?
- Sí, en los años 50 existían muy pocas universidades en España y si una persona quería estudiar (y sus padres **tenían** dinero, claro) **tenía** que irse a Salamanca, a Madrid, a Barcelona o a otra ciudad con universidad.
- ¿Y **había** chicas?
- Sí, pero **éramos** muy pocas, ¿eh? Menos del 20 %, y casi todas en carreras de letras. Muy pocas estudiaban Ciencias o Medicina.
- ¿Y qué edad **tenías** aquí?
- ¡Uy! **Era** muy joven, **tenía** 19 años.

- ¿Y esta estación?
- Es la estación de Barcelona. Yo **iba** todos los veranos a Barcelona y **pasaba** allí dos meses con mi prima, que **vivía** allí con su familia.
- ¿**Ibas** en un tren como este?
- Exacto. ¡Y en 1955 **era** muy moderno!

13.13. Cuatro temas. Detecta los siguientes temas en la conversación de la actividad 13.12. ¿Dónde se mencionan?

la situación de la mujer   la situación económica   la universidad   los transportes

13.14. Usamos el imperfecto para... Las formas verbales en negrita en la conversación de la actividad 13.12 están en un nuevo tiempo verbal: el imperfecto. Lee otra vez la conversación y marca la opción correcta para completar la regla.

Usamos el imperfecto para...

○ ... describir circunstancias o acciones habituales en el pasado.

○ ... hablar de acciones que solo ocurrieron una vez.

e **13.15.** **Conjugamos.** Observa los verbos en negrita de la actividad 13.12 y completa las conjugaciones.

	REGULARES			IRREGULARES	
	PASAR	**TENER**	**VIVIR**	**SER**	**IR**
(yo)	....	....	....	....	....
(tú)	pasabas	....	....	eras	....
(él/ella, usted)	pasaba	....	vivía	....	iba
(nosotros/nosotras)	pasábamos	....	vivíamos	....	íbamos
(vosotros/vosotras)	pasabais	teníais	vivíais	erais	íbais
(ellos/ellas, ustedes)	....	....	....	....	iban

13.16. El verbo *haber*. Ahora observa las formas destacadas en rojo en la actividad 13.12 y completa el cuadro.

La forma del verbo **haber**, correspondiente a **hay**, en imperfecto es ....

> **❶ ¿Necesitas ayuda?**
>
> Remember that **hay** is the only form to express both "there is / there are". This singular form works the same in every tense.

e **13.17.** **Completamos.** Completa estos recuerdos de otras personas sobre la España de los años 50 con la forma adecuada de estos verbos.

durar | haber (x2) | pasar (x2) | ser (x2) | tener | vivir

1. En los años 50 tus abuelos y yo .... en Irún, al lado de la frontera francesa.

2. Una vez por mes, la abuela y yo .... la frontera para comprar algunas cosas en Francia: mantequilla, pan, azúcar, etc.

3. Mi madre no .... derecho a pasar la frontera sin un permiso firmado por mi padre.

4. En mi facultad, que .... la facultad de Filosofía y Letras, ... cincuenta chicas; pero en la de Ciencias solo .... tres chicas.

5. Mis primas iban a Irún una vez al año y .... la Navidad con nosotros.

6. Casi todos los trenes .... horribles y el viaje .... más de 16 horas.

13.18. Los Estados Unidos de los años 50. ¿Qué sabes sobre los siguientes temas en los Estados Unidos de los años 50? Investiga si es necesario y escribe frases.

la situación de la mujer | la situación económica
la universidad | los transportes

En los años 50 había pocas mujeres en la universidad y...

👥 13.19. Ponemos en común nuestras frases.
En grupos, pongan en común las frases que escribieron en la actividad 13.18. ¿Hay similitudes?

Exploramos la lengua

Marcadores temporales para el presente y el pasado

13.20. ¿Siglo xv o actualidad? En un artículo sobre Cusco encontramos las siguientes frases. Léelas y marca cuáles se refieren al siglo xv (Imperio incaico) y cuáles a la actualidad.

	Siglo xv	Actualidad
1. **Hoy en día** Cusco es la 7ª ciudad más poblada de Perú.		
2. **Actualmente** es el principal destino turístico del país.		
3. **En aquella época**, era la ciudad más importante de América del Sur.		
4. **En estos momentos** la población es de unas 400 000 personas.		
5. **En aquellos tiempos**, Cusco estaba en el centro de las cuatro grandes regiones que formaban el imperio.		
6. **Ahora** es la capital del departamento del Cusco.		

13.21. Presente y pasado. Clasifica en la tabla qué expresiones de la actividad 13.20 (en negrita) sirven para hablar del presente y cuáles para hablar del pasado.

Presente	Pasado

13.22. La España de los años 50. Escribe frases sobre los años 50 en España, bajo la dictadura del general Franco, usando los conectores para hablar del pasado de la actividad 13.21 y conjugando los verbos en imperfecto.

1. No existir el **divorcio**: *En aquella época no existía el divorcio.* ....

2. Haber **censura**: ....

3. Muchas películas y libros **estar prohibidos**: ....

4. Los **partidos políticos** estar prohibidos: ....

5. Haber muchos **presos políticos**: ....

6. Miles de españoles vivir en el **exilio**: ....

7. La **libertad de expresión** ser muy limitada: ....

13.23. La España actual. Busca información sobre España en la actualidad y escribe frases usando los conectores de la actividad 13.21 para hablar del presente.

Hoy en día, España es una monarquía parlamentaria.

Cuando + imperfecto

e **13.24. Cuando...** Lee estas frases y marca aquellas con las que te identificas.

Cuando mis padres eran jóvenes, había más opciones de entretenimiento que ahora.

Cuando mi madre tenía 18 años, las mujeres no iban a la universidad: no podían.

Cuando yo iba a la escuela, los niños respetaban más a los maestros que ahora.

Cuando mis abuelos eran jóvenes, todos los **anticonceptivos** estaban prohibidos.

13.25. Comparamos con nuestra lengua. Lee de nuevo las frases de la actividad 13.24 y observa la estructura **cuando** + imperfecto. ¿Cómo expresas lo mismo en inglés? ¿Hay más de una manera de expresarlo?

13.26. Escribimos frases. Escribe frases usando **cuando** + imperfecto.

1. No haber medicamentos.
2. No existir el plástico.
3. No haber electricidad.
4. No haber automóviles.
5. Las mujeres no poder **votar**.
6. No exisitir el dinero.

1. Cuando no había medicamentos, la esperanza de vida era más corta.

13.27. Cuando mi padre era joven. Piensa en alguien de tu familia: tu padre, tu abuela... Escribe frases sobre dónde vivía cuando era joven, cómo era su casa, qué cosas hacía para pasarla bien, cómo era la vida en esa época, etc.

Ya no / todavía + presente

13.28. ¿Nos sorprende? Lee estas informaciones sobre hechos sociales o históricos del mundo hispano. ¿Alguna de ellas te parece sorprendente?

1 La base de la alimentación en el Imperio incaico eran la papa y el maíz, y la carne más consumida era la de alpaca; la papa y el maíz son **todavía** fundamentales en la alimentación de los pueblos andinos, pero la carne de alpaca **ya no** es la más consumida.

2 En 1940, solo el 12 % de los universitarios españoles eran mujeres, y en 1970 **todavía** eran minoría: solo eran el 31 %. **Ya no** es así: en este momento, más del 50 % del alumnado de la universidad española son mujeres. Sin embargo, en las carreras técnicas, como las ingenierías, **todavía** son mayoría los hombres.

13.29. Completamos la regla. Observa las palabras marcadas en negrita en los textos de la actividad 13.28 y relaciona un elemento de cada columna para completar la regla.

1. Usamos **todavía** para...   **a.** ... expresar la interrupción de una acción o de un estado.
2. Usamos **ya no** para...   **b.** ... expresar la continuidad de una acción o de un estado.

13.30. Escuchamos y reaccionamos. Vas a oír cinco afirmaciones sobre estos temas. Toma notas y escribe un comentario, según tu opinión y lo que sabes, usando **ya no** y **todavía**.

la universidad   la alimentación   la mujer   las ciudades   la tecnología

Comunicamos

¿Cómo se hacía?

 13.31. Hace 30 años. ¿Cómo se hacían estas cosas hace 30 años? ¿Cómo se hacen ahora? Coméntenlo en grupos.

| comprar | pagar | escuchar música | buscar información | buscar pareja | viajar |

comunicarse con personas que viven lejos   ver películas   tomar fotos   estar informado

• *Antes la gente tenía que ir a muchas tiendas para comprar cosas diferentes. Hoy en día hay centros comerciales en muchas ciudades y se puede comprar casi todo en el mismo sitio.*

○ *Sí, y además, ahora casi todo se puede comprar en internet y no es necesario salir de casa.*

> 🔲 **Para comunicar**
>
> **Había / se podía...**
> **La gente tenía que / podía...**
>
> **No había / no se podía...**
> **La gente no tenía que / no podía...**

Grandes inventos

 13.32. Grandes inventos. Algunos inventos y descubrimientos han sido muy importantes para la vida de la gente. Piensa cuál crees que ha sido el más importante y por qué. Antes de ese invento, ¿qué cosas eran imposibles o muy diferentes? Coméntalo con tu compañero/-a.

 LA INVENCIÓN DEL TELÉFONO

 EL DESCUBRIMIENTO DE LA PENICILINA

 LA INVENCIÓN DE LA IMPRENTA

 EL DESCUBRIMIENTO DEL FUEGO

 LA INVENCIÓN DEL AVIÓN

 LA INVENCIÓN DE LA TELEVISIÓN

 LA INVENCIÓN DE LA MÁQUINA DE VAPOR

 LA INVENCIÓN DE LA RUEDA

 OTROS

 LA APARICIÓN DE INTERNET

EL DESCUBRIMIENTO DE LA ELECTRICIDAD

• *A mí me parece muy importante la invención del avión porque, antes de los aviones, la gente viajaba mucho menos que ahora y los viajes eran mucho más lentos.*

○ *Sí, yo estoy de acuerdo. Por ejemplo, los viajes en barco de América a Europa duraban semanas y eran muy duros. Además...*

13.33. Compartimos nuestras ideas. Ahora, coméntenlo entre todos.

A nosotros nos parece...

Descubre la mentira

 13.34. Imprecisiones históricas. En grupos, repasen las informaciones de la actividad 13.6. Luego, detecten y corrijan las imprecisiones históricas de estas frases. Pueden usar internet si lo necesitan.

1. La producción de libros era una importante actividad económica en la época del imperio romano. En enormes imprentas ubicadas en diferentes lugares de todo el imperio, se producían miles de obras, principalmente de teatro y de filosofía.
2. Durante la guerra civil de los Estados Unidos, en la segunda mitad del siglo XIX, se salvaron muchas vidas gracias al uso de la penicilina.
3. Desde el siglo XVIII, la comunicación entre el continente americano y Europa es mucho más rápida gracias al uso de aviones en lugar de barcos.
4. En el siglo XX tuvieron lugar grandes avances en medicina gracias a la invención del microscopio a finales del siglo XIX.
5. En la antigua Grecia, los marineros se vacunaban antes de salir de viaje. Así evitaban contraer la gripe y otras enfermedades conocidas.

- *En la época romana no existía la imprenta.*
- *Sí, la producción de libros empezó a ser una importante actividad económica después de la invención de la imprenta en el siglo xv.*

 13.35. Comparamos. Comparen sus correcciones con las de sus compañeros/-as.

Comparamos países

 13.36. Un país de habla hispana. Elige un país de habla hispana y busca información en internet para completar esta ficha.

País:

| **Sistema político:** | **¿Las mujeres tienen los mismos derechos que los hombres?** |

Actividad económica:

| **Base de la alimentación:** | **¿Quién hace la mayoría de las labores del hogar?** |

Esperanza de vida:

13.37. Comparamos países. En grupos de tres, comparen las fichas que prepararon en la actividad 13.36. ¿Cuáles son las similitudes y las diferencias entre los distintos países?

- *El sistema político de Paraguay es una república presidencialista.*
- *Bolivia también es una república presidencialista.*
- *Ah, pues Uruguay también.*

13.38. Compartimos. Compartan con el resto de la clase los datos que más les sorprenden o que les parecen más interesantes.

Nosotros comparamos Paraguay, Bolivia y Uruguay y los tres tienen el mismo sistema político: una república presidencialista.

Ahora podemos...

Decidir cuál es la época de la historia más interesante

13.39. Una época interesante. En grupos, elijan una de estas tres épocas de la historia u otra. Piensen en sus características (positivas y negativas) y preparen una descripción para sus compañeros/-as. Pueden tener en cuenta los temas propuestos.

Imperio incaico (siglo v)	España entre los años 1939 y 1959	Los años 60 (u otra década) en Estados Unidos

- La salud: las enfermedades, la esperanza de vida...
- La convivencia: la vida familiar, el contacto con los amigos, los vecinos...
- El entretenimiento y la comunicación: la danza, la música, la radio, la televisión, los libros, los deportes...
- La tecnología: los medios de transporte, los electrodomésticos...
- La sociedad: la democracia, la justicia, la igualdad de oportunidades...

13.40. Presentamos. Ahora, cada grupo presenta la época que eligió en la actividad 13.39.

Los incas adoraban al sol. Lo llamaban "inti".

En su honor construían templos cubiertos de oro y celebraban la fiesta del sol (en quechua, "inti raymi"), que todavía se celebra hoy en día.

...

13.41. Decidimos. Entre todos, decidan cuál es la época más interesante.

Para mí, la época más interesante son los años 50 en España porque...

Video

Borinqueneer

A sus 93 años, Deogracias Rivera-Manso recuerda con orgullo y nostalgia sus años de servicio en el 65.º Regimiento de Infantería. Él y sus compañeros eran conocidos como los "Borinqueneers". Este video cuenta la historia de un hombre y de toda una vida dedicada a su país.

P Pearson
MyLab

To find out more about Deogracias and other Borinqueneers, go to MyLab to watch **Borinqueneer** and complete the video activities.

⊕ **¿Sabes que...?**

The original inhabitants of several Caribbean islands, including Puerto Rico, were the Taino. Their name for the island was Borinquen, and for this reason, many Puerto Ricans today call themselves boricuas. The Taino were virtually wiped out from the region after the arrival of the Spanish, but traces of the Taino language can be appreciated today in Spanish and English, in such loan words as *canoa* ("canoe"), *huracán* ("hurricane"), and *manatí* ("manatee").

🔍 **Hacemos conexiones**

Investiga sobre la influencia de otras lenguas en el inglés. Selecciona 10 palabras que te sorprendan y presenta su origen en la clase.

CIVILIZACIÓN MAYA

Durante 2700 años en los bosques tropicales de Mesoamérica, en territorios de lo que hoy son México, Guatemala, Belice, Honduras y El Salvador, se desarrolló una de las culturas más enigmáticas de la historia de la humanidad: la maya. **¿Qué sabemos de esta civilización?**

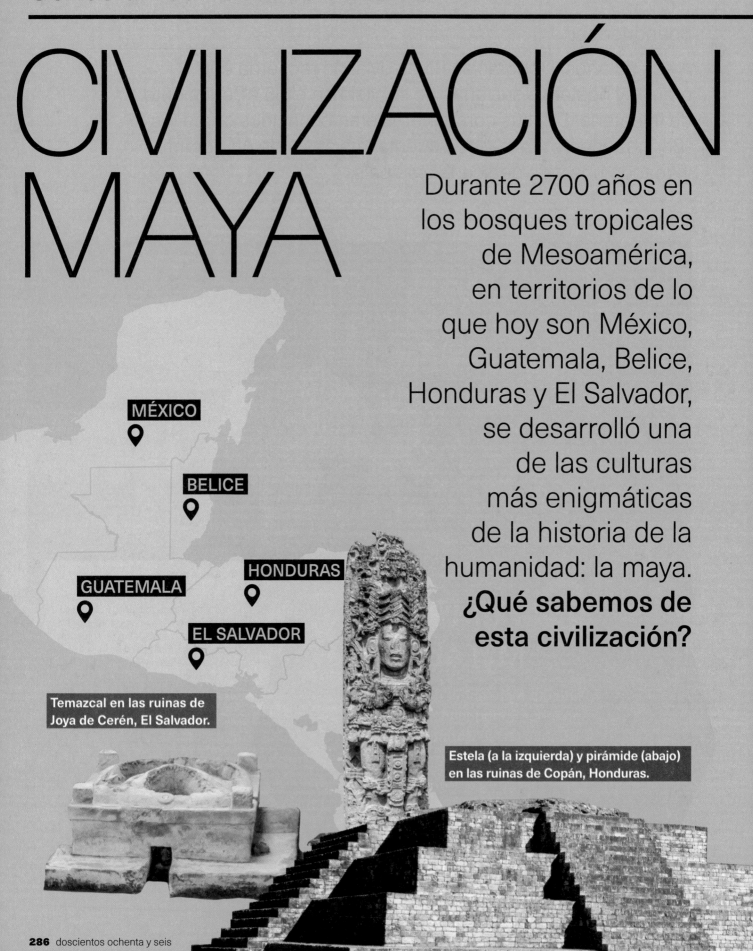

MÉXICO

BELICE

HONDURAS

GUATEMALA

EL SALVADOR

Temazcal en las ruinas de Joya de Cerén, El Salvador.

Estela (a la izquierda) y pirámide (abajo) en las ruinas de Copán, Honduras.

LA GUERRA

La guerra era una parte esencial de la cultura maya y las ciudades entraban en conflicto, unas con otras, en numerosas ocasiones. Se especula que esos conflictos son la razón de la desaparición de numerosas ciudades en el siglo VIII: Bonampak, Piedras Negras, Palenque, Yaxchilán, etc. Es el denominado "colapso maya".

EL DEPORTE: EL JUEGO DE LA PELOTA

En muchas ciudades mayas se encuentran lugares destinados a practicar el juego de la pelota. Era un juego o deporte al que jugaban hombres, mujeres y niños, pero era también, en muchos casos, un ritual relacionado con la agricultura, la guerra o la astronomía. Hoy en día, una versión moderna de este juego, llamada "ulama", se practica todavía en lugares de Guatemala y México.

LOS CENOTES SAGRADOS

Los cenotes son pozos subterráneos presentes en toda la península de Yucatán. Parece ser que los mayas consideraban estas grutas como una entrada al mundo mágico, una estación antes de llegar al cielo. En ellos se realizaban rituales relacionados con el sol y sacrificios humanos. Por esa razón, los arqueólogos encuentran en ellos esqueletos y ofrendas a los dioses.

LA ASTRONOMÍA

Los sacerdotes mayas de la época clásica (entre los siglos III y IX) eran expertos astrónomos. Conocían los movimientos de muchos planetas, los periodos de la Luna y del Sol y eran capaces de predecir eclipses. Eran especialmente importantes los movimientos del planeta Venus; parece ser que algunos rituales (incluso las batallas) se realizaban en función de este planeta.

ANTES DE LEER

 13.42. Conocimientos previos. Comenten qué saben sobre la civilización maya: territorio, costumbres, conocimientos...

LECTURA ACTIVA

13.43. Comprendemos el vocabulario. Relaciona cada palabra con su traducción en inglés.

1. desaparición (párrafo 1)
2. colapso (párrafo 1)
3. pozos (párrafo 3)
4. grutas (párrafo 3)
5. sacerdotes (párrafo 4)
6. predecir (párrafo 4)

a. priests
b. disappearance
c. downfall
d. sinkhole
e. to predict
f. cave

13.44. Verdadero o falso. Marca si estas frases son ciertas o falsas, según el texto.

	Verdadero	Falso
1. Los conflictos entre los mayas y otras culturas provocaron el colapso maya.		
2. Los mayas jugaban el juego de la pelota solamente por entretenimiento.		
3. Se practica una variedad del juego de la pelota en dos países de habla hispana.		
4. En los cenotes se celebraban rituales relacionados con el Sol.		
5. No queda ningún resto de los rituales o sacrificios humanos en los cenotes.		
6. Los mayas sabían predecir eclipses.		

13.45. Corregimos la información falsa. Corrige las frases falsas de la actividad 13.44.

DESPUÉS DE LEER

 13.46. Un pueblo nativo americano. Investiga sobre algún pueblo nativo de Estados Unidos y prepara una presentación.

Textos audiovisuales: vemos, escuchamos y presentamos

Vemos un video sobre la vida antes de los *smartphones*

13.47. Preparación. Marca si crees que estas afirmaciones sobre los *smartphones* son ventajas o desventajas.

	Ventaja	Desventaja
1. Tienes casi todo a la mano: teléfono, internet, programas de televisión, reloj, calculadora, GPS, *mail*, redes sociales, juegos, cámara, música, etc.		
2. Son caros.		
3. Necesitan batería para funcionar.		
4. Aparecen nuevos modelos constantemente y se vuelven obsoletos rápidamente.		
5. Muchas aplicaciones (*apps*) son gratis.		
6. La pantalla se rompe fácilmente.		
7. El tamaño: puedes llevarlo en tu bolsillo.		

e 13.48. Antes de los *smartphones*. Marca cuáles de estas cosas crees que ocurrían antes de la aparición de los teléfonos inteligentes. Luego, compara tus respuestas con otra persona de la clase. ¿Están de acuerdo?

- La gente conversaba más en los cafés y los restaurantes que ahora.
- La gente tomaba fotos y las publicaba en Instagram.
- La gente no daba su número de tarjeta de crédito a casi nadie.
- La gente memorizaba los números de teléfono de tiendas, servicios, familiares y amigos.
- La gente pedía comida o bebida con una *app*.
- La gente no podía corroborar información inmediatamente en su teléfono.
- Para hablar de algo la gente usaba su conocimiento de las cosas porque lo leía o lo estudiaba o alguien se lo decía.
- La gente se comunicaba con Siri en su teléfono.
- La gente prefería pagar cosas en efectivo (es decir, con dinero) que dar la información de su tarjeta de crédito.
- La gente hacía compras usando su teléfono.
- La gente necesitaba saber la dirección detallada de un lugar para poder llegar ahí.

INFORMACIÓN PREVIA   Vas a ver un video creado por Fred Lammie, un *youtuber* panameño que tiene mucho éxito con sus videos animados de su canal Casi Creativo. En este video, Lammie presenta las ventajas y las desventajas de los teléfonos inteligentes. Además, también nos presenta ejemplos de cómo era la vida en los años 90 –cuando no había *smartphones*– y compara esa época con la actual.

VEMOS EL VIDEO

13.49. Ventajas y desventajas. Ve el video hasta el minuto 1:20. ¿Qué ventajas y desventajas de la lista de la actividad 13.48 no menciona Lammie?

13.50. Ejemplos. Ahora ve el resto del video. ¿Qué aspectos de la lista de la actividad 13.48 identifica el video como ejemplos para comparar la época de los 90 y ahora? Pon estos aspectos en el orden en que aparecen en el video.

13.51. Los números de teléfono. Ve de nuevo el segmento del minuto 1:20 al minuto 1:49 y contesta:

1. Los números de teléfono que sabe de memoria el hombre son de ....

2. El hombre no recuerda el número de teléfono de su "viejo". Según el contexto, ¿a quién crees que se refiere "viejo"?
a. A su papá.
b. A su hermano mayor.

3. En el *sketch*, el hombre no recuerda un número importante. ¿Qué otro aspecto cómico tiene el final del diálogo?
a. El hombre no tiene ese número.
b. El hombre no recuerda cómo se llama su viejo.

13.52. Información incorrecta. Ve del minuto 1:49 al minuto 2:14 para contestar estas preguntas:

1. El hombre impresiona a su amigo porque...
a. ...sabe el tiempo que tarda la luz en viajar del Sol hasta la Tierra.
b. ...sabe el tamaño del Sol en comparación con el de la Tierra.

2. ¿En qué aspecto acerca de la invención del termómetro el hombre no está correcto?
a. El inventor del termómetro.
b. El año en que se inventó el termómetro.

13.53. Con efectivo o con tarjeta. Ve el segmento del minuto 2:28 al minuto 3:10 para contestar lo siguiente:

1. El hombre no quiere...
a. ...pagar con efectivo.
b. ...pagar con tarjeta de crédito.

2. El aspecto cómico de este segmento es que ahora...
a. ...le damos nuestro número de tarjeta de crédito a desconocidos.
b. ...no sabemos de memoria nuestro número de tarjeta de crédito.

DESPUÉS DE VER EL VIDEO

13.54. Comunicación interpersonal. En parejas, conversen a partir de estas preguntas.

1. ¿Qué aspecto del video les parece el más efectivo para explicar cómo ha cambiado la vida con los *smartphones*?
2. ¿Creen que alguno de los ejemplos exagera la situación? ¿Cuál? ¿Por qué?
3. Comenten qué se puede inferir sobre cómo era la gente antes del teléfono inteligente (cómo era, qué sabía hacer, qué hacía más, etc.) y cómo es ahora, de acuerdo con cada uno de los ejemplos del video.
4. ¿Se identifican con algún aspecto del video? ¿Hacen alguna de las cosas que muestra el video?
5. ¿Hay algún aspecto del video con el que no están de acuerdo?

Presentamos un ejemplo de cómo te cambia la vida un *smartphone*

13.55. Preparamos. En parejas, añadan un ejemplo al video de Fred Lammie sobre cómo te cambia la vida un *smartphone*. Sigan estas instrucciones.

INSTRUCCIONES Primero, identifica otro aspecto de la vida que ha cambiado como resultado de usar un teléfono inteligente. Después, escribe dos diálogos breves para ejemplificar ese cambio, como en el video: cómo era la vida antes y cómo es ahora. Puedes incluir un aspecto cómico si lo deseas.

13.56. Representamos. Representen los dos diálogos en clase. Los demás adivinan de qué aspecto se trata.

Recursos lingüísticos

THE IMPERFECT TENSE

REGULAR VERBS

	-AR	-ER	-IR
	ESTAR	TENER	VIVIR
(yo)	est**aba**	ten**ía**	viv**ía**
(tú)	est**abas**	ten**ías**	viv**ías**
(él/ella, usted)	est**aba**	ten**ía**	viv**ía**
(nosotros/nosotras)	est**ábamos**	ten**íamos**	viv**íamos**
(vosotros/vosotras)	est**abais**	ten**íais**	viv**íais**
(ellos/ellas, ustedes)	est**aban**	ten**ían**	viv**ían**

IRREGULAR VERBS

SER	IR	VER
era	**iba**	**veía**
eras	**ibas**	**veías**
era	**iba**	**veía**
éramos	**íbamos**	**veíamos**
erais	**ibais**	**veíais**
eran	**iban**	**veían**

▶ We use the imperfect tense to describe in the past.

*La casa de mis abuelos **era** enorme y **tenía** muchas habitaciones.* = My grandparents' house was huge and had many rooms.

▶ Additionally, the imperfect is used to talk about habitual actions in the past.

*En mi época de estudiante, **dormía** muy poco.* = In my student days, I slept / used to sleep / would sleep very little.

! We also use the imperfect tense to describe the circumstances surrounding an event in the past.
*Como **estábamos** cansados, nos quedamos en casa.* = Since we were tired, we stayed home.
*Ayer no **quería** quedarme en casa y fui al cine.* = Yesterday, I didn't want to stay home so I went to the movies.

TEMPORAL MARKERS REFERRING TO THE PAST

Temporal markers used with the imperfect tell us in general when an action took place.

en los (años) 40 = *in the '40s*
en la década de los (años) 2000 = *in the decade of the 2000s*
a principios del siglo XIX / **de** los (años) 50 = *in the beginning of the 19th century / of the '50s*
a/hasta mediados del siglo XX / **de** los (años) 60 = *in/until the mid-20th century / in the mid-'60s*
a finales del siglo XIV / **de** los años 20 = *at the end of the 14th century / at the end of the '20s*

En los años 40 *en España había una dictadura.* = In the '40s in Spain, there was a dictatorship.
En la década de los 2000 *las impresoras 3D tenían menos usos que ahora.* = In the 2000s, 3D printers had fewer uses than now.
A principios del siglo XIX *existían muchas enfermedades infecciosas y relacionadas con la mala alimentación.* = At the beginning of the 19th century, there were many infectious diseases and diseases related to poor nutrition.
Hasta mediados del siglo XX *la televisión era en blanco y negro.* = Until the mid-20th century, television was in black and white.
A finales de los años 20 *había muy pocos automóviles.* = In the late '20s, there were very few cars.

▶ To refer to a period of time in the past that we have already mentioned, we use the following expressions.

> **en esa/aquella época** = *at that/the time*
> **en aquellos tiempos** = *in those times/days*
> **entonces** = *back then*

*El trap surgió en los 90, pero **en esa época** no era tan popular como ahora.* = Trap appeared in the '90s, but at the time, it wasn't as popular as it is now.

En el siglo XIX la gente viajaba mucho en tren o en barco. **En aquellos tiempos**, *no existían los aviones de pasajeros.* = In the 19th century, people used to travel by train or boat. In those days, passenger planes did not exist.

Mi papá no recuerda la dictadura militar de Videla. **Entonces**, *era muy chico.* = My dad doesn't remember Videla's miliary dictatorship in Argentina. Back then, he was very young.

CUANDO + IMPERFECT TENSE

Cuando + the imperfect introduces a period of time when an action was taking place.

> **cuando era pequeño/-a / niño/-a / joven**
> **cuando tenía** 15 años

Cuando mis abuelos eran jóvenes, *no existía internet.*
Cuando Miguel tenía quince años, *no había* smartphones.

TEMPORAL MARKERS REFERRING TO THE PRESENT

Remember, temporal or time markers tell us when an action takes place. We use the following to talk about actions in the present.

> **ahora** = *now*   **hoy** = *today*
> **actualmente** = *currently*   **hoy en día** = *nowadays*
> **en estos momentos** = *at the moment*

Gracias a internet, **ahora** *mucha gente trabaja desde casa.* = Thanks to the internet, many people now work from home.

Mi prima, que **actualmente** *vive en Canadá, va a pasar unos días en Bogotá.* = My cousin, who currently lives in Canada, is going to spend a few days in Bogota.

En estos momentos *existen medios de transporte que funcionan por inteligencia artificial.* = At the moment, there are means of transportation that are operated by artificial intelligence.

Hoy *viajar en avión es más barato que hace treinta años.* = Today, traveling by plane is cheaper than it was thirty years ago.

Hoy en día *es difícil encontrar un buen trabajo.* = Nowadays, it's difficult to find a good job.

YA NO / TODAVÍA + PRESENTE

▶ We use **ya no** to say there was an interruption in an action or a state of being.

La mayoría de la gente **ya no** *usa disquetes para almacenar información.* = The majority of people no longer use floppy discs to store information.

▶ We use **todavía** to express the continuity of an action or state of being.

Ahora las mujeres tienen más derechos que antes, pero **todavía** *hay desigualdad.* = Now women have more rights than before, but there is still inequality.

Pronunciamos

Pronunciación de **ia** e **ía**

🔊 **13.57. Escuchamos y observamos.** Escucha estas palabras y observa la pronunciación de **ia** e **ía**.

1. d**ía**
2. polic**ía**
3. farmac**ia**
4. ped**ía**n
5. v**ia**l

6. sal**ía**mos
7. ten**ía**n
8. ser**ia**
9. quer**ía**
10. v**ía**

🔊 **ⓔ 13.58. Escuchamos y repetimos.** Escucha de nuevo las palabras de la actividad 13.57 y repite.

🔊 **ⓔ 13.59. Escuchamos y marcamos.** Escucha y marca qué palabra oyes en cada caso. ¿Cuáles son verbos en la forma del imperfecto?

1.
a. sabia   **b.** sabía

2.
a. hacia   **b.** hacía

3.
a. media   **b.** medía

🔊 **ⓔ 13.60. Escuchamos y completamos.** Escucha y completa las frases con estas palabras.

sabia   hacia   medía   sabía   hacía   media

1. Cuando tenía 12 años, ya .... 1,70 m.

2. Nos tenemos que ir ya, son las ocho y ....

3. Mi abuela era una mujer muy ....

4. Mi hermana pequeña .... leer a los 4 años.

5. No estuve mucho tiempo en la playa, ... demasiado calor.

6. Para tomar el metro tienes que ir en esta dirección, ... la Plaza de Armas.

🔊 **13.61. Escuchamos y repetimos.** Escucha de nuevo las frases de la actividad 13.60. Después, léelas en voz alta.

Vocabulario activo

 Hitos e inventos *Landmarks and inventions*

- **el ADN** *DNA*
- **la aparición** *appearance*
- **el avión** *plane*
- **el descubrimiento** *discovery*
- **el dinero** *money*
- **la electricidad** *electricity*
- **la escritura** *writing*
- **el fuego** *fire*
- **la imprenta** *press*
- **la invención** *invention*
- **el medicamento** *medicine, medication*
- **los medios de comunicación** (la comunicación) *media*
- **el microscopio** *microscope*
- **el papel** *paper*
- **la penicilina** *penicillin*
- **el petróleo** *oil*
- **la pólvora** *gunpowder*
- **la rueda** *wheel*
- **el telescopio** *telescope*
- **el termómetro** *thermometer*
- **el turismo** *tourism*
- **la vacuna** *vaccine*

Datos socioeconómicos
Socio-economic data

- **la actividad económica** *economic activity*
- **la agricultura** *agriculture*
- **el anticonceptivo** *contraceptive*
- **la base de la alimentación** *basis of nutrition*
- **el cáncer** *cancer*
- **la causa de muerte** (la muerte) *cause of death*
- **la censura** *censorship*
- **cuidar** *to take care of*
- **la democracia** *democracy*
- **el derecho** *right*
- **la desigualdad** *inequality*
- **el divorcio** *divorce*
- **la educación** *education*
- **la enfermedad** *illness*

- **la esclavitud** *slavery*
- **el/la esclavo/-a** *slave*
- **la esperanza de vida** (la vida) *life expectancy*
- **estar prohibido/-a/-os/-as** *to be forbidden*
- **el exilio** *exile*
- **existir** *to exist*
- **fabricar** *to make, to produce*
- **la forma de gobierno** (el gobierno) *form of government*
- **la guerra** *war*
- **la igualdad** *equality*
- **el imperio** *empire*
- **la industria** *industry*
- **las labores del hogar** *housework*
- **la libertad** *freedom*
- **la libertad de expresión** (la expresión) *freedom of speech*
- **la medicina** *medicine*
- **el medioambiente** *environment*
- **la monarquía (absoluta)** *(absolute) monarchy*
- **la nobleza** *nobility*
- **el partido político** *political party*
- **el poder** *power*
- **el poder económico** *economic power*
- **el poder político** *political power*
- **el preso político** *political prisoner*
- **el/la prisionero/-a** *prisoner*
- **el problema cardiovascular** *cardiovascular problem*
- **la red de caminos** (el camino) *road network*
- **la red de transporte** (el transporte) *transport network*
- **la religión** *religion*
- **los servicios** *services*
- **el sistema político** *political system*
- **votar** *to vote*

⚙ **Estrategia**

Watch out for words with multiple meanings in English. They may not have the same meaning in other contexts in Spanish. For instance:

Oil can be **petróleo** ("fuel") but also **aceite** ("liquid for cooking").
Right can be **derecho** ("things that one is entitled to do") but also **correcto** ("correct") or even **derecha** ("opposite of left").

Lección

14

¿Cómo va todo?

IN THIS LESSON WE ARE GOING TO

recreate social interactions using different levels of courtesy

LEARNING OUTCOMES
You will be able to...

• interact in social situations using the appropriate level of courtesy

• invite others to do something

• ask for items and favors

• ask for and give permission

• refuse invitations, give excuses, and explain why

VOCABULARY

• Greetings and farewells

• Verbs of courtesy: **poder**, **molestar**, and **importar**

• **Dar**, **prestar**, **traer**, and **poner** to make requests

LANGUAGE STRUCTURES

• Continuous actions in the present with **estar** + gerund

• Making requests with **poder**, **importar**, **molestar**, and similar verbs

PRONUNCIATION

• The sounds of **d** and the contrast between **d/t**

CULTURAL CONNECTIONS

• Gathering places: el Malecón de La Habana (Cuba)

El Malecón de La Habana (Cuba).

Primer contacto

14.1. Situaciones. Observa la ilustración y relaciona las diferentes situaciones con estas acciones.

○ **pedir** en un café

○ **charlar**

○ **despedirse**

○ jugar

○ tocar la guitarra

○ comer

14.2. Relaciona. Indica a qué situación de la ilustración de la actividad 14.1 corresponde cada una de estas conversaciones.

a.

○ • *Hola, ¿qué desean?*
  ○ *Un jugo de piña y un agua con gas,* **por favor**.

b.

○ • **¡Hasta luego!**
  ○ **¡Nos vemos!** *¡Adiós!*

c.

○ • **¿Qué hay de nuevo?** *Hace varios meses que no te veo.*
  ○ **Ya ves...** *Con mucho trabajo, como siempre. No tengo tiempo para casi nada.*

14.3. Representamos. Representamos las conversaciones de la actividad 14.2.

Comprendemos el vocabulario

Saludos y despedidas

14.4. Conversaciones. Lee y escucha estas cuatro conversaciones.

- *Bueno, me voy...*
- *Listo, **nos llamamos**, ¿dale?*
- *Sí, sí, **hablamos**.*
- *¡Chao!*
- *¡Nos vemos!*

- *Manuel, **¡cuánto tiempo sin verlo!** ¿Cómo va todo?**
- *Bien, bien, **todo bien**. ¿Y usted cómo está?*
- *Pues **pasándola**...*
- *¿Y la familia?*
- *Bien, bien... Gracias.*

- *¡Susana!*
- *¡Natalia! **¡Qué sorpresa!** ¿Cómo estás? ¿Qué tal todo?*
- *Bien, bien. Mucho trabajo... Y tú, **¿qué tal?***

- *Bueno, **me tengo que ir**. Tengo que ir al centro... **Me alegro** mucho de verla...*
- *Sí, yo también. Bueno, chao. ¡Y **saludos** a su familia!*
- ***Igualmente**. ¡Y **un abrazo** muy fuerte **a** su hija!*
- ***Con gusto**. ¡Chao!*
- *Chao.*

Más palabras

 abrazarse / darse un abrazo = *to hug (each other)*
besarse / darse un beso = *to kiss (each other)*
darse la mano = *to shake hands*
decir hola/adiós con la mano = *to wave hello/good-bye*

llegar tarde = *to be late*
tener cosas que hacer = *to have plans/things to do*
tener prisa = *to be in a hurry*
tocarse = *to have physical contact*

Práctica

e **14.5. Saludarse y despedirse.** ¿En qué conversaciones de la actividad 14.4 se saludan las personas? ¿En cuáles se despiden?

e **14.6. Gestos y acciones.** Observa los saludos y despedidas de la actividad 14.4. Indica en qué imagen o imágenes...

1. ... las dos personas se abrazan: ....

2. ... las dos personas se tocan los brazos: ....

3. ... las dos personas se besan: ....

4. ... las dos personas se dicen adiós con la mano: ....

14.7. Expresiones. ¿En tu lengua existen expresiones con un uso similar al de las siguientes? Si es así, escríbelas.

	Sí	No
1. Me tengo que ir. Tengo que ir a...		
2. Me alegro mucho de verla.		
3. Saludos a su familia.		
4. Un abrazo muy fuerte a su hija.		
5. Igualmente.		
6. Con gusto.		
7. Nos llamamos.		
8. Hablamos.		
9. ¿Cómo va todo?		
10. ¡Cuánto tiempo sin verlo!		
11. Todo bien.		
12. Pasándola...		

> ⚙ **Estrategia**
>
> Comparing Spanish to your language will help you discover how both languages work in similar situations. For example, standardized language or formulaic expressions are commonly used in social situations but may have little to do with their literal meaning. The English equivalent for **pasándola** is *I'm managing/doing fine* and cannot be translated literally.

14.8. Justificar. Marca si tú en tu lengua usas justificaciones como las siguientes.

		Lo digo mucho.	Lo digo a veces.	No lo digo.
Me tengo que ir.	Tengo que estudiar.			
	Tengo una reunión.			
	Tengo clase.			
	Tengo prisa.			
	Llego tarde.			
	Tengo cosas que hacer.			

14.9. Nuestras necesidades. Comenten qué otras justificaciones creen que pueden usar en español para terminar una conversación.

Comprendemos el vocabulario

Recursos para pedir y dar en diferentes situaciones

🔊 **14.10. Cortesía.** Lee y escucha este texto.

CUESTIÓN DE CORTESÍA

Cuando aprendes otra lengua, una de las cosas más importantes para no **ser descortés** o **causar malentendidos** es usar las expresiones correctas en situaciones en las que necesitamos algo de otras personas.

En nuestra vida cotidiana, todos **pedimos ayuda, pedimos permiso, pedimos un favor** a un **vecino**, pedimos dinero, **le pedimos prestado** el teléfono a un amigo, pedimos un café en una cafetería, **preguntamos la hora**, preguntamos dónde está el baño... ¿Pero cómo se hace todo eso en español? Vamos a ver algunos ejemplos que funcionan de manera general.

En la cafetería. Normalmente, los meseros pueden decir algo como **¿Qué desea?** o **¿Qué le traigo?**, y nuestra respuesta puede ser: **¿Me trae un café con leche, por favor?**. Claro que siempre podemos ser más económicos: **Un café, por favor**.

Cuando compartimos mesa (u otro espacio). Si necesitamos algo que otra persona tiene más cerca, podemos decir **¿Me pasa la sal, por favor?**

De visita en casa de unos amigos. Nuestro amigo seguramente nos va a preguntar algo como **¿Qué te provoca/apetece/quieres tomar?** Y si no nos preguntan, pero queremos pedir algo, podemos usar **¿Tienes un poco de agua?** o **¿Me puedes dar un vaso de agua?**

Y si vamos a devolver lo que pedimos... El verbo **prestar** es nuestro mejor aliado para pedir algo que tenemos la intención de **devolver: ¿Me prestas veinte pesos? ¿Me prestas tu celular?**

Las palabras mágicas. Hay palabras que suenan más amables que otras. Por ejemplo, todo suena mejor con **por favor**. Y para llamar la atención de la otra persona podemos usar expresiones como **disculpe** o **perdone: Disculpe, ¿el baño?, Perdone, ¿sabe si hay una farmacia cerca?**

También debemos ser amables cuando decimos que no a una petición. En esos casos, **Lo siento, es que...** es una buena manera de empezar.

Y también podemos usar **es que** si necesitamos justificar nuestra petición: **¿Puedo tomar un poco de agua? Es que tengo mucha sed. O: ¿Me prestas tu teléfono? Es que no tengo mi celular aquí y tengo que hacer una llamada urgente**.

⚙ **Estrategia**

Remember that learning expressions in chunks will help you communicate more naturally. Besides learning the verbs **prestar** (*to borrow/to lend*) or **tener**, for instance, try to memorize **¿Me prestas...?** or **¿Tienes un poco de...?**.

❶ **¿Necesitas ayuda?**

The pronouns **me**, **te**, and **nos** are used for both direct and indirect objects (DO and IO):

¿**Me** ves? (DO)
¿**Me** prestas tu celular? (IO)

Te llamé ayer. (DO)
¿**Te** traigo un café? (IO)

¿**Nos** ves? (DO)
¿**Nos** trae dos cafés, por favor? (IO)

❶ **¿Necesitas ayuda?**

Disculpa/Perdona (tú)

Disculpe/Perdone (usted)

❶ **¿Necesitas ayuda?**

TRAER
tra**igo**
traes
trae
traemos
traéis
traen

14.11. Comparamos. Compara estos recursos con los que se usan en tu lengua. Comenta con la clase si existen expresiones equivalentes en todos los casos.

- ¿Qué desea?
- ¿Qué le traigo?
- ¿Me trae un café, por favor?
- Un café, por favor.
- ¿Me trae un poco más de azúcar?
- ¿Me pasa la sal, por favor?
- ¿Qué le provoca/apetece tomar?

- ¿Tiene un poco de agua?
- ¿Me puede dar un poco de agua?
- ¿Me prestas veinte pesos?
- Disculpe, ¿el baño, por favor?
- Lo siento, es que estoy muy ocupada.
- ¿Puedo tomar un poco de agua? Es que tengo mucha sed.

> **⚙ Estrategia**
>
> Remember that we are not translating literally but rather looking for cultural similarities and differences.

14.12. Completamos. Completa estas frases con las expresiones más adecuadas para cada situación.

1

- ● ¡Disculpe! ¿ .... la cuenta, por .... ?
- ○ Sí, claro, ahora mismo.

2

- ● Chloe, ¿ .... el azúcar, por .... ?
- ○ Sí, claro. Aquí tienes.

3

- ● ¿ .... tu coche esta tarde? .... tengo que llevar una mesa a la casa de mi mamá.
- ○ .... Tengo cosas que hacer esta tarde y lo necesito.

4

- ● ¿Les .... algo más, señores?
- ○ Sí, por favor: ¿................... un vaso de agua y dos cafés?
- ● Con gusto.

5

- ● ...., ¿ .... un pañuelo?
- ○ Sí, cómo no. Toma.
- ● Gracias.
- ○ **De nada.**

6

- ● David, ¿ .... ayudar con la tarea de español esta tarde?
- ○ ...., es que esta tarde tengo que trabajar. ¿Qué tal mañana?

14.13. Representamos. En parejas, representen las situaciones de la actividad 14.12.

Exploramos la lengua

Estar + gerundio (formas regulares e irregulares)

14.14. Leemos y marcamos. Lee las frases, observa los verbos resaltados y marca en la tabla qué expresan.

	A. Presenta algo que ocurre en el momento exacto en el que hablamos. AHORA	**B.** Presenta algo como habitual. AHORA	**C.** Presenta algo como temporal o no definitivo. AHORA

1. Este mes **estoy viviendo** con mis padres porque hay una plaga de cucarachas en mi apartamento.
2. **Estoy trabajando** demasiado estos días. Estoy muy cansado...
3. Yo siempre **voy** a clase en metro.
4. **Estoy esperando** a Jayden. Llega en el tren de las diez.
5. Felipe y yo **estamos haciendo** un curso de yoga. Dura dos meses.
6. **Estoy leyendo** un libro muy bueno: *El túnel*, de Ernesto Sábato.
7. Ahora voy, **me estoy vistiendo**. Salgo de casa en cinco minutos.
8. ¿**Estás viendo** las noticias?
9. Últimamente **estoy comiendo** mucha fruta.
10. Normalmente **desayuno** en la cafetería de la universidad.
11. Yo **duermo** ocho horas al día. ¿Y tú?
12. Lo siento, Kora no puede hablar ahora. **Está durmiendo**.

14.15. Estructuras. Marca qué estructura se usa en A y en C. ¿Qué usas en tu lengua en esos ejemplos?

- **estar** + gerundio
- verbo en presente

14.16. Completamos la regla. Observa las formas del gerundio de la actividad 14.14 y marca la opción correcta.

1. El gerundio de los verbos terminados en **-ar** se forman añadiendo la terminación ⚪ **-ando** ⚪ **-iendo/-yendo**.

2. El gerundio de los verbos terminados en **-er/-ir** se forman añadiendo la terminación ⚪ **-ando** ⚪ **-iendo/-yendo**.

14.17. Irregulares. Ahora observa las formas irregulares **vistiendo** y **durmiendo** (frases 7 y 12 de la actividad 14.14). Escribe en tu cuaderno el infinitivo de estos verbos y marca en qué consiste la irregularidad.

- Tienen una terminación especial.
- Hay un cambio vocálico en la raíz.

14.18. Descubrimos. Estos verbos funcionan como **vestir** y **dormir**. Escribe en tu cuaderno las formas del gerundio.

decir   sentir   venir   repetir   morir   mentir   pedir   corregir   elegir

14.19. ¿Qué están haciendo? Observa la ilustración y escribe qué están haciendo en cada apartamento. Usa las siguientes expresiones.

- leer
- jugar al bingo
- dormir
- escuchar música
- tocar la batería
- cantar
- hacer yoga
- peinar a su gato
- ver la televisión

Apartamento 1: Están cantando.

14.20. ¿Qué estamos haciendo? Marca qué estás haciendo en la actualidad.

- Estoy buscando trabajo.
- Estoy leyendo un libro muy interesante.
- Estoy escribiendo un diario.
- Estoy ahorrando para comprar algo.
- Estoy trabajando los fines de semana.
- Estoy aprendiendo a tocar un instrumento.
- Estoy haciendo bastante deporte.
- Estoy viendo una serie muy buena.

¿Necesitas ayuda?

Note that **actualidad** is a false cognate.

Spanish	English
actual	= current
en la actualidad	= currently

English	Spanish
actual	= **verdadero, real**
in actuality	= **en realidad**

14.21. Cosas en común. En parejas, comparen sus respuestas de la actividad 14.20. Escriban dos cosas que tienen en común y dos cosas diferentes. Luego, coméntenlo con la clase.

Hailey y yo tenemos bastantes cosas en común. Las dos estamos leyendo un libro muy interesante y...

Exploramos la lengua

Estructuras de cortesía con los verbos **poder**, **molestar** e **importar**

e **14.22. ¿Permiso o favor?** Observa las expresiones marcadas en negrita y escribe para qué sirven: para pedir permiso (**P**) o para pedir un favor (**F**).

○ Disculpe, **¿puede abrirme** la puerta**?**

○ **¿Le importaría abrirme** la puerta, por favor**?**

○ **¿Le molesta si abro** la puerta**?**

○ **¿Puedo abrir** la puerta**?**

○ **¿Me abre** la puerta, por favor?

○ **Abro** la puerta, ¿ok?

e **14.23. ¿Quién lo hace?** Compara estos dos ejemplos y escribe quién abre la puerta en cada caso: ¿la persona que pregunta (**A**) o la otra persona (**B**)?

○ **¿Le importaría abrirme** la puerta?

○ **¿Le molesta si abro** la puerta?

> **❶ ¿Necesitas ayuda?**
>
> **Importaría** corresponds to a verb tense you haven't studied yet: the conditional. It can be translated as *would you mind*. For now, learn it as an element inside a structure: **te/le importaría** + infinitive.
> Note that it is in the same tense as: **me gustaría**.

> **❶ ¿Necesitas ayuda?**
>
> Observe that **importar** and **molestar** are similar to **gustar** and always take an indirect object pronoun:
>
> | me | |
> |---|---|
> | te | |
> | le | gusta/n |
> | nos | molesta/n |
> | os | importa/n |
> | les | |

14.24. Cortesía. Observa la pirámide de la cortesía. En cada nivel, escribe dos frases para expresar lo siguiente:

1. Pedir un favor: en una cafetería, vigilar tus cosas mientras vas al baño.

2. Pedir permiso: para poner música.

1. Favor:

¿Le importaría vigilar mis cosas, por favor? Es que tengo que ir al baño.

2. Permiso:
....
....
....

muy cortés

1. Favor:
....
....

2. Permiso:
....
....

1. Favor:
....
....
....

2. Permiso:
....
....

muy directo

14.25. Depende. Estas son algunas de las razones por las que usamos unas fórmulas u otras. Entre todos, piensen en casos concretos en los que esas razones afectan a cómo pedimos un favor o permiso.

- El grado de confianza entre las personas
- La jerarquía (la posición, la edad...)
- La molestia que implica la petición

> *No pides de la misma manera un vaso de agua a un amigo en su casa y a tu jefe en su despacho.*

14.26. Peticiones. Lee estas situaciones y escribe una petición adecuada en cada caso.

Pides…

1. … tu chaqueta a un compañero de clase que la tiene más cerca que tú.

¿Me pasas mi chaqueta, por favor?

2. … 20 dólares a un amigo. (Mañana vas a devolvérselos.)

....

3. … un poco de sal a un vecino.

....

4. … el pan, en la mesa, a un amigo de tus padres que no conoces mucho.

....

5. … su bolígrafo a un compañero.

....

6. … un café al mesero de un restaurante.

....

7. … una botella de agua del refrigerador a tu compañero de apartamento. Tú estás en la sala; él está en la cocina y va a ir a la sala.

....

> 💬 **Para comunicar**
>
> How we use **tú** and **usted** is critical in these kinds of situations, but it varies a lot from one country to another. When we don't know a person, it is a good idea to use **usted**, especially when the other person is older than us.

14.27. En un avión. Imaginen que están viajando en un avión. ¿Qué piden en las siguientes situaciones? ¿Cómo? Escríbanlo.

1 Está pasando un asistente de vuelo con un carrito con bebidas. Tienes mucha sed.

2 Unos niños están dando golpes en tu asiento. Sus padres están durmiendo.

3 Una persona está escuchando música a todo volumen.

4 Quieres leer algo. Una persona que está sentada cerca tiene muchos periódicos y revistas.

5 Quieres poner tu maleta en el compartimento superior, pero no hay sitio. Hay un asistente de vuelo cerca.

6 A tu lado hay una pareja que habla muy alto. Tú quieres dormir.

> ❶ **¿Necesitas ayuda?**
>
> **asistente de vuelo** = flight attendant
> **asiento** = seat

Comunicamos

Educado y maleducado

14.28. ¿Quién habla? Roberto, "el educado", y Liberto, "el maleducado", son hermanos gemelos, pero muy diferentes. Fíjate en cómo reaccionan en estas situaciones. Escribe quién habla en cada caso: Roberto (**R**) o Liberto (**L**).

1. **Su compañero de apartamento:** Si vas al supermercado, ¿me traes jugo de naranja, por favor?
   - **a.** ¿Por qué no vas tú?
   - **b.** Es que luego no voy a regresar a la casa. Lo siento.

2. **Un desconocido en la cola del supermercado:** Disculpe, ¿me permite pasar? Es que tengo prisa...
   - **a.** Lo siento mucho, pero es que yo también tengo prisa.
   - **b.** Todos tenemos prisa.

3. **Una señora mayor en un museo:** ¿Sabe si se pueden tomar fotos en el museo?
   - **a.** Lo siento, está prohibido. Pero si quiere, en la tienda venden postales de los cuadros.
   - **b.** Está prohibido.

4. **Una amiga (en la casa de ella):** ¿Quieres un poco de chocolate?
   - **a.** No.
   - **b.** No, gracias, es que estoy haciendo una dieta.

5. **En el cine, a una mujer que habla mucho:**
   - **a.** Disculpe... ¿Podría hablar más bajo, por favor? Es que no se oye nada.
   - **b.** Señora, ¿puede hablar en su casa?

6. **Una persona en una clase de la universidad:** Disculpa, ¿tienes un bolígrafo?
   - **a.** En esta calle hay un centro comercial.
   - **b.** Es que solo tengo este. Lo siento.

ROBERTO

LIBERTO

14.29. Nos preparamos. En grupos de tres, preparen diálogos: una persona hace una petición y las otras dos dan respuestas negativas (una educada y otra maleducada).

1. Un diccionario de español.
2. Quedarse a dormir en su apartamento (perdiste el último autobús).
3. La sal (en la mesa).
4. La hora.
5. Ir al baño (en su casa).

14.30. Representamos. Representen sus conversaciones (uno es como Roberto y otro, como Liberto). Sus compañeros/-as tienen que detectar quién es el educado y quién el maleducado.

Es que...

14.31. Excusas. Responde a estas preguntas con una excusa original, divertida o surrealista.

1. Tu profesor: ¿No hiciste los deberes? Tú: ....

2. Un amigo íntimo: ¿Me puedes prestar tu celular? Tú: ....

3. Tu madre: ¿Por qué no me llamaste ayer? Tú: ....

4. Tu vecino: ¿Puedes hacer menos ruido, por favor? Son las dos en la mañana. Tú: ....

14.32. Las mejores. En grupos, elijan las dos mejores excusas de la actividad 14.31. Luego compártanlas con la clase.

¿Me prestas 50 pesos?

14.33. Completamos. En parejas, completen estas conversaciones con los recursos que aprendieron en la lección. Luego, comparen sus respuestas con las de los otras personas de la clase.

- ...., Esteban, ¿ .... 50 pesos para desayunar? Es que dejé la cartera en mi casa.
- ○ Sí, mija, toma. ¿Seguro que 50 pesos son suficiente?
- Órale, perfecto. Mañana te los .... Muchas gracias.

- Hola, buenas tardes, ¿qué ....?
- ○ Yo, un jugo de naranja, por favor.
- ■ ¿A mí me .... un café, por favor?
- Un jugo y un café. ¿Desean alguna cosa más?
- ○ No, no, ...

- ¡Uf! ¡Qué calor! ¿Usted no tiene calor?
- ○ No, no... Estoy bien.
- ¿Puedo abrir la ventana? ...., de verdad, tengo mucho calor.
- ○ Ábrala, ábrala. No se preocupe.

- Bueno, ¿y qué ....? ¿Cómo va ....?
- ○ Pues, bien. Todo ....
- ¿Qué estás haciendo ahora?
- ○ Pues ahora .... trabajando para varias productoras de cine.
- ¡Ah, qué bien!
- ○ Sí, estoy muy contenta. ¿Y tú qué haces?
- Yo .... en la empresa de mi hermano. Lo ayudo con las redes sociales.

- Oiga, perdón. ¿ .... chequear mi equipaje? .... tengo que ir al baño. Ahorita vuelvo.
- ○ Claro, claro. Vaya tranquila. No se preocupe.
- ....
- ○ De nada. Tranquila.

14.34. Escuchamos y comprobamos. Ahora, escuchen y comprueben.

14.35. Escuchamos y representamos. Escuchen de nuevo y observen el ritmo, la entonación, la pronunciación de las palabras... Luego, representen los diálogos.

Ahora podemos...

Recrear situaciones de contacto social usando diferentes grados de cortesía

14.36. Nos preparamos. En parejas (**A/B**), van a representar una de estas tres situaciones. Elijan una y escriban su diálogo. Intenten incluir recursos adecuados para saludar, hacer peticiones, dar excusas y despedirse.

1

A Te encuentras a un vecino de 50 años en el supermercado. Llevas muchas bolsas porque compraste para todo el mes. No lo conoces mucho, pero lo saludas todos los días. Quieres volver a casa con él en su auto.

B Estás en el supermercado y te encuentras a un vecino que es un poco molesto porque escucha música muy fuerte y organiza muchas fiestas. Tienes mucha prisa porque vas a ver a un amigo.

2

A Tus padres van a visitarte en un par de días. Compartes apartamento con un amigo y tienen turnos para limpiar. La casa está desordenada y sucia. Vas a su habitación porque quieres decirle que tiene que limpiar la casa.

B Estás algo molesto con tu compañero de apartamento porque siempre está dando órdenes. Además, hace poco tiempo tú le pediste un favor y él no lo hizo.

3

A Hace dos meses prestaste 100 dólares a un compañero de trabajo, pero todavía no te los devolvió. Crees que no se acuerda, pero necesitas el dinero. Hoy se encuentran cuando entran a trabajar. ¿Cómo se lo pides?

B Hace tiempo le pediste dinero a un compañero de trabajo, pero todavía no se lo devolviste. Ahora mismo no tienes mucho dinero y quieres pedirle otros 100 dólares.

14.37. Representamos. Ahora, van a representar la situación. Sus compañeros/-as tienen que decidir si han sido corteses, demasiado directos, maleducados...

Video

Letras de hoy

Daniela del Mar creció en Estados Unidos; es una persona bilingüe y bicultural. Daniela dirige y es copropietaria de Letra Chueca Prensa, una imprenta artesana que utiliza la técnica de la impresión tipográfica. Sus impresiones mezclan motivos modernos con mensajes en Spanglish, lo que le permite conectar con comunidades tanto hispanas como angloparlantes.

ⓟ Pearson MyLab

To find out more about Daniela del Mar and her letterpress shop, go to MyLab to watch **Letras de hoy** and complete the video activities.

⊕ ¿Sabes que...?

The term *Spanglish* was originally coined as Espanglish in the 1940s by Puerto Rican poet Salvador Tió to describe the blend of Spanish and English commonly spoken in many Hispanic communities in the United States. *Spanglish* is a complex linguistic phenomenon; it includes code-switching (alternating between languages at the phrase or sentence level), borrowing (loan words), and calques (literal or word-for-word translations, sometimes with humorous effect).

🔍 Hacemos conexiones

Investiga sobre el *spanglish* y busca ejemplos que ilustren sus diferentes manifestaciones. Luego, compártelos en la clase.

El Malecón de La Habana:
lugar de encuentro

1

El paseo marítimo de La Habana, el Malecón, es el lugar de encuentro más importante de la capital cubana. En el Malecón coinciden habaneros y turistas, jóvenes y mayores, pescadores y vendedores ambulantes, parejas y amigos... Y a todas horas: siempre hay gente que pasea, que corre, que descansa, que espera a alguien, que disfruta del mar o del atardecer, gente que solo quiere estar rodeada de gente...

Con varios kilómetros de largo, este paseo conecta diferentes barrios de la ciudad (el Vedado, La Habana Vieja y Centro Habana) y la protege del mar, que no siempre es amable. Si quieres conocer de verdad La Habana y entender a los habaneros, el Malecón es una visita obligada.

2

3

4

Otros malecones en países de habla hispana

MALECÓN DE MAZATLÁN
(SINALOA, MÉXICO)

Con sus 21 kilómetros, es uno de los más largos del mundo.

MALECÓN DE MIRAFLORES
(LIMA, PERÚ)

Es un lugar perfecto para practicar parapente y disfrutar de la vista a la costa limeña.

MALECÓN SIMÓN BOLÍVAR
(GUAYAQUIL, ECUADOR)

Situado junto al río Guayas, es el lugar más visitado de la ciudad.

MALECÓN DE SANTO DOMINGO
(REPÚBLICA DOMINICANA)

Un lugar ideal para pasear. En él se encuentra el obelisco de Santo Domingo.

ANTES DE LEER

14.38. Cosas en común. Observa las imágenes. ¿Qué tienen en común esos lugares?

LECTURA ACTIVA

14.39. Relacionamos. Observa las cuatro fotos del Malecón de La Habana y relaciona cada una con palabras o fragmentos del texto.

14.40. Verdadero o falso. Marca si estas afirmaciones son verdaderas o falsas según los textos.

	Verdadero	Falso
1. El Malecón de La Habana es un lugar solo para turistas.		
2. El Malecón de La Habana no se puede visitar por la noche.		
3. Todos los malecones mencionados en el artículo están junto al mar.		

14.41. Elegimos uno. ¿Cuál de los malecones del artículo te gustaría visitar? Explica por qué.

DESPUÉS DE LEER

e 14.42. Comparamos. En tu ciudad, ¿existe un lugar de encuentro? Prepara una breve presentación.

Textos escritos: leemos y escribimos

Leemos sobre el arte de pedir

ANTES DE LA LECTURA

14.43. Anticipación. Cuando vas a pedir un favor, ¿piensas antes lo que vas a decir o cómo lo vas a hacer? Explica tu respuesta.

LECTURA ACTIVA

14.44. Lectura. Lee e indica con cuál de las seis recomendaciones del texto relacionas cada una de estas ideas.

- Es importante el contenido de nuestro mensaje, pero también cómo lo pedimos y nuestros gestos.
- Es preferible tener delante a la otra persona, así se implica emocionalmente.
- Es preferible ser conciso.

- Explicar por qué necesitas el favor resulta más efectivo que no hacerlo.
- Pedir un favor previo puede ayudarnos a conseguir nuestro objetivo.
- No es aconsejable molestar a la otra persona cuando está ocupada.

El arte de pedir

Todo el mundo necesita ayuda alguna vez. Estos son algunas recomendaciones que podemos tener en cuenta para pedir algo a los demás y conseguirlo.

1. Mirar a la cara. Según un estudio elaborado por investigadores de la Universidad de Cornell, es más efectivo pedir un favor en persona que hacerlo, por ejemplo, por correo electrónico. Leer un correo puede provocar distancia emocional con nuestro interlocutor.

2. Ir al grano y ser honesto. La clave de una buena comunicación es la claridad y la honestidad del mensaje. Es preferible no dar información innecesaria y no disfrazar nuestra petición para hacerla parecer más importante de lo que es. Si hacemos eso, podemos provocar rechazo en nuestro interlocutor en lugar de implicarlo emocionalmente.

3. Controlar el lenguaje no verbal. Si nuestra actitud corporal no es la adecuada, la otra persona puede mostrarse desconfiada. Es importante mirar a los ojos, mostrarse relajado y con una actitud abierta. Por el contrario, cruzar los brazos bloquea la comunicación.

4. Elegir bien el momento. Debemos valorar la urgencia de lo que necesitamos y elegir un momento adecuado (y, si puede ser, relajado). No es lo mismo una pausa en la oficina que un momento después de la jornada laboral, ya sin compromisos ni obligaciones. Si la otra persona está ocupada, es más difícil conseguir nuestro objetivo.

5. Dar un motivo. Hay estudios que demuestran que justificar una petición consigue más respuestas afirmativas que no hacerlo. Lo curioso es que no tiene que ser una gran excusa: parece que las personas reaccionamos positivamente al simple hecho de escuchar una justificación.

6. Manipular (un poquito). Existen técnicas de persuasión que todos podemos poner en práctica:
1. Ir de menos a más. Si pedimos un favor fácil de realizar, probablemente vamos a recibir un sí como respuesta. Y ayudar a los demás nos hace sentir bien, así que podemos aprovechar ese momento en el que la otra persona se siente bien por ayudarnos y pedirle el favor que realmente necesitamos.
2. Ir de más a menos. La técnica contraria también puede resultar efectiva: podemos empezar pidiendo algo realmente difícil que sabemos que esa persona no va a hacer y, después, pedirle el favor que realmente necesitamos.

14.45. Selección de información. Lee de nuevo el texto y completa esta tabla.

Qué hay que hacer	Qué no hay que hacer
Pedir el favor en persona	Escribir un correo electrónico

14.46. Traducimos. Encuentra en el texto la palabra o expresión que significa:

1. to keep in mind, to have in mind
2. according to
3. key
4. to disguise
5. rejection

6. relaxed
7. commitments
8. responsibilities
9. to prove
10. to put into practice

14.47. Valoramos. ¿Cuáles de los consejos te parecen más útiles? Elige tres y, después, comparte con otras personas de la clase por qué te parecen importantes.

Escribimos recomendaciones de netiqueta

INFORMACIÓN PREVIA   El término **netiqueta** se refiere al uso de aparatos electrónicos como el teléfono celular en lugares como la mesa, en el cine, en el salón de clases, conversando con un amigo, etc. También se refiere al comportamiento de las personas en las redes sociales como Facebook, Snapchat o Instagram.

14.48. Escribimos. Escribe un texto de 80-90 palabras con recomendaciones de netiqueta (y sus justificaciones) para el uso del teléfono celular. Usa el artículo de la actividad 14.44 como modelo.

Es importante/preferible/mejor Es de buena/mala educación Se debe Es aceptable Es irrespetuoso	+ infinitivo

Tener el celular en silencio durante la clase
Los sonidos del celular pueden molestar a otras personas o interrumpir la clase. Es preferible tener el teléfono en silencio.

...

14.49. Compartimos. Comparte tus recomendaciones con tus compañeros/-as. ¿Coinciden?

Recursos lingüísticos

CONTINUOUS ACTIONS IN THE PRESENT WITH ESTAR + GERUND

When we want to specify that an action is taking place as we speak, we use **estar** + gerund (also known as the present progressive in English).
No puedo hablar ahora. **Estoy trabajando**. = I can't talk right now. I'm working.

▸   For all regular verbs, the gerund is formed by replacing the **-ar** of an infinitive with **-ando**, and **-er** and **-ir** by **-iendo**.

	ESTAR	+ GERUND
(yo)	estoy	
(tú)	estás	
(él/ella, usted)	está	trabaj**ando**
(nosotros/nosotras)	estamos	com**iendo**
(vosotros/vosotras)	estáis	viv**iendo**
(ellos/ellas, ustedes)	están	

▸   Note the following exceptions for irregular gerunds:

Irregular gerunds	
leer	leyendo
oír	oyendo
decir	diciendo
dormir	durmiendo

▸   We also use the continuous form to show an action or situation that is temporary.

Estoy trabajando *de mesero en una discoteca.* = I'm working as a waiter in a club.

❗   We can sometimes express the same idea using the present tense in Spanish with temporal markers:
últimamente = *lately*
estos últimos meses = *these past few months*
desde hace algún/un tiempo = *for some time/a time*

Desde hace algún tiempo trabajo *de mesero en una discoteca.* = I've been working as a waiter in a club for some time.

MAKING REQUESTS WITH PODER, IMPORTAR, MOLESTAR, AND SIMILAR VERBS

REQUESTING AN ITEM
▸   The form we use to ask for something depends on the level of formality in the situation and the level of difficulty or the "nuisance factor" in the request.

	TÚ	USTED
↑ **más formal** **MÁS DIFÍCIL**	¿Te importaría prestarme/darme...?	¿Le importaría prestarme/darme...?
	¿Me puedes prestar/dar...?	¿Me puede prestar/dar...?
↓ **menos formal** **MENOS DIFÍCIL**	¿Me prestas/das...?	¿Me presta/da...?

▶ **Dar**: to request an item we don't intend to return.

*¿Me **das** un vaso de agua, por favor?* = Will you get me a glass of water, please?

▶ **Pasar**: to request an item that is within someone else's reach.

*¿Me **pasas** la sal, por favor?* = Will you pass me the salt, please?

▶ **Prestar**: to ask someone to lend you something.

*¿Me **prestas** tu auto este fin de semana?* = Will you lend me your car this weekend?

▶ **Tener**: to ask for something we are not sure someone has.

*¿**Tienes** un bolígrafo?* = Do you have a pen?

▶ **Traer**: to order or ask for something in a coffee shop or a restaurant.

*¿Me **trae** un café, por favor?* = Will you bring me a coffee, please?
*¿Me **trae** otro tenedor, por favor?* = Will you bring me another fork, please?

ASKING FOR A FAVOR

▶ We use the same structures to ask for a favor as we do when requesting an item.

*¿**Le importaría** ayudarme con este ejercicio?* = Would you mind helping me with this exercise?
*¿**Puede ayudarme** con este ejercicio, por favor?* = Can you help me with this exercise, please?
*¿**Me ayudas** con este ejercicio, por favor?* = Will you help me with this exercise, please?

ASKING FOR AND GIVING PERMISSION

▶ To ask for permission, we use **molestar si** + presente tense.

● *¿**Te molesta si** abro la ventana?* = Would you mind (it bother you) if I open a window?
○ *No, no. Ok.* = No. It's ok.

▶ We can also use **poder** + infinitive or even a verb in the present, if we want to be more direct.

*¿**Puedo abrir** la ventana?* = Can I open the window?
***Abro** la ventana, ¿ok?* = I'm opening the window, ok?

MAKING EXCUSES AND EXPLAINING WHY

▶ It's part of the social norm to explain why or give a reason for refusing an invitation or refusing to do a favor. These justifications are commonly introduced with **es que**.

● *¿Vienes a comer el sábado?* = Are you coming over to eat on Saturday?
○ *No puedo. **Es que** tengo que estudiar.* = I can't. (It's because) I have to study.

▶ **Es que** also serves to explain the reason for making a request.

*¿Puedo cerrar la ventana? **Es que** hace mucho frío.*
  = Can I close the window? It's just that it's very cold.

Lo siento, me tengo que ir. Es que tenemos que ir a clase.

Pronunciamos

Los sonidos de **d** y contraste **d/t**

▸ La pronunciación de la letra **d** puede variar.

▸ Generalmente, la articulación de la **d** es más débil (se pronuncia con menos fuerza) cuando se encuentra entre dos vocales o después de **n** o **l**: n<u>a</u>**d**a, m<u>o</u>**d**a, cua**n**do, fal**d**a.

▸ En algunas zonas de Latinoamérica y de España, cuando está entre dos vocales, el sonido de letra **d** puede perderse: organizado > /organizao/.

▸ En función del origen geográfico del hablante o del registro, la pronunciación de la **d** en posición final de palabra puede variar. Estos son cuatro casos comunes:

- La **d** se pronuncia como | **th** en *that o though*.
  | **th** en *think*.
  | una **t**.
- No suena.

))) **14.50. Escuchamos y observamos.** Escucha y observa cómo se pronuncia la letra **d**.

1. día - cada **d**ía **2. d**os - veinti**d**ós **3. d**ólares - cien **d**ólares **4. d**oce - canal **d**oce

))) **14.51. Escuchamos y repetimos.** Escucha de nuevo y repite.
e

))) **14.52. Escuchamos y detectamos.** Escucha y marca si la **d** suena o no suena.
e

	1. pescado	2. toda	3. casado	4. maduro	5. mercado	6. estado	7. rizado
La letra **d** suena.							
La letra **d** no suena.							

))) **14.53. Escuchamos y diferenciamos.** Escucha y marca cómo se pronuncia la letra **d** en cada caso.
e

	como **th** en *that*	como **th** en *think*	como una **t**	no suena
1. eda**d**				
2. eda**d**				
3. ciuda**d**				
4. ciuda**d**				
5. nacionalida**d**				
6. nacionalida**d**				
7. salu**d**				
8. salu**d**				

❶ **¿Necesitas ayuda?**

You will most likely encounter variations in how some words are pronounced in Spanish. When speaking, be aware of the variation of Spanish you are using and be consistent.

))) **14.54. Diferenciamos *d* y *t*.** Escucha y marca qué palabra oyes en cada caso.
e

1.
a. día **b.** tía

2.
a. domar **b.** tomar

3.
a. falda **b.** falta

4.
a. cuadro **b.** cuatro

5.
a. modo **b.** moto

6.
a. viendo **b.** viento

7.
a. cuando **b.** cuanto

8.
a. drama **b.** trama

9.
a. mido **b.** mito

❶ **¿Necesitas ayuda?**

The sounds of **d** and **t** can be difficult to distinguish. Nonetheless, it's important to listen for the difference as the sound of one or the other can result in words that are totally different in meaning.

14.55. Practicamos *d* y *t*. Lee en voz alta las palabras de la actividad 14.54 prestando especial atención a la pronunciación de las letras **d** y **t**.

Vocabulario activo

)) **Saludos y despedidas**   *Greetings and farewells*

- **¿Cómo está/s?**   *How are you?*
- **¿Cómo va todo?**   *How is everything going?*
- **con gusto**   *with pleasure*
- **¡Cuánto tiempo (sin verlo/-a)!**   *It's been a while!* (*I haven't seen you in a while*)
- **darse la mano**   *to shake hands*
- **darse un abrazo**   *to hug (each other)*
- **darse un beso**   *to kiss (each other)*
- **decir hola/adiós con la mano**   *to wave hello/ good-bye*
- **Hablamos.**   *Talk soon.*
- **¡Hasta luego!**   *See you later!*
- **Igualmente.**   *you too, same to you*
- **llegar tarde**   *to be late*
- **Me alegro de verlo/-a.**   *Glad to see you.*
- **Me tengo que ir.**   *I have to leave/to go.*
- **Nos llamamos.**   *Talk soon. (on the phone)*
- **¡Nos vemos!**   *See you!*
- **Pasándola.**   *Not bad...*
- **¿Qué hay de nuevo?**   *What's new?*
- **¡Qué sorpresa** (la sorpresa)**!**   *What a surprise!*
- **¿Qué tal?**   *How are you?*
- **¿Qué tal todo?**   *How is everything?*
- **saludos** (el saludo) **a (la familia)**   *greetings to (your family)*
- **tener cosas** (la cosa) **que hacer**   *to have things to do*
- **tener prisa** (la prisa)   *to be in a hurry*
- **tocarse**   *to have physical contact*
- **todo bien**   *all good*
- **un abrazo (a/para su familia)**   *hugs (to your family)*
- **Ya ves...**   *As you can see...*

)) **Contacto social**   *Social contact*

- **abrazarse**   *to hug (each other)*
- **ayudar**   *to help*
- **besarse**   *to kiss (each other)*
- **causar malentendidos** (el malentendido)   *to cause misunderstandings*
- **charlar**   *to chat*
- **dar**   *to give*
- **despedirse**   *to say good-bye*
- **devolver, regresar**   *to return, to give back*
- **pedir**   *to ask*
- **pedir ayuda** (la ayuda)   *to ask for help*
- **pedir permiso** (el permiso)   *to ask for permission*
- **pedir prestado**   *to borrow*
- **pedir un café**   *to order a coffee*
- **pedir un favor**   *to ask a favor*

- **preguntar la hora**   *to ask the time*
- **ser descortés**   *to be rude*
- **prestar**   *to lend*
- **el/la vecino/-a**   *neighbor*

)) **Recursos para pedir y dar en diferentes situaciones**   *Resources to ask and give in different situations*

- **de nada**   *you are welcome*
- **disculpa/-e**   *excuse me*
- **Es que...**   *It's just that...*
- **importar**   *to mind, to care*
- **Lo siento.**   *I'm sorry.*
- **¿Me pasa/s...?**   *Will you pass me...*
- **¿Me presta/s...?**   *Will you lend me...*
- **¿Me puede/s...** (+ infinitivo)**?**   *Can you... (do something for me)?*
- **¿Me trae/s...?**   *Will you bring me...?*
- **molestar**   *to bother*
- **perdona/-e**   *excuse me*
- **por favor**   *please*
- **¿Qué desea/n?**   *What would you like?*
- **¿Qué quiere/s tomar?**   *What would you like to have?, What can I get you?*
- **¿Qué te/le apetece tomar?**   *What would you like to have?, What can I get you?*
- **¿Qué te/le provoca tomar?**   *What would you like to have?, What can I get you?*
- **¿Qué te/le traigo?**   *What can I get you?*
- **¿Tiene/s (un poco de)...?**   *Do you have (some / a little)...?*

⚙ **Estrategia**

Use expressions you learned in this lesson (to greet, to say good-bye, to ask for something you need, etc.) when interacting with other people in everyday situations. They might not understand what you are saying (and may even look at you a little weird), but don't worry. Use any opportunity to practice your Spanish and talk to others about what you have learned.

Lección

15

Momentos especiales

IN THIS LESSON WE ARE GOING TO

tell a personal story

LEARNING OUTCOMES
You will be able to...

• narrate in the past

• order a series of events in the past

• express emotions

VOCABULARY
• Verbs of movement and change

• Accidents, surprises and changes

• Describing emotions

LANGUAGE STRUCTURES
• Forms and uses of the preterit (II): irregular forms

• Contrast between the preterit and the imperfect

• Adverbs of time and connectors

PRONUNCIATION
• Tongue-twisters in Spanish

CULTURAL CONNECTIONS
• Historical events in Cuba

El minero chileno Jimmy Sánchez abraza a su padre después de 10 semanas atrapado, junto a otros 32 mineros, en una mina en San José, Chile.

Primer contacto

15.1. Un día especial. Observa esta fotografía. Una de las dos personas es Emilio. ¿Por qué crees que ese día fue especial para él? Coméntalo con un compañero.

⊕ **María la Gorda** está en el extremo oeste de Cuba y forma parte del Parque Nacional Península de Guanahacabibes. El agua transparente, los arrecifes de coral, los peces exóticos y las cálidas temperaturas durante todo el año atraen a turistas de todo el mundo para practicar actividades acuáticas como el buceo o el *snorkeling*. Esta playa cubana lleva el nombre de una mujer que, según una leyenda, fue secuestrada por piratas y abandonada en esta región de la isla.

15.2. Escuchamos. Emilio habla de la fotografía con un amiga suya. Escucha y completa con los datos que da.

1. Estuvo en la playa María la Gorda (Cuba) en el año ....
2. Allí aprendió a ....
3. En ese momento estaba con ....
4. Pasó mucho miedo cuando ....

Comprendemos el vocabulario

Describir emociones

》) **15.3. Marta y sus momentos especiales.** En esta entrevista, Marta habla sobre sus "momentos especiales".
Lee y escucha.

¿Tus momentos especiales?

¿Un día que te emocionaste mucho?
Cuando vi el nacimiento de cientos de tortugas en Tortuguero, en Costa Rica. Es un espectáculo increíble, pero vi que algunas tortuguitas murieron antes de llegar al agua. **Me puse muy triste** y **lloré** mucho.

¿Un día que pasaste mucho miedo?
Un día que mi hermano y yo tuvimos un accidente en el desierto de Atacama. Nuestro auto se estropeó y nos quedamos allí solos, en medio del desierto y sin batería en el celular…

¿Un día que pasaste mucha vergüenza?
Un día que me acusaron de robar en una tienda. Compré un pantalón y la chica que me lo vendió no retiró la alarma. Cuando salí de la tienda, la alarma empezó a sonar y un guardia de seguridad me obligó a mostrarle mi bolso. **Me puse muy nerviosa**.

¿Un día que la pasaste muy bien?
El día que conocí a los que ahora son mis mejores amigos. Los conocí en la playa y pasamos todo el día juntos: me enseñaron a hacer surf, luego fuimos a su casa y pasamos toda la tarde en la piscina. Por la noche fuimos a cenar al pueblo y, después, a un concierto de música en la playa.

¿Un día que te quedaste sin palabras?
Un día que me pidieron hablar por sorpresa delante de 300 personas. Una vez, en una boda, el mejor amigo del novio hizo un discurso y, al final, dijo: "Ahora Marta va a hablarles de la novia". **Me puse colorada** porque no tenía nada preparado.

¿Un día que te reíste mucho?
Un día que fui a un espectáculo de monólogos en Buenos Aires. Estuve dos horas sin parar de reír…

¿Un día que te pusiste muy contenta?
Cuando conseguí mi permiso de conducir.

e **15.4. Identificamos emociones.** Indica qué emoción representa cada imagen.

1. Emocionarse
2. Pasar miedo

3. Llorar
4. Ponerse nervioso/-a

5. Pasar vergüenza
6. Pasarla bien

7. Ponerse contento/-a
8. Ponerse triste

9. Quedarse sin palabras
10. Reírse

11. Ponerse colorado/-a
12. Llorar

13. Ponerse nervioso/-a
14. Ponerse contento/-a

15. Pasar miedo
16. Emocionarse

e **15.5. ¿Qué sienten?** Relaciona una emoción de la actividad 15.4 con cada situación. Puede haber más de una opción posible.

1. Las personas típicamente hacen esto cuando ven algo cómico o chistoso.
2. Viendo la película *Titanic*, muchas personas lo hacen.
3. Cuando recibes una buena calificación en tu examen de español.
4. Si no hay nadie en la casa y ves una película de terror, te sientes así.

8 **15.6. Escribimos, leemos y adivinamos.** Prepara frases como las de la actividad 15.5. Después, léeselas a otra persona de la clase, que tratará de adivinar a qué emoción se refieren.

15.7. Nuestras emociones. Piensa en cosas o situaciones que te provocan las siguientes emociones y escríbelas en tu cuaderno.

Cosas que te hacen emocionarte	**Cosas que te hacen reír**	**Cosas que te hacen pasar miedo**

Cosas que te hacen pasar vergüenza	**Cosas que te hacen pasarla bien**	**Cosas que te hacen quedarte sin palabras**

Comprendemos el vocabulario

Describir el movimiento de personas y cosas

))) **15.8. ¿Qué hizo Arturo?** Una detective privada siguió a Arturo el día 1 de febrero. Lee sus notas. ¿Por qué crees que Arturo actuó de esa manera? Coméntalo con un compañero.

salió de casa por la ventana

cruzó rápidamente la calle

subió al autobús 45

el autobús **paró** y él **se bajó** en el centro

dio una vuelta por las calles comerciales

entró a una cafetería

estuvo esperando 10 minutos

se acercó una mujer con gafas oscuras y le **dijo** algo

se sentó en una mesa con ella

se oyó un ruido y **apareció** una caja de música encima de la mesa

la caja de música **se cayó**

salió un líquido verde **de** la caja

se paró y **se fue de** la cafetería

desapareció

e **15.9. Buscamos el contrario.** Escribe el contrario de estas palabras.

1. Se levantó: ....

2. Entró (a): ....

3. Apareció: ....

4. Se alejó: ....

5. Salió: ....

6. Vino: ....

15.10. Completamos. Termina estas oraciones de manera lógica.

1. Estaba caminando cuando *se acercó un chico y me dijo*..................................

2. Estaba tomando agua cuando ....

3. Estaba viendo una película con mis amigos cuando ....

4. Estaba haciendo *trick or treat* cuando ....

5. Estaba esperando el autobús cuando ....

👥 **15.11. Dibujamos.** En parejas, elijan cinco acciones de la actividad 15.8 y dibújenlas en una hoja de papel. Después, intercambien sus dibujos con otra pareja y traten de identificar qué acción representa cada dibujo.

👥 **15.12. Actuamos.** En grupos de cuatro, seleccionen una acción de la actividad 15.8. Una persona actúa y los demás adivinan.

Accidentes, sorpresas y cambios

15.13. Cosas que nos cambian la vida. Lee y escucha este artículo. ¿Crees que esos nueve eventos pueden cambiar la vida de alguien? Piensa en ejemplos de cómo y, luego, compártelos en la clase. ¿Coinciden?

¿CREES EN EL DESTINO?

¿Estás preparado o preparada para los cambios? Un día cualquiera tu vida puede cambiar de manera radical si...

... encuentras algo

... pierdes algo

... te pierdes

... te roban

... te regalan algo

... te encuentras con alguien

... descubres algo

... algo se daña

... alguien te llama

- Yo creo que tu vida puede cambiar si, un día, encuentras una mochila con un millón de dólares.
○ Sí, y también si encuentras un perro abandonado y lo adoptas.

15.14. Algo que cambió nuestras vidas. ¿Qué eventos les sucedieron a ustedes y cambiaron (un poco) su vida. Coméntenlo en grupos.

- Definitivamente, mi vida cambió cuando mis padres me regalaron una guitarra.
○ ¿Ah, sí?

15.15. Preguntamos y respondemos. Responde a estas preguntas en tu cuaderno. Después, por turnos, haz estas preguntas a otra persona de la clase.

1. ¿Qué haces si encuentras dinero en la calle?
2. ¿Qué haces cuando se daña tu celular?
3. ¿A quién llamas primero si tienes una buena noticia?
4. ¿Quién te regaló el mejor regalo?
5. ¿Qué haces si pierdes tu billetera o tus llaves?
6. Imagina que te encuentras con tu artista favorito en el supermercado. ¿Le dices algo o no?

Exploramos la lengua

Formas y usos del pretérito (II): formas irregulares

e **15.16. Acontecimientos.** Relaciona estos acontecimientos históricos con el lugar en el que ocurrieron.

1. El año 2010, 33 mineros chilenos **estuvieron** 69 días atrapados en una mina...

2. En marzo de 2011, **hubo** un gran terremoto y un tsunami....

3. El 26 de abril de 1986, se **produjo** el mayor accidente nuclear de la historia...

4. El 22 de noviembre de 1963, el presidente Kennedy **murió** asesinado...

5. Neil Armstrong **se convirtió** en el primer ser humano que tocó la superficie...

6. Durante dos años y dos meses (de 1887 a 1889), Gustave Eiffel **construyó** una torre de más de 300 metros...

7. En 2016, 2.8 millones de personas, **pidieron** asilo...

8. El 28 de agosto de 1963, Martin Luther King **dijo** su famosa frase "I have a dream" y **pidió** libertad e igualdad para los afroamericanos...

9. Los incas **construyeron** Machu Picchu en la segunda mitad del siglo xv...

10. En 2018, Veronica Escobar y Sylvia Garcia, **se convirtieron** en las primeras congresistas latinas...

A en Japón.

B en Dallas, Texas.

C en todo el mundo.

D de la Luna.

E de Texas.

F en Washington D. C., junto al monumento a Abraham Lincoln.

G en Chernóbil, actual Ucrania (en aquel momento, Unión Soviética).

H en el Campo de Marte (Champ-de-Mars) de París.

I de Caldera, región de Atacama, en el norte de Chile.

J a 80 km de Cusco, en el Perú actual.

1	2	3	4	5	6	7	8	9	10
I									

15.17. Cambios. Escribe en tu cuaderno los verbos en negrita de la actividad 15.16 y su infinitivo. Marca los cambios que hay en la raíz de esas formas verbales.

se convirtió: convertirse

e **15.18. Clasificamos.** Clasifica los verbos de la actividad 15.17 según su tipo de irregularidad.

E > I	O > U	I > Y	OTROS
convertirse			

e **15.19. Completamos.** Completa los paradigmas del pretérito de los siguientes verbos con las formas correspondientes de la actividad 15.16.

	PEDIR (e > i)	CONVERTIRSE (e > i)	CONSTRUIR (i > y)
(yo)	pedí	**me** convertí	construí
(tú)	pediste	**te** convertiste	construiste
(él/ella, usted)	....	....	....
(nosotros/nosotras)	pedimos	**nos** convertimos	construimos
(vosotros/vosotras)	pedisteis	**os** convertisteis	construisteis
(ellos/ellas, ustedes)	....	....	....

❶ ¿Necesitas ayuda?

convertirse = *to become*

e **15.20. Completamos.** Completa ahora el paradigma del verbo **morir** en pretérito.

	MORIR (o > u)
(yo)	....
(tú)	....
(él/ella, usted)	....
(nosotros/nosotras)	....
(vosotros/vosotras)	moristeis
(ellos/ellas, ustedes)	....

15.21. Buscamos información. Busquen estas informaciones; luego, por turnos, háganse preguntas sobre estos datos.

1. Autor de la frase "99 % of failures come from people who make excuses."
2. Autor de la frase "Enemies are so stimulating."
3. Fecha de la muerte de Martin Luther King.
4. Años en prisión de Nelson Mandela.
5. Año de la muerte de Steve Jobs.
6. Ciudad sede de los Juegos Olímpicos de 1992.
7. Primera mujer en ganar el Óscar a la mejor dirección.
8. Responsable de la construcción de la Estatua de la Libertad.
9. Año de construcción del Golden Gate de San Francisco.
10. Lugar de nacimiento de Ellen DeGeneres.

💬 Para comunicar

¿**Qué/cuál**...?

¿**Dónde**...?

¿**Quién**...?

¿**Cuándo**...?

¿**Cuánto/-a/-os/-as**...?

• ¿Quién dijo "99 % of failures come from people who make excuses."?
○ Fue George Washington.

15.22. Hacemos preguntas. En parejas, escriban cinco preguntas usando el pretérito sobre un hecho o un personaje histórico y tres opciones de respuesta. Después, hagan las preguntas a otra pareja.

1. ¿Cuándo se convirtió Abraham Lincoln en presidente de Estados Unidos?
a. En 1863.
b. En 1861.
c. En 1865.

Exploramos la lengua

Contraste entre pretérito e imperfecto

15.23. La experiencia de Omar. En esta conversación, Omar cuenta a un amigo una experiencia que ha vivido. ¿Cuál crees que es la explicación de lo que pasó? Coméntalo con un compañero.

- ¿Sabes qué? El otro día vi a Marcos en el parque.
- ○ ¿Marcos? ¡Qué dices! Está en Argentina.
- Sí, lo sé. Pero lo vi, te lo juro. Mira, hacía muy buen tiempo y decidí ir a dar un paseo en bici. Salí de casa y fui hasta el parque. No había casi nadie y se estaba muy bien. Entonces vi a una persona detrás de un árbol: llevaba una camisa verde y tenía un libro en la mano. Era Marcos, sin duda. Cuando me vio, empezó a correr y desapareció. Fui tras él, pero cuando llegué, ya no había nadie.
- ○ O sea, que no era él.
- No sé. Yo creo que sí. Pero lo más fuerte es que ese mismo día Marcos me llamó, supuestamente desde Argentina... pero el número estaba oculto.

- *Yo creo que Omar se equivocó.*
- ○ *Sí, vio a otra persona parecida.*

15.24. Dos tiempos verbales. En el texto de la actividad 15.23 aparecen dos tiempos del pasado: el pretérito y el imperfecto. Márcalos de manera diferente.

15.25. Completamos la regla. ¿Para qué sirve cada tiempo? Relaciona para completar la regla.

1. El **pretérito** sirve para...
2. El **imperfecto** sirve para...

a. ... presentar la información como un hecho que hace avanzar la acción.
b. ... narrar las circunstancias, lo que rodea a la acción.

15.26. Circunstancias. Este es el principio de una historia de misterio. Complétala con frases en imperfecto para describir las circunstancias indicadas sobre las ilustraciones y agrega otras frases.

(El ambiente de la estación de tren.)

Aquel día Hugo salió del trabajo a las 18:00 h y fue a la estación de tren. Compró un boleto y se sentó en un banco a esperar el tren.

(El aspecto de la mujer y del paquete.)

Bajó en la estación Plaza Central. A la salida se encontró con una mujer que le dio un beso y luego le entregó el paquete.

(Por qué Hugo no se pudo sentar en el tren y el paisaje.)

A las 18:14 h llegó el tren. Hugo subió, pero no se pudo sentar.

(El aspecto del taxista y el estado de ánimo de Hugo.)

De allí, Hugo se dirigió a una parada de taxis y esperó. Llegó un taxi a las 19:30 h y se subió.

Expresiones para relatar

e **15.27. Ordenamos una historia.** Lee esta historia y ordénala.

A **El otro día** me pasó una cosa horrible.

B **Más tarde**, cuando todo el mundo estaba charlando animadamente, saqué la torta y le di un pedazo a todo el mundo.

C **De repente**, la gente empezó a mirar la torta. Yo no entendía qué pasaba.

D **Resulta que** era el cumpleaños de mi amiga Lisa y unos amigos decidimos organizarle una fiesta sorpresa en mi casa. Decoramos la casa y yo preparé una torta, pero, sin darme cuenta, le puse sal en vez de azúcar.

E **Entonces** la probé y **me di cuenta de** que estaba malísima porque estaba salada... ¡Qué vergüenza!

F **Un poco después** Lisa llegó a casa y se encontró con la sorpresa. Se puso muy contenta y, cuando vio la torta, me dijo que tenía un aspecto fantástico.

G **Al día siguiente** volví a hacer una torta e invité a Lisa y a nuestros amigos a la casa.

H **Al final** pudimos celebrar el cumpleaños de Lisa. Esta vez la torta estaba riquísima.

1	2	3	4	5	6	7	8
A							H

15.28. ¿Qué significan? ¿Entiendes qué significan las palabras en negrita de la actividad 15.27? Tradúcelas a tu lengua.

15.29. Continuamos las frases. Continúa estas frases.

1. El otro día Daniel estaba en su casa y, de repente, ...

2. El sábado por la noche queríamos salir a bailar, pero, al final, ...

3. Renata estaba escuchando música en su casa y, de pronto, ...

4. Íbamos en autobús a la escuela y, de repente, ...

5. Era de noche y no había nadie en la calle. Un auto se paró a mi lado y entonces ....

15.30. ¿Cómo acaban? Vas a escuchar a tres personas que empiezan a contar una anécdota. Imagina cómo acaban y escríbelo usando alguna de las expresiones de la actividad 15.27.

15.31. Escuchamos y comprobamos. Escucha ahora completas las tres anécdotas de la actividad 15.30 y comprueba si acertaste.

Comunicamos

Leyendas urbanas

🗣️ **15.32. Leemos y comentamos.** Lee los hechos de dos historias. ¿Crees que son verdad? Coméntalo con algunos compañeros.

En un pueblo de mi provincia hubo el verano pasado un gran incendio forestal. Para luchar contra el fuego, se movilizaron todos los medios de emergencia ▢: más de cien voluntarios, cuarenta bomberos, cinco helicópteros y un hidroavión. Tardaron cuatro días en controlar el incendio y dos más en extinguirlo. Después, un equipo de técnicos fue al lugar para investigar las causas. Hasta aquí todo normal. Pero la sorpresa llegó cuando los técnicos encontraron en medio del bosque el cadáver de un submarinista. ▢. La única explicación que se les ocurrió fue que el hidroavión, al ir al mar a llenar el depósito de agua, absorbió a un hombre ▢. El caso nunca llegó a aclararse completamente.

▢ Cuando el hombre llegó a unos tres kilómetros del pueblo, se encontró con un control de la policía y lo hicieron parar. ▢ pero en ese momento se produjo un accidente a unos 300 metros de aquel lugar y los policías fueron hacia allí. Cuando nadie miraba, el hombre huyó, llegó a su casa y metió el automóvil en el garaje. Unas dos horas después, ▢, la policía se presentó en su casa. El hombre negó los hechos. "Estuve toda la noche en casa", les dijo. Pero los policías le preguntaron por su automóvil. "¿Dónde está su auto, señor Martínez?" Los llevó hasta el garaje y cuando lo abrieron, encontraron el automóvil policial: ▢. Parece que cuando huyó ▢ confundió el automóvil policial con su propio auto.

🗣️ **15.33. Completamos.** En los dos relatos de la actividad 15.32 se narran los hechos, pero faltan descripciones e informaciones sobre las circunstancias. En parejas, colónquenlas en el lugar adecuado.

1. ... cuando él ya estaba durmiendo
2. ... todavía tenía las luces encendidas
3. ... que estaban disponibles
4. ... una vez cerca de mi pueblo un hombre iba en automóvil hacia su casa. Conducía muy rápido
5. ... estaba tan nervioso que
6. ... que estaba practicando pesca submarina
7. ... nadie podía creer lo que estaba viendo, ya que la playa más cercana está a más de 200 kilómetros
8. ... los policías le estaban pidiendo la documentación

🗣️ **15.34. Compartimos.** ¿Conocen otras historias curiosas o leyendas urbanas? Coméntenlo. Si no conocen ninguna, pueden buscar en internet.

> Yo conozco la historia de los cocodrilos en Nueva York.

El misterio de Sara

15.35. Escribimos una historia de miedo. Hace unos días, Sara fue a la casa que sus padres tienen en el campo. Escuchen y escriban qué ocurrió cuando llegó. Usen diez de estas palabras como mínimo.

casa   automóvil   correr   luz   bosque   fósforos

copa   ojos verdes   vela   cocina   escalera   gato

piano   ruido   plato   puerta   romper

Un día en la historia

15.36. Tres personas recuerdan. Tres personas cuentan un momento de la historia que recuerdan con mucha intensidad. ¿De qué habla cada una? Escucha y escribe el número correspondiente al lado de cada imagen.

Fin de la dictadura militar en Argentina.

Crisis de los balseros en Cuba.

Mundial de fútbol de Sudáfrica.

15.37. Completamos. Vuelve a escuchar los tres testimonios de la actividad 15.36 y completa la tabla.

	Fin de la dictadura militar en Argentina	Crisis de los balseros en Cuba	Mundial de fútbol de Sudáfrica
¿Qué pasó?			
¿Cuándo ocurrió?			
¿Con quién estaba?			
¿Dónde estaba?			
¿Qué estaba haciendo?			

15.38. Comparamos nuestras notas. Comparen lo que escribieron en la actividad 15.37 y reconstruyan los hechos de los tres acontecimientos.

15.39. Recordamos juntos. ¿Y ustedes? ¿Recuerdan algún momento histórico? Coméntenlo.

- *Yo recuerdo el huracán Harvey. En esa época vivía con mis padres en Luisiana.*
- *Sí, yo también lo recuerdo. Destruyó muchas ciudades y pueblos y hubo muchas víctimas.*

Ahora podemos...

Contar una anécdota personal

15.40. Recordamos una anécdota. ¿Has vivido algún momento como los siguientes? Elige uno e intenta recordar qué pasó y las circunstancias. Toma notas en tu cuaderno. También puedes inventarte una historia.

- Un momento en el que te emocionaste mucho.
- Un momento en el que pasaste mucho miedo.
- Un momento en el que te reíste mucho.
- Un momento en el que te quedaste sin palabras.
- Un momento en el que pasaste mucha vergüenza.

Piensa en:
¿Dónde estabas? ¿Cómo era el lugar?
¿Con quién estabas?
¿Cuándo fue?
¿Qué estabas haciendo?
¿Qué tiempo hacía?
...

15.41. Compartimos nuestras anécdotas. Cuenta a tus compañeros la anécdota que preparaste en la actividad 15.40. ¿Quién tiene la anécdota más interesante o más impactante? Pueden grabar sus intervenciones para evaluar su producción oral.

- *Yo una vez pasé mucho miedo escalando.*
- *¿Cuándo?*
- *Pues hace unos seis años. Yo estaba...*

Video

Mi media naranja

Álvaro y Mariela hablan de su relación de pareja como un viaje: desde su noviazgo en Uruguay, pasando por el matrimonio, el nacimiento de su único hijo y una separación difícil, hasta la reconciliación que los llevó a comenzar una nueva vida en Florida. A pesar de ser polos opuestos, esta pareja nos muestra por qué creen que el otro es su media naranja.

P Pearson MyLab

To find out more about Mariela and Álvaro's story, go to MyLab to watch **Mi media naranja** and complete the video activities.

⊕ ¿Sabes que...?

According to Mariela, the three cultural elements that unite all Uruguayans are *mate*, *tambor*, and *fútbol*. *Mate* is an infusion, traditionally served in a gourd with a metal straw. *Tambor* ("drum") refers to the main instrument used in *candombe*, a type of Afro-Uruguayan music and dance. *Fútbol* ("soccer") is by far the most popular sport among Uruguayans.

🔍 Hacemos conexiones

Investiga sobre la importancia en Uruguay de estos tres elementos: el mate, el tambor y el fútbol. Comparte datos interesantes en la clase.

1762

Cuba era un punto comercial estratégico. En agosto de 1762 los ingleses tomaron La Habana. Once meses después, España dio Florida a los ingleses y recuperó Cuba.

1823–1895

Se creó la sociedad secreta "Los soles y rayos de Bolívar", formada por criollos que deseaban la independencia de Cuba. A mediados de siglo se produjeron varios enfrentamientos entre el ejército español y los independentistas cubanos. Durante esos años, el Gobierno español imponía impuestos, restringía el comercio entre Cuba y Estados Unidos y discriminaba a los criollos.

1492

Cuando Cristóbal Colón llegó a Cuba, la isla estaba habitada por indios guanahatabeyes, taínos y siboneyes.

1895–1898

El 24 de febrero de 1895 empezó la guerra de Independencia de Cuba. El Gobierno español tenía cada vez menos dinero y sus hombres enfermaban o morían en las luchas contra los rebeldes. En 1898, Estados Unidos entró en la guerra y Cuba se independizó de la Corona de España.

1959

El ejército rebelde derrotó a las fuerzas de Batista y entró en La Habana. Ese mismo año, Fidel Castro fue nombrado Primer Ministro e inició una serie de acuerdos comerciales con la Unión Soviética. Durante esta primera época del Gobierno de Castro, comenzaron fuertes corrientes migratorias hacia Estados Unidos, país que rompió sus relaciones diplomáticas con Cuba en enero de 1961.

1902

Se instauró la primera república, dentro del marco legal de la Constitución de 1901. La Enmienda Platt, incluida en la Constitución, permitía a Estados Unidos intervenir en asuntos cubanos. Esta situación continuó hasta 1934.

1956

Un grupo de jóvenes liderado por Fidel Castro inició la lucha guerrillera en las montañas de la Sierra Maestra. En ciudades y pueblos también tenía lugar una fuerte lucha de guerrillas urbanas. En 1958, Estados Unidos retiró la ayuda militar al régimen de Batista.

1940

Se estableció la Constitución de 1940, que dio inicio a una etapa democrática de 12 años.

Momentos importantes en la historia de Cuba

1952

Fulgencio Batista dio un golpe de Estado y se proclamó presidente de Cuba.

Estados Unidos descubrió que en Cuba había bases de misiles nucleares soviéticos y comenzó la llamada Crisis de los Misiles (conocida en Cuba como Crisis de octubre). J. F. Kennedy ordenó el bloqueo a Cuba. Tras varios días de negociaciones, Estados Unidos y la Unión Soviética firmaron un acuerdo que puso fin a la crisis.

1980 ★ ----→

El Gobierno cubano autorizó la emigración hacia los Estados Unidos. Este éxodo masivo es conocido como "éxodo del Mariel" porque así se llamaba el puerto del que partieron.

1991

La Unión Soviética puso fin a su alianza política, militar y económica con Cuba. Eso llevó a Cuba a una fuerte crisis económica, que alcanzó su punto culminante en los años 1993 y 1994.

1962 ★

2008 ★

Fidel Castro renunció a la presidencia y su hermano Raúl Castro lo sucedió.

2014

Se restituyeron las relaciones diplomáticas entre Estados Unidos y la República de Cuba.

2018

Miguel Díaz-Canel fue elegido presidente.

ANTES DE LEER

15.42. Imágenes. Observa las imágenes que acompañan el texto. ¿Pueden relacionarlas con sus conocimientos sobre Cuba? Si no, ¿qué hipótesis puedes hacer?

LECTURA ACTIVA

15.43. ¿Verdadero? Lee el texto y marca si estas afirmaciones son verdaderas o falsas. Luego, corrige las falsas.

	Verdadero	Falso
1. Cuando Cristóbal Colón llegó a Cuba, la isla estaba deshabitada.		
2. Batista llegó al poder de forma democrática.		
3. La Corona de España marginaba a las personas nacidas en sus colonias, como por ejemplo Cuba.		
4. España ganó la guerra de Independencia de Cuba.		
5. La Enmienda Platt beneficiaba a Estados Unidos.		
6. En la década de 1980, muchos cubanos emigraron a Estados Unidos.		
7. El fin de la alianza con la Unión Soviética tuvo consecuencias negativas para Cuba.		

15.44. Titulares. Lee estos titulares de noticias. ¿Con qué fechas de la historia de Cuba los relacionas?

1. Castro realiza histórica visita a la Unión Soviética.
2. Estados Unidos y Cuba abren un diálogo inédito.
3. Llegaron 4600 cubanos en un año y trámites colapsan.
4. La independencia de Cuba no está lejos.
5. Cayó Batista: el dictador huyó a la República Dominicana.
6. Los ingleses ocupan Cuba.

DESPUÉS DE LEER

15.45. De película. ¿Conocen películas que hablen sobre alguna de las etapas de la historia de Cuba mencionadas en el texto? En grupos, investiguen y comenten de qué tratan.

15.46. Momentos importantes. En grupos, preparen una cronología sobre la historia de su país.

Textos audiovisuales: vemos, escuchamos y presentamos

Vemos un video sobre un momento estresante

ANTES DE VER EL VIDEO

15.47. Preparación. ¿Qué situaciones te causan mucho estrés? ¿Has vivido algún momento estresante? Muy probablemente, sí. Lee estas situaciones y marca el grado de estrés que producen en tu opinión. Luego compara tus respuestas con las de otra persona.

	Muy estresante	Estresante	Poco estresante
1. Pedir un café y darte cuenta de que no tienes tu billetera.			
2. Llegar a tu casa y darte cuenta de que no tienes llaves para entrar.			
3. Llegar al aeropuerto y darte cuenta de que tu pasaporte está vencido.			
4. No tener tiempo de terminar un trabajo importante.			
5. Hacer una presentación en clase.			
6. Llegar a la universidad y darte cuenta de que dejaste tu celular en tu casa.			

15.48. Situaciones inesperadas. ¿Qué situaciones de la actividad 15.47 son inesperadas?

15.49. ¿Cómo terminó? ¿Has vivido alguna situación como las anteriores? Si es así, al final ¿cómo se solucionó?

INFORMACIÓN PREVIA Vas a ver un vlog en el que Rosa María habla de una experiencia inesperada que fue muy estresante en su vida.

VEMOS EL VIDEO

15.50. Una experiencia estresante. ¿Qué experiencia estresante de la actividad 15.47 tuvo Rosa María?

15.51. Expresiones. Ve el video otra vez y encuentra la expresión que mejor expresa en español el significado de estas palabras o frases en inglés.

1. student exchange
2. plane ticket
3. suitcases full with gifts
4. to board the plane
5. embassy
6. to renew the passport

15.52. Selección de información. Escucha el video otra vez y completa la información.

1. ¿Hace cuánto tiempo tuvo esta experiencia Rosa María?
2. Ciudad donde hizo el intercambio estudiantil.
3. País de destino (el país adonde viajaba).
4. Ciudad donde está el aeropuerto de Barajas.
5. Persona que compró el boleto de avión.
6. ¿Cómo se sentía Rosa María antes del incidente?
7. El pasaporte estaba vencido por (marca la respuesta correcta):

   ⬤ un mes   ⬤ un año   ⬤ un día

8. Tiempo que tuvo que quedarse en Madrid.

DESPUÉS DE VER EL VIDEO

15.53. Cómo reaccionamos. ¿Cómo reaccionas en situaciones inesperadas de estrés? Marca con qué reacción o reacciones te identificas. Luego, compártelo con la clase.

⬤ Acepto la situación.

⬤ Mantengo la calma.

⬤ Reacciono de manera emocional: lloro, río...

⬤ Uso la lógica y el razonamiento.

⬤ Discuto con las personas involucradas.

⬤ Me mantengo positivo.

15.54. Reacción personal. ¿Crees que Rosa María tuvo una actitud positiva en esta situación? Explica.

Presentamos una experiencia inesperada

15.55. Escribimos un comentario. Al final del vlog, Rosa María invita a la audiencia a compartir sus experiencias. Piensa en alguna experiencia inesperada que te causó mucho estrés en tu vida y descríbela en unas 120-150 palabras para ponerla como comentario en el sitio web del vlog de Rosa María. Menciona lo siguiente:

• Hace cuánto tiempo ocurrió.
• Dónde estabas; con quién estabas.
• Qué ocurrió.
• Cómo reaccionaste.
• Cómo se solucionó.
• Qué piensas ahora de esa experiencia.

Recursos lingüísticos

FORMS AND USES OF THE PRETERIT (II): IRREGULAR FORMS

STEM CHANGES: E > I, O > U, I > Y

▶ Remember some **-ir** verbs stem change from **e** to **i** and **o** to **u** in the third person singular and plural of the preterit. This occurs in **-ir** verbs like **pedir** and **dormir** and is true for all **-ir** verbs that stem change in the present (**e > ie, e > i, o > ue**). Remember that unlike in the present, this change only occurs in the él, ella, usted, ellos, ellas, ustedes forms of the preterit.

E > I

	PEDIR	SENTIR	CONVERTIRSE
(yo)	pedí	sentí	me convertí
(tú)	pediste	sentiste	te convertiste
(él/ella, usted)	pidió	sintió	se convirtió
(nosotros/nosotras)	pedimos	sentimos	nos convertimos
(vosotros/vosotras)	pedisteis	sentisteis	os convertisteis
(ellos/ellas, ustedes)	pidieron	sintieron	se convirtieron

O > U

	MORIR	DORMIR
(yo)	morí	dormí
(tú)	moriste	dormiste
(él/ella, usted)	murió	durmió
(nosotros/nosotras)	morimos	dormimos
(vosotros/vosotras)	moristeis	dormisteis
(ellos/ellas, ustedes)	murieron	durmieron

I > Y

▶ When the stem of **-er** and **-ir** verbs ends with a vowel, the **i** becomes **y** in the third person singular and plural forms of the preterit.

	LEER	CONSTRUIR
(yo)	leí	construí
(tú)	leíste	construiste
(él/ella, usted)	leyó	construyó
(nosotros/nosotras)	leímos	construimos
(vosotros/vosotras)	leísteis	construisteis
(ellos/ellas, ustedes)	leyeron	construyeron

El canal de Panamá se construyó a principios del siglo XX. La zona del canal fue territorio controlado por Estados Unidos hasta finales del siglo XX.

VERBS WITH IRREGULAR STEMS

▶ The following verbs have irregular stems and use special endings regardless of whether they end in **-ar**, **-er**, or **-ir**.

andar → **anduv-**	poner → **pus-**	-e
conducir* → **conduj-**	querer → **quis-**	-iste
decir* → **dij-**	saber → **sup-**	-o
estar → **estuv-**	tener → **tuv-**	+ -imos
hacer → **hic-/hiz-**	traer* → **traj-**	-isteis
poder → **pud-**	venir → **vin-**	-ieron

* Note that in third person plural, the **i** in the ending is dropped. This always occurs in verbs ending in -**ucir**.

CONTRAST BETWEEN PRETERIT AND IMPERFECT

We can use both the preterit and the imperfect in Spanish to talk about events in the past but they have different uses.

▶ We use the preterit to talk about a series of actions that tell a story.

*Silvia **visitó** Cuba por primera vez en 1988.* = Silvia visited Cuba for the first time in 1988.
***Aprendí** a cocinar en casa.* = I learned to cook at home.

▶ The imperfect is used to set the scene and describe background actions that were taking place. Think of it as what we would see if we were to pause the action and take a look around at what was going on.

*Silvia **visitó** Cuba por primera vez en 1988. <u>Era</u> septiembre y <u>hacía</u> mucho calor.* = Silvia visited Cuba for the first time in 1988. It was September and very hot.
***Aprendí** a cocinar en casa. Mi madre <u>era</u> una cocinera excelente.* = I learned to cook at home. My mother was an excellent cook.

ADVERBS OF TIME AND CONNECTORS

We use these expressions to organize information when recounting a story or anecdote.

Una vez / Un día / El otro día = *Once / One day / The other day*
(Y) entonces / (Y) en ese momento = *(And) then / (And) in the moment*
Luego / Más tarde = *Then / Later*
(Un rato/tiempo...) después = *(A while/time) later*
De repente = *Suddenly*
Resulta que = *It turns out that*

El otro día *me pasó una cosa increíble.* = The other day something incredible happened to me.
Llegué a casa, abrí la puerta **y, entonces,** *oí un ruido raro.* = I arrived home, I opened the door and then I hear a strange noise.
Luego, *cuando estaba en la cocina, oí otro ruido y,* **de repente,** *llamaron a la puerta...* = Then when I was in the kitchen I heard another noise and suddenly there was a knock on the door...

Pronunciamos

Trabalenguas en español

En todos los idiomas existen juegos de palabras formados por sonidos que, juntos, son difíciles de pronunciar. Se llaman "trabalenguas", aunque en algunos lugares también son conocidos como "destrabalenguas" o "quiebralenguas".
La gracia de estas pequeñas composiciones está en decirlas sin parar, de forma rápida y clara, y sin equivocarse.

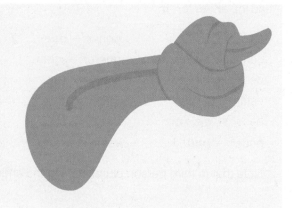

15.56. Escuchamos y repetimos. Escucha estos trabalenguas. Luego, léelos tú.

1 Los cojines de la Reina, los cajones del Sultán. ¡Qué cojines! ¡Qué cajones! ¿En qué cajonera van?

2 No me mires, que miran que nos miramos, y verán en tus ojos que nos amamos.

3 ¡Qué col colosal colocó en aquel local el loco aquel!

4 Pablito clavó un clavito. ¿Qué clavito clavó Pablito?

5 Manuel Micho, por capricho, mecha la carne de macho, y ayer dijo un muchacho: mucho macho mecha Micho.

6 Un burro comía berros y el perro se los robó, el burro lanzó un rebuzno y el perro al barro cayó.

7 El que poco coco come, poco coco compra; como poco coco como, poco coco compro.

8 El dragón tragón tragó carbón y quedó panzón. Panzón quedó el dragón por tragón. ¡Qué dragón tan panzón!

9 Cuando cuentas cuentos, nunca cuentas cuántos cuentos cuentas.

15.57. Creamos un trabalenguas. Intenta crear tu propio trabalenguas en español con sonidos difíciles y palabras con sonidos similares.

Vocabulario activo

))) Describir emociones *Describing emotions*

- **emocionar(se)** *to get excited*
- **llorar** *to cry*
- **pasar miedo** (el miedo) *to get scared*
- **pasar vergüenza** (la vergüenza) *to get embarrassed*
- **pasarla (muy) bien** *to have a (very) good time*
- **ponerse colorado/-a** *to blush, to go red*
- **ponerse (muy) contento/-a** *to get happy*
- **ponerse (muy) nervioso/-a** *to get nervous*
- **ponerse (muy) triste** *to get sad*
- **quedarse sin palabras** *to be dumbstruck*
- **reír(se)** *to laugh*

))) Describir el movimiento de personas y cosas *Verbs of movement*

- **acercar(se)** *to get close*
- **aparecer** *to appear*
- **bajar(se)** *to get off (transportation)*
- **caer(se)** *to fall*
- **cruzar** *to cross*
- **dar una vuelta** *to go for a walk, a ride*
- **decir** (e>i) *to say*
- **desaparecer** (c>zc) *to disappear*
- **entrar en (un lugar)** *to enter (a place)*
- **estar esperando** *to be waiting (for)*
- **irse (de) (un lugar)** *to leave (a place)*
- **oír** *to hear*
- **parar** *to stop*
- **pararse** *to stand up*
- **salir de (un lugar, de un recipiente...)** *to come out (something from a place, a container...)*
- **sentar(se)** (e>ie) *to sit*
- **subir** *to get on (transportation)*

))) Accidentes, sorpresas y cambios *Accidents, surprises and changes*

- **darse cuenta (de algo)** *to realize*
- **encontrar (algo)** (o>ue) *to find (something)*
- **encontrarse con (alguien)** (o>ue) *to run into (someone), to meet up with (someone)*
- **llamar (por teléfono)** *to call (on the phone)*
- **perder (algo)** (e>ie) *to lose (something)*
- **perderse** (e>ie) *to get lost*
- **regalar** *to give*
- **robar** *to rob*

Appendix 1

Verb Charts
Regular Verbs: Simple Tenses

Infinitive Present Participle Past Participle	Indicative					Subjunctive		Imperative
	Present	**Imperfect**	**Preterit**	**Future**	**Conditional**	**Present**	**Imperfect**	**Commands**
hablar hablando hablado	hablo hablas habla hablamos habláis hablan	hablaba hablabas hablaba hablábamos hablabais hablaban	hablé hablaste habló hablamos hablasteis hablaron	hablaré hablarás hablará hablaremos hablaréis hablarán	hablaría hablarías hablaría hablaríamos hablaríais hablarían	hable hables hable hablemos habléis hablen	hablara hablaras hablara habláramos hablarais hablaran	habla (tú), no hables hable (usted) hablemos hablad (vosotros), no habléis hablen (ustedes)
comer comiendo comido	como comes come comemos coméis comen	comía comías comía comíamos comíais comían	comí comiste comió comimos comisteis comieron	comeré comerás comerá comeremos comeréis comerán	comería comerías comería comeríamos comeríais comerían	coma comas coma comamos comáis coman	comiera comieras comiera comiéramos comierais comieran	come (tú), no comas coma (usted) comamos comed (vosotros), no comáis coman (ustedes)
vivir viviendo vivido	vivo vives vive vivimos vivís viven	vivía vivías vivía vivíamos vivíais vivían	viví viviste vivió vivimos vivisteis vivieron	viviré vivirás vivirá viviremos viviréis vivirán	viviría vivirías viviría viviríamos viviríais vivirían	viva vivas viva vivamos viváis vivan	viviera vivieras viviera viviéramos vivierais vivieran	vive (tú), no vivas viva (usted) vivamos vivid (vosotros), no viváis vivan (ustedes)

Regular Verbs: Perfect Tenses

Indicative										Subjunctive			
Present Perfect		**Past Perfect**		**Preterit Perfect**		**Future Perfect**		**Conditional Perfect**		**Present Perfect**		**Past Perfect**	
he has ha hemos habéis han	hablado comido vivido	había habías había habíamos habíais habían	hablado comido vivido	hube hubiste hubo hubimos hubisteis hubieron	hablado comido vivido	habré habrás habrá habremos habréis habrán	hablado comido vivido	habría habrías habría habríamos habríais habrían	hablado comido vivido	haya hayas haya hayamos hayáis hayan	hablado comido vivido	hubiera hubieras hubiera hubiéramos hubierais hubieran	hablado comido vivido

Irregular Verbs

Infinitive Present Participle Past Participle	Indicative					Subjunctive		Imperative
	Present	**Imperfect**	**Preterit**	**Future**	**Conditional**	**Present**	**Imperfect**	**Commands**
andar andando andado	ando andas anda andamos andáis andan	andaba andabas andaba andábamos andabais andaban	anduve anduviste anduvo anduvimos anduvisteis anduvieron	andaré andarás andará andaremos andaréis andarán	andaría andarías andaría andaríamos andaríais andarían	ande andes ande andemos andéis anden	anduviera anduvieras anduviera anduviéramos anduvierais anduvieran	anda (tú), no andes ande (usted) andemos andad (vosotros), no andéis anden (ustedes)

Infinitive Present Participle Past Participle	Indicative					Subjunctive		Imperative
	Present	**Imperfect**	**Preterit**	**Future**	**Conditional**	**Present**	**Imperfect**	**Commands**
caer cayendo caído	caigo	caía	caí	caeré	caería	caiga	cayera	cae (tú), no caigas
	caes	caías	caíste	caerás	caerías	caigas	cayeras	caiga (usted)
	cae	caía	cayó	caerá	caería	caiga	cayera	caigamos
	caemos	caíamos	caímos	caeremos	caeríamos	caigamos	cayéramos	caed (vosotros),
	caéis	caíais	caísteis	caeréis	caeríais	caigáis	cayerais	no caigáis
	caen	caían	cayeron	caerán	caerían	caigan	cayeran	caigan (ustedes)
dar dando dado	doy	daba	di	daré	daría	dé	diera	da (tú), no des
	das	dabas	diste	darás	darías	des	dieras	dé (usted)
	da	daba	dio	dará	daría	dé	diera	demos
	damos	dábamos	dimos	daremos	daríamos	demos	diéramos	dad (vosotros),
	dais	dabais	disteis	daréis	daríais	deis	dierais	no deis
	dan	daban	dieron	darán	darían	den	dieran	den (ustedes)
decir (i, i) diciendo dicho	digo	decía	dije	diré	diría	diga	dijera	di (tú), no digas
	dices	decías	dijiste	dirás	dirías	digas	dijeras	diga (usted)
	dice	decía	dijo	dirá	diría	diga	dijera	digamos
	decimos	decíamos	dijimos	diremos	diríamos	digamos	dijéramos	decid (vosotros),
	decís	decíais	dijisteis	diréis	diríais	digáis	dijerais	no digáis
	dicen	decían	dijeron	dirán	dirían	digan	dijeran	digan (ustedes)
estar estando estado	estoy	estaba	estuve	estaré	estaría	esté	estuviera	está (tú), no estés
	estás	estabas	estuviste	estarás	estarías	estés	estuvieras	esté (usted)
	está	estaba	estuvo	estará	estaría	esté	estuviera	estemos
	estamos	estábamos	estuvimos	estaremos	estaríamos	estemos	estuviéramos	estad (vosotros),
	estáis	estabais	estuvisteis	estaréis	estaríais	estéis	estuvierais	no estéis
	están	estaban	estuvieron	estarán	estarían	estén	estuvieran	estén (ustedes)
haber habiendo habido	he	había	hube	habré	habría	haya	hubiera	
	has	habías	hubiste	habrás	habrías	hayas	hubieras	
	ha	había	hubo	habrá	habría	haya	hubiera	
	hemos	habíamos	hubimos	habremos	habríamos	hayamos	hubiéramos	
	habéis	habíais	hubisteis	habréis	habríais	hayáis	hubierais	
	han	habían	hubieron	habrán	habrían	hayan	hubieran	
hacer haciendo hecho	hago	hacía	hice	haré	haría	haga	hiciera	haz (tú), no hagas
	haces	hacías	hiciste	harás	harías	hagas	hicieras	haga (usted)
	hace	hacía	hizo	hará	haría	haga	hiciera	hagamos
	hacemos	hacíamos	hicimos	haremos	haríamos	hagamos	hiciéramos	haced (vosotros),
	hacéis	hacíais	hicisteis	haréis	haríais	hagáis	hicierais	no hagáis
	hacen	hacían	hicieron	harán	harían	hagan	hicieran	hagan (ustedes)
ir yendo ido	voy	iba	fui	iré	iría	vaya	fuera	ve (tú), no vayas
	vas	ibas	fuiste	irás	irías	vayas	fueras	vaya (usted)
	va	iba	fue	irá	iría	vaya	fuera	vamos, no vayamos
	vamos	íbamos	fuimos	iremos	iríamos	vayamos	fuéramos	id (vosotros),
	vais	ibais	fuisteis	iréis	iríais	vayáis	fuerais	no vayáis
	van	iban	fueron	irán	irían	vayan	fueran	vayan (ustedes)
oír oyendo oído	oigo	oía	oí	oiré	oiría	oiga	oyera	oye (tú), no oigas
	oyes	oías	oíste	oirás	oirías	oigas	oyeras	oiga (usted)
	oye	oía	oyó	oirá	oiría	oiga	oyera	oigamos
	oímos	oíamos	oímos	oiremos	oiríamos	oigamos	oyéramos	oíd (vosotros),
	oís	oíais	oísteis	oiréis	oiríais	oigáis	oyerais	no oigáis
	oyen	oían	oyeron	oirán	oirían	oigan	oyeran	oigan (ustedes)

Appendix 1

Infinitive Present Participle Past Participle	Indicative					Subjunctive		Imperative
	Present	Imperfect	Preterit	Future	Conditional	Present	Imperfect	Commands
poder (ue) pudiendo podido	puedo	podía	pude	podré	podría	pueda	pudiera	
	puedes	podías	pudiste	podrás	podrías	puedas	pudieras	
	puede	podía	pudo	podrá	podría	pueda	pudiera	
	podemos	podíamos	pudimos	podremos	podríamos	podamos	pudiéramos	
	podéis	podíais	pudisteis	podréis	podríais	podáis	pudierais	
	pueden	podían	pudieron	podrán	podrían	puedan	pudieran	
poner poniendo puesto	pongo	ponía	puse	pondré	pondría	ponga	pusiera	pon (tú), no pongas
	pones	ponías	pusiste	pondrás	pondrías	pongas	pusieras	ponga (usted)
	pone	ponía	puso	pondrá	pondría	ponga	pusiera	pongamos
	ponemos	poníamos	pusimos	pondremos	pondríamos	pongamos	pusiéramos	poned (vosotros),
	ponéis	poníais	pusisteis	pondréis	pondríais	pongáis	pusierais	no pongáis
	ponen	ponían	pusieron	pondrán	pondrían	pongan	pusieran	pongan (ustedes)
querer (ie) queriendo querido	quiero	quería	quise	querré	querría	quiera	quisiera	quiere (tú), no quieras
	quieres	querías	quisiste	querrás	querrías	quieras	quisieras	quiera (usted)
	quiere	quería	quiso	querrá	querría	quiera	quisiera	queramos
	queremos	queríamos	quisimos	querremos	querríamos	queramos	quisiéramos	quered (vosotros),
	queréis	queríais	quisisteis	querréis	querríais	queráis	quisierais	no queráis
	quieren	querían	quisieron	querrán	querrían	quieran	quisieran	quieran (ustedes)
saber sabiendo sabido	sé	sabía	supe	sabré	sabría	sepa	supiera	sabe (tú), no sepas
	sabes	sabías	supiste	sabrás	sabrías	sepas	supieras	sepa (usted)
	sabe	sabía	supo	sabrá	sabría	sepa	supiera	sepamos
	sabemos	sabíamos	supimos	sabremos	sabríamos	sepamos	supiéramos	sabed (vosotros),
	sabéis	sabíais	supisteis	sabréis	sabríais	sepáis	supierais	no sepáis
	saben	sabían	supieron	sabrán	sabrían	sepan	supieran	sepan (ustedes)
salir saliendo salido	salgo	salía	salí	saldré	saldría	salga	saliera	sal (tú), no salgas
	sales	salías	saliste	saldrás	saldrías	salgas	salieras	salga (usted)
	sale	salía	salió	saldrá	saldría	salga	saliera	salgamos
	salimos	salíamos	salimos	saldremos	saldríamos	salgamos	saliéramos	salid (vosotros),
	salís	salíais	salisteis	saldréis	saldríais	salgáis	salierais	no salgáis
	salen	salían	salieron	saldrán	saldrían	salgan	salieran	salgan (ustedes)
ser siendo sido	soy	era	fui	seré	sería	sea	fuera	sé (tú), no seas
	eres	eras	fuiste	serás	serías	seas	fueras	sea (usted)
	es	era	fue	será	sería	sea	fuera	seamos
	somos	éramos	fuimos	seremos	seríamos	seamos	fuéramos	sed (vosotros),
	sois	erais	fuisteis	seréis	seríais	seáis	fuerais	no seáis
	son	eran	fueron	serán	serían	sean	fueran	sean (ustedes)
tener (ie) teniendo tenido	tengo	tenía	tuve	tendré	tendría	tenga	tuviera	ten (tú), no tengas
	tienes	tenías	tuviste	tendrás	tendrías	tengas	tuvieras	tenga (usted)
	tiene	tenía	tuvo	tendrá	tendría	tenga	tuviera	tengamos
	tenemos	teníamos	tuvimos	tendremos	tendríamos	tengamos	tuviéramos	tened (vosotros),
	tenéis	teníais	tuvisteis	tendréis	tendríais	tengáis	tuvierais	no tengáis
	tienen	tenían	tuvieron	tendrán	tendrían	tengan	tuvieran	tengan (ustedes)
traer trayendo traído	traigo	traía	traje	traeré	traería	traiga	trajera	trae (tú), no traigas
	traes	traías	trajiste	traerás	traerías	traigas	trajeras	traiga (usted)
	trae	traía	trajo	traerá	traería	traiga	trajera	traigamos
	traemos	traíamos	trajimos	traeremos	traeríamos	traigamos	trajéramos	traed (vosotros),
	traéis	traíais	trajisteis	traeréis	traeríais	traigáis	trajerais	no traigáis
	traen	traían	trajeron	traerán	traerían	traigan	trajeran	traigan (ustedes)

Infinitive Present Participle Past Participle	Indicative					Subjunctive		Imperative
	Present	**Imperfect**	**Preterit**	**Future**	**Conditional**	**Present**	**Imperfect**	**Commands**
venir (ie) viniendo venido	vengo vienes viene venimos venís vienen	venía venías venía veníamos veníais venían	vine viniste vino vinimos vinisteis vinieron	vendré vendrás vendrá vendremos vendréis vendrán	vendría vendrías vendría vendríamos vendríais vendrían	venga vengas venga vengamos vengáis vengan	viniera vinieras viniera viniéramos vinierais vinieran	ven (tú), no vengas venga (usted) vengamos venid (vosotros), no vengáis vengan (ustedes)
ver viendo visto	veo ves ve vemos veis ven	veía veías veía veíamos veíais veían	vi viste vio vimos visteis vieron	veré verás verá veremos veréis verán	vería verías vería veríamos veríais verían	vea veas vea veamos veáis vean	viera vieras viera viéramos vierais vieran	ve (tú), no veas vea (usted) veamos ved (vosotros), no veáis vean (ustedes)

Stem-Changing and Orthographic-Changing Verbs

Infinitive Present Participle Past Participle	Indicative					Subjunctive		Imperative
	Present	**Imperfect**	**Preterit**	**Future**	**Conditional**	**Present**	**Imperfect**	**Commands**

almorzar
(ue) (c)
almorzando
almorzado
	almuerzo
	almuerzas
	almuerza
	almorzamos
	almorzáis
	almuerzan
		almorzaba
		almorzabas
		almorzaba
		almorzábamos
		almorzabais
		almorzaban
			almorcé
			almorzaste
			almorzó
			almorzamos
			almorzasteis
			almorzaron
				almorzaré
				almorzarás
				almorzará
				almorzaremos
				almorzaréis
				almorzarán
					almorzaría
					almorzarías
					almorzaría
					almorzaríamos
					almorzaríais
					almorzarían
						almuerce
						almuerces
						almuerce
						almorcemos
						almorcéis
						almuercen
							almorzara
							almorzaras
							almorzara
							almorzáramos
							almorzarais
							almorzaran
								almuerza (tú),
								  no almuerces
								almuerce (usted)
								almorcemos
								almorzad
								(vosotros),
								  no almorcéis
								almuercen
								(ustedes)

buscar (qu)
buscando
buscado
	busco
	buscas
	busca
	buscamos
	buscáis
	buscan
		buscaba
		buscabas
		buscaba
		buscábamos
		buscabais
		buscaban
			busqué
			buscaste
			buscó
			buscamos
			buscasteis
			buscaron
				buscaré
				buscarás
				buscará
				buscaremos
				buscaréis
				buscarán
					buscaría
					buscarías
					buscaría
					buscaríamos
					buscaríais
					buscarían
						busque
						busques
						busque
						busquemos
						busquéis
						busquen
							buscara
							buscaras
							buscara
							buscáramos
							buscarais
							buscaran
								busca (tú),
								  no busques
								busque (usted)
								busquemos
								buscad (vosotros),
								  no busquéis
								busquen
								(ustedes)

corregir (i, i) (j)
corrigiendo
corregido
	corrijo
	corriges
	corrige
	corregimos
	corregís
	corrigen
		corregía
		corregías
		corregía
		corregíamos
		corregíais
		corregían
			corregí
			corregiste
			corrigió
			corregimos
			corregisteis
			corrigieron
				corregiré
				corregirás
				corregirá
				corregiremos
				corregiréis
				corregirán
					corregiría
					corregirías
					corregiría
					corregiríamos
					corregiríais
					corregirían
						corrija
						corrijas
						corrija
						corrijamos
						corrijáis
						corrijan
							corrigiera
							corrigieras
							corrigiera
							corrigiéramos
							corrigierais
							corrigieran
								corrige (tú),
								  no corrijas
								corrija (usted)
								corrijamos
								corregid
								(vosotros),
								  no corrijáis
								corrijan (ustedes)

Appendix 1

Infinitive	Indicative					Subjunctive		Imperative
Present Participle								
Past Participle	**Present**	**Imperfect**	**Preterit**	**Future**	**Conditional**	**Present**	**Imperfect**	**Commands**
dormir (ue, u)	duermo	dormía	dormí	dormiré	dormiría	duerma	durmiera	duerme (tú),
durmiendo	duermes	dormías	dormiste	dormirás	dormirías	duermas	durmieras	no duermas
dormido	duerme	dormía	durmió	dormirá	dormiría	duerma	durmiera	duerma (usted)
	dormimos	dormíamos	dormimos	dormiremos	dormiríamos	durmamos	durmiéramos	durmamos
	dormís	dormíais	dormisteis	dormiréis	dormiríais	durmáis	durmierais	dormid (vosotros),
	duermen	dormían	durmieron	dormirán	dormirían	duerman	durmieran	no durmáis
								duerman (ustedes)
incluir (y)	incluyo	incluía	incluí	incluiré	incluiría	incluya	incluyera	incluye (tú),
incluyendo	incluyes	incluías	incluiste	incluirás	incluirías	incluyas	incluyeras	no incluyas
incluido	incluye	incluía	incluyó	incluirá	incluiría	incluya	incluyera	incluya (usted)
	incluimos	incluíamos	incluimos	incluiremos	incluiríamos	incluyamos	incluyéramos	incluyamos
	incluís	incluíais	incluisteis	incluiréis	incluiríais	incluyáis	incluyerais	incluid (vosotros),
	incluyen	incluían	incluyeron	incluirán	incluirían	incluyan	incluyeran	no incluyáis
								incluyan (ustedes)
llegar (gu)	llego	llegaba	llegué	llegaré	llegaría	llegue	llegara	llega (tú),
llegando	llegas	llegabas	llegaste	llegarás	llegarías	llegues	llegaras	no llegues
llegado	llega	llegaba	llegó	llegará	llegaría	llegue	llegara	llegue (usted)
	llegamos	llegábamos	llegamos	llegaremos	llegaríamos	lleguemos	llegáramos	lleguemos
	llegáis	llegabais	llegasteis	llegaréis	llegaríais	lleguéis	llegarais	llegad (vosotros),
	llegan	llegaban	llegaron	llegarán	llegarían	lleguen	llegaran	no lleguéis
								lleguen (ustedes)
pedir (i, i)	pido	pedía	pedí	pediré	pediría	pida	pidiera	pide (tú), no pidas
pidiendo	pides	pedías	pediste	pedirás	pedirías	pidas	pidieras	pida (usted)
pedido	pide	pedía	pidió	pedirá	pediría	pida	pidiera	pidamos
	pedimos	pedíamos	pedimos	pediremos	pediríamos	pidamos	pidiéramos	pedid (vosotros),
	pedís	pedíais	pedisteis	pediréis	pediríais	pidáis	pidierais	no pidáis
	piden	pedían	pidieron	pedirán	pedirían	pidan	pidieran	pidan (ustedes)
pensar (ie)	pienso	pensaba	pensé	pensaré	pensaría	piense	pensara	piensa (tú),
pensando	piensas	pensabas	pensaste	pensarás	pensarías	pienses	pensaras	no pienses
pensado	piensa	pensaba	pensó	pensará	pensaría	piense	pensara	piense (usted)
	pensamos	pensábamos	pensamos	pensaremos	pensaríamos	pensemos	pensáramos	pensemos
	pensáis	pensabais	pensasteis	pensaréis	pensaríais	penséis	pensarais	pensad (vosotros),
	piensan	pensaban	pensaron	pensarán	pensarían	piensen	pensaran	no penséis
								piensen (ustedes)
producir (zc) (j)	produzco	producía	produje	produciré	produciría	produzca	produjera	produce (tú),
produciendo	produces	producías	produjiste	producirás	producirías	produzcas	produjeras	no produzcas
producido	produce	producía	produjo	producirá	produciría	produzca	produjera	produzca (usted)
	producimos	producíamos	produjimos	produciremos	produciríamos	produzcamos	produjéramos	produzcamos
	producís	producíais	produjisteis	produciréis	produciríais	produzcáis	produjerais	producid (vosotros),
	producen	producían	produjeron	producirán	producirían	produzcan	produjeran	no produzcáis
								produzcan (ustedes)

Infinitive Present Participle Past Participle	Indicative					Subjunctive		Imperative
	Present	**Imperfect**	**Preterit**	**Future**	**Conditional**	**Present**	**Imperfect**	**Commands**
reír (i, i) riendo reído	río ríes ríe reímos reís ríen	reía reías reía reíamos reíais reían	reí reíste rió/rio reímos reísteis rieron	reiré reirás reirá reiremos reiréis reirán	reiría reirías reiría reiríamos reiríais reirían	ría rías ría riamos riáis/riais rían	riera rieras riera riéramos rierais rieran	ríe (tú), no rías ría (usted) riamos reíd (vosotros), no riáis/riais rían (ustedes)
seguir (i, i) (ga) siguiendo seguido	sigo sigues sigue seguimos seguís siguen	seguía seguías seguía seguíamos seguíais seguían	seguí seguiste siguió seguimos seguisteis siguieron	seguiré seguirás seguirá seguiremos seguiréis seguirán	seguiría seguirías seguiría seguiríamos seguiríais seguirían	siga sigas siga sigamos sigáis sigan	siguiera siguieras siguiera siguiéramos siguierais siguieran	sigue (tú), no sigas siga (usted) sigamos seguid (vosotros), no sigáis sigan (ustedes)
sentir (ie, i) sintiendo sentido	siento sientes siente sentimos sentís sienten	sentía sentías sentía sentíamos sentíais sentían	sentí sentiste sintió sentimos sentisteis sintieron	sentiré sentirás sentirá sentiremos sentiréis sentirán	sentiría sentirías sentiría sentiríamos sentiríais sentirían	sienta sientas sienta sintamos sintáis sientan	sintiera sintieras sintiera sintiéramos sintierais sintieran	siente (tú), no sientas sienta (usted) sintamos sentid (vosotros), no sintáis sientan (ustedes)
volver (ue) volviendo vuelto	vuelvo vuelves vuelve volvemos volvéis vuelven	volvía volvías volvía volvíamos volvíais volvían	volví volviste volvió volvimos volvisteis volvieron	volveré volverás volverá volveremos volveréis volverán	volvería volverías volvería volveríamos volveríais volverían	vuelva vuelvas vuelva volvamos volváis vuelvan	volviera volvieras volviera volviéramos volvierais volvieran	vuelve (tú), no vuelvas vuelva (usted) volvamos volved (vosotros), no volváis vuelvan (ustedes)

Appendix 2

Spanish – English Glossary

The number following each entry in bold corresponds
to the chapter in which the word is introduced for active mastery.
Non-bold numbers correspond to the introduction of words
for receptive use.

A

a bajo precio *at a low price* 4

a cinco minutos de... *five minutes
from* **9**

a continuación *next* 4

a cualquier hora *at any time* 6

a domicilio *home delivery* 6

a finales de *at the end of (period of
time)* 7

a fuego lento *at low heat* **11**

a fuego medio *at medium heat* **11**

a lo largo de *along* 3

a mano *by hand* 4

a mediodía *at noon* **6**

a menudo *often* **6**

a mí no *not me* **5**

a mí sí *I do* **5**

a mí también *me too* **5**

a mí tampoco *me neither* **5**

a orillas de *on the shores/banks of* 3

a partir de *based on, from* 4

a primera vista *at first sight* 7

¿A qué hora...? *What time...?* **6**

a tiempo *on time* 7

a veces *sometimes* **6**

abajo *below* 6

abierto *open* **10**

abierto/-a *open* **5**

abordar *to address, deal with* 12

abrazarse *to hug (each other)* **14**

abrazo (a/para su familia), un *hugs (to
your family)* **14**

abrigo, el *coat* **4**

abrir *to open* 6

abuelo/-a, el/la *grandfather /
grandmother* **5**

abuelos, los *grandparents* **5**

aburrido/-a *boring* **5**

acceder *to consent to* 12

accesorio, el *accessory* **4**

aceite (de oliva), el *(olive) oil* **11**

aceite, el *oil* **11**

acercar(se) *to get close, to
approach* **15**

aclarar *to clarify, to clear up* 15

acogedor/a *cozy* **9**

acompañar *to accompany* 3

acontecimiento, el *event* 12

acostarse (o>ue) *to go to bed/sleep* **6**

actividad económica, la *economic
activity* **13**

actividad, la *activity* **P**

actividades de tiempo libre, las *leisure
activities* **2**

activo/-a *active* **5**

actor, el / actriz, la *actor/actress* 1, **12**

actuación en vivo, la *live
performance* **10**

actuación, la *performance* 3

actualidad, la *currently, at present* **12**

además (de) *besides, in addition (to)* 2, 4

adentrarse *to go deep into* 12

adiós *good-bye* P

adivinar *to guess* 1

adjetivo, el *adjective* 3

admirar *to admire* 1

ADN, el *DNA* **13**

adónde *where (interrogative)* 5

adquirir *to purchase, to acquire* 4

aeronáutica, la *aerospace* 3

aeropuerto, el *airport* P

afeitarse *to shave* 6

afición, la *pastime* 1

África *Africa* 3

afroamericano/-a *African-American* 7

afrocubano/-a *Afro-Cuban* 5

agradable *nice* 5

agregar *to add* **11**

agricultor/a *farmer* 6

agricultura, la *agriculture* **13**

agua con gas, el *sparkling water* **11**

agua, el *water* 4, **11**

aguacate, el *avocado* **11**

ahora *now* 6

ahorrar *to save* 4

aire acondicionado, el *air conditioner* **9**

ajo, el *garlic* **11**

al final (de) *in/at the end (of)* 4, 6

al lado (de) *next to* 3

al menos *at least* 6

alarma, la *alarm* 6

álbum, el *album, music record* 5

alcohol, el *alcohol* 4

alegre *lively* 8

alejado/-a del centro *away from the
city center* 8

alemán, el *German (language)* 5

alemán/-a *German* 1

alfombra, la *carpet* **9**

algo *something* 3

algodón, el *cotton* **4**

alguien *somebody, someone* 2

algún, alguno/-a/-os/-as *some, any* 1

alguna vez *ever* 3

alimento, el *food* **11**

allí *there* 3

almorzar (o>ue) *to have lunch* **6**

almuerzo, el *lunch* 6

alquilar *to rent* 4

altas (temperaturas) *high
(temperatures)* 3

altitud, la *altitude* 3

alto/-a *tall, high* 3, **5**

amable *kind* 3, **5**

amante, el/la *lover* 12

amarillo/-a *yellow* 4

ambicioso/-a *ambitious* 1

América Central *Central America* 3

América del Norte *North America* 3

América del Sur *South America* 3

amigo/-a, el/la *friend* 1, **2**, **5**

amistad, la *friendship* 12

amor, el *love* 1

amplio/-a *wide, spacious* 8, **9**

amueblado/-a *furnished* **9**

anaranjado/-a *orange (color)* **4**

andar *to walk* 1

angosto/-a *narrow* **8**

animado/-a *bustling, lively* **8**

antes de (+ infinitivo) *before (doing something)* 1, **6**

antesala, la *(entrance) hall* **9**

anticonceptivo, el *contraceptive* **13**

antigüedad, la *antique* **4**

antiguo/-a *old, ancient* 3, **8**

antipático/-a *mean, unpleasant* **5**

anuncio, el *advertisement, commercial* 5

añadir *to add* **11**

año, el *year* **1**

años 40, los *the forties* 5

aparecer *to appear* 3, **15**

aparición, la *appearance* **13**

apartamento, el *apartment* **8**

apasionado/-a *enthusiastic, passionate* 5

apellido, el *last name* **1**

aplastar *to crush* **11**

aportación, la *contribution* 7

apoyar *to support* 7

apoyo escolar, el *academic support* **6**

aprender a tocar un instrumento *to learn to play an instrument* **7**

aprender idiomas/lenguas (el idioma; la lengua) *to learn languages* **2**

aproximadamente *approximately* 5

aquí *here* 3

árbol genealógico, el *family tree* 5

árbol, el *tree* 15

arcilla, la *clay* 4

arena, la *sand* 3

argentino/-a *Argentinian* **1**

argumento, el *plot* **12**

árido (clima) *dry (climate)* 3

arquitecto/-a, el/la *architect* **1**

arquitectura, la *architecture* 2

arrecife de coral, el *coral reef* 3

arreglista, el/la *arranger (musical)* 5

arreglo (musical), el *(musical) arrangement* 5

arroba, la *"at" sign* 1

arroz (integral), el *(brown) rice* **11**

arte, el *art* **2**

artesanal *handcrafted* 4

artesanía, la *handicraft* **4**

artesano/-a, el/la *artisan* 4

artículo, el *article* 6

artículos de decoración, los *decorative items* **9**

artista, el/la *artist* 1, **5**

asar *to roast* **11**

asegurarse *to make sure* 12

asesinato, el *murder* 13

asesor/a *consultant* 2

Asia *Asia* 3

asiento, el *seat* **14**

asistir *to attend* 7

aspecto físico, el *physical appearance* **5**

aspirina, la *aspirin* **4**

asunto, el *subject* 5

atardecer *sunset* **8**

ático, el *attic, loft* **9**

atractivo, el *appeal* 3

atrapado/-a *caught* 15

atún, el *tuna* **11**

auge, el *growth, boom* 4

auto, el *car* 4

autobús, el *bus* 3

autopista, la *highway* 13

avena, la *oats* **11**

avenida, la *avenue* **8**

avión, el *plane* **13**

ayuda, la *help* P

ayudar *to help* 6, **14**

azúcar, el /la *sugar* **11**

azul *blue* 4

B

bailar *to dance* **1**

baile, el *dance* 5

bajar(se) *to get off (transportation)* **15**

bajas (temperaturas) *low (temperatures)* **3**

bajo los auspicios *under the auspices/ sponsorship of* 12

bajo/-a *short* **5**

balcón, el *balcony* 6, **9**

ballena, la *whale* 4

banco, el *bank* 1, **8**

banda, la *band* 5

banda sonora, la *soundtrack* **12**

bandeja de horno, la *baking sheet* **11**

baño, el *bathroom* **9**

bar, el *pub* 8

barato/-a *cheap* **4**

barba, la *beard* 5

barbería, la *barbershop* **6**

barco, el *ship, boat* 7

barra energética, la *energy bar* **11**

barra libre, la *open bar* **10**

barrio obrero, el *working-class neighborhood* **8**

barrio residencial, el *residential neighborhood* **8**

barrio, el *neighborhood* 3

base de la alimentación, la *basis of nutrition* **13**

bastante *enough* 5

batería, la *drums* 14

batir *to whip* **11**

batir un récord *to break a record* **7**

beber *to drink* 3

bebida, la *drink, beverage* 3

beige *beige* **4**

belga *Belgian* 1

bello/-a *beautiful, lovely* 3

beneficio, el *benefit* 4

besarse *to kiss (each other)* **14**

beso, el *kiss* 5

biblioteca, la *library* **8**

bien *well, good* **2**

bien ubicado/-a *well located* **9**

bigote, el *mustache* **5**

biográfico/-a *biopic* **12**

bisabuelo/-a, el/la *great grandfather/ grandmother* 7

blanco/-a *white* **4**

blog de moda, el *fashion blog* 4

blog de viajes, el *travel blog* 3

bloque de apartamentos, el *apartment building* **8**

bloque, el *block, segment* 6

blusa, la *blouse* **4**

bohemio/-a *bohemian* **8**

boleta, la *ticket* **10**

boleto, el *ticket* 4

bolígrafo, el *pen* **P**

boliviano/-a *Bolivian* 1

bolsa, la *bag* **11**

bolso, el *purse* **4**

bombero/-a, el/la *firefighter* 6

bonito/-a *nice, beautiful* 3

bosque, el *forest* 3

botas, las *boots* **4**

bote, el *jackpot* **12**

botella, la *bottle* **11**

breve *short* 3

bucear *to scuba dive* **10**

buceo, el *scuba diving* 4

Appendix 2

buena persona, la *good person* **5**

buena relación calidad-precio, la
good value for the money **10**

buena/mala distribución, la *good/bad layout* **9**

buenas tardes *good afternoon, good evening* P

buenísimo/-a *very good* 5

bueno *good* 3, 5

buenos días *good morning* P

bufanda, la *scarf* **4**

buscar *to look for, to pick up* 2, 6

buscar palabras en el diccionario/
en internet (la palabra; el/la
internet) *to look up words in the
dictionary/on the internet* 2

C

cacahuate, el *peanut* **11**

cacerola, la *saucepan* **11**

cada *each* 3

cada uno/-a *each one* 5

cadáver, el *corpse, death body* 15

caer(se) *to fall* **15**

café *brown* **4**

café, el *coffee, coffee shop* 3, 8, **11**

caja, la *box* **11**

cajero automático, el *ATM* **8**

calabacita, la *zucchini* **11**

calefacción, la *heater* **9**

calentamiento global, el *global warming* 3

calentar (e>ie) *to heat* **11**

calidad, la *quality* 3

cálido (clima) *hot (climate)* 3

calle, la *street* **8**

calmado/-a *calm* 5

calvo/-a *bald* 5

cama (doble) , la *(double) bed* **9**

cama, la *bed* 6

cambiar *to change* 6

cambiar de trabajo *to switch jobs* **7**

cambiar la historia (de la música, del
cine...) *to change the history (of
music, film...)* **7**

camello, el *camel* 6

camisa, la *shirt* **4**

camiseta, la *T-shirt* **4**

campamento de verano, el *summer
camp* 5

campeonato, el *championship* **10**

campo, el *field, countryside* 3, 4

canadiense *Canadian* 1

cáncer, el *cancer* **13**

canción, la *song* **5**

canguro, el *kangaroo* 3

cantante, el/la *singer* **1, 5**

cantar *to sing* **1**

cantidad, la *amount* 2

capital, la *capital* 1, **3**

cara, la *face* 6

carácter, el *personality traits* **5**

carcelario/-a *prison* 12

cargo político, el *political post* 7

carne, la *meat* 3, **11**

caro/-a *expensive* **4**

carrera, la *degree, major* 7

carrito, el *shopping cart* 4

carro, el *car* 5

carta, la *letter* 6

cartel, el *poster* 1

cartón, el *carton* **11**

Casa Blanca, la *White House* 3

casa, la *house* 1, **9**

casarse *to get married* **7**

casco antiguo, el *old (part of) town* **8**

casero/-a *homebody* 6

casi *almost* 3, **6**

castaño/-a *chestnut-colored* **5**

castillo, el *castle* 8

catorce *fourteen* **P**

caucho, el *rubber* 12

causa de muerte (la muerte), la
cause of death **13**

causar malentendidos (el
malentendido) *to cause
misunderstandings* **14**

cebolla, la *onion* **11**

celular, el *cellphone, smartphone* **P**

cena, la *dinner* 6

cenar *to have dinner* **6**

censura, la *censorship* **13**

centavo, el *cent* 4

céntrico/-a *central* **8, 9**

centro comercial, el *mall* **8**

centro médico, el *medical center* 1

centro, el *center, downtown* **3,** 8

Centroamérica *Central America* 7

cepillarse los dientes *to brush your
teeth* **6**

cepillo de dientes *toothbrush* **4**

cepillo, el *brush* **4**

cerámica, la *ceramic* 4

cerca de *around, about
(approximation)* 2

cerca de *close to* 3

cerdo, el *pork* **11**

cereal, el *cereal, grain* **11**

cero *zero* **P**

cerrado *closed* **10**

cerrado/-a *closed-minded* **5**

cerro, el *hill* 8

cerveza, la *beer* 1

champú, el *shampoo* **4**

chao *bye* P

chaqueta, la *jacket* **4**

charlar *to chat* **14**

chatear *to chat online* **2**

chatear con amigos *to chat with
friends* **2**

chico/-a, el/la *boy/girl* **5**

chile serrano, el *serrano chili* **11**

chileno/-a *Chilean* **1**

chino, el *Chinese (language)* 5

chocolate caliente, el *hot chocolate* 6

chocolate, el *chocolate* **11**

cien *one hundred* **P, 4**

cien mil *one hundred thousand* **4**

ciencia, la *science* 3

ciento dos *one hundred and two* **4**

ciento uno/-a *one hundred and one* **4**

cinco *five* **P**

cinco menos cuarto *a quarter to five* **6**

cinco y cuarto *a quarter after five, five
fifteen* **6**

cinco y media *half past five, five thirty* **6**

cincuenta *fifty* **P**

cine, el *film, movie theater* 1, 3, **12**

cinturón, el *belt* **4**

circo, el *circus* 1

ciudad industrial, la *industrial city* 3

ciudad turística, la *tourist destination* 3

ciudad universitaria, la *university
campus* 3

ciudad, la *city* 1

claramente *clearly* 6

claro *of course* 2

claro/-a *light (color)* 4

clase, la *class* P, 2

clima, el *climate* 3

clóset, el *closet* 9

cocer (o>ue) *to boil* **11**

cocina, la *kitchen* 9

cocina americana, la *open-floor plan kitchen* **9**

cocinar *to cook* **2**

cocinero/-a *chef, cook* **1**

cojín, el *cushion* **9**

colaborar *to collaborate* **7**

colina, la *hill* **3**

colocar *to place* **4**, **11**

colombiano/-a *Colombian* **1**

comandante, el *commander* **7**

combinar *to combine* **4**

comedia romántica, la *rom-com* **12**

comedia, la *comedy* **12**

comedor, el *dining room* **9**

comentar *to discuss* **4**

comentario, el *commentary* **3**

comer *to eat* **3**

comida, la *food* **1**

comida rápida, la *fast food* **10**

comida típica, la *typical food* **3**

comida tradicional, la *traditional food* **10**

como *like, as* **2**

¿Cómo dices? *What did you say?* **P**

¿Cómo está/s? *How are you?* **14**

como mínimo *at least* **6**

¿Cómo se dice "thank you" en español? *How do you say "thank you" in Spanish?* **P**

¿Cómo se dice esto en español? *How do you say this in Spanish?* **P**

¿Cómo se escribe...? *How do you write/spell...?* **P**

¿Cómo te llamas? *What's your name?* **P**

¿Cómo va todo? *How is everything going?* **14**

cómodo/-a *comfortable* **4, 9**

compañero/-a de clase, el/la *classmate* **5**

compañero/-a de cuarto *roommate* **5**

compañero/-a de trabajo, el/la *co-worker* **5**

compañero/-a, el/la *mate, partner* **2, 5**

compañía, la *company* **2**

compartir *to share* **1**

compositor/a, el/la *composer* **5**

compra, la *shopping* **4**

comprador/a *buyer* **4**

comprar *to buy* **4**

comprender bien una lengua *to understand a language well* **2**

comprobar (o>ue) *to check* **2**

compromiso, el *commitment* **12**

computadora, la *computer* **P**

comunidad autónoma, la *autonomous region* **3**

con *with* **1, 2**

con base en *based on* **5, 6**

con gusto *with pleasure* **14**

con mucha vida (la vida) *very lively* **8**

con mucho encanto (el encanto) *very charming* **8**

con pocas comodidades (la comodidad) *with few amenities* **8**

¿Con qué frecuencia...? *How often...?* **4**

con subtítulos (el subtítulo) *with subtitles* **10**

con vista *with views* **9**

concierto, el *concert* **2**

concordancia, la *agreement* **4**

concursante, el/la *contestant* **12**

concurso, el *contest* **3, 12**

condado, el *county* **3**

condominio, el *condominium* **9**

conductor/a, el/la *driver* **1**

conferencia, la *conference, lecture* **10**

confundir *to confuse* **15**

conjugación, la *conjugation (of verbs)* **1**

conjugar *to conjugate (verbs)* **2**

conmigo *with me* **5**

conocer (zc) *to meet, to know* **2, 5, 7**

conocido/-a *famous, well-known* **3**

conocido/-a como *known as* **3**

conocimiento, el *knowledge* **2**

conseguir *to get, to obtain* **14**

considerado/-a *considered (to be)* **2**

construcción naval, la *shipbuilding* **3**

consumo consciente, el *conscious consumerism* **4**

contacto social *social contact* **14**

contaminación, la *pollution* **8**

contaminante *contaminating* **4**

contar (o>ue) *to tell* **6, 12**

contar (o>ue) con *to have (possess)* **2**

continente, el *continent* **3**

contra *against* **4**

contratiempo, el *setback, mishap* **12**

corazón *sweetheart* **1**

cordillera, la *mountain range* **3**

corregir (i, i) *to correct* **2**

correo electrónico, el *email* **1, 2**

correr *to run, to jog* **10**

cortar *to cut* **11**

cortometraje, el *short film* **10, 12**

cosa, la *thing* **P**

costa, la *coast, coastline* **3**

costar (o>ue) *to cost* **4**

costarricense *Costa Rican* **1**

cover, la *ticket* **10**

creador/-a *creator* **4**

crear *to create* **1**

creciente *growing* **12**

creencia, la *belief* **13**

crema (hidratante), la *moisturizing cream* **6**

cristiano/-a, el/la *Christian* **3**

crítico/-a gastronómico/-a, el/la *food critic* **6**

crucero, el *cruise* **4**

cruzar *to cross* **14, 15**

cuaderno, el *notebook* **P**

cuadra, la *block* **8**

cuadrado/-a *square* **9**

cuadro, el *table, chart, painting* **5, 7**

cuál/-es *which (interrogative)* **3**

cuando *when* **4**

¿Cuántas veces? *How many times?* **6**

cuantificador, el *quantifier* **3**

¿Cuánto cuesta? *How much does it cost?* **4**

¡Cuánto tiempo (sin verlo/-a)! *It's been a while! (I haven't seen you in a while)* **14**

¿Cuánto tiempo...? *How long...?* **6**

cuántos/-as *how many* **3**

cuarenta *forty* **P**

cuarto de estudio, el *den, study* **9**

cuatro *four* **P**

cuatrocientos/-as *four hundred* **4**

cubano/-a *Cuban* **1**

cucaracha, la *cockroach* **14**

cuchara, la *spoon* **11**

cucharada, la *tablespoon* **11**

cucharadita, la *teaspoon* **11**

cuchillo, el *knife* **11**

cuenta, la *bill* **1**

cuerpo, el *body* **6**

cuidado, el *care* **6**

cuidar *to care for, to take care of* **4, 6, 13**

cuidarse *to maintain your personal appearance, to take care of yourself* **6**

cultivo, el *crops, farming* **12**

cultura, la *culture* **2**

Appendix 2

dominicano/-a *Dominican* **1**

dominio, el *command/knowledge of* 7

dónde *where (interrogative)* 3

dormilón/-a *sleepyhead* **6**

dormir (ue, u) *to sleep* **6**

dormir (ue, u) la siesta *to take a nap* 6

dormirse (ue, u) *to fall asleep* 6

dos *two* **P**

dos mil *two thousand* **4**

dos millones *two million* **4**

doscientos/-as *two hundred* **4**

doscientos/-as mil *two hundred thousand* **4**

drama, el *drama* **12**

ducharse *to take a shower* **6**

duración *length, duration* **12**

durante *during* 6

durazno, el *peach* **11**

E

echar *to pour* **11**

ecuatoguineano/-a *Equatorial Guinean* **1**

ecuatoriano/-a *Ecuadorian* **1**

edad, la *age* **1**

edición, la *editing* 7

edificio, el *building* 3, **8**

editorial, la *publishing house* 7

educación, la *education* 6, **13**

ejemplo, el *example* 3

ejercer como médico *to work as a doctor* 12

ejercicio, el *exercise, activity* 2

ejército, el *army* 7

el (día) festivo *holiday* 10

elaboración, la *preparation* 3

elaborado/-a (en/con) *made (in/with)* 4

electricidad, la *electricity* **13**

electrodomésticos, los *appliances* 9

elegante *elegant, chic* **4**

elegido/-a *selected, chosen* 3

elegir (i, i) *to select, to choose* 2, **4**

elevador *elevator* **9**

elote, el *corn on the cob* **11**

embutido, el *cold cuts* **11**

emigrar *to emigrate* 7

emitir *to emit* 12

emocionar(se) *to get excited* **15**

empaque, el *packaging* 11

empezar (e>i) a trabajar *to start to work, to get your first job* **6, 7**

empleo, el *job, employment* 12

empresa, la *company* 1

empresario/-a *businessman/ businesswoman* **1**

en *in* 1

en (la) casa de *in/at someone's house* 4

en avión *by plane* 4

en barco *by boat/ship* 4

en buen estado *in good condition* 4

en español *in Spanish* P

en función de *based on* 13

en muchos casos *in many cases* 4

en ocasiones especiales *for special occasions* **6**

en parejas *in pairs/couples* 3

en perfecto estado (el estado) *in perfect condition* **9**

en poco tiempo *in a short time* 5

en punto *o'clock, on the dot* 6

en relación con *in relation with/to* 6

en todas partes *everywhere* 5

en total *in all* 3

en varios colores (el color) *in various colors* **9**

en vez de *instead of* 15

enamorarse *to fall in love* **7**

encantado/-a *delighted* 5

encantar *to delight, to like a lot* 5

encargado/-a, el/la *manager, person in charge* 12

encargo, el *assignment, order* 12

encontrar (algo) (o>ue) *to find (something)* 4, **15**

encontrarse (en) (o>ue) *to be found (location)* 3

encontrarse con (alguien) (o>ue) *to run into (someone), to meet up with (someone)* **15**

enfermarse *to get sick, to become ill* **7**

enfermedad, la *illness* **13**

enfermero/-a, el/la *nurse* 5

enfermo/-a *patient, sick person* 6

enfrentarse *to face* 8

enloquecido/-a *deranged* 12

ensalada, la *salad* **11**

entender (e>ie) *to understand* P

enterarse *to find out (information)* 12

entonces *then* 6

entrada, la *ticket* **10**

entrada general, la *general admission* **10**

entrada gratuita, la *free admission* **10**

entrada reducida, la *reduced ticket price* **10**

entrar en (un lugar) *to enter (a place)* **15**

entre *between* 3

entre otros/-as *among others* 3

entregar *to deliver* 6

entrevista, la *interview* **12**

entrevistar *to interview* 6

enviar *to send* 12

episodio, el *episode* **12**

época, la *era, time period* 5

equipado/-a *equipped* **9**

equipo, el *team* 3

Es que... *It's just that...* **14**

escalar *to scale, to climb* **10**

escapada, la *getaway (vacation)* 4

escena, la *scene* **12**

esclavitud, la *slavery* **13**

esclavo/-a, el/la *slave* **13**

escribir *to write* P, **1**

escribir un diario/correos electrónicos/mensajes (el correo electrónico; el mensaje) *to write a diary/emails/messages* **2**

escrito/-a *written* 4

escritor/a, el/la *writer* 7

escritorio, el *desk* **9**

escritura, la *writing* **13**

escuchar *to listen to* 2

escuchar música latina (la música) *to listen to Latin music* **2**

escuela, la *school* 3, **8**

espacio en blanco, el *blank* 3

espacio, el *outer space* 7

espacio, el *room, space* 4

espacioso/-a *spacious, roomy* **9**

español, el *Spanish (language)* 2

español/a *Spaniard, Spanish* **1**

especia, la *spice* **11**

especializado/-a *specialized* 4

especialmente *especially* 3

espectáculo, el *show* **10**

espectáculo de baile/danza (baile, la danza), el *dance performance* **10**

espectáculo de circo (circo), el *circus show* **10**

espectáculo de magia (la magia), el *magic show* **10**

espejo, el *mirror* **9**

esperanza de vida (la vida), la *life expectancy* **13**

esposo/-a, el/la *husband / wife* **5**

esquiar *to ski* **1**

está bien/mal comunicado/-a *to have easy/difficult access to other areas (easy access to public transportation)* **8**

está nublado *it's cloudy* **3**

estación de metro (el metro), la *metro station* **8**

estación, la *station, season* P, **3**

estacionamiento, el *parking lot, parking garage* **8**

estado, el *state* **3**

Estados Unidos, los *United States* **1**

estadounidense *American* **1**

estar *to be* **3**

estar ambientado/a en *to be set in* **12**

estar basado/-a en *to be based on* **12**

estar casado/-a (con) *to be married (to)* **5**

estar contento/-a *to be happy* **5**

estar de acuerdo (con) *to agree (with)* **6**

estar de vuelta *to be back* **6**

estar dispuesto/-a *to be willing* **12**

estar divorciado/-a *to be divorced* **5**

estar en peligro de extinción (la extinción) *to be in danger of extinction* **3**

estar esperando *to be waiting (for)* **15**

estar incluido/-a *to be included* **3**

estar prohibido/-a *to be forbidden* **13**

estar separado/-a *to be separated* **5**

Estatua de la Libertad, la *Statue of Liberty* **3**

estatua, la *statue* **3**

este, el *east* **3**

estilo, el *style, type* **5**

estrella (del pop), la *(pop) star* **6**

estreno, el *premiere* **10**

estresante *stressful* **6**

estudiante, el/la *student* **1**

estudiar en una universidad mexicana/española *to study at a Mexican/Spanish university* **2**

estudiar español/inglés (el español; el inglés) *to study Spanish/English* **2**

estudio, el *study, studio apartment* **6, 9**

Europa *Europe* **3**

evento, el *event* **10**

excursión, la *trip* **4**

exesposo/-a, el/la *ex-husband/ex-wife* **5**

exilio, el *exile* **13**

existir *to exist* **13**

explicar *to explain* **3**

exposición, la *exhibition* **2**

exprimir *to squeeze* **11**

extenderse (e>ie) *to spread* **3**

extranjero, el *abroad* **4**

extremas (temperaturas) *extreme (temperatures)* **3**

extrovertido/-a *extrovert* **5**

F

fábrica, la *factory* **1**

fabricar *to make, to produce* **13**

fácil *easy* **4**

falda, la *skirt* **4**

falta un cuarto para las cinco *it's a quarter to five* **6**

faltar *to be missing, lacking* **3, 6**

familia, la *family* **5**

familiar *warm* **6**

familiar, el/la *relative* **5**

fantástico/-a (una película, un cortometraje...) *fantasy (movie, short film...)* **12**

farmacia, la *pharmacy* **8**

fármaco, el *drug, medicine* **7**

febrero, el *February* **3**

fecha de estreno, la *premiere date* **12**

fecha de nacimiento, la *birthdate* **7**

feo/-a *ugly* **5**

festival, el *festival* **5**

festivo (día), el *holiday* **10**

ficha, la *information card* **3**

fiel *faithful* 12

fiesta, la *party* **1**

fiesta de cumpleaños, la *birthday party* **4**

fiestero/-a *party loving, party animal* **6**

figura, la *figure* **5**

fin de semana, el *weekend* **6**

final, el *ending, end* **12**

finca, la *estate, plantation* 12

físicamente *physically* **5**

flequillo, el *hair bangs* **5**

flexibilidad de horario, la *flexible schedule* **6**

flor, la *flower* **5**

forma de gobierno (el gobierno), la *form of government* **13**

formación académica, la *academic training* **7**

formar parte (de) *to be a part ((of)* 3

fortalecer *to strengthen* 2

fotografía (foto), la *photograph, picture* 2

fotógrafo/-a, el/la *photographer* **1**

francés, el *French (language)* 5

frasco, el *jar* **11**

frecuencia, la *frequency* 6

freír (e>i) *to fry* **11**

fresa, la *strawberry* **11**

frijol, el *bean* **11**

frío (clima) *cold (climate)* **3**

frío/-a *cool (not warm)* **9**

fruta, la *fruit* 6, **11**

fruto seco, el *nut* **11**

fuego, el *fire* **13**

fuera (de casa) *outside* 6

función, la *showing* **10**

funcionar *to function, to work* 6

fundación, la *foundation* 7

fundado/-a *founded* 3

fundador/a *founder* 5

fundar una empresa *to start a company* 7

fusión, la *union, fusion* 5

fusionar *to unite, to join* 5

fútbol, el *soccer* **1**

futurista *futuristic* **12**

futuro, el *future* 2

G

gafas, las *glasses* **5**

gafas de sol, las *sunglasses* **4**

galleta, la *cookie* **11**

ganancias, las *profits* 4

ganar un Óscar *to win an Oscar* **7**

ganar un premio *to win an award* **7**

gancho, el *hanger* **4**

garaje, el *garage* **9**

gastronomía, la *gastronomy, cuisine* 3

gato/-a, el/la *cat* 1

generar *to generate, to produce* 4

género, el *genre* 5, **12**

gente mayor, la *elderly* 8

gente, la *people* 2

geografía, la *geography* **2**

gimnasio, el *gym* 1, **8**

gobierno, el *government* 2

gol, el *goal* 1

golpe, el *blow, bang* 14

gordo/-a *heavy* **5**

gorra, la *cap* 5

gorro, el *hat* **4**

grabar *to record* 3

grabar un disco *to record an album* **7**

gracias *thank you* **P**

gracias a *thanks to* 3

grado, el *degree (university)* 7

graduarse *to graduate* **7**

gráfico, el *graph, chart* 6

gramática, la *grammar* 2

gramo, el *gram* **11**

gran *great, big, huge* 2

Gran Cañón, el *Grand Canyon* 3

Gran Manzana, la *the Big Apple* 3

grande *big* **3**

Grandes Lagos *Great Lakes* 3

gratis *free* **10**

gris *gray* **4**

gritar *to yell, to scream* 6

grupo, el *band* **5**

guapo/-a *handsome, beautiful* **5**

guatemalteco/-a *Guatemalan* **1**

guerra civil, la *civil war* 7

guerra, la *war* 1, 13

guion (medio), el *hyphen* 1

guion bajo, el *underline, underscore* 1

guion, el *script* **12**

guionista, el/la *scriptwriter* **12**

guitarra, la *guitar* 1

gustar *to like* 3

gusto, el *flavor, taste, preference* **5**

H

haber *to be (in existence), to exist* 3

habitación, la *room, bedroom* **9**

habitantes, los/las *population* **3**

hábito, el *habit* 6

habla, el *speech* 2

hablador/a *talkative, chatty* **5**

Hablamos. *Talk soon.* **14**

hablante, el/la *speaker (of a language)* 2

hablar *to talk, to speak* P

hablar con amigos hispanos *to talk to Hispanic friends* **2**

hablar de temas interesantes (el tema) *to talk about interesting topics* **2**

hablar sobre *to talk about* 4

hace calor *it's hot* **3**

hace frío *it's cold* **3**

hace sol *it's sunny* **3**

hace viento *it's windy* **3**

hacer *to do, to make* 2

hacer a la plancha *to grill* **11**

hacer deporte (el deporte) *to play sports* **2, 6**

hacer ejercicios de gramática (el ejercicio) *to do grammar exercises* **2**

hacer el papel (de) *to play the role (of)* **12**

hacer hipótesis *to hypothesize* 6

hacer la cama *to make the bed* **6**

hacer la maleta *to pack a suitcase* 4

hacer preguntas *to ask questions* 3

hacer senderismo (el senderismo) *to hike* **10**

hacer un curso de cocina/escritura creativa *to take a cooking/creative writing class* **10**

hacer un intercambio *to make an exchange, to participate in an exchange program* **2**

hacer un viaje *to take a trip* **7**

hacer una pausa *to take a break* 6

hacer yoga *to do yoga* 6

hacer/organizar un pícnic *to have/organize a picnic* **10**

hacer/organizar una barbacoa *to have/organize a barbecue* **10**

hacer/organizar una fiesta *to have/organize a party* **10**

hacer/practicar artes marciales (las artes marciales) *to do martial arts* **10**

hacer/practicar meditación (la meditación) *to meditate* **10**

hacer/practicar natación (la natación) *to swim* **10**

hacer/practicar surf (el surf) *to surf* **10**

hacerse famoso/-a *to become famous* **7**

hacerse rico/-a *to become rich* **7**

hacerse una idea (de algo) *to get the idea (of something)* 3

harina, la *flour* **11**

hasta *up to* 4

¡Hasta luego! *See you later!* P, **14**

Hasta pronto. *See you soon.* P

hecho, el *fact* 7

helado, el *ice cream* **11**

herencia, la *inheritance* 4

hermanastro/-a, el/la *stepbrother / stepsister* **5**

hermano/-a, el/la *brother / sister* **5**

hermanos, los *siblings* **5**

hidroavión, el *hydroplane* 15

hierba aromática, la *aromatic herb* **11**

hijo/-a menor, el/la *youngest son/daughter* 12

hijo/-a, el/la *son / daughter* **5**

hijos, los *children* **5**

hilo, el *thread* 4

hipótesis, la *hypothesis* 4

hispano/-a *Hispanic* 1

hispanoamericano/-a *Hispanic-American* 2

historia, la *history* **2**

histórico/-a *historic, historical* **8, 12**

hito, el *landmark, milestone* 13

hoja de papel *sheet of paper* **P**

Hola. *Hello.* **P**

hombre, el *man* 4

hombre/mujer de negocios, el/la *businessman/businesswoman* 4

hondureño/-a *Honduran* **1**

hora, la *time* 6

horario, el *schedule* 6, **10**

horas trabajadas, las *hours worked* 6

hornear *to bake, to roast* **11**

horno, el *oven* **11**

hospital, el *hospital* **8**

hoy *today* 3

huevo, el *egg* **11**

huir (y) *to run away, to flee* 15

húmedo (clima) *damp, wet (climate)* **3**

I

identificar *to identify* 4

idioma, el *language* 2

iglesia, la *church* **8**

igualdad *equality* **13**

igualmente *you too, same to you* 5, **14**

imagen, la *appearance* 6

imperio, el *empire* **13**

implicar *to implicate, to involve* 4

importantísimo/-a *very important* 6

importar *to mind, to care* **14**

imprenta, la *press* **13**

incendio forestal, el *forest fire* 15

incluir *to include* 3

industria, la *industry* **13**

industria (del vidrio), la *(glass) industry* 3

industria petrolera, la *petroleum industry* 4

industria textil, la *textile industry* 4

información personal, la *personal information* **P**

informática, la *information technology* 1

informativo, el *news broadcast* **12**

infusión, la *infusion* 3

ingeniería, la *engineering* 3

Inglaterra *England* 7

inglés, el *English (language)* 2

inglés/-a *English* 1

inquebrantable *unbreakable* **12**

inteligente *intelligent, smart* 1, **5**

intentar *to try* 5

intercambio, el *exchange* 2

interés turístico, el *interesting to tourists* 3

interesado/-a (en) *interested (in)* 3

interesante *interesting* **5**

interesar *to interest* 4, **5**

interpretar *to play a role, to act* **12**

intérprete, el/la *performer* 5

invención, la *invention* **13**

inventar (un aparato, una herramienta...) *to invent (a device, a tool...)* **7**

invento, el *invention* 13

invierno, el *winter* **3**

invitado/-a *guest* 5

ir *to go* 1

ir a clase *to go to class* **6**

ir a clases de canto/dibujo/defensa personal *to go to singing/drawing/ self-defense lessons* **10**

ir a correr *to go for a run* 6

ir a la bolera (la bolera) *to go bowling* **10**

ir a la escuela *to go to school* 7

ir a la peluquería *to go to the hair salon* 6

ir a la universidad *to go to the university* 7

ir a un concierto *to go to a concert* **2**

ir a una exposición *to go to an exhibition* **2**

ir a una fiesta *to go to a party* **10**

ir a una inauguración *to go to an opening* **10**

ir al baño *to go to the bathroom* 6

ir al cine *to go to the movies* 6

ir al dentista *to go to the dentist* 6

ir al estadio (el estadio) *to go to the stadium* **10**

ir al gimnasio *to go to the gym* **1**

ir al teatro *to go to the theater* 6, **10**

ir de compras *to go shopping* **2, 4**

ir de excursión *to go on a trip* **10**

ir de vacaciones (las vacaciones) *to go on vacation* **2**

ir de viaje *to go on a trip* 4, **10**

ir en autobús *to go by bus, to go on the bus* 3

iraní *Iranian* 1

irlandés/-a *Irish* 1

irse (de) (un lugar) *to leave (a place)* 6, **15**

isla de Pascua, la *Easter Island* 3

isla volcánica, la *volcanic island* 3

isla, la *island* 3

islas Galápagos, las *Galapagos Islands* 4

J

jabón, el *soap* **4**

jalea, la *jelly* **11**

jamón, el *ham* 1, **11**

jardín, el *garden, yard* **9**

jarrón, el *vase* **9**

jeans, los *jeans* **4**

jefe/-a, el/la *boss* 1

jornada laboral, la *work day* 14

joven *young* 1

judío/-a *Jewish* 3

juego de rol, el *role-play* 3

jueves, el *Thursday* **6**

jugador/a, el/la *player* 7

jugar (u>ue) *to play* 1, 2

jugar ajedrez *to play chess* **10**

jugar boliche *to bowl* **10**

jugar juegos de mesa *to play board games* **10**

jugar póker *to play poker* **10**

jugar un partido de beisbol/voleibol *to play a volleyball/baseball game* **10**

jugar videojuegos (el videojuego) *to play videogames* **2**

jugo, el *juice* **11**

juicio, el *trial* 13

junto con *along with* 2

juntos/-as *together* 7

justo/-a *fair* 4

juventud, la *youth* 7

K

kilo, el *kilogram* **11**

kilómetro, el *kilometer* **3**

kilómetros cuadrados, los *square kilometer* **3**

L

labores del hogar, las *housework* **13**

lácteo, el *dairy* **11**

lago, el *lake* **3**

lámpara de pie, la *floor lamp* **9**

lámpara de techo (el techo), la *ceiling light* **9**

lana, la *wool* **4**

largo/-a *long* **3**

largometraje, el *feature film* 10, **12**

lata, la *can* **11**

latino/-a *Latin* 2

latinoamericano/-a *Latin American* 2

lavadero, el *laundry room* **9**

lavadora, la *washing machine* **9**

lavaplatos, el *dishwasher* **9**

leche, la *milk* **11**

lechuga, la *lettuce* **11**

lectura *reading* 4

leer *to read* 1

leer libros/periódicos/revistas/novelas (el libro; el periódico; la revista; la novela) *to read books/newspapers/ magazines/novels* **2**

leer literatura hispanoamericana/ española (la literatura) *to read Latin- American/Spanish literature* **2**

legumbre, la *legume* **11**

lejos *far* 12

lengua materna, la *primary language, mother tongue* 2

lengua oficial, la *official language* **3**

lengua, la *language* 2

letra, la *letter* 1

levantarse *to get up* **6**

Leyes, las *Law* 2

libertad de expresión (la expresión), la *freedom of speech* **13**

libertad, la *freedom* **13**

librería, la *bookstore* **8**

librero, el *bookcase* **9**

libro, el *book* **P**

licencia de conducir, la *driver's license* 4

ligero/-a (algo ligero para cenar) *light (something light to eat for dinner)* 11

lila *purple* **4**

limón, el *lemon* **11**
limpiar *to clean* 6
limpio/-a *clean* **8**
lindo/-a *beautiful* 3, **4**
listo *OK, good* 4
listo/-a para entrar a vivir *move-in ready* **9**
literatura, la *literature* 2
litro, el *liter* **11**
llamado/-a *called* 3
llamar *to call* 5
llamar (por teléfono) *to call (on the phone)* 7, **15**
llamarse *to be named* P
llegada, la *arrival* 12
llegar *to arrive* 6
llegar tarde *to be late* **14**
lleno/-a *full* 12
llorar *to cry* **15**
llueve *it rains* 3
lluvioso (clima) *rainy (climate)* **3**
lo bueno *the good thing* 6
lo contrario *the opposite* 4
lo malo *the bad thing* 6
lo más importante *the most important thing* 6
Lo siento, no entendí. *Sorry, I didn't understand.* **P**
Lo siento. *I'm sorry.* 4, **14**
local, el *premises, establishment, store* **10**
localizar *to locate* 4
loncha, la *slice* **11**
lucha activa, la *active fight, struggle* 7
luchar por una causa *to fight for a cause* 7
luego *later* 6
lugar, el *place* **3**
lugar de nacimiento, el *birthplace* 7
lugar de residencia, el *place of residence* **1**
luminoso/-a *bright* **9**
luna, la *moon* 7
lunes, el *Monday* 3, **6**

M

madre, la *mother* **5**
magacín, el *TV program with news and interviews* **12**
maíz, el *corn* **11**
mal *poorly, not well* 5

maleta, la *suitcase* **4**
manera, la *way, manner* 12
manga, la *sleeve* 4
maniático/-a *fanatical* 6
mano, la *hand* 5
mantenerse (e>ie) hidratado/-a *to keep oneself hydrated* 6
manzana, la *apple* **11**
manzanilla, la *chamomile* 6
mañana *tomorrow* 3
maquillarse *to put on make-up* **6**
mar (Caribe), el *sea (Caribbean)* 3
maravilloso/-a *wonderful, amazing* 3
marisco, el *shellfish* **11**
marroquí *Moroccan* 1
martes, el *Tuesday* **6**
más *more* P, 3
materia, la *matter* 2
mayor *older* 5
mayoría, la *the majority* 6
Me alegro de verlo/-a. *Glad to see you.* **14**
¿Me pasa/s...? *Will you pass me...?* **14**
¿Me presta/s...? *Will you lend me...?* **14**
¿Me puede/s... (+ infinitivo)? *Can you... (do something for me)?* **14**
Me tengo que ir. *I have to leave/to go.* **14**
¿Me trae/s...? *Will you bring me...?* **14**
medicamento, el *medicine, medication* **13**
medicina, la *medicine* **13**
médico/-a, el/la *doctor* **1**
medida, la *measure* 11
medio/-a hermano/-a, el/la *half-brother / half-sister* **5**
medioambiente, el *environment* **13**
medios de comunicación (la comunicación), los *media, means of communication* **13**
medir (i, i) *to measure* 5
mejor *better, best* 2
mejor amigo/-a, el/la *best friend* **5**
mejorar mi inglés *to improve my English* **2**
menos *less* 4
mensaje, el *message* 2
mercado, el *market* 3, **4**
mesa de centro, la *coffee table* **9**
mesa, la *table* **P, 9**

mesero/-a, el/la *bartender, waiter/waitress* **1**
mesita de noche, la *nightstand* **9**
metro, el *meter, subway* 3, **8**
metros lisos, los 100 *one hundred meters (race)* 7
mexicano/-a *Mexican* **1**
mezclar *to mix, to blend* **11**
mezquita, la *mosque* **8**
microondas, el *microwave oven* **9**
microscopio, el *microscope* **13**
miedo, el *fear* 12
miel, la *honey* **11**
miembros de la familia, los *family members* 5
mientras *while* 5
miércoles, el *Wednesday* **6**
mijo/-a *my son/daughter (colloquial)* 14
mil *one thousand* **4**
mil millones *one billion* **4**
millón/-es *million(s)* 3
ministro, el *minister* 7
minuto, el *minute* 3
mirador, el *lookout, overlook* **8**
mirar mal *to give a dirty look* 11
mirar(se) *to look at (oneself)* 4
mismo/-a, el/la *himself/herself* 1, **3**
moái, el *Easter Island statue* 3
mochila, la *backpack* **P**
moderno/-a *modern* **4**
moler (o>ue) *to grind* **11**
molestar *to bother* **14**
monarquía (absoluta), la *(absolute) monarchy* **13**
moneda, la *currency, coin* **3**
montaña, la *mountain* **3**
montar *to ride* 3
montar a caballo *to ride a horse* 4
monte, el *hill, mount* 3
moreno/-a *dark-haired / brunette* **5**
morir (ue, u) *to die* **7**
mostaza, la *mustard* **11**
mostrar (o>ue) *to show* 6
muchas gracias *thank you very much* 4
mucho *a lot* 2, 3
mucho/-a/-os/-as *many* 2, 3
mudarse *to move away* 12
muebles, los *furniture* 9
mujer, la *woman* 5
mundial *worldwide* 10
mundo, el *world* 2

Appendix 2

música clásica, la *classic music* **5**
música electrónica, la *electronic music* **5**
música en vivo, la *live music* **5**
música independiente, la *indie/ alternative music* **5**
música instrumental, la *instrumental music* **5**
música soul, la *soul music* 5
música, la *music* 2, 5
musical, el *musical* **12**
músico/-a, el/la *musician* 5
musulmán/a el/la *Muslim* 3
muy *very* 3

N

nacer (zc) *to be born* 5, **7**
nacimiento, el *birth* 5
nacionalidad, la *nationality* **1**
nada *nothing, not anything* 6
nadie *no one, not anyone* 7
naranja, la *orange (fruit)* **11**
narrar *to narrate* 7
nativo/-a *native* 2
naturaleza, la *nature* **2**
necesitar *to need* P
negar *to deny* 15
negocio, el *business* 4
negro/-a *black* 3, **4**
nevar (e>ie) *to snow* 3
nicaragüense *Nicaraguan* **1**
nieto/-a, el/la *grandson / granddaughter* 5
nietos, los *grandchildren* **5**
nieva *it snows* **3**
ninguno/-a *none, not any* 3
niño/-a, el/la *child* 4
nivel avanzado, el *advanced level* 7
no *no* P
no hacer nada *to do nothing, not do anything* **10**
no importa *does not matter* 3
no lo sé *I don't know (it, that)* 3
no sé *I don't know* 3
¿no? *right?* P
nobleza, la *nobility* **13**
noche, la *night* 2
nombre completo, el *full name* **1**
nombre, el *first name* P, **1**
nombre, el *noun* 2
normal *normal* **5**

normalmente *normally* 5, **6**
norte, el *north* **3**
Nos llamamos. *Talk soon. (on the phone)* **14**
¡Nos vemos! *See you!* P, **14**
nosotros/-as *we* 1
noticia, la *news* **12**
novecientos/-as *nine hundred* **4**
novedad, la *new, novelty* 4
novela, la *novel* 2, **4**
noventa *ninety* P
noventa y nueve *ninety-nine* **P**
novio/-a, el/la *boyfriend / girlfriend* 2, **5**
nuera, la *daughter-in-law* 12
nuestro/-a *our* P
nueve *nine* **P**
nuevo/-a *new* 5
numerado/-a *numbered* 3
número, el *number* P
numeroso/-a *numerous* 3
nunca *never, not ever* **6**

O

obra de arte, la *work of art* **10**
obra de teatro, la *play* **10**
obra, la *work* 7
obtener (e>ie) *to obtain, to get* 4
Oceanía *Oceania* 3
océano Atlántico, el *Atlantic Ocean* **3**
océano Índico, el *Indian Ocean* **3**
océano Pacífico, el *Pacific Ocean* **3**
océano, el *ocean* 3
ochenta *eighty* **P**
ocho *eight* **P**
ochocientos/-as *eight hundred* **4**
ocupar *to occupy* 4
oeste, el *west* **3**
oficina, la *office* 6
oficina de correos (el correo), la *post office* **8**
ofrecer (zc) *to offer* 2
oír *to hear* **15**
ojos, los *eyes* **5**
olimpiadas, las *Olympics* 7
olla, la *pot* **11**
once *eleven* **P**
ONU (Organización de las Naciones Unidas), la *UN (United Nations)* 7
ópera, la *opera* **5**
opinar *to opine, give an opinion* 3
oponerse *to oppose* 12

optar por *to opt for* 4
órale *wow, ok (colloquial)* 14
original *original* **4**
oscuro/-a *dark* **4**
oso, el *bear* 3
otoño, el *fall, autumn* **3**
otra vez *again* 6
otro/-a/-os/-as *other* 3

P

padre, el *father* **5**
padres, los *parents* **5**
pagar *to pay* 4
página web, la *web page* 2
página, la *page* **P**
país, el *country* 1
paisaje, el *landscape* 12
palabra, la *word* P
palacio, el *palace* 3
palillos, los *sticks, chopsticks* 11
palma, la *palm* 4
pan, el *bread* **11**
panameño/-a *Panamanian* **1**
pantalones, los *pants, trousers* **4**
pantalones cortos, los *shorts* **4**
papa, la *potato* **11**
papás, los *parents* 5
papel, el *role, part, paper* 4, **12, 13**
papelera, la *wastepaper basket* **P**
paquete, el *packet, package* **11**
para *to, for* 2
Para mí... *For me (In my opinion)* 2
parada de autobús (el autobús), la *bus stop* **8**
parado/-a *standing* 11
paraguayo/-a *Paraguayan* **1**
parapente, el *paraglider* 14
parar *to stop* 6, **15**
parar(se) *to stand up* 15
parecer (zc) *to seem* 4, 5
pared, la *wall* **9**
pareja, la *partner, couple* 3, 4, **5**
parentesco, el *relationship, kinship* 5
parque nacional, el *national park* P, **3**
parque natural, el *nature park* 3
parque, el *park* 8
parte, la *part* 6
participar en una carrera/competición/ maratón *to participate in a race/ competition/marathon* **10**
partido político, el *political party* **13**

partido, el *game, match (sports)* **10**

Pasándola. *Not bad. / Doing OK.* **14**

pasaporte, el *passport* **4**

pasar *to spend (time), to pass, to happen* 3, 4, 7

pasar el día con la familia/(los) amigos *to spend the day with the family/friends* **10**

pasar el día en casa/la playa *to spend the day at home/at the beach* **10**

pasar miedo (el miedo) *to get scared* **15**

pasar vergüenza (la vergüenza) *to get embarrassed* **15**

pasarla (muy) bien *to have a (very) good time* **15**

pasatiempo, el *pastime* 1

pasear *to go for a walk* 2

paseo, el *promenade* **8**

paso, el *passing* 11

pasta, la *pasta* **11**

pasta de dientes, la *toothpaste* **4**

Patrimonio de la Humanidad, el *World Heritage Site* 2

patrimonio, el *heritage* **2**

pavo, el *turkey* **11**

peculiar *strange* 6

pedazo, el *piece, chunk, bit* **11**

pedir (i, i) *to ask for* **14**

pedir (i, i) ayuda (la ayuda) *to ask for help* **14**

pedir (i, i) permiso (el permiso) *to ask for permission* **14**

pedir (i, i) un café *to order a coffee* **14**

pedir (i, i) un crédito / un préstamo para... *to ask for a loan to...* **7**

pedir (i, i) un favor *to ask a favor* **14**

peinar *to comb* 6

pelar *to peel* **11**

película bélica, la *war movie* **12**

película, la *movie* 2

pelirrojo/-a *red-haired* **5**

pelo liso, el *straight hair* **5**

pelo rizado, el *curly hair* **5**

pelo rubio, el *blonde hair* **5**

penicilina, la *penicillin* **13**

península, la *peninsula* 3

pensamiento, el *thought* 3

pensar (e>ie) *to think* 3

pequeño/-a *small, little, young* **3**, 6

pera, la *pear* **11**

perder (e>ie) (algo) *to lose (something)* 6, **15**

perderse (e>ie) *to get lost* **15**

perdona/-e *excuse me* **14**

perezoso/-a *lazy* **5**

perfil, el *profile* 5

perfume, el *perfume* 6

perilla, la *goatee* 5

periódico, el *newspaper* 2

periodismo, el *journalism* 7

periodista, el/la *journalist* 5

permiso de conducir, el *driver's licence* 15

permitir *to permit, to allow* 4

pero *but* 1

perro/-a, el/la *dog* 6

persona mayor, la *older person, elder* 6

personaje, el *character* 5, **12**

pertenecer (zc) *to belong* 5

peruano/-a *Peruvian* 1

pescado, el *fish* **11**

pescar *to fish* **10**

peso, el *weight* 11

petróleo, el *oil* 13

picar *to chop* **11**

pico, el *peak (mountain)* 3

piedra, la *stone* 8

piel, la *leather* **4**

pieza (de automóvil), la *part (auto)* 3

pieza de fruta, la *piece of fruit* **11**

pimiento, el *pepper* **11**

pingüino, el *penguin* 1

pintado/-a *painted* 4

pintar un cuadro *to paint a painting* **7**

piña, la *pineapple* **11**

pisar *to step (on)* 7

piso, el *floor* **9**

pista de baile, la *dance floor* 5

pista de esquí, la *ski slope* 3

pizarra (digital), la *chalkboard (whiteboard)* **P**

pizca de, una *a pinch of* **11**

plaga, la *plague* 14

plan de estudios, el *curriculum* 3

planchar *to iron* 6

planificar *to plan* 6

planta, la *story, level, plant* **9**

plata, la *silver* 2

plátano, el *plantain* **11**

plato típico, el *typcal dish* 3

plato, el *dish* 4, 11

plaza, la *townsquare, seat* 3, **8**, 9

población, la *population, inhabitants* 3

poblado/-a *populated* **3**

pobre *poor* **8**

poco *few, a little* 3

poco tiempo después *soon after* 7

poder (ue, u) *can, to be able* **P**

poder económico, el *economic power* **13**

poder político, el *political power* **13**

poder votar *to be able to vote* **7**

poder, el *power* **13**

poderoso/-a *powerful* 12

policiaco/-a *crime thriller* 12

Polinesia, la *Polynesia* 7

polinesio/-a *Polynesian* 7

pollo, el *chicken* **11**

pólvora, la *gunpowder* **13**

poner *to put* 6, **11**

poner(se) crema *to put on moisturizer* **6**

poner(se) perfume *to put on perfume* **6**

ponerse (muy) contento/-a *to get (very) happy* **15**

ponerse (muy) nervioso/-a *to get (very) nervous* **15**

ponerse (muy) triste *to get (very) sad* **15**

ponerse rojo/-a *to blush, to go red* **15**

pop latino *Latin pop* **5**

por *for the sake of, because of* **2**

por *along, through* 3

por *by* 2

por ejemplo *for example* 3

por favor *please* **P**, **14**

por la calle *along the street* 5

por la mañana *in the morning* **6**

por la noche *at night* **6**

por la tarde *in the afternoon* **6**

por peso *by weight* **11**

por primera vez *for the first time* 7

por qué *why (interrogative)* 6

por unidades *by unit* **11**

porque *because* 1, **2**

portátil, el *laptop* 6

practicar español/inglés *to practice Spanish/English* **2**

practicar la pronunciación *to practice pronunciation* **2**

precio promedio, el *average price* **10**

precio, el *price* 4

precioso/-a *precious, beautiful* 3

preferir (e>ie) *to prefer* 3, **4**

pregunta, la *question* 1

Appendix 2

relación de parentesco, la *kinship* 5
relacionado/-a (con) *related (to)* 2
relajarse *to relax* **10**
religión, la *religion* **13**
rellenar *to fill, to stuff* **11**
remover (o>ue) *to stir* **11**
rendimiento, el *performance* 10
rendirse (e>i) *to give up, to surrender* 12
renovado *renovated, restored* 8
repartir *to distribute* 4
reparto, el *cast* **12**
repetir (i, i) *to repeat* P
reportaje, el *article, report* **12**
reprimido *repressed* 10
res, la *veal, beef* **11**
reservar *to book, to reserve, to save* **10, 11**
resolver (o>ue) *to solve* 3
respectivamente *respectively* 4
responder *to answer* 2
restaurante, el *restaurant* **8**
resultado, el *result* 5
resumir *to summarize* 3
retirar *to move away* **11**
retirarse *to retire* **7**
retransmisión deportiva, la *sports broadcast* **12**
revelar *to reveal* 12
revista, la *magazine* 2
rey, el *king* 6
rico/-a *delicious, rich* 3, 4, **8**
río Amazonas, el *Amazon River* 3
río, el *river* **3**
ritmo latino, el *Latin rhythm* **5**
rival, el/la *rival* 3
robar *to rob* **15**
rodeado/-a *surrounded* 14
rojo/-a *red* **4**
romántico/-a *romantic* 5, **12**
ropa, la *clothes* **4**
ropa de marca, la *designer clothes* 4
ropa deportiva, la *sportswear* **4**
ropa interior, la *underwear* **4**
rosa *pink* **4**
rubio/-a *blonde* **5**
rueda, la *wheel* **13**
ruidoso/-a *noisy* **8**
ruinas (mayas), las *ruins (Mayan)* 3
ruso, el *Russian* 5

S

sábado, el *Saturday* **6**
saber *to know* 1
sacar *to remove, to take out* **11**
sagrado/-a *sacred* 12
sal, la *salt* **11**
sala de juegos (el juego), la *game room, playroom* **9**
sala-comedor, la *living-dining room* **9**
salado/-a *salty* 15
salir *to appear* **12**
salir (algo) de (un lugar, de un recipiente...) *to come out (something from a place, a container...)* **15**
salir (con alguien) *to go out (with someone)* 7
salir a correr *to go out for a run* 6
salir de (un lugar) *to leave (a place)*
salir de casa *to leave the house* **6**
salir de noche (la noche) *to go out at night* 2
salir del trabajo *to leave work* **6**
salón, el *living room* **6**
salsa, la *sauce* **11**
saltear *to sauté, to stir-fry* **11**
saludo, el *greeting* P, 14
saludos (el saludo) a (la familia) *greetings to (your family)* **14**
¡saludos! *greetings* 5
salvadoreño/-a *Salvadoran* **1**
sandalias, las *sandals* **4**
sano/-a *healthy* 6
sartén, la *frying pan* **11**
secador de pelo, el *hair dryer* **4**
secarse el pelo *to dry your hair* 6
seco (clima) *dry (climate)* **3**
seco/-a *dry* 3
secuestro, el *kidnap* 12
seda, la *silk* **4**
sede, la *headquarters* 15
seguir (i, i) *to continue* 6
segundo, el *second (time)* 3
segundo/-a *second (ordinal number)* 3
seguramente *surely* 6
¿Seguro? *Are you sure?* 5
seguro/-a *safe, secure* 4
seis *six* **P**
seiscientos/-as *six hundred* **4**
sello, el *seal* 4
selva, la *rain forest, jungle* **3**
semana, la *week* 3

sensible *sensitive* 5
sentar(se) (e>ie) *to sit* 6, **15**
sentir (ie, i) *to feel* P
sentirse (ie, i) bien *to feel good* 6
señalar *to point out, to indicate* 3
señor/a, el/la *man/woman* 1
ser *to be* 1
ser descortés *to be rude* **14**
ser doctor/a en *to have a PhD in* 7
ser el/la mejor (en algo) *to be the best (in something)* **7**
ser el/la primero/-a en (+ infinitivo) *to be the first to (+ infinitive)* 7
ser hijo/-a único/-a *to be an only child* 5
ser número uno *to be number one* 7
ser verdad *to be true* 4
ser/estar soltero/-a *to be single* 5
ser/estar viudo/-a *to be widowed* 5
serie, la *TV series* 2
serio/-a *serious* 5
servicio, el *service* **10**
servicios, los *services* 8, **13**
servir (i, i) *to serve* **11**
servir (i, i) (para) *can be used for* 6
sesenta *sixty* **P**
setecientos/-as *seven hundred* **4**
setenta *seventy* **P**
sexto/-a *sixth* 4
si *if* 4
sí *yes* P
sí mismo/-a *himself/herself* 5
siempre *always* 2, **6**
siete *seven* **P**
siglo, el *century* 2
significar *to mean* P
siguiente *next* 3
silla, la *chair* **P, 9**
sillón, el *armchair* **9**
simpático/-a *likeable, amusing* 3, **5**
sin *without* 3
simplemente *simply* 6
sin amueblar *unfurnished* **9**
sin duda *without a doubt* **4**
sin mangas *sleeveless* **4**
sinagoga, la *synagogue* **8**
sinopsis, la *synopsis* **12**
sistema político, el *political system* **13**
sitio cultural, el *cultural site* 2
sitio, el *place, location* 4
sobre *about* 1
sobre todo *mainly, mostly* 5

Appendix 2

sobrino/-a, el/la *nephew / niece* **5**
sociable *sociable* **5**
sofá, el *sofa, couch* **9**
soler (o>ue) *to tend to do something* **6**
solo *just, only* **3**
solo/-a *alone* **2**
sombrero, el *hat* **4**
sonar (o>ue) *to sound* **5**
sonido, el *sound* **1**
sopa, la *soup* **11**
soportar *to tolerate* **12**
sorprendido *surprised* **12**
sospechar *to suspect* **12**
sospechoso/-a *suspicious* **12**
Soy argentino/-a. *I'm Argentinian/ from Argentina.* **1**
Soy estudiante. *I'm a student.* **1**
suaves (temperaturas) *mild (temperatures)* **3**
subir *to upload, to get on (transportation)* **4, 6, 15**
submarinista, el/la *submariner* **15**
subrayar *to underline* **12**
subtitulado/-a *subtitled* **10**
sucio/-a *dirty* **8**
suerte, la *luck* **12**
suéter, el *sweater* **4**
sugerencia, la *suggestion* **2**
sujeto, el *subject* **1**
supermercado, el *supermarket* **8**
superviviente, el/la *survivor* **12**
supuestamente *supposedly* **15**
sur, el *south* **3**
surgir *to appear* **5**
sustantivo, el *noun* **3**
sustentable *sustainable* **4**

T

tabla, la *chart, table* **3**
talentoso/-a *talented* **1**
talla, la *size* **4**
también *too, also* **1**
tampoco *neither* **5**
tapar *to cover* **11**
tardar *to be late* **15**
tarea, la *task, homework* **3**
tarjeta, la *card* **3**
tarjeta de crédito, la *credit card* **4**
tasa de participación, la *participation fee* **6**
taxi, el *taxi* **P**

taxista, el/la *taxi driver* **1**
taza, la *cup* **11**
té, el *tea* **11**
tejeduría (wayúu), la *weaving* **4**
teléfono, el *telephone* **4**
telescopio, el *telescope* **13**
televisión, la *TV* **2**
televisor, el *television set* **P**
tema, el *topic, theme* **2**
temperatura, la *temperature* **3**
templado (clima) *temperate , mild (climate)* **3**
temporada, la *season* **12**
temprano *early* **6**
tenedor, el *fork* **11**
tener (e>ie) *to have* **P**
tener (e>ie) amigos hispanos (el amigo; la amiga) *to have Hispanic friends* **2**
tener (e>ie) buen aspecto *to look good* **6**
tener (e>ie) cosas (la cosa) que hacer *to have things to do* **14**
tener (e>ie) en cuenta *to take into account* **14**
tener (e>ie) éxito *to be succesful* **7**
tener (e>ie) hijos *to have children* **5, 7**
tener (e>ie) lugar *to take place* **5**
tener (e>ie) prisa (la prisa) *to be in a hurry* **14**
tener (e>ie) que *to have to* **3, 4**
tener (e>ie) un accidente *to have an accident* **7**
Tengo 22 años. *I'm 22 years old.* **1**
Tengo una empresa de informática. (la informática) *I own a software company.* **1**
tenis, el *tennis* **1**
tenis, los *sneakers* **4**
tenista, el/la *tennis player* **1**
terminación, la *ending* **1**
terminar *to finish, to end* **7**
terminar los estudios *to graduate* **7**
termómetro, el *thermometer* **13**
terraza, la *terrace* **9**
terremoto, el *earthquake* **15**
testimonio, el *testimony* **6**
tiempo (libre), el *(free) time* **2**
tiempo, el *weather* **3**
tienda de lujo (el lujo), la *luxury store (boutique)* **8**
tienda de ropa, la *clothing store* **8**
tienda, la *store, shop* **1**

tiene un/a novio/-a colombiano/-a (porque) *(because) he/she has a Colombian boyfriend/girlfriend* **2**
¿Tiene(s) hora/s? *Do you have the time?* **6**
¿Tiene/s (un poco de)...? *Do you have (some / a little)...?* **14**
tímido/-a *shy* **5**
tina, la *bathtub* **9**
tío/-a, el/la *uncle / aunt* **5**
tíos, los *aunt + uncle* **5**
típico/-a *typical* **3**
tipo (de), el *type (of)* **3**
título, el *title* **12**
toalla de playa, la *beach towel* **4**
tocar *to touch* **15**
tocar (un instrumento) *to play (an instrument)* **1**
tocar la guitarra *to play guitar* **1**
tocarse *to have physical contact* **14**
todavía *still* **6**
todo *all, everything* **2**
todo bien *all good* **14**
todo el año *all year* **3**
todo el mundo *whole world* **3**
todos los días *every day* **3, 6**
todos/-as junto/-as *all together* **6**
tomar *to take* **3**
tomar algo *to have a drink* **10**
tomar el sol *to sunbathe* **10**
tomar fotos (la fotografía) *to take pictures* **2**
tomate, el *tomato* **11**
torta, la *cake* **11**
tortuga, la *turtle* **3**
total, el *total* **4**
totalmente *totally* **7**
trabajador/a *hard worker* **6**
trabajar en una compañía (para) *(in order to) to work in a company* **2**
trabajo, el *job, work* **1**
trabajo (por su) *(for the sake of) his/ her job* **2**
Trabajo en un restaurante. *I work in a restaurant.* **1**
Trabajo en una fábrica. *I work in a factory.* **1**
Trabajo en una tienda. *I work in a store.* **1**
trabajo no remunerado, el *unpaid work* **6**

traducción, la *translation* 4
traductor/a, el/la *translator* 7
traer *to bring* 12
traición, la *treason* 12
traje de baño, el *bathing suit* 4
trama, la *plot, storyline* **12**
tranquilo/-a *calm* **5**
trapecista, el/la *trapeze artist* 7
trasladar *to move* 8
tratar (de/sobre) *to be about* 3, 6, **12**
trece *thirteen* **P**
treinta *thirty* **P**
treinta y cinco *thirty-five* **P**
treinta y cuatro *thirty-four* **P**
treinta y dos *thirty-two* **P**
treinta y nueve *thirty-nine* **P**
treinta y ocho *thirty-eight* **P**
treinta y seis *thirty-six* **P**
treinta y siete *thirty-seven* **P**
treinta y tres *thirty-three* **P**
treinta y uno *thirty-one* **P**
tres *three* **P**
trescientos/-as *three hundred* **4**
triturar *to blend* **11**
trocear *to dice* **11**
tropical (clima) *tropical (climate)* **3**
truco, el *trick* 4
turismo, el *tourism* **13**

U

ubicar *to locate* 3
último/-a *last* 6
un millón *one million* **4**
un montón de *a lot of* 4
un poco de *a little bit of* 1, **11**
un poco más *a little bit more* 6
único/-a *only one* 4
unidad de medida, la *unit of measure* **3**
universidad, la *university* 2
uno *one* **P**
unos/-as *about, approximately* 5
uruguayo/-a *Uruguayan* **1**
usado/-a *used* 3
usar internet *to use the internet* 2
uso cotidiano, el *everyday use* 4
usuario/-a, el/la *user* 4
utensilio de cocina, el *kitchen utensil* 11
uva, la *grape* **11**

V

vacaciones, las *vacation* 2
vacuna, la *vaccine* **13**
valer *to be worth* 3
valer la pena *to be worthwhile* **12**
valle, el *valley* **3**
vanidoso/-a *vain* 6
variado/-a *varied* 3
variedad, la *variety* 2
vaso, el *glass* **11**
veces a la semana (tres) *(three) times a week* 6
veces al año (tres) *(three) times a year* **6**
veces al día (tres) *(three) times a day* **6**
veces al mes *times a month* 6
vecino/-a, el/la *neighbor* **14**
veinte *twenty* **P**
veinte mil *twenty thousand* **4**
veinticinco *twenty-five* **P**
veinticuatro *twenty-four* **P**
veintidós *twenty-two* **P**
veintinueve *twenty-nine* **P**
veintiocho *twenty-eight* **P**
veintiséis *twenty-six* **P**
veintisiete *twenty-seven* **P**
veintitrés *twenty-three* **P**
veintiuno *twenty-one* **P**
vendedor/a, el/la *vendor, seller* 4
vender *to sell* **4**
venezolano/-a *Venezuelan* **1**
venganza, la *revenge, vengeance* 12
vengarse *to take revenge* 12
venta, la *sale* 4
ventaja, la *advantage* 6
ventana, la *window* **9**
ver (la) televisión *to watch TV* 2
ver a los amigos *to meet some friends* **2**
ver películas/series en español (la película; la serie) *to watch movies / TV series in Spanish* 2
ver una serie *to watch a TV series* 2
ver videos *to watch videos* 1
verano, el *summer* **3**
¿verdad? (la verdad) *right?* 4
verdadero/-a *true* 2
verde *green* **4**
verdura, la *green vegetable* **11**
vestido, el *dress* **4**
vestir(se) (i, i) *to get dressed* 4, **6**
vez, la *time, occasion* 3

viajar *to travel* **1**
viajar (para) *to travel (in order to)* **2**
viaje de fin de semana, el *weekend trip* 4
viaje de placer, el *leisure trip* 4
viaje de trabajo, el *work trip* 4
viaje, el *trip* 3
vida, la *life* 6
videojuego, el *video game* 2
viernes, el *Friday* **6**
villa, la *villa, vacation property* **9**
vinagre, el *vinegar* **11**
vincular *to link* 13
vinilo, el *vinyl* 5
vino, el *wine* 3, **11**
visitado/-a *visited* 2
vista, la *view* 8
vistoso/a *attractive* 8
vivienda, la *housing* **8**
vivir *to live* 1, **2**
vivir en (un país) (para) *to live in (a country) (in order to)* **2**
vivir en otro país *to live in another country* 7
Vivo en Boulder. *I live in Boulder.* **1**
volcán, el *volcano* **3**
volver (o>ue) *to return* 6
votar *to vote* **13**
voz, la *voice* 3

Y

¿Y tú? *And you?* **P**
Ya ves... *As you can see...* **14**
Yo me llamo... *My name is...* **P**
yogur, el *yogurt* **11**
yuca, la *yuca, manioc* **11**

Z

zanahoria, la *carrot* **11**
zapatos, los *shoes* **4**
zona peatonal, la *pedestrian zone* **8**
zonas verdes, las *green zones* **8**
zoológico, el *zoo* 1

Appendix 3

English – Spanish Glossary

The number following each entry in bold corresponds
to the chapter in which the word is introduced for active mastery.
Non-bold numbers correspond to the introduction of words
for receptive use.

A

"at" sign *arroba, la* 1
a little *poco* 3
a little bit more *un poco más* 6
a little bit of *un poco de* 1, **11**
a lot *mucho* 2, 3
a lot of *un montón de* 4
a pinch of *pizca de, una* **11**
a quarter after five *cinco y cuarto* **6**
a quarter to five *cinco menos cuarto* **6**
about *sobre; cerca de, unos/-as*
    (approximation) 1, 2, 5
abroad *extranjero, el* 4
academic support *apoyo escolar, el* 6
academic training *formación*
    académica, la 7
accessory *accesorio, el* **4**
accompany, to *acompañar* 3
accomplish, to *realizar* 6
action *de acción* **12**
active *activo/-a* **5**
active fight *lucha activa, la* 7
activity *ejercicio, el* 2
acquire, to *adquirir* 4
activity *actividad, la* **P**
act, to *interpretar* **12**
actor *actor, el* **1, 12**
actress *actriz, la* **1, 12**
add, to *agregar, añadir* **11**
address, to *abordar* 12
adjective *adjetivo, el* 3
admire, to *admirar* 1
advanced level *nivel avanzado, el* 7
advantage *ventaja, la* 6
adventure *de aventuras* **12**
advertisement *anuncio, el* 5
aerospace *aeronáutica, la* 3
Africa *África* **3**
African-American *afroamericano/-a* 7
Afro-Cuban *afrocubano/-a* 5
after *después* 3, **6**

after (doing something) *después de*
    (+ infinitivo) 1, **6**
again *de nuevo* 3
again *otra vez* 6
against *contra* 4
age *edad, la* **1**
agree (with), to *estar de acuerdo (con)* 6
agreement *concordancia, la* 4
agriculture *agricultura, la* **13**
air conditioner *aire acondicionado,*
    el **9**
airport *aeropuerto, el* P
alarm *alarma, la* 6
album *álbum, el* 5
alcohol *alcohol, el* 4
all *todo* 2
all audiences *público general* **10**
all good *todo bien* **14**
all together *todos/-as junto/-as* 6
all year *todo el año* 3
allow, to *permitir* 4
almost *casi* 3, **6**
alone *solo/-a* 2
along *por* 3
along *a lo largo de* 3
along the street *por la calle* 5
along with *junto con* 2
also *también* 1
alternative music *música*
    independiente, la **5**
altitude *altitud, la* 3
always *siempre* 2, **6**
amazing *maravilloso/-a* 3
Amazon River *río Amazonas, el* 3
ambitious *ambicioso/-a* **1**
American *estadounidense* **1**
among others *entre otros/-as*
amount *cantidad, la* 2
amusing *simpático/-a* 3, **5**
ancient *antiguo/-a* 3, **8**
And you? *¿Y tú?* **P**

animated *de animación* **12**
answer, to *responder* 2
antique *antigüedad, la* **4**
any *algún, alguno/-a/-os/-as* 1
apartment *apartamento, el* **8**
apartment building *bloque de*
    apartamentos, el **8**
appeal *atractivo, el* 3
appear, to *aparecer* **3, 15**
appear, to *salir* 12
appear, to *surgir* 5
appearance *aparición, la* **13**
appearance *imagen, la* 6
apple *manzana, la* **11**
appliances *electrodomésticos, los* 9
approach, to *acercar(se)* **15**
approximately *aproximadamente,*
    unos/-as 5
architect *arquitecto/-a, el/la* **1**
architecture *arquitectura, la* **2**
Are you sure? *¿Seguro?* 5
Argentinian *argentino/-a* **1**
argue, to *discutir* 3
armchair *sillón, el* **9**
army *ejército, el* 7
aromatic herb *hierba aromática, la* **11**
around (approximation) *cerca de* 2
arrangement, (musical) *arreglo*
    (musical), el 5
arranger, (musical) *arreglista, el/la* 5
arrival *llegada, la* 12
arrive, to *llegar* 6
art *arte, el* **2**
article *artículo, el* 6
article *reportaje, el* **12**
artisan *artesano/-a, el/la* 4
artist *artista, el/la* 1, **5**
as *como* 2
As you can see... *Ya ves...* **14**
Asia *Asia* **3**
ask, to *preguntar* 3

ask a favor, to *pedir (i, i) un favor* **14**

ask for, to *pedir (i, i)* **14**

ask for a loan to..., to *pedir (i, i) un crédito/préstamo para...* **7**

ask for help, to *pedir (i, i) ayuda (la ayuda)* **14**

ask for permission, to *pedir (i, i) permiso (el permiso)* **14**

ask questions, to *hacer preguntas* **3**

ask the time, to *preguntar la hora* **14**

aspirin *aspirina, la* **4**

assignment *encargo, el* 12

at a low price *a bajo precio* 4

at any time *a cualquier hora* 6

at first sight *a primera vista* 7

at least *al menos* 6

at least *como mínimo* 6

at low heat *a fuego lento* **11**

at medium heat *a fuego medio* **11**

at night *por la noche* **6**

at noon *a mediodía* **6**

at the end of (period of time) *a finales de* 7

athlete *deportista, el/la* 5

athletic *deportista* 5

Atlantic Ocean *océano Atlántico, el* **3**

ATM *cajero automático, el* **8**

attend, to *asistir* 7

attic *ático, el* **9**

attractive *vistoso/a* 8

aunt *tía, la* **5**

aunt + uncle *tíos, los (la tía + el tío)* **5**

autonomous region *comunidad autónoma, la* **3**

autumn *otoño, el* **3**

availability *disponibilidad, la* 7

avenue *avenida, la* **8**

average price *precio promedio, el* **10**

avocado *aguacate, el* **11**

award *premio, el* 6, 7

away from the city center *alejado/-a del centro* **8**

B

backpack *mochila, la* **P**

bag *bolsa, la* **11**

bake, to *hornear* **11**

baking sheet *bandeja de horno, la* **11**

balcony *balcón, el* 6, **9**

bald *calvo/-a* **5**

banana *plátano, el* **11**

band *banda, la* 5

band *grupo, el* **5**

bang *golpe, el* 14

bank *banco, el* 1, **8**

barbershop *barbería, la* 6

bartender *mesero/-a, el/la* **1**

based on *con base en, en función de* 5, 6, 13

based on, from *a partir de* 4

basis of nutrition *base de la alimentación, la* **13**

bathing suit *traje de baño, el* **4**

bathroom *baño, el* **9**

bathtub *tina, la* **9**

be, to *ser* 1

be (in existence), to *haber* 3

be a part (of), to *formar parte (de)* 3

be able, to *poder (ue, u)* P

be able to vote, to *poder (ue, u) votar* **7**

be about, to *tratar (de/sobre)* 3, 6, **12**

be an only child, to *ser hijo/-a único/-a* **5**

be back, to *estar de vuelta* 6

be based on, to *estar basado/-a en* **12**

be born, to *nacer (zc)* 5, **7**

be divorced, to *estar divorciado/-a* **5**

be dumbstruck, to *quedarse sin palabras* **15**

be forbidden, to *estar prohibido/-a* **13**

be found (location), to *encontrarse (en) (o>ue)* 3

be happy, to *estar contento/-a* **5**

be in a hurry, to *tener (e>ie) prisa (la prisa)* **14**

be in danger of extinction, to *estar en peligro de extinción (la extinción)* 3

be included, to *estar incluido/-a* 3

be lacking, to *faltar* 3, 6

be late, to *llegar tarde* **14**

be late, to *tardar* 15

be married (to), to *estar casado/-a (con)* **5**

be missing, to *faltar* 3, 6

be named, to *llamarse* P

be number one, to *ser número uno* **7**

be rude, to *ser descortés* **14**

be separated, to *estar separado/-a* **5**

be set in, to *estar ambientado/a en* **12**

be single, to *ser/estar soltero/-a* **5**

be succesful, to *tener (e>ie) éxito* **7**

be the best (in something), to *ser el/la mejor (en algo)* **7**

be the first to (+ infinitive), to *ser el/la primero/-a en (+ infinitivo)* **7**

be true, to *ser verdad* 4

be waiting (for), to *estar esperando* **15**

be widowed, to *ser/estar viudo/-a* **5**

be willing, to *estar dispuesto/-a* 12

be worth, to *valer* 3

be worthwhile, to *valer la pena* **12**

beach towel *toalla de playa, la* **4**

bean *frijol, el* **11**

bear *oso, el* 3

beard *barba, la* **5**

beautiful *lindo/-a, bello/-a, bonito/-a, precioso/-a, guapo/-a* 3, **4, 5**

because *porque* 1, **2**

because of *por* **2**

become famous, to *hacerse famoso/-a* **7**

become ill, to *enfermarse* **7**

become rich, to *hacerse rico/-a* **7**

bed *cama, la* 6

bed, (double) *cama (doble), la* **9**

bedroom *habitación, la* **9**

beef *res, la* **11**

beer *cerveza, la* 1

before (doing something) *antes de (+ infinitivo)* 1, **6**

beginning *principio, el* 5

beige *beige* **4**

Belgian *belga* 1

belief *creencia, la* 13

belong, to *pertenecer (zc)* 5

below *abajo* 6

belt *cinturón, el* **4**

benefit *beneficio, el* 4

besides *además (de)* 2, 4

best *mejor* 2

best friend *mejor amigo/-a, el/la* **5**

better *mejor* 2

between *entre* 3

beverage *bebida, la* 3

big *gran, grande* 2, **3**

bill *cuenta, la* 1

biopic *biográfico/-a* **12**

birth *nacimiento, el* 5

birthdate *fecha de nacimiento, la* 7

birthday *cumpleaños, el* 4

birthday party *fiesta de cumpleaños, la* 4

birthplace *lugar de nacimiento, el* 7

bit *pedazo, el* **11**

black *negro/-a* 3, **4**

blank *espacio en blanco, el* 3

Appendix 3

chopsticks *palillos, los* 11

chosen *elegido/-a* 3

Christian *cristiano/-a, el/la* 3

chunk *pedazo, el* **11**

church *iglesia, la* **8**

circus *circo, el* 1

circus show *espectáculo de circo (el circo), el* **10**

city *ciudad, la* 1

civil war *guerra civil, la* 7

clarify, to *aclarar* 15

class *clase, la* P, 2

classic music *música clásica, la* **5**

classmate *compañero/-a de clase, el/la* 5

clay *arcilla, la* 4

clean *limpio/-a* **8**

clean, to *limpiar* 6

clear up, to *aclarar* 15

clearly *claramente* 6

climate *clima, el* **3**

climb, to *escalar* **10**

close to *cerca de* 3

closed *cerrado* **10**

closed-minded *cerrado/-a* **5**

closet *clóset, el* **9**

cloth, (made of) *de tela* **9**

clothes *ropa, la* 4

clothing items *prendas de vestir, las* 4

clothing store *tienda de ropa, la* **8**

club *discoteca, la* **5**

co-worker *compañero/-a de trabajo, el/la* 5

coast *costa, la* **3**

coastline *costa, la* **3**

coat *abrigo, el* 4

cockroach *cucaracha, la* 14

coffee *café, el* **11**

coffee table *mesa de centro, la* **9**

coin *moneda, la* 3

cold (climate) *frío (clima)* 3

cold cuts *embutido, el* **11**

collaborate, to *colaborar* 7

Colombian *colombiano/-a* **1**

colored *de colores* 6, **9**

comb, to *peinar* 6

combine, to *combinar* 4

come out (something from a place, a container...), to *salir (algo) de (un lugar, de un recipiente...)* **15**

comedy *comedia, la* **12**

comfortable *cómodo/-a* **4, 9**

command *dominio, el* 7

commander *comandante, el* 7

commentary *comentario, el* 3

commercial *anuncio, el* 5

commitment *compromiso, el* **12**

company *compañía, la* **2**

company *empresa, la* 1

composer *compositor/a, el/la* 5

computer *computadora, la* **P**

concert *concierto, el* 2

condominium *condominio, el* **9**

conference *conferencia, la* **10**

confuse, to *confundir* 15

conjugate (verbs), to *conjugar* 2

conjugation (of verbs) *conjugación, la* 1

conscious consumerism *consumo consciente, el* 4

consent to, to *acceder* 12

considered, (to be) *considerado/-a* 2

consultant *asesor/a* 2

container *recipiente, el* 11

contaminating *contaminante* 4

contest *concurso, el* 3, **12**

contestant *concursante, el/la* **12**

continent *continente, el* **3**

continue, to *seguir (i, i)* 6

contraceptive *anticonceptivo, el* **13**

contribute to, to *propiciar* 8

contribution *aportación, la* 7

cook *cocinero/-a* **1**

cook, to *cocinar, preparar la comida* **2, 6**

cookie *galleta, la* **11**

cool (not warm) *frío/-a* **9**

coral reef *arrecife de coral, el* 3

corn *maíz, el* **11**

corn on the cob *elote, el* **11**

corpse *cadáver, el* 15

correct, to *corregir (i, i)* 2

cost, to *costar (o>ue)* 4

Costa Rican *costarricense* 1

cotton *algodón, el* 4

couch *sofá, el* **9**

Could you speak louder, please? *¿Puedes hablar más alto, por favor?* **P**

Could you speak more slowly, please? *¿Puedes hablar más despacio, por favor?* **P**

country *país, el* 1

countryside *campo, el* 3, 4

county *condado, el* 3

couple *pareja, la* 3, 4, **5**

course *curso, el* 2

cousin *primo/-a, el/la* **5**

cousins *primos, los* **5**

cover, to *tapar* **11**

cozy *acogedor/a* **9**

create, to *crear* 1

creator *creador/-a* 4

credit card *tarjeta de crédito, la* **4**

crime thriller *policiaco/-a* **12**

crops *cultivo, el* 12

cross, to *cruzar* 14, **15**

cruise *crucero, el* 4

crush, to *aplastar* **11**

cry, to *llorar* **15**

Cuban *cubano/-a* **1**

cuisine *gastronomía, la* 3

cultural site *sitio cultural, el* 2

culture *cultura, la* **2**

cup *taza, la* **11**

curly hair *pelo rizado, el* **5**

currency *moneda, la* **3**

currently *actualidad, la* **12**

curriculum *plan de estudios, el* 3

cushion *cojín, el* **9**

cut, to *cortar* **11**

D

daily *diariamente* 4

daily *diario/-a* 6

dairy *lácteo, el* **11**

damp (climate) *húmedo* **3**

dance *baile, el* 5

dance, to *bailar* **1**

dance floor *pista de baile, la* 5

dance performance *espectáculo de baile/danza (baile, la danza), el* **10**

dark *oscuro/-a* 4

dark-haired *moreno/-a* **5**

daughter *hija, la* **5**

daughter-in-law *nuera, la* 12

day *día, el* 3

days of the week *días de la semana, los* **6**

deal with, to *abordar* 12

death body *cadáver, el* 15

decisive *determinante* 7

decorative items *artículos de decoración, los* **9**

dedicate, to *dedicar* 6

defense *defensa, la* 3

Appendix 3

excuse me *disculpa/-e* **14**
excuse me *perdona/-e* **14**
exercise *ejercicio, el* 2
exhibition *exposición, la* 2
exile *exilio, el* **13**
exist, to *haber, existir* 3, **13**
expensive *caro/-a* **4**
explain, to *explicar* 3
extreme (temperatures) *extremo/-a* **3**
extrovert *extrovertido/-a* 5
eyes *ojos, los* **5**

F

face *cara, la* 6
face, to *enfrentarse* 8
fact *hecho, el* 7
factory *fábrica, la* 1
fair *justo/-a* 4
faithful *fiel* 12
fall asleep, to *dormirse (ue, u)* 6
fall in love, to *enamorarse* 7
fall *otoño, el* **3**
fall, to *caer(se)* **15**
family *familia, la* 5
family members *miembros de la familia, los* 5
family tree *árbol genealógico, el* 5
famous *conocido/-a* 3
fanatical *maniático/-a* 6
fantasy (movie, short film...) *fantástico/-a (una película, un cortometraje...)* **12**
far *lejos* 12
farewell *despedida, la* P, **14**
farmer *agricultor/a* 6
farming *cultivo, el* 12
fashion blog *blog de moda, el* 4
fast food *comida rápida, la* **10**
father *padre, el* **5**
fear *miedo, el* 12
feature film *largometraje, el* 10, **12**
February *febrero, el* 3
feel, to *sentir (ie, i)* P
feel good, to *sentirse (ie, i) bien* 6
festival *festival, el* **5**
few *poco* 3
fiancé/-e *prometido/-a, el/la* **5**
field *campo, el* 3, 4
fifteen *quince* P
fifty *cincuenta* P
fight for a cause, to *luchar por una causa* 7

figure *figura, la* 5
fill, to *rellenar* **11**
film *cine, el* 1, 3, **12**
find (something), to *encontrar (algo) (o>ue)* 4, **15**
find out (information), to *enterarse* 12
finish, to *terminar* 7
fire *fuego, el* **13**
firefighter *bombero/-a, el/la* 6
first *primer, primero/-a/-os/-as* 2, **6**
first name *nombre, el* P, **1**
fish *pescado, el* **11**
fish, to *pescar* 10
five *cinco* P
five fifteen *cinco y cuarto* **6**
five hundred *quinientos/-as* **4**
five minutes from... *a cinco minutos de...* **9**
five thirty *cinco y media* **6**
flavor *gusto, el* 5
flee, to *huir (y)* 15
flexible schedule *flexibilidad de horario, la* **6**
floor *piso, el* **9**
floor lamp *lámpara de pie, la* **9**
flour *harina, la* **11**
flower *flor, la* 5
food *comida, la* 1
food *alimento, el* **11**
food critic *crítico/-a gastronómico/-a, el/la* 6
for *para* 2
for example *por ejemplo* 3
For me... (In my opinion) *Para mí...* **2**
for special occasions *en ocasiones especiales* 6
for the first time *por primera vez* 7
for the sake of *por* **2**
forest *bosque, el* **3**
forest fire *incendio forestal, el* 15
fork *tenedor, el* **11**
form of government *forma de gobierno (el gobierno), la* **13**
forty *cuarenta* P
foundation *fundación, la* 7
founded *fundado/-a* 3
founder *fundador/a* 5
four *cuatro* P
four hundred *cuatrocientos/-as* **4**
fourteen *catorce* P
free *gratis* 10

free admission *entrada gratuita, la* **10**
freedom *libertad, la* **13**
freedom of speech *libertad de expresión (la expresión), la* **13**
French *francés, el* 5
frequency *frecuencia, la* 6
Friday *viernes, el* **6**
friend *amigo/-a, el/la* 1, **2, 5**
friendship *amistad, la* 12
from *de, desde* P, 5
fruit *fruta, la* 6, **11**
fry, to *freír (e>i)* **11**
frying pan *sartén, la* **11**
full *lleno/-a* 12
full name *nombre completo, el* **1**
fun *divertido/-a* **5**
function, to *funcionar* 6
funny *divertido/-a* **5**
furnished *amueblado/-a* **9**
furniture *muebles, los* 9
fusion *fusión, la* 5
future *futuro, el* 2
futuristic *futurista* **12**

G

Galapagos Islands *islas Galápagos, las* 4
game room *sala de juegos (el juego), la* **9**
game *partido, el* **10**
garage *garaje, el* **9**
garden *jardín, el* **9**
garlic *ajo, el* **11**
gastronomy *gastronomía, la* 3
general admission *entrada general, la* **10**
generate, to *generar* 4
genre *género, el* 5, **12**
geography *geografía, la* **2**
German *alemán/-a* 1
German (language) *alemán, el* 5
get, to *obtener (e>ie), conseguir (i, i)* 4, **14**
get (very) happy, to *ponerse (muy) contento/-a* **15**
get (very) nervous, to *ponerse (muy) nervioso/-a* **15**
get (very) sad, to *ponerse (muy) triste* **15**
get close, to *acercar(se)* **15**
get divorced, to *divorciarse* 7
get dressed, to *vestir(se) (i, i)* 4, **6**
get embarrassed, to *pasar vergüenza (la vergüenza)* **15**

get excited, to *emocionar(se)* **15**

get lost, to *perderse (e>ie)* **15**

get married, to *casarse* **7**

get off (transportation), to *bajar(se)* **15**

get on (transportation), to *subir* 4, 6, **15**

get rid of, to *desechar* 4

get scared, to *pasar miedo (el miedo)* **15**

get sick, to *enfermarse* **7**

get the idea (of something), to *hacerse una idea (de algo)* 3

get up, to *levantarse* **6**

get your first job, to *empezar (e>ie) a trabajar* **6, 7**

getaway (vacation) *escapada, la* 4

gift *regalo, el* 5

girl *chica, la* **5**

girlfriend *novia, la* 2, **5**

give, to *dar, regalar* 1, **14, 15**

give a dirty look, to *mirar mal* 11

give an opinion, to *opinar* 3

give back, to *devolver (o>ue)* **14**

give priority to, to *dar prioridad a* 4

give up, to *rendirse (e>i)* 12

Glad to see you. *Me alegro de verlo/-a.* **14**

glass *vaso, el* **11**

glass, (made of) *de vidrio* 9

glasses *gafas, las* 5

global warming *calentamiento global, el* 3

go, to *ir* 1

go bowling, to *ir a la bolera (la bolera)* **10**

go by bus, to *ir en autobús* 3

go deep into, to *adentrarse* 12

go for a run, to *ir a correr* 6

go for a walk/ride, to *pasear, dar un paseo* 2, **15**

go on a trip, to *ir de viaje / de excursión* 4, **10**

go on the bus, to *ir en autobús* 3

go on vacation, to *ir de vacaciones (las vacaciones)* 2

go out (with someone), to *salir (con alguien)* 7

go out at night, to *salir de noche (la noche)* 2

go out for a run, to *salir a correr* 6

go red, to *ponerse rojo/-a* **15**

go shopping, to *ir de compras* **2, 4**

go to a concert, to *ir a un concierto* 2

go to a party, to *ir a una fiesta* **10**

go to an exhibition, to *ir a una exposición* 2

go to an opening, to *ir a una inauguración* **10**

go to bed/sleep, to *acostarse (o>ue)* **6**

go to class, to *ir a clase (la clase)* **6**

go to school, to *ir a la escuela* **7**

go to singing/drawing/self-defense lessons, to *ir a clases de canto/dibujo/defensa personal* **10**

go to the bathroom, to *ir al baño* **6**

go to the dentist, to *ir al dentista* 6

go to the gym, to *ir al gimnasio* **1**

go to the hair salon, to *ir a la peluquería* **6**

go to the movies, to *ir al cine* 6

go to the stadium, to *ir al estadio (el estadio)* **10**

go to the theater, to *ir al teatro* 6, **10**

go to the university, to *ir a la universidad* **7**

goal *gol, el* 1

goatee *perilla, la* 5

good *bien, bueno, listo* **2**, 3, 4, 5

good afternoon *buenas tardes* P

good evening *buenas tardes* P

good morning *buenos días* P

good person *buena persona, la* **5**

good value for the money *buena relación calidad-precio, la* **10**

good-bye *adiós* P

good/bad layout *buena/mala distribución, la* **9**

government *gobierno, el* 2

graduate, to *graduarse* **7**

graduate, to *terminar los estudios* **7**

grain *cereal, el* **11**

gram *gramo, el* **11**

grammar *gramática, la* 2

Grand Canyon *Gran Cañón, el* 3

grandchildren *nietos, los* **5**

granddaughter *nieta, la* **5**

grandfather *abuelo, el* **5**

grandmother *abuela, la* **5**

grandparents *abuelos, los* **5**

grandson *nieto, el* **5**

grape *uva, la* **11**

graph *gráfico, el* 6

grate, to *rallar* **11**

gray *gris* 4

great grandfather *bisabuelo, el* 7

great grandmother *bisabuela, la* 7

Great Lakes *Grandes Lagos* 3

great *gran, grande* 2

green *verde* **4**

green vegetable *verdura, la* **11**

green zones *zonas verdes, las* **8**

greeting *saludo, el* P, 14

greetings *¡saludos! (el saludo)* 5

greetings to (your family) *saludos (el saludo) a (la/su familia)* **14**

grill, to *hacer a la plancha* **11**

grind, to *moler (o>ue)* **11**

growing *creciente* 12

growth *auge, el* 4

Guatemalan *guatemalteco/-a* **1**

guess, to *adivinar* 1

guest *invitado/-a* 5

guitar *guitarra, la* 1

gunpowder *pólvora, la* **13**

gym *gimnasio, el* 1, **8**

H

habit *hábito, el* 6

hair bangs *flequillo, el* **5**

hair dryer *secador de pelo, el* **4**

half past five *cinco y media* 6

half-brother *medio hermano, el* **5**

half-sister *medio hermana, la* **5**

hall, (entrance) *antesala, la* 9

ham *jamón, el* 1, **11**

hand *mano, la* 5

handcrafted *artesanal* 4

handicraft *artesanía, la* **4**

handsome *guapo/-a* **5**

hanger *gancho, el* 4

happen, to *pasar, producirse* 3, 4, 7, 15

hard *difícil* 7

hard worker *trabajador/a* 6

hat *gorro, el* **4**

hat *sombrero, el* 4

have, to *tener (e>ie); contar (o>ue) con (possess)* P, 2

have a (very) good time, to *pasarla (muy) bien* **15**

have a drink, to *tomar algo* **10**

have a PhD in, to *ser doctor/a en* 7

have an accident, to *tener (e>ie) un accidente* 7

have breakfast, to *desayunar* 6

have children, to *tener (e>ie) hijos* 5, **7**

have dinner, to *cenar* 6

have easy/difficult access to other areas (easy access to public transportation), to *está bien/mal comunicado/-a* **8**

have Hispanic friends, to *tener (e>ie) amigos hispanos (el amigo; la amiga)* **2**

have lunch, to *almorzar (o>ue)* **6**

have physical contact, to *tocarse* **14**

have the leading role, to *protagonizar* **7, 12**

have things to do, to *tener (e>ie) cosas (la cosa) que hacer* **14**

have to, to *tener (e>ie) que* **3, 4**

have a barbecue, to *hacer/organizar una barbacoa* **10**

have a party, to *hacer/organizar una fiesta* **10**

have a picnic, to *hacer/organizar un pícnic* **10**

he/she has a Colombian boyfriend/ girlfriend, (because) *tiene un/a novio/-a colombiano/-a, (porque)* **2**

headquarters *sede, la* 15

healthy *sano/-a* 6

hear, to *oír* **15**

heat, to *calentar (e>ie)* **11**

heater *calefacción, la* **9**

heavy *gordo/-a* 5

Hello. *Hola.* **P**

help *ayuda, la* P

help, to *ayudar* 6, **14**

here *aquí* 3

heritage *patrimonio, el* **2**

herself *misma, la; sí misma* 1, 3, 5

high *alto/-a* **3, 5**

high-rise *rascacielos, el* **8**

highway *autopista, la* 13

hike, to *hacer senderismo (el senderismo)* **10**

hill *monte, el; colina, la; cerro, el* 3, 8

himself *mismo, el; sí mismo* 1, 3, 5

Hispanic *hispano/-a* 1

Hispanic-American *hispanoamericano/-a* 2

historic *histórico/-a* **8, 12**

historical *histórico/-a* **8, 12**

history *historia, la* **2**

holiday *(día) festivo, el* **10**

home delivery *a domicilio* 6

homebody *casero/-a* 6

homework *tarea, la; deberes, los* 3, 6

Honduran *hondureño/-a* **1**

honey *miel, la* **11**

horror *de terror* **12**

hospital *hospital, el* **8**

hot (climate) *cálido/-a* **3**

hot chocolate *chocolate caliente, el* 6

hours worked *horas trabajadas, las* 6

house *casa, la* 1, **9**

household chores *quehaceres domésticos, los* 6

housework *labores del hogar, las* **13**

housing *vivienda, la* **8**

How about...? *¿Qué te/le parece...?* 7

How are you? *¿Cómo está/s?, ¿Qué tal?* **14**

How do you say "thank you" in Spanish? *¿Cómo se dice "thank you" en español?* **P**

How do you say this in Spanish? *¿Cómo se dice esto en español?* **P**

How do you write/spell...? *¿Cómo se escribe...?* **P**

How is everything going? *¿Cómo va todo?* **14**

How is everything? *¿Qué tal todo?* **14**

How long...? *¿Cuánto tiempo...?* 6

how many *cuántos/-as* 3

How many times? *¿Cuántas veces?* 6

How much does it cost? *¿Cuánto cuesta?* 4

how nice *qué bien* 2

How often...? *¿Con qué frecuencia...?* 4

hug (each other), to *abrazarse , darse un abrazo* **14**

huge *gran, grande* 2

hugs (to your family) *abrazo (a/para la/su familia), un* **14**

husband *esposo, el* 5

hydroplane *hidroavión, el* 15

hyphen *guion (medio), el* **1**

hypothesis *hipótesis, la* 4

hypothesize, to *hacer hipótesis* 6

I

I do *a mí sí; yo sí* **5**, 6

I don't know *no sé* 3

I don't know (it, that) *no lo sé* 3

I have to leave/go. *Me tengo que ir.* **14**

I live in Boulder. *Vivo en Boulder.* **1**

I own a software company. *Tengo una empresa de informática (la informática).* **1**

I work in a factory. *Trabajo en una fábrica.* **1**

I work in a restaurant. *Trabajo en un restaurante.* **1**

I work in a store. *Trabajo en una tienda.* **1**

I'm 22 years old. *Tengo 22 años.* **1**

I'm a student. *Soy estudiante.* **1**

I'm Argentinian / from Argentina. *Soy argentino/-a.* **1**

I'm sorry. *Lo siento.* 4, **14**

ice cream *helado, el* **11**

identify, to *identificar* 4

if *si* 4

illness *enfermedad, la* **13**

implicate, to *implicar* 4

important product *producto importante, el* **3**

improve my English, to *mejorar mi inglés* **2**

in *en* 1

in a short time *en poco tiempo* 5

in addition (to) *además (de)* 2, 4

in all *en total* 3

in couples *en parejas* 3

in good condition *en buen estado* 4

in many cases *en muchos casos* 4

in pairs *en parejas* 3

in perfect condition *en perfecto estado (el estado)* 9

in relation with/to *en relación con* 6

in Spanish *en español* P

in the afternoon *por la tarde* **6**

in the morning *por la mañana* **6**

in various colors *en varios colores (el color)* **9**

in/at someone's house *en (la) casa de* 4

in/at the end (of) *al final (de)* 4, 6

include, to *incluir* 3

Indian Ocean *océano Índico, el* **3**

indicate, to *señalar* 3

indie music *música independiente, la* **5**

industrial city *ciudad industrial, la* 3

industrial style *de estilo industrial* 9

industry *industria, la* **13**

industry, (glass) *industria (del vidrio), la* 3

inequality *desigualdad, la* **13**

information card *ficha, la* 3

information technology *informática, la* 1

locate, to *ubicar, localizar* 3, 4
location *sitio, el* 4
loft *ático, el* **9**
long *largo/-a* **3**
long-sleeve *de manga larga (la manga)* **4**
look at (oneself), to *mirar(se)* 4
look for, to *buscar* 2, 6
look good, to *tener (ie) buen aspecto* 6
look up words in the dictionary / on the internet, to *buscar palabras en el diccionario / en internet (la palabra; el/la internet)* **2**
lookout *mirador, el* 8
lose (something), to *perder (algo) (e>ie)* 6, **15**
lose your job, to *quedarse sin trabajo (el trabajo)* 7
love *amor, el; de amor* 1, **12**
lovely *bello/-a* 3
lover *amante, el/la* 12
low (temperatures) *bajo/-a* 3
luck *suerte, la* 12
lunch *almuerzo, el* 6
luxury store (boutique) *tienda de lujo (el lujo), la* **8**

M

made (in/with) *elaborado/-a (en/con)* 4
magazine *revista, la* 2
magic show *espectáculo de magia (la magia), el* **10**
main *principal* 1
main character *protagonista, el/la* **12**
mainly *sobre todo* 5
maintain your personal appearance, to *cuidarse* **6**
major *carrera, la* 7
make, to *hacer, fabricar* 2, **13**
make an exchange, to *hacer un intercambio* **2**
make sure, to *asegurarse* 12
make the bed, to *hacer la cama* **6**
mall *centro comercial, el* **8**
man *hombre, el; señor, el* 1, 4
manager *encargado/-a, el/la* 12
manioc *yuca, la* **11**
manner *manera, la* 12
many *mucho/-a/-os/-as* 2, 3
market *mercado, el* 3, **4**
match (sports) *partido, el* **10**
mate *compañero/-a, el/la* 2, **5**

matter *materia, la* 2
me neither *a mí tampoco; yo tampoco* 5, 6
me too *a mí también; yo también* 5, 6
mean, to *significar* P
mean *antipático/-a* **5**
means of communication *medios de comunicación (la comunicación), los* **13**
measure *medida, la* 11
measure, to *medir (i, i)* 5
meat *carne, la* 3, **11**
media *medios de comunicación (la comunicación), los* **13**
medical center *centro médico, el* 1
medication *medicamento, el* **13**
medicine *fármaco, el; medicamento, el; medicina, la* 7, **13**
meditate, to *hacer/practicar meditación (la meditación)* **10**
meet, to *conocer (zc)* 2, 5, **7**
meet some friends, to *ver a los amigos* 2
meet up with (someone), to *encontrarse con (alguien) (o>ue)* **15**
memory *recuerdo, el* 12
message *mensaje, el* 2
metal, (made of) *de metal* **9**
meter *metro, el* **3**
metro station *estación de metro (el metro), la* **8**
Mexican *mexicano/-a* **1**
microscope *microscopio, el* **13**
microwave oven *microondas, el* **9**
mild *suaves (temperaturas); templado (clima)* **3**
milestone *hito, el* 13
milk *leche, la* **11**
million(s) *millón/-es, (el/los)* 3
mind, to *importar* **14**
minimalist style *de estilo minimalista* **9**
minister *ministro, el* 7
minute *minuto, el* 3
mirror *espejo, el* **9**
mishap *contratiempo, el* 12
mix, to *mezclar* **11**
modern *moderno/-a* **4**
moisturizing cream *crema hidratante, la* 6
monarchy, (absolute) *monarquía (absoluta), la* **13**

Monday *lunes, el* 3, **6**
money *dinero, el* **4, 13**
moon *luna, la* 7
more *más* P, 3
Moroccan *marroquí* 1
mosque *mezquita, la* **8**
mostly *sobre todo* 5
mother *madre, la* **5**
mother tongue *lengua materna, la* 2
mount *monte, el* 3
mountain *montaña, la* **3**
mountain range *cordillera, la* **3**
move, to *trasladar* 8
move away, to *retirar, mudarse* **11**, 12
move-in ready *listo/-a para entrar a vivir* **9**
movement *desplazamientos, los* 6
movie *película, la* 2
movie theater *cine, el* 1, 3, **12**
mucho *mucho* 2, 3
murder *asesinato, el* 13
music *música, la* 2, 5
music program *programa musical, el* **12**
music record *álbum, el* 5
musical *musical, el* **12**
musician *músico/-a, el/la* 5
Muslim *musulmán/a el/la* 3
mustache *bigote, el* **5**
mustard *mostaza, la* **11**
My name is... *Yo me llamo...* **P**
my son/daughter (colloquial) *mijo/-a* 14

N

narrate, to *narrar* 7
narrow *angosto/-a* 8
national park *parque nacional, el* P, **3**
nationality *nacionalidad, la* **1**
native *nativo/-a* 2
nature *naturaleza, la* **2**
nature park *parque natural, el* **3**
need, to *necesitar* P
neighbor *vecino/-a, el/la* **14**
neighborhood *barrio, el* 3
neither *tampoco* 5
nephew *sobrino, el* **5**
never *nunca* 6
new *nuevo/-a* 5
new construction *de nueva construcción* **9**
new *novedad, la* 4
news *noticia, la* **12**

news broadcast *informativo, el* **12**

newspaper *diario, el; periódico, el* 2

next *a continuación* 4

next *siguiente* 3

next to *al lado (de)* 3

Nicaraguan *nicaragüense* **1**

nice *agradable* **5**

nice *bonito/-a* 3

niece *sobrina, la* **5**

night *noche, la* 2

nightstand *mesita de noche (la noche), la* **9**

nine *nueve* **P**

nine hundred *novecientos/-as* **4**

nineteen *diecinueve* **P**

ninety *noventa* **P**

ninety-nine *noventa y nueve* **P**

no *no* P

no any *ninguno/-a* 3

no one *nadie* 7

nobility *nobleza, la* **13**

noisy *ruidoso/-a* **8**

none *ninguno/-a* 3

normal *normal* **5**

normally *normalmente* 5, **6**

north *norte, el* **3**

North America *América del Norte* **3**

not anyone *nadie* 7

not anything *nada* 6

Not bad. *Pasándola.* **14**

not ever *nunca* **6**

not me *a mí no* **5**

not well *mal* 5

notebook *cuaderno, el* **P**

nothing *nada* 6

noun *nombre, el; sustantivo, el* 2, 3

novel *novela, la* 2, **4**

novelty *novedad, la* 4

now *ahora* 6

number *número, el* P

numbered *numerado/-a* 3

numerous *numeroso/-a* 3

nurse *enfermero/-a, el/la* 5

nut *fruto seco, el* **11**

O

oats *avena, la* **11**

obtain, to *obtener (e>ie)* 4, **14**

o'clock *en punto* **6**

occasion *vez, la* 3

ocean *océano, el* **3**

Oceania *Oceanía* **3**

ocupy, to *ocupar* 4

of *de* P

of course *claro* 2

offer, to *ofrecer (zc)* 2

office *oficina, la* 6

official language *lengua oficial, la* **3**

often *a menudo* **6**

oil *aceite, el; petróleo, el* **11, 13**

OK *listo, órale* 4, 14

old (part of) town *casco antiguo, el* **8**

old *antiguo/-a* 3, **8**

older *mayor* 5

older person *persona mayor, la* 6

olive oil *aceite de oliva (la oliva), el* **11**

Olympics *olimpiadas, las* 7

on the dot *en punto* **6**

on the shores/banks of *a orillas de* 3

on time *a tiempo* 7

on your behalf *de tu parte* 5

one *uno* **P**

one billion *mil millones (el millón)* **4**

one hundred *cien* **P, 4**

one hundred and one *ciento uno/-a* **4**

one hundred and two *ciento dos* **4**

one hundred meters (race) *metros lisos, los 100* 7

one hundred thousand *cien mil* **4**

one million *un millón* **4**

one thousand *mil* **4**

onion *cebolla, la* **11**

only *solo* 3

only one *único/-a* 4

open *abierto/-a* **5, 10**

open, to *abrir* 6

open bar *barra libre, la* **10**

open-floor plan kitchen *cocina americana, la* **9**

opera *ópera, la* **5**

opine, to *opinar* 3

oppose, to *oponerse* 12

opt for, to *optar por* 4

orange (color) *anaranjado/-a* **4**

orange (fruit) *naranja, la* **11**

order *encargo, el* 12

order a coffee, to *pedir (i, i) un café* 14

organize a barbecue, to *hacer/organizar una barbacoa* **10**

organize a party, to *hacer/organizar una fiesta* **10**

organize a picnic, to *hacer/organizar un pícnic* **10**

original *original* **4**

other *otro/-a/-os/-as* 3

our *nuestro/-a* P

outside *fuera (de casa)* 6

oven *horno, el* **11**

overlook *mirador, el* 8

own *propio/-a/-os/-as* 5

P

Pacific Ocean *océano Pacífico, el* **3**

pack a suitcase, to *hacer la maleta* 4

package *paquete, el* **11**

packaging *empaque, el* 11

packet *paquete, el* **11**

page *página, la* **P**

paint a painting, to *pintar un cuadro* **7**

painted *pintado/-a* 4

palace *palacio, el* 3

palm *palma, la* 4

Panamanian *panameño/-a* **1**

pants *pantalones, los* **4**

paper *papel, el* 4, **12, 13**

paraglider *parapente, el* 14

Paraguayan *paraguayo/-a* **1**

parents *padres, los; los papás* **5**

park *parque, el* **8**

parking garage *estacionamiento, el* **8**

parking lot *estacionamiento, el* **8**

part *papel, el; parte, la* 4, 6, **12, 13**

part (auto) *pieza (de automóvil), la* 3

participate in a race/competition/marathon, to *participar en una carrera/competición/maratón* **10**

participate in an exchange program, to *hacer un intercambio* 2

participation fee *tasa de participación, la* 6

partner *pareja, la; compañero/-a, el/la* 2, 3, 4, **5**

party *fiesta, la* 1

party animal *fiestero/-a* 6

party loving *fiestero/-a* 6

pass, to *pasar* 3, 4, 7

passing *paso, el* 11

passionate *apasionado/-a* 5

passport *pasaporte, el* **4**

pasta *pasta, la* **11**

pastime *afición, la; pasatiempo, el* **1**

patient *enfermo/-a* 6

pay, to *pagar* 4

peach *durazno, el* **11**

peak (mountain) *pico, el* **3**

peanut *cacahuate, el* **11**

pear *pera, la* **11**

pedestrian zone *zona peatonal, la* **8**

peel, to *pelar* **11**

pen *bolígrafo, el* **P**

penguin *pingüino, el* **1**

penicillin *penicilina, la* **13**

peninsula *península, la* **3**

people *gente, la* **2**

pepper *pimiento, el* **11**

perform, to *desempeñar* **12**

performance *actuación, la* **3**

performance *rendimiento, el* **10**

performer *intérprete, el/la* **5**

perfume *perfume, el* **6**

permit, to *permitir* **4**

person in charge *encargado/-a, el/la* **12**

personal information *datos personales, los* **1**

personal information *información personal, la* **P**

personality traits *carácter, el* **5**

Peruvian *peruano/-a* **1**

petroleum industry *industria petrolera, la* **4**

pharmacy *farmacia, la* **8**

photograph *fotografía (foto), la* **2**

photographer *fotógrafo/-a, el/la* **1**

physical appearance *aspecto físico, el* **5**

physically *físicamente* **5**

pick up, to *ir a buscar, recoger* **2, 6, 12**

picture *fotografía (foto), la* **2**

piece of fruit *pieza de fruta (la fruta), la* **11**

piece *pedazo, el* **11**

pineapple *piña, la* **11**

pink *rosa* **4**

place *lugar, el; sitio, el* **3**

place, to *colocar* **4, 11**

place of residence *lugar de residencia (la residencia), el* **1**

plague *plaga, la* **14**

plaid *de cuadros* **5**

plan, to *planificar* **6**

plane *avión, el* **13**

plant *planta, la* **9**

plantation *finca, la* **12**

play *obra de teatro, la* **10**

play, to *jugar (u>ue)* **1, 2**

play (an instrument), to *tocar (un instrumento)* **1**

play a role, to *interpretar* **12**

play a volleyball/baseball game, to *jugar un partido de voleibol (el voleibol)/beisbol (el beisbol)* **10**

play board games, to *jugar juegos (el juego) de mesa (la mesa)* **10**

play chess, to *jugar ajedrez (el ajedrez)* **10**

play guitar, to *tocar la guitarra* **1**

play poker, to *jugar póker (el póker)* **10**

play sports, to *hacer deporte (el deporte)* **2, 6**

play the role (of), to *hacer el papel (de)* **12**

play videogames, to *jugar videojuegos (el videojuego)* **2**

played by *protagonizado/-a por* **7**

player *jugador/a, el/la* **7**

playroom *sala de juegos (el juego), la* **9**

please *por favor (el favor)* **P, 14**

plot *argumento, el; trama, la* **12**

point *punto, el* **1**

point out, to *señalar* **3**

political party *partido político, el* **13**

political post *cargo político, el* **7**

political power *poder político, el* **13**

political prisoner *preso político, el* **13**

political system *sistema político, el* **13**

pollution *contaminación, la* **8**

Polynesia *Polinesia, la* **7**

Polynesian *polinesio/-a* **7**

poor *pobre* **8**

poorly *mal* **5**

populated *poblado/-a* **3**

population *habitantes, los/las* **3**

population *población, la* **3**

pork *cerdo, el* **11**

portion *ración, la* **11**

post office *oficina de correos (el correo), la* **8**

poster *cartel, el* **1**

pot *olla, la* **11**

potato *papa, la* **11**

pour, to *echar* **11**

power *poder, el* **13**

powerful *poderoso/-a* **12**

practice pronunciation, to *practicar la pronunciación* **2**

practice Spanish/English, to *practicar español/inglés* **2**

precious *precioso/-a* **3**

prefer, to *preferir (e>ie)* **3, 4**

preference *gusto, el* **5**

premiere *estreno, el* **10**

premiere date *fecha de estreno, la* **12**

premises *local, el* **10**

prepare a meal, to *preparar la comida* **6**

preparation *elaboración, la* **3**

preposition *preposición, la* **2**

present *regalo, el* **5**

press *imprenta, la* **13**

price *precio, el* **4**

primary language *lengua materna, la* **2**

prison *carcelario/-a* **12**

prisoner *prisionero/-a, el/la* **13**

prize *premio, el* **6, 7**

produce, to *generar, fabricar* **4, 13**

producer *productor/a, el/la* **2**

profession *profesión, la* **1**

profile *perfil, el* **5**

profits *ganancias, las* **4**

program *programa, el* **12**

program, to *programar* **6**

programming *programación, la* **6**

projector *proyector, el* **P**

promenade *paseo, el* **8**

promote, to *promover (o>ue)* **2**

pronoun *pronombre, el* **5**

pronounce, to *pronunciar* **1**

pronunciation *pronunciación, la* **2**

propose, to *proponer* **1**

protect, to *proteger* **2**

provide, to *proporcionar* **3**

provider *proveedor/a, el/la* **4**

province *provincia, la* **3**

provoke, to *provocar* **3**

pub *bar, el* **8**

publish, to *publicar* **3**

publish a book, to *publicar un libro* **7**

published *publicado/-a* **3**

publishing house *editorial, la* **7**

Puerto Rican *puertorriqueño/-a* **1**

purchase, to *adquirir* **4**

purple *lila* **4**

purse *bolso, el* **4**

put, to *poner* **6, 11**

put on make-up, to *maquillarse* **6**

put on moisturizer, to *poner(se) crema (la crema)* **6**

put on perfume, to *poner(se) perfume* **6**

Appendix 3

Q

quality *calidad, la* 3
quantifier *cuantificador, el* 3
question *pregunta, la* 1

R

racquetball player *raquetbolista, el/la* 7
radio *radio, la* **5**
rain forest *selva, la* **3**
rainy (climate) *lluvioso/-a* **3**
reaction, (personal) *reacción (personal), la* 3
read, to *leer* **1**
read books/newspapers/magazines/ novels, to *leer libros/periódicos/ revistas/novelas (el libro; el periódico; la revista; la novela)* **2**
read Latin-American/Spanish literature, to *leer literatura hispanoamericana/ española (la literatura)* **2**
reading *lectura, la* 4
reaffirm, to *reafirmar* 12
real *real, de verdad* 6
reality *realidad, la* 7
realize, to *darse cuenta* **15**
reason *razón, la* **2**
receive a Nobel prize, to *recibir el premio Nobel* **7**
recent *reciente* 6
reclaim, to *reivindicar* 11
recognition *reconocimiento, el* 3
recognize, to *reconocer (zc)* 5
recommend, to *recomendar (e>ie)* 2
recommendation *recomendación, la* 2
record *disco, el* **4**
record, to *grabar* 3
record an album, to *grabar un disco* **7**
recover, to *recuperar* 12
recruit, to *reclutar* 12
red *rojo/-a* **4**
red-haired *pelirrojo/-a* **5**
reduced ticket price *entrada reducida, la* **10**
refer to, to *referirse (ie, i) a* 3
reflect, to *reflejar* 9
refrigerator *refrigerador, el* **9**
refuse, to *rechazar* 12
reggaeton *reguetón, el* **5**
reject, to *rechazar* 12
related (to) *relacionado/-a (con)* 2

relationship *parentesco, el* 5
relative *familiar, el/la* 5
relax, to *relajarse* **10**
religion *religión, la* **13**
remember, to *recordar (o>ue)* 6
remove, to *quitar, sacar* **11**
renovated *renovado* 8
rent, to *alquilar* 4
repeat, to *repetir (i, i)* P
report *reportaje, el* **12**
repressed *reprimido* 10
reserve, to *reservar* 10
residential neighborhood *barrio residencial, el* **8**
resource *recurso, el* P
respectively *respectivamente* 4
rest, to *descansar* 6
restaurant *restaurante, el* **8**
restored *renovado* 8
result *resultado, el* 5
résumé *currículum, el* 7
retire, to *retirarse* **7**
return, to *volver (o>ue); regresar; devolver (o>ue)* 6, **14**
return home, to *regresar a casa* **6**
reveal, to *revelar* 12
revenge *venganza, la* 12
rice, (brown) *arroz (integral), el* **11**
rich *rico/-a* 3, 4, **8**
ride, to *montar* 3
ride a horse, to *montar a caballo (el caballo)* 4
right *derecho, el* 7, **13**
right? *¿no?; ¿verdad? (la verdad)* P, 4
rival *rival, el/la* 3
river *río, el* **3**
road network *red de caminos (el camino)* **13**
roast, to *asar, hornear* **11**
rob, to *robar* **15**
role-play *juego de rol, el* 3
role *papel, el* 4, **12, 13**
rom-com *comedia romántica, la* **12**
romantic *romántico/-a* 5, **12**
room *espacio, el; habitación, la* 4, **9**
roommate *compañero/-a de cuarto* 5
roomy *espacioso/-a* **9**
round *redondo/-a* **9**
rubber *caucho, el* 12
ruins, (Mayan) *ruinas (mayas), las* 3
rule *regla, la* 2

run, to *correr* **10**
run away, to *huir (y)* 15
run into (someone), to *encontrarse con (alguien) (o>ue)* **15**
Russian *ruso, el* 5

S

sacred *sagrado/-a* 12
safe *seguro/-a* 4
salad *ensalada, la* **11**
sale *venta, la* 4
salt *sal, la* **11**
salty *salado/-a* 15
Salvadoran *salvadoreño/-a* 1
same to you *igualmente* 5, **14**
sand *arena, la* **3**
sandals *sandalias, las* **4**
Saturday *sábado, el* **6**
sauce *salsa, la* **11**
saucepan *cacerola, la* **11**
sauté, to *saltear* **11**
save, to *ahorrar, reservar* 4, **11**
say good-bye, to *despedirse (i, i)* **14**
say, to *decir (i, i)* P, **15**
scale, to *escalar* **10**
scarf *bufanda, la* **4**
scene *escena, la* **12**
schedule *horario, el* 6, **10**
school *escuela, la* 3, **8**
science *ciencia, la* 3
science fiction (sci-fi) *de ciencia ficción* **12**
scream, to *gritar* 6
script *guion, el* **12**
scriptwriter *guionista, el/la* **12**
scuba dive, to *bucear* **10**
scuba diving *buceo, el* 4
sea, (Caribbean) *mar (Caribe), el* **3**
seal *sello, el* 4
season *estación, la; temporada, la* **3, 12**
season *estación, la* P, **3**
seat *plaza, la; asiento, el* 3, **8**, 9, **14**
second (ordinal number) *segundo/-a* 3
second (time) *segundo, el* 3
second hand *de segunda mano (la mano)* 4
secure *seguro/-a* 4
See you later! *¡Hasta luego!* P, **14**
See you soon. *Hasta pronto.* P
See you! *¡Nos vemos!* P, **14**
seem, to *parecer (zc)* 4, 5

segment *bloque, el* 6
select, to *elegir (i, i)* 2, **4**
selected *elegido/-a* 3
sell, to *vender* **4**
seller *vendedor/a, el/la* 4
send, to *enviar* 12
sensitive *sensible* 5
serious *serio/-a* **5**
serrano chili *chile serrano, el* **11**
serve, to *servir (i, i)* **11**
service *servicio, el* **10**
services *servicios, los* 8, **13**
setback *contratiempo, el* 12
seven *siete* **P**
seven hundred *setecientos/-as* **4**
seventeen *diecisiete* **P**
seventy *setenta* **P**
shake hands, to *darse la mano* **14**
shampoo *champú, el* **4**
share, to *compartir* 1
shave, to *afeitarse* **6**
sheet of paper *hoja de papel (el papel),
    la* **P**
shellfish *marisco, el* **11**
ship *barco, el* 7
shipbuilding *construcción naval, la* 3
shirt *camisa, la* **4**
shoes *zapatos, los* **4**
shop *tienda, la* 1
shopping *compra, la* **4**
shopping cart *carrito, el* 4
short *breve; bajo/-a* 3, **5**
short film *cortometraje, el* 10, **12**
short-sleeve *de manga corta (la
    manga)* **4**
shorts *pantalones cortos, los* **4**
show *espectáculo, el* **10**
show, to *mostrar (o>ue)* 6
shower *regadera, la* 9
showing *función, la* **10**
shy *tímido/-a* **5**
siblings *hermanos, los* **5**
sick person *enfermo/-a* 6
silk *seda, la* **4**
silver *plata, la* 2
simply *simplemente* 6
sing, to *cantar* **1**
singer *cantante, el/la* **1, 5**
sister *hermana, la* **5**
sit, to *sentar(se) (e>ie)* 6, **15**
six *seis* **P**

six hundred *seiscientos/-as* **4**
sixteen *dieciséis* **P**
sixth *sexto/-a* 4
sixty *sesenta* **P**
size *talla, la* **4**
ski slope *pista de esquí, la* 3
ski, to *esquiar* **1**
skirt *falda, la* **4**
skyscraper *rascacielos, el* **8**
slave *esclavo/-a, el/la* **13**
slavery *esclavitud, la* **13**
sleep, to *dormir (ue, u)* **6**
sleepyhead *dormilón/-a* 6
sleeve *manga, la* 4
sleeveless *sin mangas (la manga)* **4**
slice *loncha, la* **11**
slowly *despacio* P
small *pequeño/-a* 3, **6**
smart *inteligente* 1, **5**
smartphone *celular, el* **P**
sneakers *tenis, los* **4**
snow, to *nevar (e>ie)* 3
soap *jabón, el* **4**
soccer *fútbol, el* **1**
sociable *sociable* **5**
social contact *contacto social, el* **14**
socio-economic data *datos
    socioeconómicos, los* **13**
soda *refresco, el* **11**
sofa *sofá, el* 9
soft drink *refresco, el* **11**
solve, to *resolver (o>ue)* 3
some *algún, alguno/-a/-os/-as* 1
somebody *alguien* 2
someone *alguien* 2
something *algo* 3
sometimes *a veces* **6**
son *hijo, el* **5**
song *canción, la* **5**
soon after *poco tiempo después* 7
Sorry, I didn't understand. *Lo siento,
    no entendí.* **P**
soul music *música soul, la* 5
sound *sonido, el* 1
sound, to *sonar (o>ue)* 5
soundtrack *banda sonora, la* **12**
soup *sopa, la* **11**
south *sur, el* **3**
South America *América del Sur* **3**
space *espacio, el* 4, 7
spacious *amplio/-a, espacioso/-a* **8, 9**

spaghetti straps *de tirantes (el tirante)* 4
Spaniard *español/a* **1**
Spanish *español/a; español, el* **1**, 2
Spanish teacher *profesor/a de español
    (el español), el/la* **1**
sparkling water *agua con gas, el* **11**
speak, to *hablar* **P**
speaker (of a language) *hablante, el/la* 2
specialized *especializado/-a* 4
speech *habla, el* 2
speech *discurso, el* 15
spell, to *deletrear* 1
spend (time), to *pasar* 3, 4, 7
spend the day at home / the beach, to
    pasar el día en casa / la playa **10**
spend the day with the family/friends, to
    *pasar el día con la familia/(los)
    amigos* **10**
spice *especia, la* **11**
spoon *cuchara, la* **11**
sports *deporte, el* 2
sports broadcast *retransmisión
    deportiva, la* **12**
sportswear *ropa deportiva, la* **4**
sporty *deportista* **5**
spread, to *extenderse (e>ie)* 3
spring *primavera, la* **3**
square *cuadrado/-a* **9**
square kilometer *kilómetros
    cuadrados, los* **3**
squeeze, to *exprimir* **11**
stand out, to *destacar* 3
stand up, to *parar(se)* **15**
standing *parado/-a* 11
star, (pop) *estrella (del pop), la* 6
start a company, to *fundar una
    empresa* **7**
start to work, to *empezar (e>ie) a
    trabajar* **6, 7**
state *estado, el* 3
station *estación, la* P
statue *estatua, la* 3
Statue of Liberty *Estatua de la
    Libertad, la* 3
stay at home, to *quedarse en casa (la
    casa)* **10**
step (on), to *pisar* 7
stepbrother *hermanastro, el* **5**
stepsister *hermanastra, la* **5**
sticks *palillos, los* 11
still *todavía* 6

Appendix 3

stir, to *remover (o>ue)* **11**
stir-fry, to *saltear* **11**
stone *piedra, la* 8
stop, to *parar* 6, **15**
store *tienda, la; local, el* 1, **10**
story *planta, la* **9**
storyline *trama, la* **12**
straight hair *pelo liso, el* **5**
strange *peculiar* 6
strawberry *fresa, la* **11**
street *calle, la* **8**
strengthen, to *fortalecer* 2
stressful *estresante* 6
struggle *lucha activa, la* 7
student *estudiante, el/la* **1**
studio *estudio, el* **9**
study *estudio, el* 6
study at a Mexican/Spanish university, to *estudiar en una universidad mexicana/española* **2**
study Spanish/English, to *estudiar español/inglés (el español; el inglés)* **2**
studying room *cuarto de estudio, el* **9**
stuff, to *rellenar* **11**
style *estilo, el* 5
subject *asunto, el* 5
subject *sujeto, el* 1
submariner *submarinista, el/la* 15
subtitled *subtitulado/-a* **10**
sugar *azúcar, el/la* **11**
suggestion *sugerencia, la* 2
suitable for general public *público (el público) general* **10**
suitcase *maleta, la* **4**
summarize, to *resumir* 3
summer *verano, el* **3**
summer camp *campamento de verano (el verano), el* 5
sunbathe, to *tomar el sol* **10**
Sunday *domingo, el* **6**
sunglasses *gafas de sol, las* **4**
sunscreen *protector solar, el* **4**
sunset *atardecer* **8**
superhero *de superhéroes* **12**
supermarket *supermercado, el* **8**
support, to *apoyar* 7
supposedly *supuestamente* 15
surely *seguramente* 6
surf, to *hacer/practicar surf (el surf)* **10**
surprised *sorprendido/-a* 12
surrender, to *rendirse (e>i)* 12

surrounded *rodeado/-a* 14
survivor *superviviente, el/la* 12
suspect, to *sospechar* 12
suspicious *desconfiado/-a* 14
suspicious *sospechoso/-a* 12
sustainable *sustentable* 4
sweater *suéter, el* **4**
sweetheart *corazón* 1
swim, to *hacer/practicar natación (la natación)* **10**
switch jobs, to *cambiar de trabajo* 7
synagogue *sinagoga, la* **8**
synopsis *sinopsis, la* **12**

T

T-shirt *camiseta, la* **4**
table *mesa, la* **P, 9**
table *tabla, la; cuadro, el* 3, 5
tablespoon *cucharada, la* **11**
take, to *tomar* 3
take a break, to *hacer una pausa* 6
take a cooking/creative writing class, to *hacer un curso de cocina (la cocina)/ escritura (la escritura) creativa* **10**
take a nap, to *dormir (ue, u) la siesta* 6
take a shower, to *ducharse* **6**
take a trip, to *hacer un viaje* 7
take care of, to *cuidar* 4, **6, 13**
take care of yourself, to *cuidarse* **6**
take into account, to *tener (e>ie) en cuenta* 14
take out, to *sacar* **11**
take pictures, to *tomar fotos (la fotografía)* **2**
take place, to *tener (e>ie) lugar (el lugar)* 5
take revenge, to *vengarse* 12
talented *talentoso/-a* 1
talk, to *hablar* P
talk about interesting topics, to *hablar de temas (el tema) interesantes* **2**
talk about, to *hablar sobre* 4
Talk soon. *Hablamos.* **14**
Talk soon. (on the phone) *Nos llamamos.* **14**
talk to Hispanic friends, to *hablar con amigos hispanos* **2**
talkative *hablador/a* **5**
tall *alto/-a* **3, 5**
tank *depósito, el* 15
task *tarea, la* 3

taste *gusto, el* 5
taxi *taxi, el* P
taxi driver *taxista, el/la* **1**
tea *té, el* **11**
team *equipo, el* 3
teaspoon *cucharadita, la* **11**
telephone *teléfono, el* **4**
telescope *telescopio, el* **13**
television set *televisor, el* **P**
tell, to *decir (i, i), contar (o>ue)* P, 6, **12, 15**
temperate (climate) *templado/-a* **3**
temperature *temperatura, la* **3**
ten *diez* P
ten thousand *diez mil* **4**
tend to do something, to *soler (o>ue)* 6
tennis *tenis, el* **1**
tennis player *tenista, el/la* 1
terrace *terraza, la* **9**
testimony *testimonio, el* 6
textile industry *industria textil, la* 4
thank you *gracias* **P**
thank you very much *muchas gracias* 4
thanks to *gracias a* 3
that *que* 5
that way *de ese modo* 4
the bad thing *lo malo* 6
the Big Apple *Gran Manzana, la* 3
the forties *años 40, los* 5
the good thing *lo bueno* 6
the majority *mayoría, la* 6
the most important thing *lo más importante* 6
the opposite *lo contrario* 4
theme *tema, el* 2
then *entonces* 6
there *allí* 3
thermometer *termómetro, el* **13**
thin *delgado/-a* **5**
thing *cosa, la* P
think, to *pensar (e>ie)* 3
thirteen *trece* **P**
thirty *treinta* **P**
thirty-eight *treinta y ocho* **P**
thirty-five *treinta y cinco* **P**
thirty-four *treinta y cuatro* **P**
thirty-nine *treinta y nueve* **P**
thirty-one *treinta y uno* **P**
thirty-seven *treinta y siete* **P**
thirty-six *treinta y seis* **P**
thirty-three *treinta y tres* **P**

thirty-two *treinta y dos* **P**

this way *de esta forma* 5

thought *pensamiento, el* 3

thread *hilo, el* 4

three *tres* **P**

three hundred *trescientos/-as* **4**

Three Kings Day *Día de Reyes, el* 6

through *por* 3

Thursday *jueves, el* **6**

ticket *boleto, el; boleta, la; cover, la; la entrada* 4, **10**

time *vez, la; hora, la* 3, 6

time, (free) *tiempo (libre), el* 2

time period *época, la* 5

times a day, (three) *veces (la vez) al día, (tres)* **6**

times a month *veces (la vez) al mes* 6

times a week, (three) *veces (la vez) a la semana (tres)* **6**

times a year, (three) *veces (la vez) al año (tres)* **6**

title *título, el* **12**

to work in a company, (in order to) *trabajar en una compañía (para)* **2**

to *para* **2**

today *hoy* 3

together *juntos/-as* 7

tolerate, to *soportar* 12

tomato *tomate, el* **11**

tomorrow *mañana* 3

too *también* 1

too much *demasiado/-a* 6

toothbrush *cepillo de dientes (el diente), el* **4**

toothpaste *pasta de dientes (el diente), la* **4**

topic *tema, el* 2

total *total, el* 4

totally *totalmente* 7

touch, to *tocar* 15

tourism *turismo, el* **13**

tourist destination *ciudad turística, la* 3

town *pueblo, el* 6

townsquare *plaza, la* 3, **8**, 9

traditional food *comida tradicional, la* **10**

translation *traducción, la* 4

translator *traductor/a, el/la* 7

transport network *red de transporte (el transporte)* **13**

trapeze artist *trapecista, el/la* 7

travel, (in order to) *viajar, (para)* **2**

travel blog *blog de viajes (el viaje), el* 3

travel, to *viajar* **1**

treason *traición, la* 12

tree *árbol, el* 15

trial *juicio, el* 13

trick *truco, el* 4

trip *excursión, la* 4

trip *viaje, el* 3

tropical (climate) *tropical* **3**

trousers *pantalones, los* **4**

true *verdadero/-a* 2

try, to *intentar* 5

Tuesday *martes, el* **6**

tuna *atún, el* **11**

turkey *pavo, el* **11**

turtle *tortuga, la* 3

TV *televisión, la* 2

TV program with news and interviews *magacín, el* **12**

TV series *serie, la* 2

twelve *doce* **P**

twenty *veinte* **P**

twenty thousand *veinte mil* **4**

twenty-eight *veintiocho* **P**

twenty-five *veinticinco* **P**

twenty-four *veinticuatro* **P**

twenty-nine *veintinueve* **P**

twenty-one *veintiuno* **P**

twenty-seven *veintisiete* **P**

twenty-six *veintiséis* **P**

twenty-three *veintitrés* **P**

twenty-two *veintidós* **P**

two *dos* **P**

two hundred *doscientos/-as* **4**

two hundred thousand *doscientos/-as mil* **4**

two million *dos millones (el millón)* **4**

two thousand *dos mil* **4**

typical dish *plato típico, el* 3

type *estilo, el* 5

type (of) *tipo (de), el* 3

typical *típico/-a* 3

typical food *comida típica, la* **3**

U

ugly *feo/-a* 5

UN (United Nations) *ONU (Organización de las Naciones Unidas), la* 7

unbreakable *inquebrantable* 12

uncle *tío, el* **5**

under *debajo* 5

under the auspices/sponsorship of *bajo los auspicios* 12

underline, to *subrayar* 12

underline *guion bajo, el* 1

underscore *guion bajo, el* 1

understand, to *entender (e>ie)* P

understand a language well, to *comprender bien una lengua* **2**

underwear *ropa interior, la* **4**

unfurnished *sin amueblar* **9**

union *fusión, la* 5

unit of measure *unidad de medida, la* **3**

unite, to *fusionar* 5

United States *Estados Unidos, los* 1

university *universidad, la* 2

university campus *ciudad universitaria, la* 3

unknown *desconocido/-a* 7

unpaid work *trabajo no remunerado, el* 6

unpleasant *antipático/-a* **5**

up to *hasta* 4

upload, to *subir* 4, 6, **15**

Uruguayan *uruguayo/-a* **1**

use the internet, to *usar internet (el/la)* **2**

used *usado/-a* 3

user *usuario/-a, el/la* 4

V

vacation *vacaciones, las* 2

vacation property *villa, la* **9**

vaccine *vacuna, la* 13

vain *vanidoso/-a* 6

valley *valle, el* **3**

varied *variado/-a* 3

variety *variedad, la* 2

vase *jarrón, el* **9**

veal *res, la* **11**

vendor *vendedor/a, el/la* 4

Venezuelan *venezolano/-a* **1**

vengeance *venganza, la* 12

very *muy* 3

very charming *con mucho encanto (el encanto)* **8**

very good *buenísimo/-a* 5

very good quality *de buena calidad (la calidad)* 3

very important *importantísimo/-a* 6

very lively *con mucha vida (la vida)* **8**

video game *videojuego, el* 2

Appendix 3

view *vista, la* **8**
villa *villa, la* **9**
village *pueblo, el* **6**
vinegar *vinagre, el* **11**
vinyl *vinilo, el* **5**
visited *visitado/-a* **2**
voice *voz, la* **3**
volcanic island *isla volcánica, la* **3**
volcano *volcán, el* **3**
vote, to *votar* **13**

W

waiter *mesero, el* **1**
waitress *mesera, la* **1**
wake up, to *despertarse (e>ie)* **6**
walk, to *andar* **1**
wall *pared, la* **9**
want, to *querer (e>ie)* **2**
war *guerra, la* **1, 13**
war movie *película bélica, la* **12**
warm *familiar* **6**
washing machine *lavadora, la* **9**
waste *desecho, el* **4**
wastepaper basket *papelera, la* **P**
watch a TV series, to *ver una serie* **2**
watch movies/series in Spanish, to *ver películas (la película) / series (la serie) en español* **2**
watch TV, to *ver (la) televisión* **2**
watch videos, to *ver videos (el video)* **1**
water *agua, el* **4, 11**
water sport *deporte acuático, el* **5**
wave hello/good-bye, to *decir hola/ adiós con la mano* **14**
way *manera, la* **12**
we *nosotros/-as* **1**
weather *tiempo, el* **3**
weaving *tejeduría (wayúu), la* **4**
web page *página web, la* **2**
Wednesday *miércoles, el* **6**
week *semana, la* **3**
weekend *fin de semana (la semana), el* **6**
weekend trip *viaje de fin de semana (la semana), el* **4**
weight *peso, el* **11**
well *bien, pues* **2, 3**
well located *bien ubicado/-a* **9**
well-known *conocido/-a* **3**
west *oeste, el* **3**

western *del oeste* **12**
wet (climate) *húmedo/-a* **3**
whale *ballena, la* **4**
what (interrogative) *qué* P
What a surprise! *¡Qué sorpresa (la sorpresa)!* **14**
What can I get you? *¿Qué te/le traigo?, Qué te/le apetece tomar?, ¿Qué quiere/s tomar?* **14**
What did you say? *¿Cómo dices?* P
What time is it? *¿Qué hora es?* **6**
What time...? *¿A qué hora...?* **6**
What would you like to have? *Qué te/ le apetece tomar?, ¿Qué quiere/s tomar?* **14**
What would you like to have?, What can I get you? *¿Qué te/le provoca tomar?* **14**
What would you like? *¿Qué desea/n?* **14**
What's new? *¿Qué hay de nuevo?* **14**
What's the meaning of...? *¿Qué significa...?* **P**
What's your name? *¿Cómo se/te llama/s?* **P**
wheel *rueda, la* **13**
when *cuando* **4**
where (interrogative) *adónde* **5**
where (interrogative) *dónde* **3**
which (interrogative) *cuál/-es* **3**
while *mientras* **5**
whip, to *batir* **11**
white *blanco/-a* **4**
White House *Casa Blanca, la* **3**
who (interrogative) *quién* **1**
why (interrogative) *por qué* **6**
wide *amplio/-a* **8, 9**
wife *esposa, la* **5**
Will you bring me...? *¿Me trae/s...?* **14**
Will you lend me... *¿Me presta/s...?* **14**
Will you pass me... *¿Me pasa/s...?* **14**
win an award, to *ganar un premio* **7**
win an Oscar, to *ganar un Óscar* **7**
window *ventana, la* **9**
wine *vino, el* **3, 11**
winter *invierno, el* **3**
with *con* **1, 2**
with few amenities *con pocas comodidades (la comodidad)* **8**
with me *conmigo* **5**
with pleasure *con gusto (el gusto)* **14**

with subtitles *con subtítulos (el subtítulo)* **10**
with views *con vista (la vista)* **9**
without *sin* **3**
without a doubt *sin duda (la duda)* **4**
woman *señora, la; mujer, la* **1, 5**
wonderful *maravilloso/-a* **3**
wood, (made of) *de madera* **9**
wool *lana, la* **4**
word *palabra, la* **P**
work *trabajo, el; obra, la* **1, 7**
work, to *funcionar* **6**
work as a doctor, to *ejercer como médico* **12**
work day *jornada laboral, la* **14**
work of art *obra de arte, la* **10**
work trip *viaje de trabajo (el trabajo), el* **4**
working-class neighborhood *barrio obrero, el* **8**
world *mundo, el* **2**
world, (whole) *mundo, (todo el)* **3**
World Heritage Site *Patrimonio de la Humanidad, el* **2**
worldwide *mundial* **10**
wow (colloquial) *órale* **14**
write a diary/emails/messages, to *escribir un diario/correos electrónicos/mensajes (el correo electrónico; el mensaje)* **2**
write, to *escribir* P, **1**
writer *escritor/a, el/la* **7**
writing *escritura, la* **13**
written *escrito/-a* **4**

Y

yard *jardín, el* **9**
year *año, el* **1**
yell, to *gritar* **6**
yellow *amarillo/-a* **4**
yes *sí* P
yogurt *yogur, el* **11**
you are welcome *de nada* **14**
you too *igualmente* **5, 14**
young *joven, pequeño/-a* **1, 3, 6**
youngest daughter *hija menor, la* **12**
youngest son *hijo menor, el* **12**
youth *juventud, la* **7**
yuca *yuca, la* **11**

Z

zero *cero* **P**
zoo *zoológico, el* **1**
zucchini *calabacita, la* **11**

Credits

TEXT CREDITS

Lesson 6
p. 134: http://blog.freniche.com (used with permission of Diego Freniche)

Lesson 8
p. 178: www.yaencontre.com (used with permission from the publisher)

IMAGE CREDITS

Preliminary lesson
p. 2: kali9/iStockphoto.com; **p. 3 (t):** shironosov/iStockphoto.com; **p. 3 (b):** MarkVorobev/Dreamstime.com; **p. 4:** Alejandro Milà; **p. 6-1:** Difusión/Pearson; **p. 6-2:** Vykkdraygo/Dreamstime.com; **p. 6-3:** Roberto Pirola/Dreamstime.com; **p. 6-4:** Richard Thomas/Dreamstime.com; **p. 6-5:** Greenland/Dreamstime.com; **p. 6-6:** Eskaylim/Dreamstime.com; **p. 6-7:** victorgeorgiev/iStockphoto.com; **p. 6-8:** Surut Wattanamaetee/Dreamstime.com; **p. 6-9:** Ijansempoi/Dreamstime.com; **p. 6-10:** Vasabii/Dreamstime.com; **p. 6-11:** Firmafotografen/iStockphoto.com; **p. 6-12:** Rangizzz/Dreamstime.com; **p. 6-13:** Dio5050/Dreamstime.com; **p. 8-1a:** Matyas Rehak/Dreamstime.com; **p. 8-1b:** FrankvandenBergh/iStockphoto.com; **p. 8-1c:** Toniflap/Dreamstime.com; **p. 8-2a:** Christin Millhill/Dreamstime.com; **p. 8-2b:** Steven Cukrov/Dreamstime.com; **p. 8-3:** Bruno Monteny/Dreamstime.com; **p. 8-4a:** Czuber/Dreamstime.com; **p. 8-4b:** Markjonathank/Dreamstime.com; **p. 8-4c:** Abril Sanchez/Dreamstime.com

Lesson 1
p. 10: Rawpixel/iStockphoto.com; **p. 11 (t):** Sam74100/Dreamstime.com; **p. 11 (ml):** Rawpixel images/Dreamstime.com; **p. 11 (mr):** Sam74100/Dreamstime.com; **p. 11 (b):** Sam74100/Dreamstime.com; **p. 12-1:** Huntstock/Photaki; **p. 12-2:** Sandro Bedini; **p. 12-3:** VMJones/iStockphoto.com; **p. 12-4:** Sandro Bedini; **p. 12-5:** Sandro Bedini; **p. 12-6:** Kanittha Promsakul/Dreamstime.com; **p. 13:** Frazer Harrison / Fotógrafo de plantilla / Getty Images Entertainment; **p. 15-1a:** Antonio Diaz/iStockphoto.com; **p. 15-1b:** Muhammad Annurmal/Dreamstime.com; **p. 15-1c:** Georgejmclittle/Dreamstime.com; **p. 15-2a:** Aspenphoto/Dreamstime.com; **p. 15-2b:** Intararit/Dreamstime.com; **p. 15-2c:** Damaisin/Dreamstime.com; **p. 15-3a:** martin-dm/iStockphoto.com; **p. 15-3b:** Kadettmann/Dreamstime.com; **p. 15-3c:** Vladimir Galkin /Dreamstime.com; **p. 15-4a:** Kdshutterman/Dreamstime.com; **p. 15-4b:** Vladimir Galkin/Dreamstime.com; **p. 15-4c:** Zhukovsky/Dreamstime.com; **p. 17:** monkeybusinessimages/iStockphoto.com; **p. 18 (tl):** Juliatimchenko/Dreamstime.com; **p. 18 (tc):** Pius Lee/Dreamstime.com; **p. 18 (tr):** Provectorstock/Dreamstime.com; **p. 18 (ml):** Roger Jegg/Dreamstime.com; **p. 18 (mr):** Seventyfour Images/Dreamstime.com; **p. 18 (bl):** DESKCUBE/iStockphoto.com; **p. 18 (bc):** Kawee Wateesatogkij/Dreamstime.com; **p. 18 (br):** Liliya Krivoruchko/Dreamstime.com; **p. 20 (background):** Matt Antonino/Dreamstime.com; **p. 20 (illustrations):** Paco Riera; **p. 20 (b):** abzee/iStockphoto.com; **p. 21 (t):** Pearson; **p. 21 (b):** Irina_Strelnikova/iStockphoto.com; **p. 22-23:** Man Carot; **p. 24:** Difusión; **p. 27:** Alejandro Milà; **p. 28:** Yobro10/Dreamstime.com

Lesson 2
p. 30: Nicolas McComber/iStockphoto.com; **p. 31-a:** Fotonoticias / Colaborador / WireImage; **p. 31-b:** Arturo Osorno/Dreamstime.com; **p. 31-c:** Saiko3p/Dreamstime.com; **p. 31-d:** Angel Delgado/Clasos.com/LatinContent/Getty Images; **p. 31-e:** Kmiragaya/Dreamstime.com; **p. 31-f:** Jeff Greenberg / Alamy Stock Photo; **p. 32-1a:** Pablo Hidalgo/Dreamstime.com; **p. 32-1b:** Fat Camera/iStockphoto.com; **p. 32-1c:** Xalanx /Dreamstime.com; **p. 32-2a:** Monkey Business Images/Dreamstime.com; **p. 32-2b:** Carlos Mora/Dreamstime.com; **p. 32-2c:** Christian Bertrand/Dreamstime.com; **p. 32-3a:** Czuber/Dreamstime.com; **p. 32-3b:** Silverblack/Dreamstime.com; **p. 32-3c:** Kerkez/iStockphoto.com; **p. 32-4a:** g-stockstudio/iStockphoto.com; **p. 32-4b:** Pekic/iStockphoto.com; **p. 32-4c:** David Molina/Dreamstime.com; **p. 33 (tl):** Annie Su Yee Yek/Dreamstime.com; **p. 33 (tc):** Rawpixelimages/Dreamstime.com; **p. 33 (tr):** Anke Van Wyk/Dreamstime.com; **p. 33 (ml):** Enrique Gomez/Dreamstime.com; **p. 33 (mc):** Hyunsuss/Dreamstime.com; **p. 33 (mr):** Voyagerix/Dreamstime.com; **p. 33 (bl):** Tomislav Pinter/Dreamstime.com; **p. 33 (br):** Igorr/Dreamstime.com; **p. 34 (tl):** Kadettmann/Dreamstime.com; **p. 34 (tr):** Tyler Olson/Dreamstime.com; **p. 34 (bl):** Wavebreakmedia Ltd/Dreamstime.com; **p. 34 (br):** Georgii Dolgykh/Dreamstime.com; **p. 35-1:** Kadettmann/Dreamstime.com; **p. 35-2:** MangoStar_Studio/iStockphoto.com; **p. 35-3:** Snappylens/Dreamstime.com; **p. 35-4:** Mangpor2004/Dreamstime.com; **p. 35-5:** Mcpics/Dreamstime.com; **p. 35-6:** Yunuli123/Dreamstime.com; **p. 36 (l):** Kadettmann/Dreamstime.com; **p. 36 (r):** Olena Hromova/Dreamstime.com; **p. 37:** Paul Bradbury/iStockphoto.com; **p. 38:** Roger Zanni; **p. 39:** Ulf Huebner/Dreamstime.com; **p. 40 (tl):** Robert Reyl/Dreamstime.com; **p. 40 (tr):** Leo Rosenthal/Pix Inc./The LIFE Images Collection; **p. 40 (bl):** Kseniya Ragozina/Dreamstime.com; **p. 40 (br):** Marlene Vicente/Dreamstime.com; **p. 41 (l):** LysenkoAlexander/iStockphoto.com; **p. 41 (r):** .shock/Dreamstime.com; **p. 42:** Alejandro Milà; **p. 43 (t):** Pearson; **p. 43 (b):** Irina_Strelnikova/iStockphoto.com; **p. 46-1:** Rawpixelimages/Dreamstime.com; **p. 46-2:** Lunamarina/Dreamstime.com; **p. 46-3:** Jesús Eloy Ramos Lara/Dreamstime.com; **p. 46-4:** Cameron Craig/Dreamstime.com; **p. 47:** dlewis33/iStockphoto.com; **p. 49:** Gvictoria/Dreamstime.com; **p. 50: (t)** Yobro10/Dreamstime.com; **p. 50 (b):** Martín Tognola

Lesson 3
p. 52: Sean Pavone Photo/iStockphoto.com; **p. 53 (tl):** Betty Leung/Dreamstime.com; **p. 53 (tr):** Tomas Griger/Dreamstime.com; **p. 53 (ml):** khyim/iStockphoto.com; **p. 53 (mr):** Tomas Griger/Dreamstime.com; **p. 53 (bl):** Venemama/Dreamstime.com; **p. 53 (br):** Tomas Griger/Dreamstime.com; **p. 54 (l):** Colin Young/Dreamstime.com; **p. 54 (r):** Carlito/Fotolia.com; **p. 55 (t):** Alejandro Milà; **p. 55 (ml):** GiorgioMorara/iStockphoto.com; **p. 55 (mc):** Fbxx/iStockphoto.com; **p. 55 (mr):** Thomas Barrat/Dreamstime.com; **p. 55 (bl):** Pretoperola/Dreamstime.com; **p. 55 (bc):** sara_winter/iStockphoto.com; **p. 55 (br):** robertiez/iStockphoto.com; **p. 56 (t):** hobbitfoot; **p. 56-1a (m):** Eva Kali/AdobeStock.com; **p. 56-1b (m):** HansUntch/iStockphoto.com; **p. 56-1c (m):** mmac72/iStockphoto.com; **p. 56-1d (m):** Ferguswang/Dreamstime.com; **p. 56-1e (m):** Delphotostock/AdobeStock.com; **p. 56-1f (m):** aragami123345/iStockphoto.com; **p. 56-2a (m):** filipefrazao/iStockphoto.com; **p. 56-2b (m):** MarioGuti/iStockphoto.com; **p. 56-2c (m):** Praxoss/iStockphoto.com; **p. 56-2d (m):** CampPhoto/iStockphoto.com; **p. 56-2e (m):** moofushi/AdobeStock.com; **p. 56-2f (m):** Erlantz Pérez Rodríguez/iStockphoto.com; **p. 56 (b):** MarcelC/iStockphoto.com; **p. 57:** Alejandro Milà; **p. 58 (t):** tomfot/iStockphoto.com; **p. 58 (b):** Peek Creative Collective/Dreamstime.com; **p. 59:** Ivan Feoktistov/Dreamstime.com; **p. 60:** Dayzeren/Dreamstime.com; **p. 61 (t):** Orbon Alija/iStockphoto.com; **p. 61 (b):** MBPROJEKT_Maciej_Bledowski/iStockphoto.com; **p. 62 (CA):** UbjsP/AdobeStock.com; **p. 62 (MT):** Justinreznick/iStockphoto.com; **p. 62 (CO):** aluxum/iStockphoto.com; **p. 62 (IA):** Jens Lambert Photography/iStockphoto.com; **p. 62 (NY):** Jan Pokorný/Dreamstime.com; **p. 62 (AZ):** DavorLovincic/iStockphoto.com; **p. 62 (AR):** Linettesimoes photography/Dreamstime.com; **p. 62 (AK):** Rkpimages/Dreamstime.com; **p. 62 (TX):** uschools/iStockphoto.com; **p. 62 (FL):** Dibrova/Dreamstime.com; **p. 64:** Alejandro Milà; **p. 65 (t):** Pearson; **p. 65 (b):** Irina_Strelnikova/iStockphoto.com; **p. 66-67:** freevectormaps.com; **p. 66:** Ron_Thomas/iStockphoto.com; **p. 67:** Sean Pavone Photo/iStockphoto.com; **p. 68:** cinoby/iStockphoto.com; **p. 69 (t):** PorFang/iStockphoto.com; **p. 69 (bl):** Valentin Armianu/Dreamstime.com; **p. 69 (br):** Paco Romero/iStockphoto.com; **p. 71:** Piotr Pawinski/Dreamstime.com; **p. 72:** Yobro10/Dreamstime.com

Lesson 4
p. 74: LUIS ROBAYO/Colaborador/AFP/Getty Images; **p. 75 (tl):** Lord_Kuernyus/iStockphoto.com; **p. 75 (tc):** LisaEPerkins/iStockphoto.com; **p. 75 (tr):** E.Westmacott / Alamy Stock Photo; **p. 75 (bl):** Tangophotography/Dreamstime.com; **p. 75 (bc):** Studio_Grand_Web/Dreamstime.com; **p. 75 (br):** Jevgeni_Mironov/Dreamstime.com; **p. 76:** Alejandro Milà; **p. 78-1a:** Deemakdaksina/Dreamstime.com; **p. 78-1b:** PARNTAWAN/iStockphoto.com; **p. 78-1c:** RossiAgung/iStockphoto.com; **p. 78-1d:** Tina Zovteva/Dreamstime.com; **p. 78-1e:** Gordana Sermek/

Lesson 5

Lesson 6

Lesson 7

Credits

Shannon Finney / Fotógrafo autónomo / Getty Images Entertainment; **p. 155 (r):** Pablo Blazquez Dominguez / Colaborador / Getty Images Entertainment; **p. 156:** Bettmann / Colaborador; **p. 157 (tl):** Vladimir Velickovic/Dreamstime.com; **p. 157 (tr):** Miceking/Dreamstime.com; **p. 157 (bl):** Artenz/Dreamstime.com; **p. 157 (br):** Sjgh/Dreamstime.com; **p. 159:** Alejandro Milà;

Lesson 8

p. 162: marshalgonz/iStockphoto.com; **p. 163:** Dimarik16/Dreamstime.com; **p. 164:** Roger Zanni; **p. 165-1:** clu/iStockphoto.com; **p. 165-2:** AdrianHancu/iStockphoto.com; **p. 165-3:** vichie81/Fotolia.com; **p. 165-4:** NoSystem images/iStockphoto.com; **p. 165-5:** tupungato/iStockphoto.com; **p. 165-6:** vizualni/iStockphoto.com; **p. 166 (t):** tupungato/iStockphoto.com; **p. 166 (m):** Charlie Bautista; **p. 166 (b):** Victor Torres/Dreamstime.com; **p. 167:** Jjfarq/Dreamstime.com; **p. 168:** Maurie Hill/Dreamstime.com; **p. 170 (t):** Roger Zanni; **p. 170 (b):** Roger Zanni; **p. 171:** Alejandro Milà; **p. 172 (l):** mountlynx/iStockphoto.com; **p. 172 (c):** tifonimages/iStockphoto.com; **p. 172 (r):** Rudimencial/iStockphoto.com; **p. 174:** Alejandro Milà; **p. 175 (t):** Pearson; **p. 175 (b):** Irina_Strelnikova/iStockphoto.com; **p. 176 (l):** Robert Lerich/Dreamstime.com; **p. 176 (r):** Blackalex/Dreamstime.com; **p. 177 (l):** Delpixart/iStockphoto.com; **p. 177 (c):** Pablo Hidalgo/Dreamstime.com; **p. 177 (r):** Starcevic/iStockphoto.com; **p. 178:** Owsspawg/Dreamstime.com; **p. 180:** holgs/istockphoto.com

Lesson 9

p. 184: Taiga/Dreamstime.com; **p. 185 (tl):** Starcevic/iStockphoto.com; **p. 185 (tr):** Aneese/iStockphoto.com; **p. 185 (bl):** InStock/iStockphoto.com; **p. 185 (br):** FluxFactory/iStockphoto.com; **p. 186:** Alejandro Milà; **p. 187 (l):** ESB Professional/Shutterstock.com; **p. 187 (c):** Luxy Images/Getty Images; **p. 187 (r):** Imtmphoto/iStockphoto.com; **p. 188:** vicnt/iStockphoto.com; **p. 189-1:** Evgeny Kosharsky/Dreamstime.com; **p. 189-2:** Photobac /Dreamstime.com; **p. 189-3:** Firmafotografen/iStockphoto.com; **p. 189-4:** Michaelfair/Dreamstime.com; **p. 189-5:** Anastasiia Guseva/Dreamstime.com; **p. 189-6:** George Mdivanian /Dreamstime.com; **p. 189-7:** tiler84/iStockphoto.com; **p. 189-8:** ilyarexi/iStockphoto.com; **p. 190 (t):** Alejandro Milà; **p. 190 (b):** Alejandro Milà; **p. 191:** gerenme/iStockphoto.com; **p. 193 (tl):** diegograndi/iStockphoto.com; **p. 193 (tr):** LUke1138/iStockphoto.com; **p. 193 (ml):** Magaiza/iStockphoto.com; **p. 193 (mr):** stockcam/iStockphoto.com; **193 (bl):** Melpomenem/iStockphoto.com; **193 (br):** Torresigner/iStockphoto.com; **p. 194-1a:** Anthony Paz Photographer/iStockphoto.com; **p. 194-1b:** myasinirik/iStockphoto.com; **p. 194-1c:** pattonmania/iStockphoto.com; **p. 194-1d:** AlexLMX/iStockphoto.com; **p. 194-1e:** archideaphoto/iStockphoto.com; **p. 194-2a:** trismile/iStockphoto.com; **p. 194-2b:** Sabuhi Novruzov/Dreamstime.com; **p. 194-2c:** Artem Perevozchikov/iStockphoto.com; **p. 194-2d:** Vitalii Shkliarov/Dreamstime.com; **p. 194-3a:** Srki66/Dreamstime.com; **p. 194-3b:** photojournalis/iStockphoto.com; **p. 194-3c:** H368k742/Dreamstime.com; **p. 194-3d:** CTRPhotos/iStockphoto.com; **p. 194-3e:** Wojciechzalewski/Dreamstime.com; **p. 194-3f:** Liliia Khuzhakhmetova/Dreamstime.com; **p. 195 (l):** Difusión; **p. 195 (r):** Difusión; **p. 196 (tl):** Silverblack/Dreamstime.com; **p. 196 (tc):** Ljupco/iStockphoto.com; **p. 196 (tr):** andresr/iStockphoto.com; **p. 196 (bl):** cokada/iStockphoto.com; **p. 196 (bc):** Sidekick/iStockphoto.com; **p. 196 (br):** Maksym Drozd/Dreamstime.com; **p. 197 (t):** Pearson; **p. 197 (b):** Irina_Strelnikova/iStockphoto.com; **p. 198-1:** Alexandre Fagundes De Fagundes/Dreamstime.com; **p. 198-2:** Coralimages2020/Dreamstime.com; **p. 198-3:** Pablo Hidalgo/Dreamstime.com; **p. 199-a:** Markpittimages/Dreamstime.com; **p. 199-b:** Coralimages2020/Dreamstime.com; **p. 199-c:** Mandy Pirch/Dreamstime.com; **p. 200-1:** Karina Azaretzky / Alamy Stock Photo; **p. 200-2:** Martinotero/iStockphoto.com; **p. 200-3:** Xenomanes/Dreamstime.com; **p. 200 (b):** iquiquetv; **p. 201:** RonTech2000/iStockphoto.com; **p. 202:** Roger Zanni; **p. 204:** Oksun70/Dreamstime.com

Lesson 10

p. 206: Marcelo Endelli / Fotógrafo autónomo / Getty Images Sport; **p. 207-a:** sfgp/Album; **p. 207-b:** Nobara Hayakawa (used by permission); **p. 207-c:** chaoss/iStockphoto.com; **p. 207-d:** Pablo Garrido; **p. 207-e:** havanaworldmusic (used by permission); **p. 209:** louhan/iStockphoto.com; **p. 210-1a:** BraunS/iStockphoto.com; **p. 210-1b:** Armastas/iStockphoto.com; **p. 210-1c:** Andreea Dobrescu/Dreamstime.com; **p. 210-1d:** Ilandrea/iStockphoto.com; **p. 210-2a:** FatCamera/iStockphoto.com; **p. 210-2b:** Weedezign/iStockphoto.com; **p. 210-2c:** pamirc/iStockphoto.com; **p. 210-3a:** NoSystem images/iStockphoto.com; **p. 210-3b:** Yobro10/Dreamstime.com; **p. 210-4a:** matzaball/iStockphoto.com; **p. 210-4b:** vladacanon/iStockphoto.com; **p. 212:** chanvito/iStockphoto.com; **p. 213 (t):** YinYang/iStockphoto.com; **p. 213 (m):** MaboHH/iStockphoto.com; **p. 213 (b):** Mihalec/Dreamstime.com; **p. 214 (l):** Naphat_Jorjee/iStockphoto.com; **p. 214 (r):** Susan M. Santa Maria/Dreamstime.com; **p. 215:** Alejandro Milà; **p. 217:** Cunaplus_M.Faba/iStockphoto.com; **p. 218 (lt):** Lunamarina/Dreamstime.com; **p. 218 (lb):** Triciadaniel/Dreamstime.com; **p. 218 (r):** Wenling01/Dreamstime.com; **p. 219 (t):** Pearson; **p. 219 (b):** Irina_Strelnikova/iStockphoto.com; **p. 220:** Marco Livolsi/Dreamstime.com; **p. 222:** irina_levitskaya/Adobe Stock; **p. 225:** Roger Zanni

Lesson 11

p. 228: Mychal Watts / Fotógrafo autónomo / Getty Images Entertainment; **p. 229-1:** Difusión; **p. 229-2:** Sandro Bedini; **p. 229-3:** Sandro Bedini; **p. 229-4:** DGLimages/iStockphoto.com; **p. 229-5:** Sandro Bedini; **p. 230-1a:** Gita Kulinica/Dreamstime.com; **p. 230-1b:** Raja RC/Dreamstime.com; **p. 230-1c:** Nevinates/Dreamstime.com; **p. 230-1d:** Anphotos /Dreamstime.com; **p. 230-1e:** Ronald Van Der Beek/Dreamstime.com; **p. 230-1f:** Siripun/Dreamstime.com; **p. 230-2a:** Anton Eine/Dreamstime.com; **p. 230-2b:** kaanates/iStockphoto.com; **p. 230-2c:** Floortje/iStockphoto.com; **p. 230-2d:** chengyuzheng/iStockphoto.com; **p. 230-2e:** pigtar/iStockphoto.com; **p. 230-2f:** © Airborne77/Dreamstime.com; **p. 230-3a:** Turnervisual/iStockphoto.com; **p. 230-3b:** Elovich/Dreamstime.com; **p. 230-3c:** jirkaejc/iStockphoto.com; **p. 230-3d:** Picsfive /Dreamstime.com; **p. 230-3e:** kolesnikovserg/iStockphoto.com; **p. 230-3f:** Mamuka Gotsiridze/Dreamstime.com; **p. 231-1:** Ingrampublishing/Photaki; **p. 231-2:** Pablo Hidalgo/Dreamstime.com; **p. 231-3:** Jiann Ho/iStockphoto.com; **p. 231-4:** Riderfoot /iStockphoto.com; **p. 232-1a:** Floortje/iStockphoto.com; **p. 232-1b:** Stable400/Dreamstime.com; **p. 232-1c:** Photology1971/iStockphoto.com; **p. 232-1d:** MileA/iStockphoto.com; **p. 232-1e:** alenkadr/iStockphoto.com; **p. 232-2a:** Alexandr Kornienko/Dreamstime.com; **p. 232-2b:** artisteer/iStockphoto.com; **p. 232-2c:** Johnfoto/iStockphoto.com; **p. 232-2d:** RedHelga/iStockphoto.com; **p. 232-2e:** xamtiw/iStockphoto.com; **p. 233:** Alejandro Milà; **p. 234:** JJAVA/Fotolia.com; **p. 235 (l):** interplanetary; **p. 235 (c):** Victorpr/iStockphoto.com; **p. 235 (r):** FG Trade/iStockphoto.com; **p. 236:** Mallivan/iStockphoto.com; **p. 237 (l):** Alejandro Milà; **p. 237 (r):** Alejandro Milà; **p. 238:** Alejandro Milà; **p. 239 (l):** N Po/Dreamstime.com; **p. 239 (r):** Dimjul/Dreamstime.com; **p. 240:** Cienpies Design/Illustrations/Dreamstime.com; **p. 241 (t):** Pearson; **p. 241 (b):** Irina_Strelnikova/iStockphoto.com; **p. 242 (t):** The Washington Post/Contributor; **p. 242 (m):** Daniel Zuchnik/Colaborador/Getty Images Entertainment; **p. 242 (b):** Dave Kotinsky/Fotógrafo autónomo/Getty Images Entertainment; **p. 243:** LUIS ACOSTA/Fotógrafo de plantilla/AFP; **p. 244 (t):** Difusión; **p. 244-1a (b):** Feng Yu/iStockphoto.com; **p. 244-1b (b):** Nevinates/Dreamstime.com; **p. 244-2 (b):** Cretolamna/Dreamstime.com; **p. 244-3 (b):** Maxim Tatarinov/Dreamstime.com; **p. 245:** EzumeImages/iStockphoto.com; **p. 247:** Alejandro Milà

Lesson 12

p. 250: Rachel Murray/Fotógrafo autónomo/Getty Images Entertainment; **p. 251-1:** Arau Films Internacional/Photo 12 / Alamy Stock Photo; **p. 251-2:** ScreenProd/Photononstop/Alamy Stock Photo; **p. 251-3:** TCD/Prod.DB/Alamy Stock Photo; **p. 251-4:** AF archive/Alamy Stock Photo; **p. 251-5:** United Archives GmbH/Alamy Stock Photo; **p. 251-6:** Lifestyle pictures/Alamy Stock Photo; **p. 252 (t):** Lifestyle pictures/Alamy Stock Photo; **p. 252 (b):** Lifestyle pictures/Alamy Stock Photo; **p. 253-1a:** Aleksander Kovaltchuk/Dreamstime.com; **p. 253-1b:** Sdecoret/Dreamstime.com; **p. 253-1c:** Hayati Kayhan/Dreamstime.com; **p. 253-1d:** aijohn784/iStockphoto.com; **p. 253-1e:** Issele/Dreamstime.com; **p. 253-1f:** Eike Leppert/Dreamstime.com; **p.**

253-1g: Elena Gladkaya /Dreamstime.com; **p. 253-2a:** South_agency/ iStockphoto.com; **p. 253-2b:** Duncan Noakes/Dreamstime.com; **p. 253-2c:** Kuprevich/Dreamstime.com; **p. 253-2d:** Alexei Novikov/ Dreamstime.com; **p. 253-3a:** Tudor Stanica/Dreamstime.com; ; **p. 253-3b:** Angelo Gilardelli/Dreamstime.com; **p. 253-3c:** Steffen Højager/ Dreamstime.com; **p. 253-3d:** laluve/iStockphoto.com; **p. 253-3e:** Iana Zyrianova/Dreamstime.com; **p. 253-3f:** Elnur/Dreamstime.com; **p. 254:** Clasos/Colaborador/LatinContent Editorial; **p. 255 (tl):** KONTROLAB/ Colaborador Getty Images; **p. 255 (mc):** Herianus/iStockphoto.com; **p. 255 (tr):** Juan Naharro Gimenez/Colaborador/WireImage; **p. 255 (br):** Charnsitr/Dreamstime.com; **p. 256-1:** VIRGIN FILMS/Album; **p. 256-2:** ROSAFREY S.r.l./SUSY SURANYI ASOCIADOS/Album; **p. 256-3:** Everett Collection, Inc./Alamy Stock Photo; **p. 256-4:** Everett Collection, Inc./Alamy Stock Photo; **p. 257 (t):** Everett Collection, Inc./Alamy Stock Photo; **p. 257 (m):** Entertainment Pictures/Alamy Stock Photo; **p. 257 (b):** AF archive/Alamy Stock Photo; **p. 258:** JUANJO MARTIN/EFE/lafototeca.com/Album; **p. 259:** Ulf Andersen/ Colaborador/Hulton Archive; **p. 260:** chipstudio/iStockphoto.com; **p. 261-1a:** Pictorial Press Ltd/Alamy Stock Photo; **p. 261-1b:** AF archive/ Alamy Stock Photo; **p. 261-1c:** Atlaspix/Alamy Stock Photo; **p. 261-1d:** Allstar Picture Library/Alamy Stock Photo; **p. 261-2a:** Allstar Picture Library/Alamy Stock Photo; **p. 261-2b:** Moviestore collection Ltd/Alamy Stock Photo; **p. 261-2c:** Allstar Picture Library/Alamy Stock Photo; **p. 261-2d:** Pictorial Press Ltd/Alamy Stock Photo; **p. 262:** ensup/123RF; **p. 263 (t):** Pearson; **p. 263 (b):** Irina_Strelnikova/iStockphoto.com; **p. 264:** RTI TELEVISION/Album; **p. 265:** David Bergman/Colaborador/ Getty Images Entertainment; **p. 267:** mizoula/iStockphoto.com; **p. 270:** Yobro10/Dreamstime.com

Lesson 13

p. 272: MIGUEL ROJO/Fotógrafo autónomo/AFP; **p. 273 (tl):** Underwood Archives/Colaborador/Archive Photos; **p. 273 (mr):** Francois Lochon/Colaborador/The LIFE Images Collection; **p. 273 (bl):** Photo 12/Colaborador/Universal Images Group; **p. 274-1a:** sbayram/ iStockphoto.com; **p. 274-1b:** Altayb/iStockphoto.com; **p. 274-1c:** Herzstaub/iStockphoto.com; **p. 274-1d:** sprng23/iStockphoto.com; **p. 274-2a:** vavlt/iStockphoto.com; **p. 274-2b:** scanrail/iStockphoto.com; **p. 274-2c:** Ekaterina Tarasenkova/Dreamstime.com; **p. 274-2d:** Cassis/iStockphoto.com; **p. 274-2e:** underworld111/iStockphoto.com; **p. 274-3a:** Claudio Ventrella/iStockphoto.com; **p. 274-3b:** BraunS/ iStockphoto.com; **p. 274-3c:** hohl/iStockphoto.com; **p. 274-3d:** Stefan032/iStockphoto.com; **p. 274-4a:** MarcPo/iStockphoto.com; **p. 274-4b:** YinYang/iStockphoto.com; **p. 274-4c:** tupungato/ iStockphoto.com; **p. 274-4d:** hanhanpeggy/iStockphoto.com; **p. 274-4e:** Vertigo3d/iStockphoto.com; **p. 276 (l):** Saiko3p/Dreamstime.com; **p. 276 (r):** Eloi_Omella/iStockphoto.com; **p. 278 (t):** Justin Locke/ Colaborador/National Geographic Image Collection; **p. 278 (m):** Three Lions/Fotógrafo autónomo/Hulton Archive; **p. 278 (b):** Edouard BOUBAT/Colaborador/Gamma-Legends; **p. 279:** Allan Cash Picture Library/Alamy Stock Photo; **p. 284 (l):** chrisfarrugia/iStockphoto.com; **p. 284 (r):** jeffwqc/iStockphoto.com; **p. 285 (t):** Pearson; **p. 285 (b):** Irina_ Strelnikova/iStockphoto.com; **p. 286 (l):** Matyas Rehak | Dreamstime. com; **p. 286 (c):** Diego Grandi/Dreamstime.com; **p. 286 (r):** Maria Teresa Weinmann/Dreamstime.com; **p. 288:** Casi creativo/Fred Lammie; **p. 292:** Yobro10/Dreamstime.com

Lesson 14

p. 294: IulianU/iStockphoto.com; **p. 295:** Alejandro Milà; **p. 296-1:** Sandro Bedini; **p. 296-2:** Sandro Bedini; **p. 296-3:** FG Trade/iStockphoto.com; **p. 296-4:** Difusión; **p. 298:** monkeybusinessimages/iStockphoto.com; **p. 299:** Alejandro Milà; **p. 301:** Alejandro Milà; **p. 303:** Paco Riera; **p. 304 (t):** Difusión; **p. 304 (b):** Difusión; **p. 305:** Alejandro Milà; **p. 306 (t):** Alejandro Milà; **p. 306 (m):** Alejandro Milà; **p. 306 (b):** Vijay kumar/iStockphoto.com; **p. 307 (t):** Pearson; **p. 307 (b):** Irina_Strelnikova/iStockphoto.com; **p. 308-1:** taikrixel/iStockphoto.com; **p. 308-2:** Flavio Vallenari/iStockphoto.com; **p. 308-3:** Giacomo Scandroglio/Dreamstime.com; **p. 308-4:** Ziya Akturer/Dreamstime.com; **p. 309 (tl):** Fiskness/Dreamstime.com; **p. 309 (tr):** MediaProduction/iStockphoto.com; **p. 309 (bl):** Rudimencial/

iStockphoto.com; **p. 309 (br):** holgs/iStockphoto.com; **p. 310:** Mykola Kravchenko/Dreamstime.com; **p. 311:** bowie15/iStockphoto.com

Lesson 15

p. 316: AFP; **p. 317:** jonathanfilskov-photography/iStockphoto.com; **p. 318 (t):** Evgeny Krutakov/Dreamstime.com; **p. 318 (m):** Evgeny Krutakov/ Dreamstime.com; **p. 318 (b):** Evgeny Krutakov/Dreamstime.com; **p. 319-1a:** Mykola Kravchenko/Dreamstime.com; **p. 319-1b:** Dtiberio/ Dreamstime.com; **p. 319-1c:** Javiindy/Dreamstime.com; **p. 319-1d:** Khosrork/Dreamstime.com; **p. 319-2a:** shock/Dreamstime.com; **p. 319-2b:** Kiosea39/Dreamstime.com; **p. 319-2c:** AaronAmat/ iStockphoto.com; **p. 319-2d:** Zegers06/Dreamstime.com; **p.320:** olegback/iStockphoto.com; **p. 321:** Alejandro Milà; **p. 324:** Alejandro Milà; **p. 325:** Alejandro Milà; **p. 326 (t):** Bruno ismael da silva Alves/ Dreamstime.com; **p. 326 (b):** Artzzz/Dreamstime.com; **p. 327 (t):** Alejandro Milà; **p. 327 (bl):** Alain MINGAM/Colaborador/Gamma-Rapho; **p. 327 (bc):** philippe giraud/Sygma; **p. 327 (br):** Matthew Ashton/ Colaborador/Corbis Sport; **p. 328:** aluxum/iStockphoto.com; **p. 329 (t):** Pearson; **p. 109 (b):** Irina_Strelnikova/iStockphoto.com; **p. 330 (tl):** Grafissimo/iStockphoto.com; **p. 330 (tr):** Picturenow/Universal Images Group; **p. 330 (ml):** Photo 12/Colaborador/Universal Images Group; **p. 330 (mr):** Photo 12/Alamy Stock Photo; **p. 330 (b):** Lois Herman/Corbis Historical; **p. 331 (l):** Julio Etchart/Alamy Stock Photo; **p. 331 (r):** YAMIL LAGE/Colaborador/AFP; **p. 332:** Difusión; **p. 334:** Manakin/Istockphoto; **p. 336:** Maryvalery/Dreamstime.com

RICH MEDIA CREDITS

Lesson 1
p. 21: Pearson; **p. 24:** Difusión
Lesson 2
p. 43: Pearson
Lesson 3
p. 65: Pearson; **p. 68:** Difusión
Lesson 4
p. 87: Pearson
Lesson 5
p. 109: Pearson; **p. 112:** Difusión
Lesson 6
p. 131: Pearson
Lesson 7
p. 153: Pearson; **p. 156:** Difusión
Lesson 8
p. 175: Pearson
Lesson 9
p. 197: Pearson; **p. 200:** iquiquetv (used by permission)
Lesson 10
p. 219: Pearson
Lesson 11
p. 241: Pearson; **p. 244:** Difusión
Lesson 12
p. 263: Pearson
Lesson 13
p. 285: Pearson; **p. 288:** Casi creativo/Fred Lammie (used by permission)
Lesson 14
p. 307: Pearson
Lesson 15
p. 329: Pearson; **p. 332:** Difusión

Index

Index